lonely planet

Croatia

Jeanne Oliver

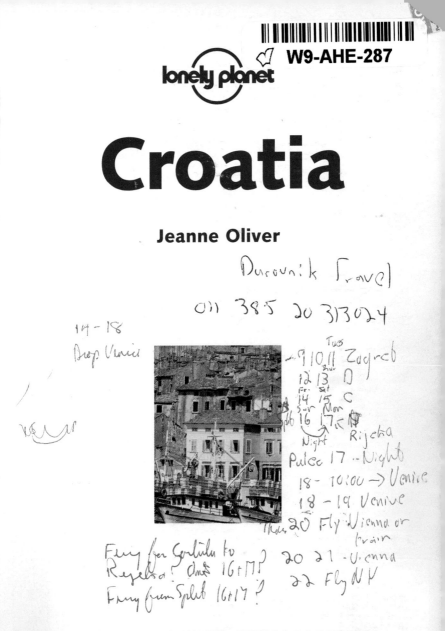

Dubrovnik Travel

011 385 20 313024

14 - 18
Drop Venice

Tue
9 10 11 Zagreb
12 13 D
Fri Sat
14 15 C
Sun Mon
16 17 B
Night   Rijeka
Pulec 17 -- Night
18 - 10:00 → Venice
18 - 19 Venice
Thur 20 Fly Vienna or
train
20 21 - Vienna
22 Fly N V

Ferry for Korčula to
Rejelson? Out 16 + 17?
Ferry from Split 16 + 17 ?

LONELY PLANET PUBLICATIONS
Melbourne • Oakland • London • Paris

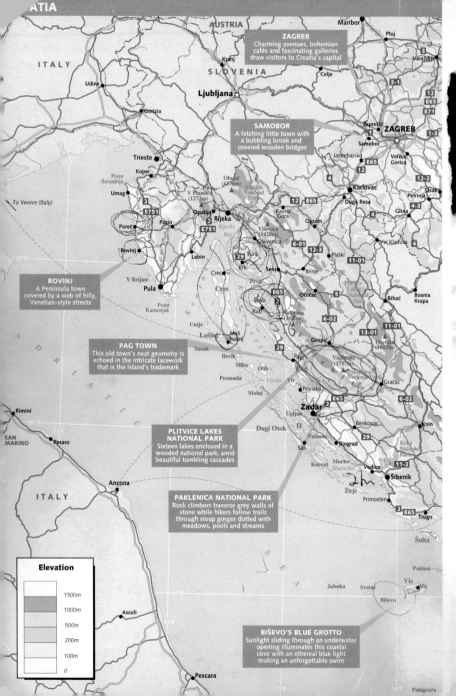

ATIA

AUSTRIA

ZAGREB
Charming avenues, bohemian cafés and fascinating galleries draw visitors to Croatia's capital

Maribor

Ptuj

ITALY

Kranj

SLOVENIA

Celje

Varaždin

Ljubljana

SAMOBOR
A fetching little town with a bubbling brook and covered wooden bridges

Zaprešić

ZAGREB

Gorizia

Samobor

Velika Gorica

Udine

Jastrebarsko

Trieste

Koper

Point Savudrija

Obruč (776m)

Karlovac

Sisak

Petrinja

Umag

V Planik (1272m)

Ravna Gora

Ogulin

Duga Resa

Glina

To Venice (Italy)

Opatija

Rijeka

Rijecki Bay

Vel Kladuša

Poreč

Pazin

Višnevica (1428m)

Plaški

Labin

Krk

Senj

Brinje

Bihać

ROVINJ
A Peninsula town covered by a web of hilly, Venetian-style streets

Rovinj

V Brijun

Cres

Krk

Prvić

Bosna Krupa

Pula

Cres

Point Kamenjak

Rab

Otočac

Unije

Lošinj

Rab

Gospić

Ozeblin (1657m)

Mali Lošinj

PAG TOWN
This old town's neat geometry is echoed in the intricate lacework that is the island's trademark

Susak

Ilovik

Silba

Pag

Vaganski (1757m)

Rimini

Premuda

Olib

Vir

Gračac

Molat

Privlaka

PLITVICE LAKES NATIONAL PARK
Sixteen lakes enclosed in a wooded national park, amid beautiful tumbling cascades

Virska

SAN MARINO

Pesaro

Zadar

Ancona

Ugljan

Benkovac

Knin

ITALY

Dugi Otok

Iž

Pašman

Biograd

PAKLENICA NATIONAL PARK
Rock climbers traverse grey walls of stone while hikers follow trails through steep gorges dotted with meadows, pools and streams

Sali

Murter

Vodice

Šibenik

Kornat

Murtersko

Primošten

Žirje

Trogir

Šolta

Pakleni

Elevation

	1500m
	1000m
	500m
	200m
	100m
	0

Ascoli

Jabuka

Svetac

Vis

Vis

Biševo

BIŠEVO'S BLUE GROTTO
Sunlight sliding through an underwater opening illuminates this coastal cove with an ethereal blue light making an unforgettable swim

Pescara

Palagruža

HVAR TOWN
A beautiful town on a beautiful island that attracts beautiful people

BRELA
A pine-tree lined coastal promenade winds around a long string of white, pebbled beaches dipping into pristine waters

MLJET
Fall under the spell of this magical island of caves, coves and lakes: bike, boat, hike or simply dream the day away

DUBROVNIK
The pearl of the Adriatic: Renaissance architecture and massive walls rising from a sparkling sea

HUNGARY

YUGOSLAVIA

BOSNIA HERCEGOVINA

YUGOSLAVIA

ALBANIA

Croatia
1st edition – April 1999

Published by
Lonely Planet Publications Pty Ltd A.C.N. 005 607 983
192 Burwood Rd, Hawthorn, Victoria 3122, Australia

Lonely Planet Offices
Australia PO Box 617, Hawthorn, Victoria 3122
USA 150 Linden St, Oakland, CA 94607
UK 10a Spring Place, London NW5 3BH
France 1 rue du Dahomey, 75011 Paris

Photographs
Many of the images in this guide are available for licensing from
Lonely Planet Images.
email: lpi@lonelyplanet.com.au

Front cover photograph
Rovinj Harbour (Jon Davison)

ISBN 0 86442 646 1

Contents – Text

THE AUTHOR   **5**

THIS BOOK   **7**

FOREWORD   **8**

INTRODUCTION   **11**

FACTS ABOUT CROATIA   **13**

History 13	National Parks 27	Arts 30
Geography 25	Government & Politics 27	Society & Conduct 34
Climate 25	Economy 29	Religion 34
Ecology & Environment 26	Population & People 30	
Flora & Fauna 26	Education 30	

FACTS FOR THE VISITOR   **35**

Highlights 35	Radio & TV 44	Public Holidays & Special
Suggested Itineraries 35	Time 44	Events 50
Planning 36	Electricity 44	Activities 50
Tourist Offices 37	Weights & Measures 44	Courses 53
Visas & Documents 38	Laundry 44	Work 54
Embassies & Consulates 39	Toilets 46	Accommodation 54
Customs 40	Health 46	Food 57
Money 40	Women Travellers 49	Drinks 58
Post & Communications 42	Gay & Lesbian Travellers 49	Entertainment 59
Internet Resources 43	Disabled Travellers 49	Shopping 60
Books 43	Legal Matters 49	
Newspapers & Magazines 44	Business Hours 50	

GETTING THERE & AWAY   **61**

Air 61	Land 65	Sea 67

GETTING AROUND   **68**

Air 68	Boat 69	Hitching 72
Bus 68	Car & Motorcycle 70	Local Transport 72
Train 68	Bicycle 71	Organised Tours 72

ZAGREB   **73**

History...............74	Places to Stay.....................88	**Around Zagreb** **95**
Orientation 75	Places to Eat 90	Hrvatsko Zagorje 95
Information 78	Entertainment 93	Banija-Kordun Region 97
Things to See......80	Spectator Sport 93	Samobor 99
Activities 87	Shopping 94	Varaždin 100
Organised Tours 88	Getting There & Away 94	
Special Events 88	Getting Around 95	

SLAVONIA   **103**

Osijek 104	Around Osijek 109

KVARNER REGION 111

Rijeka ...113	Krk Island ...132	Rab Town ...141
Opatija ...119	Krk Town ...134	Lopar ...145
Around Opatija ...122	Around Krk Town ...137	Barbat ...146
Lošinj & Cres Islands ...122	Baška ...137	Suha Punta ...146
Lošinj Island ...124	Punat ...139	
Cres Island ...128	Around Punat ...139	

ISTRIA 147

Pula ...151	Poreč ...163
Around Pula ...157	Around Poreč ...168
Rovinj ...158	

ZADAR REGION 170

Zadar ...170	Paklenica National Park ...181	Pag ...190
Around Zadar ...178	Stari Grad ...186	
Plitvice Lakes National Park ..178	Dugi Otok ...186	

ŠIBENIK REGION 195

Šibenik ...195	Krka National Park ...202
Around Šibenik ...201	Kornati Islands ...203

CENTRAL DALMATIA 205

Split ...205	Makarska ...221	Hvar ...237
Around Split ...216	Around Makarska ...224	
Trogir ...218	Vis ...225	
Around Trogir ...221	Brač ...228	

SOUTHERN DALMATIA 246

Dubrovnik ...246	Korčula Island ...264	Vela Luka ...272
Around Dubrovnik ...260	Korčula ...266	Orebić ...272
Mljet ...261	Lumbarda ...271	

LANGUAGE 274

GLOSSARY 276

FOOD GLOSSARY 278

INDEX 284

Text ...284	Boxed Text ...287

MAP LEGEND back page

METRIC CONVERSION inside back cover

Contents – Maps

INTRODUCTION

Locator Map 11

ZAGREB

Zagreb 76-7   Zagreb Region & Northern
                                Croatia................................96

SLAVONIA

Slavonia 104   Osijek 106

KVARNER

Kvarner Region 112   Mali Lošinj 125   Rab Island 140
Rijeka 114-15   Krk Island..........................133   Rab Town 142
Lošinj & Cres 123   Krk Town............................135

ISTRIA

Istria 148   Rovinj 159
Pula 152   Poreč 164

ZADAR

Zadar Region 171   Plitvice Lakes National Park 179   Sali......................................188
Zadar..................................174   Paklenica Naional Park........182   Pag Town 192

ŠIBENIK

Šibenik 198-9   Šibenik-Knin Region 202-3

CENTRAL DALMATIA

Central Dalmatia 206   Trogir..................................219   Hvar Island 238-9
Split....................................208   Brač 228-9   Hvar Town........................240
Solin 217   Bol Town 234-5

SOUTHERN DALMATIA

Southern Dalmatia 248-9   Dubrovnik – Old Town 254   Korčula Island & Pelješac 264-5
Dubrovnik 252-3   Mljet................................262-3   Korčula Town......................267

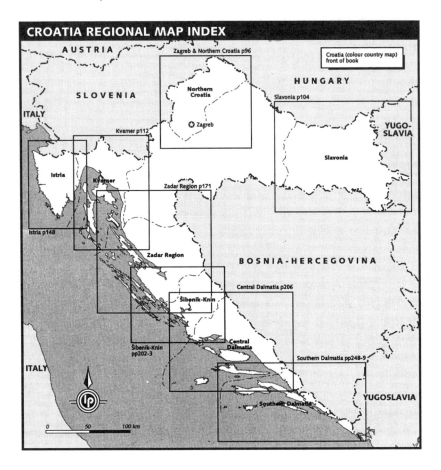

CROATIA REGIONAL MAP INDEX

AUSTRIA

Zagreb & Northern Croatia p96

Croatia (colour country map)
front of book

HUNGARY

SLOVENIA

Northern
Croatia

Zagreb

Slavonia p104

ITALY

YUGO-
SLAVIA

Kvarner p112

Istria

Kvarner

Slavonia

Zadar Region p171

Istria p148

Zadar Region

BOSNIA-HERCEGOVINA

Central Dalmatia p206

Šibenik-Knin

Šibenik-Knin
pp202-3

Central
Dalmatia

Southern Dalmatia pp248-9

ITALY

YUGOSLAVIA

Southern Dalmatia

0   50   100 km

The Author

Born in New Jersey, Jeanne Oliver spent her childhood mulling over the *New York Times* travel section and plotting her future voyages. She received a BA in English at the State University of New York at Stony Brook and then moved to New York City to work at the *Village Voice* newspaper. After a law degree, she set up a legal practice that was interrupted by ever-more-frequent trips to Central and South America, Europe and the Middle East. Her love of travel eventually prevailed and in 1989 she set off on a round-the-world trip that took her through Africa, India and south-east Asia. She moved to Paris in 1992, taught law, translated and worked in the tourist business before turning to journalism. She now makes her living as a freelance travel writer, authoring guidebooks and articles. Jeanne can be found in cyberspace at j-oliver@worldnet.fr.

FROM THE AUTHOR

A number of people assisted in the research and preparation of this book. Mirjana Žilić of the Croatian National Tourist Office provided patient support far beyond the call of duty and was unfailingly generous with her time and energy. Hvala, Mirjana. Thanks also to Antun Kenda and the staff of the National Tourist Office, Martina Grilec of the Zagreb Tourist Office, Vlatka Erceg in Varaždin and Damir Macanić of the Osijek Tourist Association.

In Split, I would like to thank the knowledgeable Zdravko Banović of the Split Tourist Office and Ankica Bokšić of the Split-Dalmatia County Tourist Board who worked hard to make my travels through Dalmatia comfortable. Thanks also to her boss, Mili Razović of the Split-Dalmatia County Tourist Board, Ante Škarpa of HPT and the Dorotić family. Other helpful tourism workers in Split-Dalmatia County include Nikola Bulic in Vis, Vinko Bakija in Supetar, Ante-Ćićo Ruićin Šolta, Davor Glavina in Makarska, the staff of the Hvar Tourist Board and the Vis Tourist Association.

In Zadar County, Gordana Perić went out of her way to coordinate my trip and provide necessary information. I also appreciate the help provided by Dragica Jović in Paklenica National Park, Mariana Lonžarić in Stari Grad and Nera Usalj in Dugi Otok.

In Kvarner County, thanks to Gordana Medved and the staff of the county Tourist Board as well as Olga Sinčić in Mali Lošinj, Josip Karabaić and Mr Crnčić in Krk, Marie-Rose Kordić in Rab and the tourist boards of Opatija and Rijeka.

Thanks to the Istrian Tourist Board headed by Veljko Ostojić for providing such a large quantity of useful maps and brochures as well as Albino Sinožić and Roberto Poropat of Poreč and Marino Brečević of Pula. A special thanks to my friend Vesna Jovićić of Pula for her invaluable support and assistance.

In Dubrovnik-Neretva County I would like to thank Vladimir Bakic and in Dubrovnik, Antonjeta-Nives Miloš made my visits pleasant. Stanka Kraljević in Korčula is always a reliable source of information and help.

And, finally, at Lonely Planet thanks to my editors Liz Filleul and Clay Lucas for their patience and good cheer.

This Book

This first edition of Croatia was researched and written by Jeanne Oliver, who also updated the Croatia chapter from LP's *Eastern Europe* and *Mediterranean Europe* guides.

From the publisher

Clay Lucas was the coordinating editor of this first edition of Croatia. Mark Griffiths took the book through layout and Tony Fankhauser drew all the maps, produced the colour wraps and found us some little boats for chapter ends. Clay was assisted by Janet Austin, Ada Cheung, Kate Daly, Martine Lleonart and Chris Wyness. Thanks to Rebecca Turner for technical support, Maria Vallianos for the cover, Tim Uden for his Quark XPress expertise and ever-so-fond memories of Croatia and Alison Brown for her work on the Health section. Quentin Frayne and our phrasebook department produced the Language chapter.

Foreword

ABOUT LONELY PLANET GUIDEBOOKS

The story begins with a classic travel adventure: Tony and Maureen Wheeler's 1972 journey across Europe and Asia to Australia. Useful information about the overland trail did not exist at that time, so Tony and Maureen published the first Lonely Planet guidebook to meet a growing need.

From a kitchen table, then from a tiny office in Melbourne (Australia), Lonely Planet has become the largest independent travel publisher in the world, an international company with offices in Melbourne, Oakland (USA), London (UK) and Paris (France).

Today Lonely Planet guidebooks cover the globe. There is an ever-growing list of books and there's information in a variety of forms and media. Some things haven't changed. The main aim is still to help make it possible for adventurous travellers to get out there – to explore and better understand the world.

At Lonely Planet we believe travellers can make a positive contribution to the countries they visit – if they respect their host communities and spend their money wisely. Since 1986 a percentage of the income from each book has been donated to aid projects and human rights campaigns.

Updates Lonely Planet thoroughly updates each guidebook as often as possible. This usually means there are around two years between editions, although for more unusual or more stable destinations the gap can be longer. Check the imprint page (following the colour map at the beginning of the book) for publication dates.

Between editions up-to-date information is available in two free newsletters – the paper *Planet Talk* and email *Comet* (to subscribe, contact any Lonely Planet office) – and on our Web site at www.lonelyplanet.com. The *Upgrades* section of the Web site covers a number of important and volatile destinations and is regularly updated by Lonely Planet authors. *Scoop* covers news and current affairs relevant to travellers. And, lastly, the *Thorn Tree* bulletin board and *Postcards* section of the site carry unverified, but fascinating, reports from travellers.

Correspondence The process of creating new editions begins with the letters, postcards and emails received from travellers. This correspondence often includes suggestions, criticisms and comments about the current editions. Interesting excerpts are immediately passed on via newsletters and the Web site, and everything goes to our authors to be verified when they're researching on the road. We're keen to get more feedback from organisations or individuals who represent communities visited by travellers.

Lonely Planet gathers information for everyone who's curious about the planet – and especially for those who explore it first-hand. Through guidebooks, phrasebooks, activity guides, maps, literature, newsletters, image library, TV series and Web site we act as an information exchange for a worldwide community of travellers.

Research Authors aim to gather sufficient practical information to enable travellers to make informed choices and to make the mechanics of a journey run smoothly. They also research historical and cultural background to help enrich the travel experience and allow travellers to understand and respond appropriately to cultural and environmental issues.

Authors don't stay in every hotel because that would mean spending a couple of months in each medium-sized city and, no, they don't eat at every restaurant because that would mean stretching belts beyond capacity. They do visit hotels and restaurants to check standards and prices, but feedback based on readers' direct experiences can be very helpful.

Many of our authors work undercover, others aren't so secretive. None of them accept freebies in exchange for positive write-ups. And none of our guidebooks contain any advertising.

Production Authors submit their raw manuscripts and maps to offices in Australia, USA, UK or France. Editors and cartographers – all experienced travellers themselves – then begin the process of assembling the pieces. When the book finally hits the shops, some things are already out of date, we start getting feedback from readers and the process begins again ...

WARNING & REQUEST

Things change – prices go up, schedules change, good places go bad and bad places go bankrupt – nothing stays the same. So, if you find things better or worse, recently opened or long since closed, please tell us and help make the next edition even more accurate and useful. We genuinely value all the feedback we receive. Julie Young coordinates a well travelled team that reads and acknowledges every letter, postcard and email and ensures that every morsel of information finds its way to the appropriate authors, editors and cartographers for verification.

Everyone who writes to us will find their name in the next edition of the appropriate guidebook. They will also receive the latest issue of *Planet Talk*, our quarterly printed newsletter, or *Comet*, our monthly email newsletter. Subscriptions to both newsletters are free. The very best contributions will be rewarded with a free guidebook.

Excerpts from your correspondence may appear in new editions of Lonely Planet guidebooks, the Lonely Planet Web site, *Planet Talk* or *Comet*, so please let us know if you *don't* want your letter published or your name acknowledged.

Send all correspondence to the Lonely Planet office closest to you:

Australia: PO Box 617, Hawthorn, Victoria 3122
USA: 150 Linden St, Oakland, CA 94607
UK: 10A Spring Place, London NW5 3BH
France: 1 rue du Dahomey, 75011 Paris

Or email us at: talk2us@lonelyplanet.com.au

For news, views and updates see our Web site: www.lonelyplanet.com

HOW TO USE A LONELY PLANET GUIDEBOOK

The best way to use a Lonely Planet guidebook is any way you choose. At Lonely Planet we believe the most memorable travel experiences are often those that are unexpected, and the finest discoveries are those you make yourself. Guidebooks are not intended to be used as if they provide a detailed set of infallible instructions!

Contents All Lonely Planet guidebooks follow the same format. The Facts about the Country chapters or sections give background information ranging from history to weather. Facts for the Visitor gives practical information on issues like visas and health. Getting There & Away gives a brief starting point for researching travel to and from the destination. Getting Around gives an overview of the transport options when you arrive.

The peculiar demands of each destination determine how subsequent chapters are broken up, but some things remain constant. We always start with background, then proceed to sights, places to stay, places to eat, entertainment, getting there and away, and getting around information – in that order.

Heading Hierarchy Lonely Planet headings are used in a strict hierarchical structure that can be visualised as a set of Russian dolls. Each heading (and its following text) is encompassed by any preceding heading that is higher on the hierarchical ladder.

Entry Points We do not assume guidebooks will be read from beginning to end, but that people will dip into them. The traditional entry points are the list of contents and the index. In addition, however, there is a complete list of maps and an index map illustrating map coverage.

There's also a colour map that shows highlights. These highlights are dealt with in greater detail in the Facts for the Visitor chapter, along with planning questions and suggested itineraries. Each chapter covering a geographical region begins with a locator map and another list of highlights. Once you find something of interest in a list of highlights, turn to the index.

Maps Maps play a crucial role in Lonely Planet guidebooks and include a huge amount of information. A legend is printed on the back page. We seek to have complete consistency between maps and text, and to have every important place in the text captured on a map. Map key numbers usually start in the top left corner.

Although inclusion in a guidebook usually implies a recommendation we cannot list every good place. Exclusion does not necessarily imply criticism. In fact there are a number of reasons why we might exclude a place – sometimes it is simply inappropriate to encourage an influx of travellers.

Introduction

Croatia (Hrvatska) is a peaceful country, which may sound surprising considering the well-publicised strife that followed its declaration of independence from Yugoslavia in 1991. Yet even at the height of the conflict most of the country remained untouched by war, and there has been no fighting on Croatian soil since 1995. Despite years of peace, Croatia's reputation as a war zone distracts attention from the country's many treasures which include crystal-clear seas, remote islands, unspoilt fishing villages, beaches, vineyards, Roman ruins and medieval walled cities.

Before Croatia separated from Yugoslavia, it had a booming tourist industry that attracted some 10 million visitors a year. For most of the 1970s and 1980s, Germans, Italians, Austrians and Brits packed Croatia's coastal and island resorts each summer from Istria to Dubrovnik, making Croatian tourism a cornerstone of the former Yugoslav economy. Although tourists are slowly starting to drift back to their favourite haunts, it will be many years before tourism reaches prewar levels, which means that there's a window of opportunity for travellers to explore one of the world's newest countries before the crowds return.

A glance at a map will explain a large part of Croatia's appeal. With a surface area of over 56,538 sq km, the country is not large but it has a spectacular 1778km coastline on the Adriatic and 1185 offshore islands. All

11

told, almost 6000km of coastline winds around innumerable bays and inlets, rising to steep mountainous backdrops or flattening out to sandy beaches. An abundance of natural harbours lures yachties, and naturists have a wide choice of secluded coves. There's an island for every taste, ranging from stark, sunbaked outcrops to softly contoured Shangri-las replete with meadows, lakes and forested hills.

It's easy to binge on sun and sea in Croatia but that would be to miss out on the country's rich cultural heritage. Evolving from centuries of occupation by foreign empires, Croatian culture is divided between the Latin-influenced coast and the Central European-style interior. Along the Adriatic coast, you'll find remains of palaces, temples and amphitheatres from the Roman empire as well as forts, fishing villages and fortified towns built during the many centuries of Venetian rule. The Austro-Hungarian empire left a strong imprint on the architecture of the interior, particularly in the baroque cities that flourished in the 17th and 18th centuries.

Now that Croatia has achieved its hard-won independence, there's a new emphasis on the traditions that have kept its sense of nationhood alive throughout the era of foreign domination. Religion, in the form of the Catholic Church, has been essential to the Croatian identity and many of the recently revived folk traditions revolve around religious holidays. Carnival festivals marking the observance of Lent are becoming increasingly popular and the Holy Week that precedes Easter is celebrated with songs and processions. Many towns celebrate the feast day of their patron saint, while others commemorate historic battles. Colourful embroidered costumes, traditional music and dances and regional culinary specialties link today's Croats with their ancestors.

But Croatia is no Balkan backwater locked in a time warp. Croatians perceive themselves as part of modern Europe, not the troubled Balkans – a region they would cheerfully snip off and mail to another part of the globe if they could. Croatia's historical ties to Western Europe were maintained throughout its absorption into Yugoslavia as many Croatians worked and travelled abroad and Europeans vacationed in Croatia. Whether or not it bears any resemblance to the reality of modern Europe, Croatians model themselves after their idea of European values – good food and wine, nice clothes, vacations at the seashore, attention to the environment, preservation of historical treasures and a calm, polite demeanour.

All this adds up to a relaxed, easy-going country. Croatians are justifiably proud of the wealth of vacation opportunities they can offer – from national parks, modern beach resorts, hiking and scuba diving to museums, churches and archaeological sites. All the country lacks is the kind of clearly defined image that has turned more modest European destinations into international hot spots. No famous writer has extolled its culture, no film-makers have set car chases on its dramatic coastal cliffs, and bikini-clad movie stars are not regularly photographed on its shores. Yet the absence of a prepackaged fantasy can be liberating. Unburdened by preconceptions and expectations, a visitor to Croatia can experience the increasingly rare sense of wonder that transforms mere tourism into travel.

Facts about Croatia

HISTORY
Early Inhabitants

Excavations in north-western Croatia have revealed that the area has been inhabited since the Paleolithic Age. The discovery of Neanderthal bones in a cave near Krapina at the turn of the century unleashed an archaeological controversy that has not yet been entirely resolved. Excavated between 1899 and 1911, it appeared that the 100,000-year-old bones had been roasted and split open to extract the marrow. Were our ancestors cannibals or practicing strange funerary rites? Archaeologists disagree, but the more recent excavation of the nearby Vindija cave in the 1970s lends support to the cannibal theory. It appears that both the animal and human bones showed cut marks, signs of burning and had been broken up and strewn about the cave in what would seem a joyous food fest.

Apart from their unusual diet and poor table manners, little is known about the Paleolithic cave-dwellers that inhabited the region. Stone tools were found in the Krapina cave and tools from the Upper Paleolithic age were also found at a cave in Lokve near Rijeka. The discovery of a bear skull at the Veternica cave near Zagreb seem to point to some sort of bear-cult ceremonies. Excavations in the Grabac cave on Hvar island turned up ornamented red-painted pottery from the Neolithic Age that recalls pottery found in other Mediterranean cultures. Still, the main activities through the Paleolithic period were hunting and foraging for food.

Fast forward tens of thousands of years to 6000 BC when the Starcevo fishing and farming culture spread throughout eastern Europe as far as eastern Slavonia. People settled down, raised livestock, began to construct permanent dwellings and made pottery. Excavations at Vucedol (near Vukovar) reveal a culture that flourished from the late Stone Age to the Bronze Age,

3000-2000 BC. It is believed that they built their houses on piles over marshy lands in order to conserve fertile land for agriculture. The population grew during the Bronze Age and crafts multiplied. Although early pottery was crude, fragments from the later period were ornamented with geometric figures and decorated with a white glaze. Eastern Slavonia was the base for what became known as the Vucedol culture which reached Slovakia, Slovenia, Austria, Germany, Hungary and the Czech Republic before moving southward to the Adriatic islands.

Most of what is known about Middle Bronze Age to Iron Age inhabitants has been surmised from examining their funerary practices. The Glasinac culture which centred in eastern Bosnia-Hercegovina maintained their tradition of covering graves with earthen mounds from the late Neolithic period through the Bronze Age (700 BC) against pressure from the growing vogue for flat grave burial. The late Bronze Age was characterised by the practice of cremation and placing the bones in urns surrounded by food, drink, jewellery and weapons. In the early Iron Age, graves of tribal chiefs often contained bronze vessels, swords, and glass from Germany and Greece indicating that trade flourished during this period. Excavations in Vukovar have raised the possibility that fierce Cimmerian horsemen from Crimea may have inhabited the region around the 8th century BC.

The Illyrians, an Indo-European people, began migrating into the region around 1000 BC, spreading iron tools and implements from the Hallstatt settlements in modern day Austria southward to the Adriatic. Although Greeks set up trading posts on the eastern Adriatic coast in the 6th century BC, their influence was kept in check by the warlike Illyrians. Invading Celts pushed the Illyrians further south in the 4th century, towards what is today Albania.

The last powerful Illyrian ruler was King Agron, who formed an alliance with Demetrius of Macedonia to defeat the Aetolian Greeks in the latter shalf of the 3rd century BC. Upon King Agron's death, his widow, Queen Teuta, antagonised Rome by refusing to punish those responsible for attacking a Roman delegation that had been sent to complain about the notorious Illyrian pirates. She then attacked Greek colonies along the coast which provoked a punitive strike by the Romans in 229 BC. The Romans continued to push their way into the region and, in 168 BC, they finally conquered Genthius, the last Illyrian king.

The Romans

The initial Roman colony of Illyricum was gradually enlarged in a series of wars (156, 119, 78-77 BC) which brought much of the Dalmatian coast within their control. Until the reign of Emperor Augustus (30 BC to 14 AD), the Roman province of Illyricum stretched from the Drin River in modern Albania to Istria in the north and the Sava River in the east. During 12-11 BC Rome conquered much of the interior which was inhabited by the Pannonian tribe, extending the empire's reach to the middle and lower Danube. The realm was reorganised into Dalmatia (the former Illyricum), and Upper and Lower Pannonia which covered much of the interior of modern Croatia. After an unsuccessful Illyrian revolt that lasted from 6 to 9 AD, the territory was finally subjugated in 12 AD with the defeat of the Illyrian tribe of the Ardeioi (whose name gradually evolved into the Adriatic).

The Romans ruled the area for five centuries, making Salona (Solin) their administrative headquarters. The Romans believed they had brought peace and prosperity to a barbarous land. The Illyrians might have expressed it a little differently, perhaps pointing out that things were working out fine until they had to expend resources defending themselves from Roman expansion. It is clear that the Romans built a network of roads, linking the coast with the Aegean and Black seas, and with the Danube River which facilitated trade. The mining industry that was already in place in the central and western lands continued to prosper and the fertile Pannonian plains produced a wealth of agricultural products. The region was profitable for the Romans, but its prosperity was partly based on their introduction of the slave trade. As in other parts of the empire, cities flourished as rural inhabitants flocked to the forums, temples, theatres, baths and circuses that characterised Roman rule. In addition to Salona, other important Roman towns included Zadar (Jadera), Poreč (Parentium), Pula (Polensium) and, later, Split (Spalato).

In addition to providing riches for Rome, Dalmatia also provided warriors to serve in the Roman legions, five of whom were to rise through the ranks to become emperor. When the Roman empire began to crack in the late third century AD, two strong Dalmatian emperors emerged. Emperor Diocletian was born in Salona in 236 AD and was chosen by the army to succeed Numerian as emperor in 285. While establishing strong central control, he divided Dalmatia into Dalmatia Salonitana with its capital at Salona and Dalmatia Praevalitana with its capital at Scodra (Schkoder in modern Albania). By placing the two regions in separate dioceses, he sowed the seeds for the later division into the Eastern and Western Roman empire. In 305 Diocletian retired to his palace in Split, today the greatest Roman ruin in eastern Europe.

In contrast to Diocletian's persecution of Christians, Emperor Constantine was ostentatiously Christian (to the point that the Eastern Orthodox Church today recognises Constantine as a saint). Born in Niš (modern Yugoslavia) in 285, Constantine began his rule in 306 as Emperor of the Western Empire, becoming Emperor of the entire Roman empire in 324. In 330 he founded a new capital of the Roman empire at the ancient Greek city of Byzantium, renaming the city Constantinople and thus providing a nucleus for the later Byzantine empire.

Constantine: ostentatiously Christian and a saint to the Eastern Orthodox church

The last Roman leader to rule a united empire was Theodosius ('the Great'), who adeptly managed to stave off serious threats from the northern Visigoths. On Theodosius death in 395, the empire was divided between his two sons: Honorius to rule the West and Arcadius the East. Although the intention was to create a merely administrative division, his rather dull-witted sons were easily manipulated by ambitious underlings which led to the empire's formal division into eastern and western realms. What is now Slovenia, Croatia and Bosnia-Hercegovina were assigned to the Western Roman Empire, while present-day Serbia, Kosovo and Macedonia went to what was to become the Byzantine Empire.

Migration

Visigoth, Hun and Lombard invasions marked the fall of the Western Roman Empire in the 5th century. Dalmatia briefly became part of the Ostrogoth kingdom at the turn of the 6th century, before the Byzantine Emperor Justinian grabbed it for the Eastern Roman Empire in 535. Meanwhile, nomadic Avars established an empire for themselves on the Hungarian plain between the Danube and Tisza rivers from which they launched attacks against Byzantium.

While the Roman empire was disintegrating, the Croats and other Slavic tribes were living in a swampy terrain that roughly covered the area of modern Ukraine, Poland and Belarus. The region was later called White Croatia and, within its bounds, the Slavs tended fields and raised livestock.

Little is known about the origins of these early Slavs, but it appears that early in the 7th century they moved south across the Danube and joined the Avars in their attacks on Byzantine Dalmatia. Salona and Epidaurus were ravaged, their inhabitants taking refuge in Spalato (Split) and Ragusa (Dubrovnik) respectively.

Although the exact dates and motives of the migrating Slavs remain uncertain, there was clearly a slow movement of peoples southward that probably lasted for most of the 7th and 8th centuries. Sometimes the Croats and Slavic tribes joined Avars in their attacks on Byzantium and other times they were persuaded by Byzantium to attack the Avars.

By the middle of the 7th century the Croatian tribe had begun to settle in Pannonia and Dalmatia, mingling with earlier Slav settlers on the Pannonian plains and forming communities around the Dalmatian towns of Jadera (Zadar), Aeona (Nin) and Tragurium (Trogir). During the course of the 8th century the Dalmatian and Pannonian Croats organised themselves around powerful clans, one of which was called Hrvat (Croat), a name that the clan gave to their territory in central Dalmatia, Bijela Hrvatska (White Croatia).

Croatian Kings

Charlemagne's Frankish army seized Dalmatia in 800, which led to the Christianisation of the Croat rulers in a series of mass baptisms. After Charlemagne's death in 814, the Pannonian Croats revolted unsuccessfully against Frankish rule without the support of the Dalmatian Croats, whose major coastal cities remained under the influence of the Byzantine empire throughout the 9th century. Even as Dalmatia accepted the political domination of Byzantium, the spread of Christianity encouraged cultural ties with Rome which proved to be the unifying factor in forging a national identity.

The first ruler to unite Pannonia and Dalmatia was Tomislav, who was crowned in 925 and was recognised by the pope as king. His territory included virtually all of modern Croatia as well as part of Bosnia and the coast of Montenegro.

Although parts of this epoch remain vague, it appears that Croatia had become a military power of some importance. At least it was strong enough to repel the first of many Hungarian attacks on their soil in 924.

By the mid 10th century, the country's fragile unity was threatened by power struggles in its ruling class. Venice took advantage of the disarray to launch an invasion of Dalmatia at the turn of the 11th century that established its first foothold on the coast.

Krešimir IV (1058-74) regained control over Dalmatia with the help of the papacy, but the kingdom once again descended into anarchy upon his death. A new leader emerged from Pannonia who took the name Zvonimir. King Zvonimir (1075-89) also cemented his authority with the help of the pope but the independent land he forged did not survive his death.

King Ladislav of Hungary was the brother of Zvonimir's widow and acted quickly to secure the throne by invading northern Croatia in 1091. The queen and many nobles supported him but his plans to conquer Dalmatia were thwarted by a Byzantine attack on Hungary which successfully kept Dalmatia under Byzantine control. Although Ladislav's successor, King Koloman, managed to persuade the Dalmatian nobility to accept his rule in exchange for self-government, his victory was somewhat limited by the increasing control that Venice was exerting over the Dalmatian coast.

Hungary versus Venice

The hope that Hungary would save Dalmatia from Venetian control proved ephemeral. Upon Koloman's death in 1116 Venice launched new assaults on Biograd, Zadar, and the islands of Lošinj, Pag, Rab and Krk. Venice laid siege to Zadar for ten years but managed to capture it only after the Doge of Venice paid 13th century Crusaders handsomely to attack and sack the town before proceeding on to Constantinople.

The 13th century also brought new troubles in the form of a Mongol invasion that pushed the Hungarian King Bela IV down to Trogir. Dalmatian cities warred with each other and Venice again took advantage of the confusion to consolidate its hold on Zadar. The death of King Bela in 1270 led to another power struggle among the Croatian nobility which allowed Venice to add Šibenik and Trogir to its possessions.

King Ludovik I of Hungary (1342-82) re-established control over the country and even persuaded Venice to relinquish Dalmatia. The Hungarian victory was short-lived. New conflicts emerged upon Ludovik's death and the Croatian nobility rallied around Ladislas of Naples who was crowned King in Zadar in 1403. Short of funds, Ladislas then sold Zadar to Venice in 1409 for a paltry 100,000 ducats and renounced his rights to Dalmatia. In the early 15th century Venice solidified its grip on the Dalmatian coastline from Zadar to Dubrovnik and remained in control until the Napoleonic invasion of 1797.

Habsburgs 1 Ottomans 0

The rise of the Ottoman empire brought new threats to 16th century Croatia. Ottoman conquests in the 15th century brought Byzantine rule to a crashing end. The defeat of the Serbs in 1389 at Kosovo opened the door to Bosnia, which did not last long after the fall of Constantinople in 1453. Sensing nasty weather from the east, the Croatian nobility desperately appealed to foreign powers for help but to no avail. The Ottomans continued their relentless advance, virtually wiping out the cream of Croatian leadership at the 1493 battle of Krbavsko Polje. Despite the sudden unity of the remaining noble families, one city after another fell to the Ottoman sultans. The important bishopric at Zagreb heavily fortified the cathedral in Kaptol which remained untouched, but the gateway town of Knin fell in 1521. Towns and villages were burned, churches and monasteries sacked, and tens of thousands of citizens were either killed or dragged off into slavery.

Hungary was no help. Inept and outmatched, King Ludovik II was killed in the disastrous battle of Mohacs in southern Hungary in 1526 which opened the way for the Ottoman occupation of Buda (Budapest). The Archduke Ferdinand of Austria established his claim to the Hungarian throne against bitter opposition and the Croatian Sabor (Parliament) elected him king of Croatia with the explicit proviso that he was expected to provide help against the Turkish enemy. Unfortunately, the Habsburgs were unable to protect Croatia against the Ottoman onslaught and the Croats continued to lose territory. By the end of the century only a narrow strip of territory around Zagreb, Karlovac and Varaždin was under Habsburg control. The Adriatic coast was threatened by the Turks but never captured and Ragusa (Dubrovnik) maintained its independence throughout the turmoil.

To form a buffer against the Turks the Austrians maintained a string of forts south of Zagreb called the Vojna Krajina (Military Frontier). Initially open to anyone who wanted to live on the marshy land, the Habsburgs invited Vlachs to settle the land in the 16th century. At the time most Vlachs belonged to the Serbian Orthodox Church which irritated the Croatian Sabor, although they were much more irritated by the arrangement allowing the settlers to escape the harsh feudal system that the Hungarians had instituted in the country. Despite repeated efforts by the Croatian nobility to either turn them into serfs or get rid of them completely, the free peasants stayed on their land until they were expelled in 1995.

The first major defeat suffered by the Ottomans was the battle of Lepanto in 1571 which ended the Turkish naval threat in the Mediterranean. From the Balkan point of view however, it was the Ottoman rout at the siege of Vienna in 1683 that marked the beginning of the end of Turkish hegemony. With the myth of Turkish invincibility shattered, more victories followed. Slavonia was liberated within a few years. The Turks were evicted from Buda, Osijek, Vukovar and Belgrade. In the Treaty of Sremski Karlovci of 1699 the Turks renounced all claims to Hungary and Croatia. During the 18th century, Croat and Serb immigrants flooded into Slavonia joined by Hungarians, Slovaks, Albanian Catholics and Jews. Much land was awarded to the Catholic and Orthodox churches and distributed as awards for good service to wealthy landlords and generals. Under the rule of Maria Theresa of Austria, the region returned to stability.

Venetian Empire

Venetian rule in Dalmatia and Istria was a ruthless record of nearly unbroken economic exploitation. Early in their rule, the Venetians ordered the destruction of Dalmatian mulberry trees in order to kill the silk trade for no other apparent reason than to keep the region poor and dependent. Other trees also suffered as the Venetians systematically denuded the landscape in order to provide wood for their ships. Olive oil, figs, wine, fish and salt were in effect confiscated, since merchants were forced to sell only to Venetians and only at the price the Venetians were willing to pay. Dalmatian fisherman were unable to salt their fish for preservation because salt was kept unreasonably expensive by a state monopoly. Shipbuilding was effectively banned since Venice tolerated no competition with its own ships. No roads or schools were built, no investment made in local industry. All manufactured articles had to be imported and, by the latter half of the 18th century, even agricultural products had to be imported to keep the population – barely surviving on roots and grass – from starving to death. In addition to Venice's iron fisted economic policies, the population was also subject to malaria and plague epidemics that ravaged the region.

Enter Napoleon

Habsburg support for the restoration of the monarchy in France led to Napoleon's invasion of Austria's Italian states in 1796. After conquering Venice in 1797 he agreed to transfer Dalmatia to Austria in the Treaty of Campo Formio in exchange for other concessions. Croatian hopes that Dalmatia would be united with Slavonia were soon dashed as the Habsburgs made it clear that the two territories would retain separate administrations.

Austrian control of Dalmatia only lasted until Napoleon's 1805 victory over Austrian and Prussian forces at Austerlitz forced Austria to cede the Dalmatian coast to France. Ragusa (Dubrovnik) quickly surrendered to French forces. Napoleon renamed his conquest the 'Illyrian provinces' and moved with characteristic swiftness to reform the crumbling territory. A tree planting program was established to reforest the barren hills. Since almost the entire population was illiterate, the new government set up primary schools, high schools and a college at Zadar. Roads and hospitals were built and new crops introduced. A program was instituted to drain the marshes that were breeding malarian mosquitoes. Yet the French regime remained unpopular, partly because the anti-clerical French were staunchly opposed by the clergy and partly because the population was heavily taxed to pay for the reforms.

The fall of the Napoleonic empire after his disastrous Russian campaign led to the 1815 Congress of Vienna which recognised Austria's claims to Dalmatia and placed the rest of Croatia under the jurisdiction of Austria's Hungarian province. For the Dalmatians, the new regime meant a return to the status quo since the Austrians restored the former Italian elite to power. For the Croats the agreement meant submission to

Napoleon Bonaparte: conqueror, educator and marsh drainer to the people of Croatia

Hungary's insistent desire to impose the Hungarian language and culture on the population.

The 1848 Revolution

One of the effects of Hungarian heavy-handedness was to create the first stirrings of a national identity among the southern Slavic people. The sense of a shared identity first found expression in an 'Illyrian' movement in the 1830s that centred on the revival of the Croatian language. Traditionally, upper-class Dalmatians spoke Italian, and northern Croats spoke German or Hungarian. The establishment of the first 'Illyrian' newspaper in 1834, written in the Zagreb dialect prompted the Croatian Sabor to call for the teaching of the Slavic language in schools and even the unification of Dalmatia with Slavonia. Despite Hungarian threats, in 1847 the Sabor voted to make 'Illyrian' the national language.

The increasing desire for more autonomy and the eventual unification of Dalmatia and Slavonia led the Croats to intervene on the side of the Habsburgs against a Hungarian revolutionary movement that sought to free the country from Austrian rule. The Croatian Sabor informed Austria that it would send the Croatian commander Josip Jelačić to fight the Hungarian rebels in return for the cancellation of Hungary's jurisdiction over Croatia, among other demands. Unfortunately Jelačić's military campaign was unsuccessful. Russian intervention quelled the Hungarian rebellion and Austria firmly rejected any further demands for autonomy from its Slavic subjects.

Dreams of Yugoslavia

Disillusionment spread after 1848, amplified by the birth of the Austro-Hungarian Dual Monarchy in 1867. The monarchy placed Croatia and Slavonia within the Hungarian administration, while Dalmatia remained within Austria. For the first time Rijeka and the Medjimurje region were also handed over to Hungary. Whatever limited form of self-government the Croats enjoyed under the Habsburgs disappeared along with 55% of their revenues earmarked for the imperial treasury.

The river of discontent running through late 19th century Croatia forked into two streams that dominated the political landscape for the next century. The old 'Illyrian' movement became the National Party, dominated by the brilliant Bishop Josif Juraf Strossmayer. Strossmayer believed that the differences between Serbs and Croats were magnified by the manipulations of the Habsburgs and the Hungarians, and that only through south-Slavic unity (*Jugoslavenstvo*) could the aspirations of both peoples be realised. Strossmayer supported the Serbian independence struggle in Serbia but favoured a Yugoslav entity within the Austro-Hungarian empire rather than complete independence.

By contrast, the Party of Rights led by Ante Starčević envisioned an independent Croatia made up of Slavonia, Dalmatia, the Krajina, Slovenia, Istria, and part of Bosnia and Hercegovina. Starčević was also militantly anti-Serbian. At the time, the Orthodox church was encouraging the Serbs to form a national identity based upon their religion. Until the 19th century, Orthodox inhabitants of Croatia identified themselves as Vlachs, Morlachs, Serbs, Orthodox or even Greeks but, with the help of Starčević's attacks, the sense of a separate Serbian, Orthodox identity within Croatia developed.

Under the theory of 'divide and rule', the Hungarian-appointed Ban (viceroy) of Croatia blatantly favoured the Serbs and the Orthodox church, but his strategy backfired. The first organised resistance formed in Dalmatia. Croat representatives in Rijeka and Serb representatives in Zadar joined together in 1905 to demand the unification of Dalmatia and Slavonia with a formal guarantee of Serbian equality as a nation. The spirit of unity mushroomed, and by 1906 Croat-Serb coalitions had taken over local government in Dalmatia and Slavonia, forming a serious threat to the Hungarian power structure.

The Kingdom of Serbs, Croats & Slovenes

With the outbreak of WWI, Croatia's future was again up for grabs. According to the Treaty of London (1915) an Allied victory would have carved up Croatia between Italy and Serbia. Sensing that they would once again be pawns to the Great Powers, a Croatian delegation, the 'Yugoslav Committee', convinced the Serbian government to agree to the establishment of a parliamentary monarchy that would rule over the two countries. The Yugoslav Committee became the National Council of Slovenes, Croats and Serbs after the collapse of the Austro-Hungarian empire in 1918 and they quickly negotiated the establishment of the Kingdom of Serbs, Croats and Slovenes to be based in Belgrade. Although many Croatians were unsure about Serbian intentions, they were very sure about Italian intentions since Italy lost no time in seizing Pula, Rijeka and Zadar in November 1918.

Given, in effect, a choice between throwing in their lot with Italy or Serbia, the Croats chose Serbia.

Problems with the kingdom began almost immediately. Currency reforms benefited Serbs at the expense of the Croats. A treaty between Yugoslavia and Italy gave Istria, Zadar and a number of islands to Italy. The new constitution abolished Croatia's Sabor and centralised power in Belgrade while new electoral districts under-represented the Croats.

Opposition to the new regime was led by the Croat Stjepan Radić who remained favourable to the idea of Yugoslavia but wished to transform it into a federal democracy. His alliance with the Serb Svetpzar Pribićevic proved profoundly threatening to the regime and Radić was assassinated. Exploiting fears of civil war, on January 6, 1929 King Aleksandar in Belgrade proclaimed a royal dictatorship, abolished political parties and suspended parliamentary government, thus ending any hope of democratic change.

WWII & the Rise of Ustashe

One day after the proclamation, a Bosnian Croat, Ante Pavelić, set up the Ustashe Croatian Liberation Movement in Zagreb with the stated aim of establishing an independent state by force if necessary. Fearing arrest, he fled to Sofia, Bulgaria and made contact with anti-Serbian Macedonian revolutionaries before fleeing to Italy. There, he established training camps for his organisation under Mussolini's benevolent eye. After organising various disturbances, in 1934 he and the Macedonians succeeded in assassinating King Aleksandar in Marseilles while he was on a state visit. Italy responded by closing down the training camps and imprisoning Pavelić and many of his followers.

Meanwhile, the process of providing more autonomy for Croatia within the Kingdom of Yugoslavia was slowly being advanced by King Aleksandar's successor, his cousin Prince Paul, governing as regent until the majority of the King's son, King Petar. An agreement with the Croatian leader Vlado Maček would have granted self-rule to the Croatians but the threat from Nazi Germany drove a further wedge between the two sides. Prince Paul was ousted by a Serbian population infuriated by his pact with Hitler, while Croatia remained determined not to wage war on behalf of England and France who were viewed as too closely affiliated with the increasingly discredited Kingdom of Yugoslavia. When Germany invaded Yugoslavia on 6 April 1941 the exiled Ustashe were quickly installed by the Germans, with the support of the Italians who hoped to see their own territorial aims in Dalmatia realised.

Within days the Independent State of Croatia (NDH) headed by Pavelić issued a range of decrees designed to persecute and eliminate the regime's 'enemies' who were mainly Jews, gypsies and Serbs. Over 80% of the Jewish population was rounded up and packed off to extermination camps between 1941 and 1945. Serbs fared no better. The Ustashe program called for 'one-third of Serbs killed, one-third expelled and one-third converted to Catholicism,' a program that was carried out with a brutality that appalled even the Nazis. Villages conducted their own personal pogroms against Serbs and extermination camps were set up, most notoriously at Jasenovac south of Zagreb. The exact number of Serb victims is uncertain, ranging from 60,000 to 600,000 but, whatever the number, it is clear that the NDH and their supporters made a diligent effort to exterminate the entire Serb population.

Tito & the Partisans

Not all Croats supported these policies. The Ustashe regime drew most of its support from the Lika region south-west of Zagreb and western Hercegovina but Pavelić's agreement to cede a good part of Dalmatia to Italy was highly unpopular to say the least and the Ustashe had almost no support in that region.

Armed resistance to the regime took the form of Serbian 'Chetnik' formations led by

General Draza Mihailovic which began as an antifascist rebellion but soon degenerated into massacres of Croats in eastern Croatia and Bosnia.

The most effective antifascist struggle was conducted by National Liberation Partisan units and its leader, Josip Broz, known as Tito. With its roots in the outlawed Yugoslavian Communist party, the Partisans attracted long-suffering Yugoslav intellectuals, Croats disgusted with Chetnik massacres, Serbs disgusted with Ustashe massacres, and antifascists of all kinds. The Partisans gained wide popular support with their early program which, although vague, appeared to envision a post-war Yugoslavia that would be based on a loose federation.

Although the Allies initially backed the Serbian Chetniks, it became apparent that the Partisans were waging a far more focused and determined fight against the Nazis. With the diplomatic and military support of Churchill and other Allied powers the Partisans controlled much of Croatia by 1943. The Partisans established functioning local governments in the territory they seized, which later eased their transition to power. On 20 October 1944 Tito entered Belgrade with the Red Army and was made Prime Minister. When Germany surrendered in 1945, Pavelić and the Ustashe fled and the Partisans entered Zagreb. Tito's attempt to retain control of the Italian city of Trieste and parts of southern Austria faltered in the face of Allied opposition, but Dalmatia was made a permanent part of post-war Yugoslavia.

Yugoslavia

The good news was that Tito was determined to create a state in which no ethnic group dominated the political landscape. Croatia became one of six republics – Macedonia, Serbia, Montenegro, Bosnia and Hercegovina, and Slovenia – in a tightly configured federation. The bad news was that Tito effected this delicate balance by creating a one-party state and rigorously stamping out all opposition whether nationalist, royalist or religious. The government's hostility to organised religion, particularly the Catholic church, stemmed from its perception that the Church was complicit in the murderous nationalism that surfaced during WWII.

Economic power was initially as centralised as political power in Tito's Yugoslavia. Modelling his policies after the centrally planned economy of Stalin's Soviet Union, Tito became less hard-line after his break with Stalin in 1948. The abandonment of the plan to collectivise agriculture in 1953 was followed by further deviations from Soviet-style communism. The ease with which Yugoslavs were able to travel abroad, for example, distinguished the country from other Soviet-bloc nations.

During the 1960s, the concentration of power in Belgrade became an increasingly testy issue as it became apparent that money from the more prosperous republics of Slovenia and Croatia was being distributed to the poorer republics Montenegro and Bosnia-Hercegovina. The problem seemed particularly blatant in Croatia which saw money from its prosperous tourist business on the Adriatic coast flow into Belgrade. At the same time Serbs in Croatia were over-represented in the government, armed forces and the police, partly because state-service offered an opportunity for a chronically disadvantaged population.

In Croatia the unrest reached a crescendo in the 'Croatian Spring' of 1971. Led by reformers within the Communist Party of Croatia, intellectuals and students first called for greater economic autonomy and then constitutional reform to loosen Croatia's ties to Yugoslavia. Tito's eventual crackdown was ferocious. Leaders of the movement were 'purged' – either jailed or expelled from the Party. Careers were abruptly terminated, some dissidents chose exile and emigrated to the United States. Serbs viewed the movement as the Ustashe reborn and jailed reformers blamed the Serbs for their troubles. The stage was set for the later rise of nationalism and war that followed Tito's death in 1980, even though his 1974 constitution afforded the republics more autonomy.

Independence

Tito's habit of borrowing from abroad to flood the country with cheap consumer goods produced an economic crisis after his death. The country was unable to service the interest on its loans and inflation soared. The authority of the central government sank along with the economy and long suppressed mistrust among Yugoslavia's ethnic groups resurfaced.

In 1989 severe repression of the Albanian majority in Serbia's Kosovo province sparked renewed fears of Serbian hegemony and heralded the end of the Yugoslav Federation. With political changes sweeping Eastern Europe, many Croats felt the time had come to end more than four decades of communist rule and attain complete autonomy into the bargain. In the free elections of April 1990 Franjo Tudjman's Croatian Democratic Union (Hrvatska Demokratska Zajednica) secured 40% of the vote, to the 30% won by the Communist Party which retained the loyalty of the Serbian community as well as voters in Istria and Rijeka. On 22 December 1990 a new Croatian constitution was promulgated, changing the status of Serbs in Croatia from that of a 'constituent nation' to a national minority.

The constitution's failure to guarantee minority rights, and mass dismissals of Serbs from the public service, stimulated the 600,000-strong ethnic Serb community within Croatia to demand autonomy. In early 1991 Serb extremists within Croatia staged provocations designed to force federal military intervention. A May 1991 referendum (boycotted by the Serbs) produced a 93% vote in favour of independence, but when Croatia declared independence on 25 June 1991, the Serbian enclave of Krajina proclaimed its independence from Croatia.

War & Peace

Heavy fighting broke out in Krajina, Baranja (the area north of the Drava River opposite Osijek) and Slavonia in June 1991. The 180,000-member, 2000-tank Yugoslav People's Army, dominated by Serbian communists, began to intervene on its own authority in support of Serbian irregulars under the pretext of halting ethnic violence. After European Community (now the European Union) mediation, Croatia agreed to freeze its independence declaration for three months to avoid bloodshed.

In the three months following 25 June, a quarter of Croatia fell to Serbian militias and the Serb-led Yugoslav People's Army. In September the Croatian Government ordered a blockade of 32 federal military installations in the republic, lifting morale and gaining much-needed military equipment. In response, the Yugoslav navy blockaded the Adriatic coast and laid siege to the strategic town of Vukovar on the Danube.

In early October 1991 the federal army and Montenegrin militia moved against Dubrovnik to protest against the ongoing blockade of their garrisons in Croatia, and on 7 October the presidential palace in Zagreb was hit by rockets fired by Yugoslav air force jets in an unsuccessful assassination attempt on President Tudjman. On 19 November heroic Vukovar finally fell when the army culminated a bloody three-month siege by concentrating 600 tanks and 30,000 soldiers there. During six months of fighting in Croatia 10,000 people died, hundreds of thousands fled and tens of thousands of homes were destroyed.

In early December the United Nations special envoy, Cyrus Vance, began successful negotiations with Serbia over the deployment of a 14,000-member UN Protection Force (UNPROFOR) in the Serb-held areas of Croatia. Beginning on 3 January 1992, a ceasefire generally held. The federal army was allowed to withdraw from its bases inside Croatia without having to shamefully surrender its weapons and thus tensions diminished.

When the three-month moratorium on independence expired on 8 October 1991, Croatia declared full independence. To fulfil a condition for EC (now EU) recognition, in December the Croatian parliament belatedly amended its constitution to protect minority and human rights. In January 1992 the EC, succumbing to strong pressure from Germany, recognised Croatia. This was followed three months later by US recognition and in May 1992 Croatia was admitted to the United Nations.

The UN peace plan in Krajina was supposed to have led to the disarming of local Serb paramilitary formations, the repatriation of refugees and the return of the region to Croatia. Instead it only froze the existing situation and offered no permanent solution.

In January 1993 the Croatian army suddenly launched an offensive in southern Krajina, pushing the Serbs back as much as 24km in some areas and recapturing strategic points such as the site of the destroyed Maslenica bridge, Zemunik airport near Zadar and the Perućac hydroelectric dam in the hills between Split and Bosnia-Hercegovina. The Krajina Serbs vowed never to accept rule from Zagreb and in June 1993 they voted overwhelmingly to join the Bosnian Serbs (and eventually Greater Serbia).

The self-proclaimed 'Republic of Serbian Krajina' held elections in December 1993 which no international body recognised as legitimate or fair. Meanwhile, continued 'ethnic cleansing' left only about 900 Croats in the Krajina out of an original population of 44,000. Although no further progress was made in implementing the Vance Peace Plan, the Krajina Serbs signed a comprehensive ceasefire on 29 March 1994 which substantially reduced the violence in the region and established demilitarised 'zones of separation' between the parties.

While world attention turned to the grim events unfolding in Bosnia-Hercegovina, the Croatian government quietly began procuring arms from abroad. On 1 May 1995, the Croatian army and police entered occupied western Slavonia, east of Zagreb, and seized control of the region within days. The Krajina Serbs responded by shelling Zagreb in an attack that left seven people dead and 130 wounded. As the Croatian military consolidated its hold in western Slavonia, some 15,000 Serbs fled the region despite assurances from the

War & Peace

1980

Death of President Tito; strains appear in Yugoslavia's federated system of six republics and two auonomous provinces.

1990

Collapse of communist system in Eastern Europe; elections in Yugoslavia bring nationalist and independence-minded governments to power in republics of Croatia, Slovenia and Serbia.

1991

June
Croatia and Slovenia declare independence: brief conflict between Slovenes and Yugoslav federal army; protracted conflict between newly independent Croatia and the Serbian minority in Croatia (Krajina Serbs). Krajina Serbs supported by the 180,000-member Yugoslav federal army.

August
Vukovar besieged by Yugoslav federal army in response to Croat blockade of military installations belonging to former Yugoslavia.

September
UN Security Council imposes arms embargo against all of former Yugoslavia.

October
Dubrovnik attacked by Yugoslav federal army and Montenegrin militia; unsuccessful assination attempt on President Franjo Tudjman.

November
Vukovar surrenders to Yugoslav federal army, after Yugoslav forces amass 600 tanks and 30,000 troops in the area.

December
14,000-member UN Protection Forces established. In the six months between June and December, an estimated 10,0000 Croatians die.

War & Peace

1992

January
  UN-brokered ceasefire takes effect; EC recognises Croatian independence. Yugoslav federal army withdraws from Croatia.
August
  Presidental elections in Croatia; Franjo Tudjman returned to office.
May
  Croatia admitted into UN.
October
  No-fly zone over Bosnia and Hercegovina declared by NATO.

1993

January
  Croatia signs pact with Bosnia. Croatian army launches offensive in southern Krajina to re-establish road connections between northern and southern Dalmatia. Krajina Serbs pushed back, but vow never to accept rule from Zagreb.
June
  Krajina Serbs vote overwhelmingly to join Bosnian Serbs.

1994

March
  Ceasefire signed in Zagreb between Croatia and Serbia.

1995

May
  Croat offensive in western Slavonia recaptures most of the territory held for three years by Krajina Serbs; Krajina Serbs retaliate by shelling Zagreb and other cities.
August
  Croatian offensive begins in Krajina Serb capital of Knin; Krajina Serb army flees, along with up to 150,000 civilians.
December
  Dayton Accord signed in Paris.

Croatian government that they were safe from retribution.

Belgrade's silence throughout this campaign made it clear that the Krajina Serbs had lost the support of their Serbian sponsors, encouraging the Croats to forge ahead. At dawn on 4 August the military launched a massive assault on the rebel Serb capital of Knin, pummelling it with shells, mortars and bombs. Outnumbered by two to one, the Serb army fled towards northern Bosnia, along with 150,000 civilians whose roots in the Krajina stretched back centuries. The military operation ended in days, but was followed by months of terror. Widespread looting and burning of Serb villages, as well as attacks upon the few remaining elderly Serbs, seemed designed to ensure the permanence of this massive population shift.

The Dayton agreement signed in Paris in December 1995 recognised Croatia's traditional borders and provided for the return of eastern Slavonia which was effected in January 1998. The transition has proceeded relatively smoothly with less violence than was expected. Local institutions have been re-established with an eye toward restoring the ethnic composition that existed before the war. Ethnic Serb representatives began to fill government posts in Slavonia and the Cyrillic script is now allowed to be taught in primary school.

Although stability has returned to the country, a key provision of the agreement was the promise by the Croatian government to facilitate the return of Serbian refugees, a promise that is far from being fulfilled. Housing, local industry and agriculture in Slavonia and the Krajina were devastated by the war, making resettlement both costly and complicated. To the frustration of the international community, the government has clearly manifested more enthusiasm for re-settling Croatian refugees while Serbian refugees face a tangle of bureaucratic obstacles and a political environment they fear may be less than welcoming. Since regional peace depends upon the return of refugees, international pressure upon the Croatian government has been unrelenting.

GEOGRAPHY

Croatia is half the size of present-day Yugoslavia in area (56,538 sq km) and population. The topography of the country is divided into the lowland basin between the Sava and Drava rivers which expands to mountains and hills in the north, the mountainous *karst* region of the Dinaric range and the littoral which runs from Istria south through Dalmatia along the Adriatic.

The narrow Croatian coastal belt at the foot of the Dinaric Alps is only about 600km long as the crow flies, but it's so indented that the actual length is 1778km. If the 4012km of coastline around the offshore islands is added to the total, the length becomes 5790km.

Croatia's offshore islands are every bit as beautiful as those in Greece. There are 1185 islands and islets along the tectonically submerged Adriatic coastline, 66 of them inhabited. The largest are: Cres, Krk, Lošinj, Pag and Rab in the north; Dugi otok in the middle; and Brač, Hvar, Korčula, Mljet and Vis in the south. Most are elongated from north-west to south-east and run parallel to the coastal mountains. Although islands such as Korčula, Rab, Hvar and Mljet are lush most of the smaller islands are barren, with high mountains that drop right into the sea.

The most outstanding geological feature of Croatia is the prevalence of the highly porous limestone and Dolomitic rock called *karst*. Stretching from Istria to Montenegro and covering large parts of the interior, karst is formed by the absorption of water into the surface limestone, which then corrodes and allows the water to seep into the harder layer underneath. Eventually the water forms underground streams, carving out fissures and caves before resurfacing, disappearing into another cave and finally emptying into the sea. The jagged, sparsely vegetated landscape is dramatic, but deforestation, wind and erosion makes the land unsuitable for agriculture. When the limestone collapses, a kind of basin is formed known as *polje* which is then cultivated despite the fact that this kind of field drains poorly and can easily turn into a temporary lake.

CLIMATE

The climate varies from Mediterranean along the Adriatic coast to continental inland. The sunny coastal areas experience hot, dry summers and mild, rainy winters,

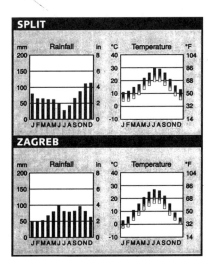

while the interior regions are cold in winter and warm in summer. Wind patterns cool the coast with refreshing breezes in the summer but high mountains shield the coast from bitter winter weather. Because of a warm current flowing north up the Adriatic coast, sea temperatures never fall below 10°C in winter, and in August they go as high as 26°C. The sea also stores heat in the summer and radiates the heat onto the land in the winter, warming the surrounding air.

In spring and early summer a sea breeze called the *maestral* keeps the temperature down along the coast. It generally starts blowing around 9 am, increases until early afternoon and dies down in late afternoon. This strong steady wind makes good sailing weather.

Winter weather is defined by two winds. The south-easterly *široko* from the Sahara brings warm moist air to the mainland and can produce a heavy cloud cover. This wind also has the steady strength that sailors love. The north-easterly *bura* blows from the interior to the coast in powerful gusts, bringing dry air and blowing away clouds.

Sun-lovers should note that the island of Hvar gets 2715 hours of sun a year, followed by Split with 2697 hours, Vela Luka on Korčula island with 2671 hours and Dubrovnik with 2584 hours. The lack of rainfall along the coast, especially on islands further removed from the mainland has produced severe water shortages in Dalmatia throughout its history. Summer dry periods can last up to 100 days, nearly as long as Sicily and Greece. Before pipelines to the Cetina and Neretva rivers were laid, islanders often had to collect rainwater in cisterns.

ECOLOGY & ENVIRONMENT

Although 23% of Croatia is covered by forests, they are under serious threat. It's estimated that about 50% of the forests are imperilled as a result of acid rain, mostly from neighbouring countries. Logging and building projects are cutting into forested land at the rate of about 1000 hectares a year.

Coastal and island forests face particular problems. First logged by Venetians to build ships, then by local people desperate for fuel, centuries of neglect have left many island and coastal mountains barren. The dry summers and brisk *maestral* winds also pose substantial fire hazards along the coast. In the last 20 years, fires have destroyed 7% of Croatia's forests.

Animal pasturing in the Kornati islands, Krka National Park and the Velebit mountain range have also damaged the landscape even though sheep and goat herds are disappearing. Although the sea along the Adriatic coast is among the cleanest in the world, overfishing has greatly reduced the fish population and scavenging for coral has nearly eliminated reefs.

FLORA & FAUNA

The Gorski Kotar highland region in western Croatia is the most densely forested part of Croatia; Risnjak Mountain is within this region, and has beech, fir, spruce and sycamore maple. Deer are plentiful as well as brown bear, wild cat and lynx (*ris*) from which the park gets its name. Occasionally a wolf or wild boar may appear but only rarely. Plitvice National Park however is an important refuge for wolves. A rare sea otter is also protected in Plitvice as well as in Krka National Park.

The griffon vulture with a wing span of 2.6m has a permanent colony in Paklenica National Park which is rich in peregrine falcons, goshwaks, sparrow hawks, buzzards and owls. Krka National Park is an important migration route and winter habitat for marsh birds like heron, wild duck, geese, cranes and the rare golden eagle and short-toed eagle. Kopački Rit swamp near Osijek in eastern Croatia is an extremely important bird refuge but, as of the writing of this book, is no longer safe to visit because of extensive land mining during the recent war.

Two venomous snakes are endemic in Paklenica – the nose-horned viper and the European adder – and the non-venomous leopard snake, four-lined snake, grass snake and snake lizard species can also be found in Krka National Park.

The richest plant life is found in the Velebit mountain range, part of the Dinaric range. Botanists have counted 2700 species and 78 endemic plants there including the increasingly threatened edelweiss. Risnjak National Park is another good place to find edelweiss along with black vanilla orchids, lilies and hairy alpenrose which looks a lot better than it sounds. The dry Mediterranean climate along the coast is perfect for maquis, a low brush which flourishes all along the coast but especially on the island of Mljet. You'll also find oleander, jasmine and juniper trees along the coast and lavender is cultivated on the island of Hvar. Typically Mediterranean olive and fig trees are also abundant.

NATIONAL PARKS

When the Yugoslav Federation collapsed, seven of its finest national parks ended up in Croatia, which now has 472 sq km of national park on land and 224km that compose the Kornati island group. Risnjak National Park south of Zagreb is the most untouched forested park, partly because the climate at its higher altitudes is somewhat inhospitable – an average temperature of 12.6°C in July. The winters are long and snowy but when spring finally comes in late May or early June, everything blooms at once. The park has been kept deliberately free of tourist facilities with the idea that only mountain lovers need apply.

The dramatically formed karstic gorges and cliffs make Paklenica National Park along the coast a rock climbing favourite and the scene of a European rock-climbing competition held each year in early May. Large grottoes and caves filled with stalactites and stalagmites make it an interesting park for cave explorers and there are many kilometres of trails for hiking. Tourist facilities are well-developed here.

The waterfalls of Plitvice Lakes National Park were formed by mosses that retain calcium carbonate as river water rushes through the karst. Travertine or tufa builds up sprouting plants which grow on top of each other to create barriers to the river. The park has been named a world heritage site and is easily accessible from either Zagreb or Zadar. The falls are at their watery best in the spring.

The Kornati Islands consist of 140 islands, islets and reefs scattered over 300 sq km. It is sparsely inhabited and sparsely vegetated but the great indentedness of the islands and extraordinary rock formations make it an Adriatic highlight. Unless you have your own boat, however, you'll need to join an organised tour from Zadar.

Only the western third of Mljet island has been named a national park for the two highly indented salt water lakes surrounded by lush vegetation. Maquis is thicker and taller on Mljet than nearly anywhere else in the Mediterranean which makes it a natural refuge for many animals. Snakes nearly overran the island until the Indian mongoose was introduced in 1909. This idyllic island is accessible by regular boats from Dubrovnik.

The Brijuni (Brioni) Islands are the most cultivated national park since they were developed as a tourist resort at the end of the 19th century. They were the getaway paradise for Tito and now provide an escape for President Tudjman. Most of the exotic animals and plants were introduced (elephants are not normally found in the Adriatic) but the islands are lovely. An organised tour is required.

Krka National Park is an even more extensive series of lakes and waterfalls than Plitvice. The Zrmanja, Krka, Cetina and Neretva rivers form waterfalls, but Manojlovac's power plant upstream can interfere with the flow, which can slow considerably in July or August. The main access point in Skradinski buk, with the largest cascade covering 800m.

GOVERNMENT & POLITICS

The constitution adopted on 22 December 1990 established a parliamentary democracy in Croatia with a strong presidency. The legislative branch consists of the 68-seat

House of Districts (Zupanijski Dom), of which 63 are directly elected by popular vote (five are appointed by the president) and the House of Representatives (Zastupnicki Dom), which has 127 members directly elected by popular vote. Members of both branches serve four-year terms. The president is the head of state, commander of the armed forces and is elected by popular vote for a five-year term. The prime minister and deputy prime ministers are appointed by the president. The Supreme Court is the highest judicial authority. Its judges are appointed for eight-year terms by the Judicial Council of the Republic, which is elected by the House of Representatives. Although nominally democratic, the concentration of power in the presidency, coupled with strong control over the media and extensive power over the judiciary makes the regime a highly authoritarian one-party state.

Croatia is divided into 21 counties (*županijas*) that closely parallel the historical development of the nation. The counties are Bjelovar-Bilogora, Dubrovnik-Neretva, City of Zagreb, Istra, Karlovac, Koprivnica-Krizevci, Kotar, Krapina-Zagorje, Lika-Senj, Medimurje, Pozega-Slavonija, Primorje-Gorski, Osijek-Baranja, Šibenik-Knin, Sisak-Moslavina, Slavonski Brod-Posavina, Split-Dalmatia, Virovitica-Podravina, Zadar, Varaždin, Vukovar-Srijem, and Zagreb county.

There are 13 political parties in Croatia, led by the Croatian Democratic Union (Hrvatska Demokratska Zajednica) or HDZ, founded in 1989 by Franjo Tudjman. Other important parties include the Social Liberal Party led by Vlado Gotovac and the ex-communist Social Democratic Party led by Zdravko Tomac. Some political parties represent regions such as the Istrian Democratic Party or the Primorje Gorski Kotar Alliance (representing the Gulf of Kvarner) while others stem from pre-independence parties such as the Croatian Party of Rights or the Croatian Peasants' Party.

In 1997 Franjo Tudjman was re-elected to a second five-year term as President, in an election that foreign observers characterised as 'fundamentally flawed' and 'free, but not fair'. State control of the media, especially television, strongly favoured the HDZ. A report by the OSCE (Organisation of South Central Europe) found that 300 times more coverage was devoted to Tudjman's campaign than that of Zdravko Tomac of the Social Democratic party – his nearest rival. Following the election, support for the ruling party fell amid widespread allegations of corruption and cronyism, particularly in the privatisation of state-owned assets. The imposition of the 22% value-added tax was widely perceived as an unfair burden on an increasingly impoverished population, while the ruling elite continued to enrich themselves at taxpayers' expense. The opposition was too fractured to mount a serious challenge to the HDZ leadership though the Social Democratic Party which won 21% of the vote in 1997, was expected to benefit in the 1999 legislative elections from widespread discontent.

At the time of writing, relations with other republics of the former Yugoslavia remained strained. Croatia and Slovenia had a list of issues to resolve including bank deposits, property rights and a disputed border in Piran Bay, off Sečovlje. The Prevlaka Peninsula east of Dubrovnik was being monitored by UN observers because of an unresolved border dispute between Croatia and Montenegro.

The international community also had a number of problems with Tudjman's regime, largely involving the issue of resettlement of Serbian refugees discussed above. Government repression of the press also alienated the international community. The HDZ's uncomfortably cosy relationship with Croat nationalists in Bosnia complicated peace efforts there and foot-dragging before the International War Crimes Tribunal in the Hague undermined the prosecution of war criminals. Although the government extradited Jasenovac camp commander Dinko Sakić from Argentina to stand trial in Croatia for war crimes,

Tudjman refused to confront and unequiv-ocally repudiate the evil perpetrated by the wartime Ustashe regime. On the contrary, his government attempted to recast Pavelić and the Ustashe as patriots and founding fathers, making Serbs throughout the region uneasy. Threats to withdraw the life-support of international loans and bar Croatia from participation in international organisations forced concessions from the government. The Croatians were under no illusions that they could go it alone however, either economically or politically: their determination to exit the problems of the Balkans and enter 'civilised' Europe looked like a wedge that would open the door to a more open, democratic society.

ECONOMY

The years since independence have pre-sented the government with formidable challenges. As a new country, the govern-ment must switch from a state-controlled to a privatised economy while rebuilding its infrastructure after a devastating war, re-housing returning refugees and finding new markets for its products after the loss of markets in the southern regions of former Yugoslavia. Vital transfusions of money from the International Monetary Fund and the World Bank have kept the economy functioning until a long-term solution emerges.

The former communist government of Yugoslavia emphasised heavy industry, es-pecially in aluminium, chemicals, petroleum and shipbuilding.

The shipyards of Pula, Rijeka and Split made Croatia the world's third largest shipbuilder. The chemical industry was concentrated at Krk, Rijeka, Split and Zagreb; machine-tool manufacture at Karlovac, Slavonski Brod and Zagreb; heavy electrical engineering at Zagreb; and textiles at Zagreb and in north-west Croatia. Unfortunately, many of these industries have stagnated since the war, their prob-lems compounded by large debts that have inhibited necessary restructuring. Growth in industrial output has been slow, ham-pered by an overvalued kuna that penalises exports while making imports cheap.

In the past a third of Croatia's national income came from tourism, but between 1991 and 1995 tourism fell dramatically. Dalmatia was the hardest hit and has yet to recover while Istria and Krk have begun to rebound, with an influx of Germans, Aus-trians, Italians and Czechs. It may be years before tourism reaches pre-war levels however, and attracting tourism requires capital outlays. Many hotels along the coast require costly renovation after years of shel-tering refugees. Investment in air, road and boat connections along the coast are also necessary if tourism is to be the cornerstone of the Croatian economy.

Unlike the trade and industrial sectors, agriculture has been in private hands since the failure of collectivisation just after WWII. Private farmers with small plots continue to work most of the land. The in-terior plains produce fruit, vegetables and grains (especially corn and wheat), while olives and grapes are cultivated along the coast. The return of fertile eastern Slavonia should eventually give the economy a boost once the war damage is repaired.

Economic reform without political reform is problematic however. Confi-dence in the banking sector has been weakened by a series of scandals involving low or no-interest loans to politically con-nected tycoons. Dubrovačka Banka, a financial powerhouse on the coast, required a costly taxpayer-funded bailout to keep afloat after 'sweetheart deals' with HDZ loyalists drove it to the edge of bankruptcy.

From the point of view of the average Croatian, life is difficult with no gleaming light at the end of the tunnel. The average wage is less than 2500KN (US$400) a month, and a high percentage of the popu-lation is unemployed (17.6% in 1997). Although inflation is low (3.6% in 1997), the recent imposition of a 22% value-added tax has eroded purchasing power, particularly for pensioners on fixed incomes. There's a widespread perception that the standard of living has fallen since the pre-war years and that the social safety net has been abruptly snatched away. A middle class faced with growing insecurity could eventually pose a serious threat to further economic reform.

POPULATION & PEOPLE

Before the war, Croatia had a population of nearly five million, of which 78% were Croats and 12% Serbs. With a constant flow of refugees in both directions, reliable statistics since the war have been difficult to compile but it is estimated that only 5% of the Serbian population remains. Small communities of Slavic Muslims, Hungarians, Slovenes, Italians, Czechs and Albanians complete the mosaic. The largest cities in Croatia are Zagreb (one million), Split (300,000), Rijeka (225,000), Osijek (175,000) and Zadar (150,000).

Another million Croats live in the other states of ex-Yugoslavia, especially Bosnia-Hercegovina, northern Vojvodina and around the Bay of Kotor in Montenegro. Some 2.3 million ethnic Croats live abroad, including almost 1.5 million in the USA, 270,000 in Germany, 240,000 in Australia, 150,000 in Canada and 150,000 in Argentina. Pittsburgh and Buenos Aires have the largest Croatian communities outside Europe. The Croatian diaspora actively supported Croatia's recent bid for independence, providing financial and other aid. The HDZ has assiduously cultivated links· with Croatian citizens abroad who can, of course, vote.

EDUCATION

Primary school (*osnovna škola*) is free and compulsory for eight years. Secondary school (*srednja škola*) students can either choose a three-year technical course or apprenticeship or head on to the *gymnazija* for further studies. At the end of their secondary education, all students must pass a national examination in order to qualify for university admission and then another examination for specialised studies such as law, medicine or journalism. Although education through university level is free, students must pay for their own living expenses if schools in their field of interest are far from their hometown. Scholarships may be available for outstanding students.

There are four universities – at Zagreb, Osijek, Rijeka and Split – but competition for places is stiff. Croatia's literacy rate is 97%. Of the total population over age 15, 40% have completed secondary education and 5.3% have a university degree or higher.

ARTS
Music

Although Croatia has produced many fine classical musicians and composers, their most original musical contribution lies in their rich tradition of folk music. Franz Joseph Haydn was born in a Croatian enclave in Austria and was strongly influenced by traditional Croatian airs. Croatian folk music bears many influences. The *kolo*, a lively Slavic round dance in which men and women alternate in the circle, is accompanied by Gypsy-style violinists or players of the *tamburitza*, a three or five-string mandolin popular in Croatia. The measured guitar-playing and rhythmic accordions of Dalmatia have a gentle Italian air.

A recommended recording available locally on compact disc (DD-0030) is the *Narodne Pjesme i Plesovi Sjeverne Hrvatske* (Northern Croatian Folk Songs and Dances) by Croatian folkloric ensemble Lado. The 22 tracks on this album represent nine regions, with everything from haunting Balkan voices reminiscent of Bulgaria to lively Mediterranean dance rhythms.

Literature

The Croatian language developed in the centuries following the great migration into Slavonia and Dalmatia. Originally influenced by Latin, Greek and the language of Franciscan and Benedictine monks, the oldest Slavic influence was the Church-Slavonic language which became influential around the 10th century. In order to convert the Slavs to Christianity, Greek missionaries Cyril and Methodius learned the language. It was Cyril who first put the language into writing which became known as Glagolitic script. The earliest known example of Glagolitic script was an 11th century inscription in a Benedictine abbey on Krk island and ecclesiastical works in Glagolitic continued to appear until the Middle Ages.

The first literary flowering in Croatia, however, took place in Dalmatia, which was strongly influenced by the Italian Renaissance. The works of the scholar and poet, Marko Marulić (1450-1524) from Split are still venerated in Croatia. His play *Judita* was the first work produced by a Croatian writer in his native tongue. Ivan Gundulić (1589-1638) from Ragusa (Dubrovnik) is widely considered to be the greatest Croatian poet. His epic poem *Osman* celebrated the Polish victory over the Turks in 1621, which the author saw as heralding the destruction of the detested Ottoman rule. The plays of Marin Držić (1508?-1567), especially *Dundo Maroje*, express humanistic Renaissance ideals and are still performed, especially in Dubrovnik.

Croatia's towering literary figure is 20th century novelist and playwright Miroslav Krleža. Always politically active, Krleža broke with Tito in 1967 over the writer's campaign for equality between the Serbian and Croatian literary languages. Depicting the concerns of a changing Yugoslavia, his most popular novels include *The Return of Philip Latinovicz* (1932), which has been translated into English, and *Banners* (1963-65), a multivolume saga about middle-class Croatian life at the turn of the century.

Mention should also be made of Ivo Andrić (1892-1975) who won the Nobel Prize for literature in 1961 for his Bosnian historical trilogy *The Bridge on the Drina, Bosnian Story*, and *Young Miss*. Born as a Catholic Croat in Bosnia, the writer used the Serbian dialect and lived in Belgrade, but identified himself as a Yugoslav.

Architecture, Painting & Sculpture

Examples of Roman architecture are abundant in Dalmatia, and the Euphrasian basilica in Poreč is an outstanding example of Byzantine art; however, the first distinctively Croatian design also appeared along the coast. Plaited ornamentation (*pleter*) first appeared around 800 AD on the baptismal font of Duke Višeslav of Nin in the church of the Holy Cross in Nin. This ornamentation appears frequently on church entrances and on church furniture from the early medieval period. Around the end of the 10th century, the lattice-work began to acquire leaves and tendrils. The design is so linked with Croatian culture that President Franjo Tudjman used it in a campaign poster in his first election to signal a return to traditional Croat culture.

The oldest example of Glagolitic script – the Baška slab, on display at the Strossmayer Gallery of Old Masters in Zagreb

The best example of pre-Romanesque architecture is found along the Dalmatian coast beginning with the 11th century church of the Holy Cross in Nin built in the shape of a cross with two apses and a dome above the centre point. Although there are the remains of circular pre-Romanesque churches in Split, Trogir and Ošalj, the most impressive is the Church of St Donat in Zadar, dating from the 9th century. The round central structure and three semi-circular apses make it most unusual. Other smaller churches in Šipan and Lopud from the 10th and 11th centuries are built with a cross-shaped ground plan indicating the growing influence of Byzantine culture.

The Romanesque tradition persisted along the coast long after the Gothic style had swept the rest of Europe. In the 13th century the earliest examples of the Gothic style appeared usually still mixed with Romanesque forms. The most stunning work from this period is the portal on the Cathedral of Trogir carved by the master-artisan Radovan. Depicting human figures performing everyday chores was a definite break with traditional Byzantine reliefs of saints and apostles. The unusual wooden portal on the Cathedral in Split (1240), made up of 28 square reliefs by Andrija Buvina, is another masterpiece from the Gothic period. St Stephen's Cathedral in Zagreb was the first venture into the Gothic style in northern Croatia. Although reconstructed several times, the sacristy has remnants of 13th century murals.

Late Gothic building was dominated by the builder and sculptor Juraj Dalmatinac, born in Zadar in the 15th century. His most outstanding work was the Cathedral of St Jacob in Šibenik, which marks a transition from the Gothic to the Renaissance period. In addition to constructing the church entirely of stone, without timber, Dalmatinac adorned the apses with a wreath of realistically carved local people.

At the same time the painter Vincent of Kastav was producing lovely church frescoes in Istria. The small church of St Maria near Beram contains his frescoes, most notably the *Dance of Death*. Another notable Istrian painter in the 15th century is Ivan of Kastav who has left frescoes throughout Istria, mostly in Slovenia.

Many artists born in Dalmatia were influenced by and in turn influenced Italian Renaissance style. The sculptors Lucijano Vranjanin and Frano Laurana, the minituarist Julije Klović and the painter Andrija Medulić left Dalmatia while the region was under threat from the Turks and worked in Italy. Museums in London, Paris and Florence contain examples of their work, but few of their creations are in Croatia.

In independent Ragusa (Dubrovnik) however, the Renaissance flourished. By the second half of the 15th century, Renaissance flourishes were appearing on late-Gothic structures. The Sponza Palace, formerly the Customs House, is a fine example of this mixed style. By the mid-16th century, Renaissance features began to supplant the Gothic style in the palaces and summer residences built in and around Ragusa by the wealthy nobility. Unfortunately, much was destroyed in the 1667 earthquake and now Dubrovnik is more notable for the mixed Gothic-Romanesque Franciscan Church, the 15th century Orlando column and Onofrio fountain, and the baroque church of St Blaise, the Jesuit church and Dubrovnik Cathedral.

Northern Croatia is more notable for the baroque style that was introduced by Jesuit monks in the 17th century. The city of Varaždin was a regional capital in the 17th and 18th centuries and, because of its location, enjoyed a steady interchange of artists, artisans and architects with northern Europe. The combination of wealth and creatively fertile environment led it to become Croatia's foremost city of baroque art. You'll notice the style in the elaborately restored houses, churches and, especially the impressive castle.

In Zagreb good examples of baroque style are found in the upper town. Notice the church of St Catherine and the church of St Xavier and the restored baroque mansions that are now the Croatian History

Dolac's produce market provides for locals

One of Zagreb's charming avenues

Street life on Tkalčića ulica

Grožnjan hill town in Istria

Opatija in the Kvarner region

The four bell-towers of Rab town on Rab island

Did you know . . .

That Dalmatian dogs probably did not originate in Dalmatia? The origins of the breed are uncertain but some experts believe the dogs may have been brought into Dalmatia by gypsies and used to guard the Dalmatian border.

That the ball-point pen and fountain pen were invented in 1906 by the Croatian Slavoljub Penkala (1871-1922)?

That the neck tie is a descendant of the 'cravat' which originated in Croatia as part of military attire and was adopted by the French in the 17th century? The name 'cravat' is a corruption of Croat and Hrvat.

That Shakespeare's *Twelfth Night* was set in Dalmatia?

That the writer Vladimir Nabokov vacationed regularly in Opatija when he was a child?

That Ivan Vučetić (1858-1925), the man who developed dactyloscopy – or fingerprint identification – was born on the island of Hvar?

That Nikola Tesla (1856-1943), the father of the radio and alternating electric current technology, was born in Croatia? The Tesla unit for magnetic induction was named after him.

That Šibenik-born Faust Vrančić (1551-1617) made the first working parachute?

That Agatha Christie spent her second honeymoon in Dubrovnik and Split?

That James Joyce taught English in Pula from 1904 to 1905?

That the Duke of Windsor and Wallis Simpson vacationed in Dalmatia?

Museum and the Gallery of Primitive Art. Wealthy families built baroque mansions around Zagreb, including mansions at Brezovica, Milyana, Lobor and Bistra.

In the 19th century, Dalmatian style stagnated as the region fell prey to political problems, but Zagreb underwent a revival. Vlaho Bukovac (1855-1922) was the most notable painter in the late 19th century. After working in London and Paris, he came to Zagreb in 1892 and produced portraits and paintings on historical themes in a lively style. Early 20th century painters of note include Miroslav Kraljević (1885-1913) and Josip Račić (1885-1908), but the most internationally recognised artist was the sculptor Ivan Meštrović who created many masterpieces on Croatian themes. Antun Augustinčić (1900-1979) was another internationally recognised sculptor whose Monument to Peace is outside the United Nations in New York. A small museum of his work can be visited in the town of Klanjec, north of Zagreb.

Post-war artists experimented with abstract expressionism but this period is best remembered for the naive art that began with the 1931 'Zemlja' (soil) exhibition in Zagreb that introduced the public to works by Ivan Generalić (1914-1992) and other peasant-painters. Committed to producing art that could be easily understood and appreciated by ordinary people, Generalić was joined by painters Franjo Mraz and Mirko Virius and sculptor Petar Smajic in a campaign to gain acceptance and recognition for naive art.

Recent trends have included minimalism, conceptual art and pop art. The Art Pavilion in Zagreb, designed by Vlaho Bukovac is a good place to keep up with the latest developments in Croatian art. Built as an exhibition space for large exhibits, this elaborate structure presents the finest contemporary local artists.

SOCIETY & CONDUCT

Croats take pride in keeping up appearances. Despite a fragile economy, money can usually be found to brighten up the town centre with a fresh coat of paint or to repair a historic building. Even as their own bank accounts diminish most people will cut out restaurants and movies in order to afford a shopping trip to Italy for some new clothes.

The tidy streets and stylish clothes are rooted in the Croats' image of themselves as western Europeans, not Yugoslavs, a word that makes Croats wince. Dressing neatly will go a long way towards gaining a traveller acceptance.

Because of the intense propaganda surrounding the recent war, Croats are inclined to see themselves as wholly right and the other side as wholly wrong. Comments questioning this assumption are not particularly appreciated. People who have had their lives disrupted if not shattered by war are generally uninterested in the political niceties of their situation.

RELIGION

According to 1991 figures, 76.6% of the population is Roman Catholic, 11.1% Orthodox, 1.1% Muslim, 3.9% atheist and 7.3% are 'others' including a tiny Protestant and Jewish population. Croats are overwhelmingly Roman Catholic, while virtually all Serbs belong to the Eastern Orthodox Church, a division that has its roots in the fall of the Roman Empire. In fact, religion is the only factor separating the ethnically identical populations. In addition to various doctrinal differences, Orthodox Christians venerate icons, allow priests to marry and do not accept the authority of the Pope.

It would be difficult to overstate the extent to which Catholicism shapes the Croatian national identity. The Croats pledged allegiance to Roman Catholicism as early as the 9th century and were rewarded with the right to conduct Mass and issue religious writings in the local language, which eventually became the Glagolitic script. The popes supported the early Croatian kings who in turn built monasteries and churches to further promote Catholicism. Throughout the long centuries of domination by foreign powers, Catholicism was the unifying element in forging a sense of nationhood.

Tragically, the profound faith that had animated Croatian nationalism was perverted into a murderous intolerance under the wartime Ustashe regime. The complicity of local parishes in 'cleansing' the population of Jews and Serbs, prompted Tito to suppress religion – and, he hoped, nationalism – when he took power. Although religion was not officially forbidden, it was seen as 'politically incorrect' for ambitious Croats to attend mass. Small wonder that the Vatican was the first entity to recognise an independent Croatia in 1991.

In today's Croatia, it's not only politically correct but politically necessary to be seen as a good Catholic. Churches are strongly attended every Sunday and religious holidays are taken seriously. The pope's visit to Croatia in October 1998 to beatify the controversial Cardinal Stepinac was the event of the year (especially since Croatia failed to win the World Cup) and inevitably served to bolster the prestige of the Tudjman regime.

There are signs that the Church's patience with the Croatian government is wearing thin, however. The new Archbishop of Zagreb, Monsignor Josip Bozanic, has rattled the government with speeches denouncing official corruption and a government policy that results in the 'quick enrichment of a few and the impoverishment of the many'. Clearly uncomfortable with this cold blast of criticism from a reliable ally, President Tudjman has resorted to public snubs but the Archbishop's remarks struck a chord with his disenchanted parishioners. With an Easter message titled *The Church Cannot Remain Quiet*, it appears that the Archbishop is defining a new role for the Church in modern Croatia.

Facts for the Visitor

HIGHLIGHTS
Natural Wonders
The spectacular beauty of Croatia's 1778km coastline and 1185 islands is undoubtedly the country's greatest natural asset. The 140 islands of the Kornati archipelago are a sailor's paradise, the Brijuni islands were Tito's paradise and lush islands such as Korčula, Hvar, and Rab could easily become anyone's paradise.

The Velebit mountain range includes the distinctive *karst* formations of Paklenica National Park, with it's great opportunities for hiking and rock climbing. Plitvice Lakes National Park has been named a world heritage site for its 16 lakes linked by crashing, tumbling, trickling waterfalls.

Museums & Galleries
Art museums and galleries are easier for a foreign visitor to enjoy than historical museums, which are usually captioned in Croatian only. In Zagreb the Museum Mimara contains an outstanding collection of Spanish, Italian and Dutch paintings as well as an archaeological collection, exhibits of ancient art from the Far East and collections of glass, textiles, sculpture and furniture. The Strossmayer Gallery, also in Zagreb, is worthwhile for its exhibits of Italian, Flemish, French and Croatian paintings.

The Meštrović Gallery in Split is worth a detour to see and in Zagreb the Meštrović Studio gives a fascinating insight into the life and work of this remarkable sculptor. Admission to museums runs about 10KN but is slightly higher in Zagreb.

Castles
The palace of the Roman emperor Diocletian in Split has been named a world heritage site by UNESCO. Despite a weathered façade, this sprawling imperial residence and fortress is considered the finest intact example of classical defence architecture in Europe.

Just outside Zagreb is an impressive circle of castles. To the north is Veliki Tabor, a fortified medieval castle in the process of restoration, but the most impressive is Trakošćan, beside a long lake. Medvedgrad, west of Zagreb, was built by bishops in the 13th century. The Varaždin Castle in northern Croatia has recently been restored and hosts an annual music festival. Trsat Castle in Rijeka offers a stunning view of the Kvarner Gulf.

Historic Towns
All along the Adriatic coast are white-stone towns with narrow, winding streets enclosed by defensive walls. Each town has its own flavour. Hilly Rovinj looks out over the sea, while the peninsula of Korčula town burrows into it. Zadar retains echoes of its original Roman street plan while Hvar and Trogir are traditional medieval towns. But none can match the exquisite harmony of Dubrovnik, with its blend of elements of medieval and Renaissance architecture.

Beaches
Now you're talking. Whether rocky, pebbly, gravelly or (rarely) sandy, Croatian beaches are often on the edge of a pine grove and slope into crystalline water that always seems to be the right temperature. The coastline is indented with wide bays and cosy coves where you just might be tempted to cast off your bathing suit along with the many naturists that flock to the Croatian shores each summer.

SUGGESTED ITINERARIES
Your itinerary will vary according to your interests, when you travel and how much time you have, but the following suggestions may help you plan your trip. Before

organising an itinerary that includes boat travel, it's essential to check the latest available Jadrolinija schedule (see Getting There & Away) to make sure that there's a boat that will take you where you want to go, when you want to go there. Bus transport is much more frequent.

The Coastal Route

Going from Rijeka to Dubrovnik by boat, stopping off at the many islands and cities, is one of the great journeys in Central Europe. You can combine a through-ticket on the large Jadrolinija ferry with trips on local ferries to visit fishing villages, Roman ruins, sprawling resorts and remote islands. A leisurely month is ideal.

Spend a few days in Zagreb for the museums and historic old town, then head to the coast. Before leaving for your cruise down the Dalmatian coast, stop in Istria – maybe Rovinj or Poreč – and Krk or Rab island in the Gulf of Kvarner. Your boat may stop at rustic Dugi Otok before docking at Zadar where you can spend a few days exploring the town centre and then visit Pag, Mali Lošinj or Cres islands. Your next stop will be Split where you could easily spend a week taking day trips to Brač, Vis and Šolta islands, relaxing on the beaches of Makarska or poking around in the ancient cities of Trogir and Salona. Hvar island is your next stop with the architectural treasure, Hvar town, and a wealth of beautiful coves and bays to explore. On to the walled town of Korčula and lush Korčula island before arriving in Dubrovnik, an enchanting city of medieval, Renaissance and baroque splendours.

Active Vacations

For hiking, rock climbing and swimming, the best itinerary would include at least a two week stay in and around Paklenica National Park. The best time to visit is late spring or early fall when the mountains are cool enough for hiking and the water is still warm enough for swimming. You can make brief forays into the park from a base at Stari Grad or hike all the way through it, staying at remote mountain lodges.

Culture Buffs

Croatia has a rich cultural heritage that spans the classical European features of northern Croatia and the Italianised cities along the coast. If you only have a week you could divide it between Zagreb and Dubrovnik. If you have two weeks you could include Plitvice Lakes, Zadar, Pag island and Split with day trips to Trogir and Salona. In three weeks, you could cover the Istrian cities of Rovinj, Poreč and Pula with side trips to the hill villages of Motovun and Grošnjan.

Beach Lovers

If you have little time but a large yearning for a sand beach, then you could divide a week long beach holiday between Baška on Krk island and Lopar on Rab island, both with wide swathes of sand. For a more varied topography, a week long stay in Split would give you a taste of central Dalmatian beaches. In addition to the beaches outside of Split, you can make day trips to the unusual Zlatni Rat beach on Brač, the rocky coves of Šolta, and the pebble, pine-lined beaches of Makarska. In two weeks you could add on Hvar or Korčula island with easy access to the beaches of Orebić.

PLANNING
When to Go

April through September is a great time to visit Croatia. Although the coast is too cool for swimming in April, you'll enjoy warm, clear skies south of Split. Zagreb is likely to be chilly, but the cultural season is in full swing at this time. Accommodation prices are low in April but book ahead since many hotels, camping grounds and hostels along the coast are likely to be closed.

May and June are great months for all outdoor activities (except skiing). Italian and German tourists have yet to arrive, accommodation prices are still reasonable and you'll enjoy long, sunny days. Watch out for battalions of students from grade school through high school on class field trips at the end of May and beginning of June. Hotels and transport around cultural highlights can suddenly fill up with boisterous youths and their harried chaperones.

July and August are the most expensive months to visit Croatia as the tourist season swings into gear. Accommodation prices are highest in summer and popular places such as Krk, Istria, Rab, Hvar, Korčula and Dubrovnik can become uncomfortably crowded. The advantages of high-season travel are the extra boat lines to whisk you to the islands and organised excursions to take you to out-of-the-way highlights.

September is perhaps the best month since it's not as hot as summer, though the sea remains warm, the crowds will have thinned out as children return to school, off-season accommodation rates will be in place and fruit such as figs and grapes will be abundant. In October it may be too cool for camping, but the weather should still be fine along the coast, and private rooms will be plentiful and inexpensive.

Maps

Kimmerley & Frey's map *Croatia & Slovenia* (1:500,000) is detailed and depicts the latest borders. Most of the free maps handed out by local tourist offices are not detailed enough to be useful, but in big cities the tourist office or a local bookstore will sell good quality city maps. Make sure the street names are up-to-date before you buy a map since there's been an epidemic of name changing in recent years.

What to Bring

Remember that the climate on the coast can be much warmer than the inland climate, which may require both light and medium-weight clothing from May to September. Croats are casual but neat dressers. Trainers are generally not appropriate for an evening restaurant meal but soft-soled shoes make cobblestone streets a lot easier on your feet.

Bring a swimsuit if you'll be spending time along the coast. A light sarong can work as a beach towel, cover-up or sheet. A sleeping sheet with a pillow cover (case) is a good idea if you plan to stay in hostels. Ear plugs can block out noisy neighbours, late night street action and other impediments to a good nights sleep. A eye mask can allow you to sleep late in a sunny hotel room or leave a window open without a street light shining in your face. A padlock is useful to secure your hostel locker and a pocket knife with a bottle opener and corkscrew usually comes in handy. Soap, toothpaste and toilet paper are readily obtainable, as are tampons and condoms, both locally made and imported.

Few hotels bother to produce a decent cup of coffee for breakfast. Coffee lovers can either pay for a brewed espresso or bring instant coffee. You can always switch to tea but bring your own bags if you're used to a strong, flavourful brew.

Sun protection gear is essential in summer along the coast. Sunglasses, a brimmed hat and plenty of sunscreen should be brought and worn. Bring a universal sink plug, a length of cord to use as a washing line and packets of laundry detergent to wash your own clothes since laundry facilities are scarce. Books in English are also scarce and expensive; it's best to bring your own reading material. Don't forget an adaptor for electrical appliances.

TOURIST OFFICES
Local Tourist Offices

Transport, accommodation, prices and even street names are changing rapidly in Croatia as the country embraces independence and a privatised economy at the same time. Your first stop in every town should be at the official tourist office, which is usually called *Turistički Ured, Turistički Zajednica* or *Tourist Information Centar*. In addition to brochures and sometimes free 'City Guides', the tourist offices often sell local guidebooks that are excellent value if you'll be staying long in one place. In remote places a commercial travel agency or *Turist biro* may have more complete information on accommodation and excursions and may also be able to provide maps, brochures and transportation schedules. Ask if they have the schedule for coastal and local ferries and then ask them to explain how to read it since the format is extremely complicated.

Sightseeing excursions are usually arranged by commercial travel agencies. Some of the main commercial travel agencies are Kompas, Atlas, Generalturist, Croatia Express and KEI-Kvarner Express. Keep in mind that these are profit-making businesses, so don't be put off if you're asked to pay for a town map etc. Depending on the town, either a commercial travel agency or the official tourist office will arrange for private accommodation for rooms or apartments.

Tourist Offices Abroad

The Croatian Ministry of Tourism – sometimes in conjunction with local travel agencies – maintains the following tourist offices that will gladly mail brochures containing much information on the country:

Austria
  (☎ 01-585 3884) Kroatische Zentrale für Tourismus, Operngasse 5, 1010 Vienna
Czech Republic
  (☎ 02-231 7166) Hrvatska turistiška zajednica O.S., Jachymova 4, 11630 Prague
Germany
  (☎ 069-252 045) Kroatische Zentrale für Tourismus, Karlsluher Strasse 18, D-60329 Frankfurt, or (☎ 089-223 344) Kroatische Zentrale für Tourismus, Rumfordstrasse 7, D-80469 Munich
Hungary
  (☎ 01-339 8255) Horvát Idegenforgalmi Közösség Magyar u. 36, 1053 Budapest
Italy
  (☎ 02-86 45 44 97) Ente nazionale Croato per il turismo, Piazzale Cadorna 9, 20123 Milan
Netherlands
  (☎ 020-405 7066) Kroatische Centrale voor Tourisme, Schipholboulevard 205 WTC, 1118 BH Luchthaven Schiphol
UK
  (☎ 0181-563 7979; from 22 April 2000 ☎ 020-8563 7979) Phoenix Holidays, 2 The Lanchesters, 162-164 Fulham Palace Rd, London W69ER
USA
  (☎ 201-428 0707) Croatian National Tourist Office, 300 Lanidex Plaza, Parsippany, NJ 07054

VISAS & DOCUMENTS
Passport

A valid passport is necessary in order to enter Croatia. To avoid problems, it's best to insure that your passport will remain valid for the entire course of your stay. Always make a photocopy of your passport and keep the photocopy in a separate place. In case your passport is lost or stolen, producing a photocopy of the original at your embassy or consulate will greatly facilitate the replacement. If your passport disappears right before your departure take your flight tickets to your embassy or consulate and you will normally get a temporary passport enabling you to at least re-enter your home country.

Visas

Croatia has relaxed entry requirements considerably in recent years in order to bring greater numbers of tourists to the country. Citizens of US, Canada, Australia, New Zealand, Israel, Ireland and the UK no longer need a visa for stays of up to 90 days. Citizens of Singapore must apply in Jakarta for a 90-day visa and South Africans must apply for a 90-day visa in Pretoria. The price is roughly 148KN and you may have to show a return ticket. Contact any Croatian embassy, consulate or travel agency abroad for information. If you're looking on-line, go to www.lonelyplanet.com for hot links to up-to-date information.

If you want to stay in Croatia longer than three months, the easiest thing to do is cross the border into Italy or Austria and return.

Croatian authorities require foreigners to register with local police when they arrive in a new area of the country, but this is a routine matter normally handled by the hotel, hostel, camp site or agency securing private accommodation. That's why they need to take your passport away for the night.

If you're staying elsewhere (eg with relatives or friends), your host will have to take care of this for you. Failing to register would have more repercussions for your host than for you.

Travel Insurance

A travel insurance policy to cover theft, loss and medical problems is a good idea. The policies handled by STA Travel and other student travel organisations are usually good value. Some policies offer lower and higher medical-expense options; the higher ones are chiefly for countries such as the USA, which have extremely high medical costs.

There's a variety of policies available so check the small print. Some policies specifically exclude 'dangerous activities', which can include scuba diving, motorcycling, even trekking. A locally acquired motorcycle license is not valid under some policies.

You may prefer a policy that pays doctors or hospitals directly rather than you having to pay on the spot and claim later. If you have to claim later make sure you keep all documentation. Some policies ask you to call back (reverse charges) to a centre in your home country where an immediate assessment of your problem is made. Check that the policy covers ambulances or an emergency flight home.

Student & Youth Cards

Most museums, galleries, theatres and festivals in Croatia offer student discounts of up to 30%. Although any proof of attendance at an educational institution is acceptable, most people get an International Student Identity Card (ISIC), which is the best international proof of your student status. Emergency medical coverage is also included among the benefits.

To get an ISIC card, you must be enrolled full or part-time in a degree program. The application must include proof of student registration (transcript or bursar's receipt, for example), a US$20 registration fee and one passport-size photo. The 1999 card is valid from September 1998 through December 1999. It comes with a Travel Handbook listing discounts for cardholders.

People under the age of 25 who are not students qualify for the GO25 Card, but in Croatia few discounts in this category are offered. Applicants must present proof of age (a copy of your birth certificate, passport, or driver's license), a $20 fee, and one passport-size photo. The card, valid one year from the date of issuance, also comes with a Travel Handbook.

Both the ISIC and GO25 cards carry basic accident and sickness insurance coverage, and cardholders have access to a worldwide hotline for help in medical, legal or financial emergencies.

Other programs for students and travellers under 26 include USIT travel discounts, which offer reduced rates on air tickets, and the European Youth Card, which offers reductions on shops, services, restaurants and libraries in participating countries. Travel agencies specialising in youth travel issue ISIC, GO25 and European Youth Cards and USIT air fares. In Croatia, contact Dali Travel, Dežmanova 9, Zagreb 1000 (☎ 422 953). The Council on International Educational Exchange (www.ciee.org) is another good source of information and can be contacted at one of the following addresses:

Australia
(☎ 02-9373 2730, info@ciee.org.au) The University Centre, Level 8, 210 Clarence St, Sydney 2000
UK
(☎ 0171-478 20 00; from 22 April 2000 ☎ 020-7478 2000, infoUK@ciee.org) 52 Poland St, London WIV 4JQ
USA
(☎ 800-GETANID or ☎ 212-822-2600, info@ciee.org) 205 E. 42nd St, New York, NY 10017

EMBASSIES & CONSULATES
Croatian Embassies & Consulates

Croatian embassies and consulates abroad include:

Australia
(☎ 062-86 6988) 6 Bulwarra Close, O'Malley, Canberra, ACT 2606
(☎ 03-9699 2633) 9-24 Albert Rd, South Melbourne, Victoria 3205
(☎ 02-9299 8899) 379 Kent St, Level 4, Sydney, NSW 2000
(☎ 09-321 6044) 68 St George's Terrace, Perth, WA 6832

Bosnia-Hercegovina
(☎ 71-444-428) Borise Kovacevica 20 Sarajevo
Bulgaria
(☎ 02-467 262) Ulica Krakra 18, Sofia
Canada
(☎ 613-230 7351) 130 Albert St, Suite 1700, Ottawa, ON K1P 5G4
(☎ 905-277 9051) 918 Dundas St E, Suite 302, Mississauga ON L4Y 2B8
Czech Republic
(☎ 02-627 1936) Vinohradska 69, 120 00 Prague
Hungary
(☎ 01-155 1522) Nogradi ut. 28/B, 1125 Budapest
Italy
(☎ 33-265 567) Via Santi Cosma e Damiano 26, 00189 Rome
Slovakia
(☎ 07-361 413) Groslingova 47, Bratislava
Slovenia
(☎ 61-125 6220) Gubajevo nabrezje 6, 61000 Ljubljana
New Zealand
(☎ 09-836 5581) 131 Lincoln Rd, Henderson, Box 83200, Edmonton, Auckland
Romania
(☎ 01-638 4982) Stirbei uoda 87, Bucharest
UK
(☎ 0171-387 0022; from 22 April 2000 ☎ 020-7387 0022) 21 Conway St, London W1P 5HL
USA
(☎ 202-588 5899) 2343 Massachusetts Ave NW, Washington, DC 20008
Yugoslavia
(☎ 11-668-063) Cakorska 1a, 11000 Belgrade

Embassies & Consulates in Croatia

All addresses following are in Zagreb unless otherwise noted:

Albania
(☎ 01-48 10 679) Jurišiaeva 2a
Australia
(☎ 01-45 77 433) Mihanovićeva 1
Bosnia-Hercegovina
(☎ 01-46 83 767) Torbarova 9
Bulgaria
(☎ 01-45 52 288) Novi Goljak 25
Canada
(☎ 01-45 77 905) Mihanovićeva 1
Czech Republic
(☎ 01-61 15 914) Savska 41

Hungary
(☎ 01-422 654) Krležin Gvozd 11a
Poland
(☎ 01-278 818) Krležin Gvozd 3
Romania
(☎ 01-23 36 091) Srebrnjak 150a
Slovakia
(☎ 01-48 48 941) Prilaz Gjure Deželića 10
Slovenia
(☎ 01-61 56 945) Savska 41
UK
(☎ 01-45 55 310) Vlaška 121;
Split:
(☎ 021-341 464) Obala hrvatskog narodnog preporoda 10, Split 21000
USA
(☎ 01-45 55 500) Andrije Hebranga 2
Yugoslavia
(☎ 01-46 80 553) Mesićeva 19

CUSTOMS

Travellers can bring their personal effects into the country as well as one litre of liquor, one litre of wine, 500g of coffee, 200 cigarettes and 50ml of perfume. The import or export of kuna is limited to 2000 per person. Camping gear, boats and electronic equipment should be declared upon entering the country. There is no quarantine for bringing animals into the country but you should have a recent vaccination certificate from your veterinarian. Otherwise the animal is subject to inspection by a local veterinarian who, needless to say, may not be immediately available.

MONEY
Currency

In May 1994 the Croatian dinar was replaced by the kuna, which takes its name from the marten, a fox-like animal whose pelt served as a means of exchange in the Middle Ages. Commonly circulated banknotes come in denominations of 500, 200, 100, 50, 20, 10 and 5 kunas bearing likenesses of Croat heroes such as Stjepan Radić and Ban Josip Jelačić. Each kuna is divided into 100 lipa. You'll find silver-coloured 50 and 20 lipa coins and bronze-coloured 10 lipa coins.

The government deliberately overvalues the kuna to obtain cheap foreign currency.

The kuna is tied to the Deutschmark and thus the exchange rate has remained fairly stable. Inflation has also been stable and is likely to remain so since the country is trying to present an image of fiscal stability to international investors.

Exchange Rates
Exchange rates are as follows:

country	unit	kuna
Austria	AS1	0.53KN
Australia	A$1	4.07KN
Canada	C$1	4.19KN
Czech Republic	1K	0.21KN
European Union	€1	7.38KN
France	1FF	1.11KN
Germany	DM1	3.75KN
Hungary	Ft100	2.90KN
Italy	L1000	3.79KN
Japan	¥100	5.22KN
UK	UK£1	10.62KN
USA	US$1	6.42KN

Changing Money
There are numerous places to change money, all offering similar rates; ask at any travel agency for the location of the nearest exchange. Post offices change money and keep long hours. Most places deduct a commission of 1 to 1.5% to change cash or travellers cheques but some banks do not. Kuna can be converted into hard currency only at a bank and if you submit a receipt of a previous transaction. Hungarian currency is difficult to change in Croatia.

Credit Cards Visa credit cards are accepted for cash advances in Croatia only at Splitska Banka and Dubrovačka Banka (American Express, MasterCard and Diners Club cards are easier). Cirrus cards can be used for cash withdrawals and you get the best rate. Diners Club cards can also be used for cash withdrawals in many places. Note that MasterCard, Eurocard and Cirrus are all part of the same system throughout Europe.

To report a lost or stolen Diners Club card call their 24-hour hotline (☎ 423 123) or their office (☎ 45 54 511) at Praška 5a, Zagreb 10000 for any other information.

Visa cardholders who need to replace a lost or stolen card can call the hotline in Split (☎ 021-342 944) or go to Splitska banka (☎ 48 14 410) at Zrinskog 16, Zagreb 10000 (Monday to Friday between 9 am and 3 pm). Holders of lost or stolen Eurocards or MasterCards cannot get a replacement in Croatia, but if you call Zagrebačka banka (☎ 01–37 89 789), Samoborska 145, Zagreb 10000, they will send a fax to your bank to block the card. The hotline is available 24 hours a day.

All post offices will allow you to make a cash withdrawal on MasterCard or Cirrus and a growing number work with Diners Club as well. Major cities have 'bank-o-mats' (Automatic Teller Machines – ATMs) that accept MasterCard, Cirrus and Diners Club but many of the islands are not yet hooked up to the system. Make sure you have a four-digit Personal Identification Number (PIN). American Express cardholders can contact Atlas agencies in Dubrovnik, Zagreb, Pula, Poreč, Zadar, Opatija and Split for the full range of American Express services including cashing personal checks and holding clients' mail.

Costs
Accommodation is more expensive than it should be for a country trying to lure more tourists; real budget accommodation is in short supply. Transport, concert and theatre tickets, and food are reasonably priced for Europe.

Average prices per person are around 90KN for a private room, 25KN for a meal at a self-service restaurant and 25 to 45KN for an average intercity bus fare. It's not that hard to do it on 200KN a day if you stay in hostels or private rooms and you'll pay less if you camp and self-cater. Eating only things such as bread, cheese, yoghurt and canned fish or meat will help to cut costs (cooking facilities are seldom provided).

Your daily expenses will come way down if you can find a private room to use as a base for exploring nearby areas.

Coastal towns that lend themselves to this include Rovinj, Rab, Zadar, Split, Korčula and Dubrovnik.

You will also escape the 30 to 50% surcharge on private rooms rented for under four nights.

Tipping & Bargaining

In restaurants a service charge is automatically added to the bill. However, if the service is good you should round up the bill as you're paying (don't leave money on the table). Bar bills and taxi fares can also be rounded up. Tour guides on day excursions expect to be tipped; a tip of 15KN for an excursion is appropriate.

Prices are fixed in stores, making bargaining impossible, but it's good idea to bargain at street markets. Some street markets have their prices posted but where prices are not posted foreigners are sometimes quoted a higher price on the logical assumption that they are probably richer than the average Croatian.

Taxes & Refunds

Travellers who spend more than 500KN in one store are entitled to a refund of the VAT, which is equivalent to 18% of the purchase price. In order to claim the refund, the merchant must fill out the required forms in triplicate and you must present this to the customs office upon leaving the country. Mail a stamped copy to the store, which will then credit your credit card with the appropriate sum. There is also a service called Tax Free Shopping that will give you your refund in cash at the airport if you shop at participating stores, but your refund is only 14% of the purchase price. Both the VAT and the refund system are newfangled notions in Croatia, so don't be surprised if merchants don't have the necessary forms.

POST & COMMUNICATIONS
Post

HPT Hrvatska, recognised by its red, white and blue sign offers a wide variety of services – from selling stamps and telephone cards to sending faxes. If you want to avoid a trip to the post office and just want to send a few postcards, you can buy *pismo* (stamps) at any *Tisak* (newsstand) and drop your mail into any of the yellow letterboxes on the street.

Domestic mail costs 1.80KN for up to 20g and 3KN for up to 100g. Postcards are 1.80KN. For international mail, the base rate is 2.65KN for a postcard, 7.20KN for a letter up to 20g, and 12.20KN for a letter up to 100g. Then you have to add on the airmail charge for every 10g, which is 0.80KN for Europe, 1.20KN for North America, 1KN for Asia, 1.35KN for southern Africa and 1.65KN for Australia. Therefore, standard size postcards sent via air mail to friends in London, New York, Hong Kong, Sydney or Johannesburg will cost 3.45, 3.85, 3.65, 4.30, and 4KN respectively.

Mail sent to Poste Restante, 10000 Zagreb, Croatia, is held at the post office next to Zagreb railway station, which is open 24 hours a day. A good coastal address to use is c/o Poste Restante, Main Post Office, 21000 Split, Croatia.

If you have an American Express card or you've travelling with American Express travellers cheques, you can have your mail addressed to branches of Atlas travel agencies in Dubrovnik, Zagreb, Pula, Poreč, Zadar, Opatija and Split; mail will be held for up to two months.

Telephone & Fax

To call Croatia from abroad, dial your international access code, ☎ 385 (the country code for Croatia), the area code (without the initial zero) and the local number. Phone numbers with a prefix 060 are free and phone numbers that begin with 098 are cellular phone numbers, which are billed at a higher rate than regular numbers.

To make a phone call from Croatia, go to the main post office – phone calls placed from hotel rooms are much more expensive.

There are few coin-operated phones, so you'll need a telephone card to use public telephones. Most public telephones use phonecards which are sold according to units (*impulsa*). You can buy cards of 50, 100,

200, and 500 units at any post office and most tobacco shops and newspaper kiosks. Many new phone boxes are equipped with a button on the upper left with a flag symbol. Press the button and you get instructions in English.

Telephone calls within Croatia are 25% cheaper if made in the period between 4 pm and 10 pm and 75% cheaper if made between 10 pm and 7 am as well as on Sunday and holidays. A three minute call from Croatia will be around 20KN to the UK and 23KN to the USA or Australia. The international access code is ☎ 00. Some other useful numbers are ☎ 92 for the police, ☎ 93 for the fire department, ☎ 94 for emergency medical assistance and ☎ 901 to place an operator-assisted call.

Faxes can be sent from any post office at a cost of 21.30KN, 14.20KN and 21.30KN a page to the USA, UK and Australia respectively.

Email & Internet Access

In order to have email and Internet access you'll need to have a dial-up connection to the Internet, normally provided through an Internet service provider. In Croatia, the post office is the country's main Internet service provider and offers a connection at up to 56000bps in some places. Unfortunately much of the country is stuck with outdated phone lines that can only handle much slower speeds if they can handle Internet access at all. The government is working hard to modernise the telecommunications system but work is proceeding in patches so it is entirely possible to have a good, fast connection in some parts of a city and none whatsoever in other neighbourhoods. Currently Zagreb offers the best Internet hook-up but that could change soon.

America Online subscribers can get a dial-up connection from Zagreb, Split, Rijeka and Dubrovnik for a surcharge of US$6 a month. Otherwise, if you're going to be in Croatia for some time, it may be worthwhile to take out a subscription with the post office. The fee is based on the speed at which you want to connect but,

before paying the top price for a fast connection, make sure the place where you'll be staying has modernised their phone lines. Generally the most practical speed is 33600bps for which you'll pay 70KN a month plus a 35KN subscription fee.

Cybercafés are in short supply. Currently, the only reliable outlets are in Zagreb, Rijeka and Korčula but that should change soon. Local tourist bureaus and travel agencies should be able to point the way to any others that may have sprung up and may even let you use their connection in an emergency.

INTERNET RESOURCES

Croatia has exploded into cyberspace with the speed of the Starship Enterprise. Cultural and historical sites are proliferating madly as Croats in the country and abroad aim to tell the world about their new country. The struggle to attract more tourism has led companies and municipalities to rush regional and commercial information onto the web. The National Tourist Board (www.htz.hr) maintains a web site with good links to other sources such as bus, train and plane information, contact information for tourist offices throughout the nation and abroad, and practical information on accommodation and outdoor activities. The jazzy site at www.dalmatia.net has a grab bag of cultural, political, practical and entertainment information as well as links to other sites.

BOOKS
Travel

The classic travel book on Yugoslavia and indeed one of the all-time great travel books is Rebecca West's *Black Lamb and Grey Falcon*. Written in 1941 as the world was becoming enmeshed in WWII, this massive volume recounts several trips that the writer took through Croatia, Serbia, Bosnia, Macedonia and Montenegro, weaving her observations into a seamless narrative. Passionate, forthright and wise, West's encyclopedic knowledge of Balkan history and culture illuminates many of the region's current difficulties. Robert Kaplan is a contemporary journalist who travelled through the Balkans in the 1980s and early 1990s as Yugoslavia began to fall apart. His book *Balkan Ghosts* vividly presents the people and places that form the tangled web of Balkan culture.

History & Politics

The most comprehensive recent account of Croatian history is Marcus Tanner's *Croatia: A Nation Forged in War*. The writer was an award-winning correspondent for the UK's *Independent* newspaper from 1988 to 1994, covering the former Yugoslavia as it descended into chaos. From the Roman era to President Tudjman, the complicated history of Croatia is presented in a lively, readable style.

If you're still trying to sort out who did what to whom in the recent war, it would be hard to surpass *The Death of Yugoslavia* by Laura Silber & Allan Little, based on the 1995 BBC television series of the same name. The drama of ineffectual Western peace initiatives trying to reign in power-driven regional despots makes riveting, if depressing reading. Richard Holbrooke's *To End a War* recounts the personalities and events surrounding the Dayton peace agreement. As the American official who prodded the warring parties to the negotiating table to hammer out a peace accord, Mr Holbrooke was in a unique position to evaluate the personalities and politics of the region.

General

Café Europa is a series of essays by a Croatian journalist, Slavenka Drakulić, which provides an inside look at life in the country since independence. Branded with the word 'dissident' in her home country, this Istrian expatriate unravels the contradictions and ambivalence that have formed Croatians growing up in the post-Tito era.

NEWSPAPERS & MAGAZINES

The most respected daily newspaper in Croatia is *Vjesnik* but the most daring is the satirical newsweekly *Feral Tribune*. Its investigative articles and sly graphics target increasingly unamused political parties,

who have responded with taxes, libel suits and general harassment. German and Italian newspapers are widely available and a daily newspaper in Italian, *La Voce del Popolo*, is published in Rijeka. American, British and French newspapers and magazines can be hard to find outside of large cities.

RADIO & TV

The three national television stations in Croatia fill a lot of air time with foreign programming; usually American, Italian and German and always in the original language. For local news, residents of Zadar, Split, Vinkovci and Osijek turn to their regional stations. Croatian Radio broadcasts news in English four times a day (8 am, 10 am, 2 pm and 11 pm) on frequencies 88.9, 91.3 and 99.3.

TIME

Croatia is on Central European Time (GMT/UTC plus one hour). Daylight saving comes in to effect at the end of March when clocks are turned forward an hour. At the end of September they're turned back an hour.

ELECTRICITY

Electricity is 220V, 50 Hz AC. Croatia uses the standard European round-pronged plugs.

WEIGHTS & MEASURES

The metric system is used. Like other continental Europeans, Croats indicate decimals with commas and thousands with points.

LAUNDRY

Self-service laundromats are virtually unknown. In Zagreb and a few other places you can leave laundry for a fee that will be based on either the weight or the article of clothing. An average load, without ironing will cost about 50KN. Most camping grounds have laundry facilities, hotels will wash clothes for a (hefty) fee or you could make arrangements with the proprietor if

The Trials and Travails of the Feral Tribune

The splashy graphics and catchy title of the *Feral Tribune* make the tabloid stand out amid a forest of newspapers crowding the local kiosks. Even if you don't understand Croatian, a front page photo montage that may blend President Tudjman's face into that of Franco, Stalin or Milošević quickly makes the paper's political viewpoint clear. The government has not been slow to grasp the paper's subversive message either and has subjected Croatia's leading independent newspaper to an unrelenting campaign of harassment.

Founded as a satirical weekly supplement to the Dalmatian newspaper, *Slobodna Dalmacija*, the Split-based *Feral Tribune* began its independent life in 1992 when the parent paper was taken over by the government. The tabloid's barbs became increasingly pointed, leading the government to slam a 50% sales tax on it in 1994, characterising it as a 'pornographic publication'. The tax was annulled by the Supreme Court but the news weekly's troubles were far from over.

In 1996 the Croatian Parliament passed a law making it a criminal offence to publicly criticise high officials. Within three months the paper's editor-in-chief, Viktor Ivančić, and commentator Marinko Čulić were indicted for two articles in which they compared Tudjman's proposal to rebury the bones of Ustashe activists with their concentration camp victims in Jasenovac to a similar scheme by Spanish dictator, General Francisco Franco. In December 1997, a lower court judge threw the case out, ruling that he would need to petition the Spanish Justice Ministry for its expert assessment in order to decide the case. An appeals court reinstated the case which, at the time of writing, is still pending. If convicted, Ivančić and Čulić could face up to three years in jail.

Aside from the criminal case, the *Feral Tribune* is facing dozens of civil defamation suits adding up to about US$3 million. President Tudjman's daughter is suing because of an article alleging that government connections enabled her to set up a prosperous business. Former Health Minister Andrija Hebrang is suing over an article dealing with the deaths of six children in a Zagreb hospital.

So far, the *Feral Tribune* has managed to stave off fines by adroit legal manoeuvring but lawyers' bills are taking their toll on the paper's finances. Because of the current economic situation in Croatia, money from distributors is slow to roll in, adding to their financial woes. Despite the headaches, the feisty tabloid is doing quite well where it counts – circulation is ever-increasing.

For the latest information go to www.cpj.org – the web page of the Committee to Protect Journalists.

The Feral Tribune's unofficial masthead, a court jester, gives us a sign

you're staying in private accommodation. Otherwise, bring your own detergent, washing line and clothes pegs.

TOILETS

Toilets are usually clean and well-stocked. In bus or train stations you'll normally have to pay about 2KN, but there's rarely a problem using the free facilities in cafés, restaurants or bars.

HEALTH

No special inoculations are needed before visiting Croatia and tap water is 100% safe, if somewhat overchlorinated. There are few dangerous snakes or bugs although mosquitoes can be a pain around lakes. Make sure you're armed with insect repellent and wear trousers and long sleeved shirts around sundown.

The standard of medical care in Croatia is high, although more expensive than it used to be before independence. All foreigners are entitled to emergency medical aid at the very least; for subsequent treatment entitlement varies. Some EU countries (including the UK) have contractual agreements with Croatia which allow their citizens free care while travelling in the country. This may require carrying a special form so check with your Ministry of Health or equivalent before setting out. Others have to pay and medical care can be expensive.

A travel insurance policy that covers medical problems is highly advisable (see Travel Insurance above). Remember, however, that some policies specifically exclude 'dangerous activities' such as scuba diving, rock-climbing or even trekking – the very activities you may be coming to Croatia for.

Predeparture planning

Make sure you're healthy before you start travelling. If you are going to be in Croatia for a while make sure your teeth are okay. If you wear glasses take a spare pair and your prescription.

If you require a particular medication take an adequate supply, as it may not be available locally. Take part of the packaging showing the generic name, rather than the brand, which will make getting replacements easier.

It's a good idea to have a legible prescription or letter from your doctor to show that you use the medication legally.

It's also wise to bring a basic medical kit, even though most of what you will need should be readily available in pharmacies in the main towns.

Basic Rules

Water Purification If you are planning on trekking or camping in one of Croatia's national parks and are unsure about the water, the simplest way of purifying water is to boil it thoroughly.

Chlorine tablets (Puritabs, Steritabs or other brand names) will kill many pathogens, but not some parasites like giardia and amoebic cysts. Iodine is more effective in purifying water and is available in tablet form (such as Potable Aqua). Follow the directions carefully and remember that too much iodine can be harmful.

Environmental Hazards

Motion Sickness Although car ferries and cruise lines rarely produce motion sickness, susceptible individuals may have problems. Eating lightly before and during a trip will reduce the chances of motion sickness.

If you are prone to motion sickness try to find a place that minimises movement – usually close to midship. Fresh air usually helps; reading and cigarette smoke don't. Commercial motion-sickness preparations, which can cause drowsiness, have to be taken before the trip commences. Ginger (available in capsule form) and peppermint (including mint-flavoured sweets) are natural preventatives.

Prickly Heat Prickly heat is an itchy rash caused by excessive perspiration trapped under the skin. It usually strikes people who have just arrived in a hot climate. Keeping cool, bathing often, drying the skin and using a mild talcum or prickly heat powder or resorting to air-conditioning may help.

Sunburn You can get sunburned surprisingly quickly in the Adriatic sun, even through a cloud. Use a sunscreen, hat, and barrier cream for your nose and lips. Calamine lotion or stingose are good for mild sunburn.

Heat Exhaustion Dehydration and salt deficiency can cause heat exhaustion. Take time to acclimatise to high temperatures, drink sufficient liquids and do not do anything too physically demanding.

Salt deficiency is characterised by fatigue, lethargy, headaches, giddiness and muscle cramps; salt tablets may help, but adding extra salt to your food is better.

Heatstroke This serious, occasionally fatal condition can occur if the body's heat regulating mechanism breaks down and the body temperature rises to dangerous levels. Long, continuous periods of exposure to high temperatures and insufficient fluids can leave you vulnerable to heatstroke.

The symptoms are feeling unwell, not sweating very much (or at all) and a high body temperature (39°C to 41°C or 102°F to 106°F). Where sweating has ceased the skin becomes flushed and red. Severe, throbbing headaches and lack of coordination will also occur, and the sufferer may be confused or aggressive. Eventually the victim will become delirious or convulse. Hospitalisation is essential, but in the interim get victims out of the sun, remove their clothing, cover them with a wet sheet or towel and then fan continually. Give fluids if they are conscious.

Hypothermia Too much cold can be just as dangerous as too much heat. Hypothermia occurs when the body loses heat faster than it can produce it and the core temperature of the body falls. It is surprisingly easy to progress from very cold to dangerously cold due to a combination of wind, wet clothing, fatigue and hunger, even if the air temperature is above freezing.

It is best to dress in layers; silk, wool and some of the new artificial fibres are all good insulating materials. A hat is important, as a lot of heat is lost through the head. A strong, waterproof outer layer (and a 'space' blanket for emergencies) is essential.

Carry basic supplies, including food containing simple sugars, to generate heat quickly, and fluid to drink.

Symptoms of hypothermia are exhaustion, numb skin (particularly toes and fingers), shivering, slurred speech, irrational or violent behaviour, lethargy, stumbling, dizzy spells, muscle cramps and violent bursts of energy. Irrationality may take the form of sufferers claiming they are warm and trying to take off their clothes.

WARNING

! Land mines left over from the recent war in Croatia pose no threat to the average visitor but it's important to be aware that certain areas of the country are still dangerous. Although the government moved with lightning speed to remove mines from any area even remotely interesting to tourists, the former confrontation line between Croat and federal forces is still undergoing de-mining operations which will not be complete for many years.

Slavonia was the most heavily mined region, followed by the Krajina region from Knin to Karlovac and the hinterlands of Zadar. Main towns and paved roads in these regions are perfectly safe but under no circumstances should you stray off the road into fields or abandoned villages. As a general rule, you should avoid any area along this route in which shattered roofs or artillery-pocked walls indicate that rebuilding and, possibly, de-mining has not yet occurred. If a place is still abandoned, there may be a reason.

Conflict in Yugoslavia in mid-1999 has made travel in Slavonia even more dangerous. We do not recommend visiting this region.

To treat mild hypothermia, first get the person out of the wind and/or rain, remove their clothing if it's wet and replace it with dry, warm clothing. Give them hot liquids – not alcohol – and some high-kilojoule, easily digestible food.

Do not rub victims, instead allow them to slowly warm themselves. This should be enough to treat the early stages of hypothermia. The early recognition and treatment of mild hypothermia is the only way to prevent severe hypothermia, which is a critical condition.

Infectious Diseases

Diarrhoea Simple things like a change of water, food or climate can all cause a mild bout of diarrhoea, but a few rushed toilet trips with no other symptoms is not indicative of a major problem.

Dehydration is the main danger with any diarrhoea, particularly in children or the elderly as dehydration can occur quite quickly. Under all circumstances fluid replacement (at least equal to the volume being lost) is the most important thing to remember. Weak black tea with a little sugar, soda water, or soft drink allowed to go flat and diluted 50% with clean water are all good.

HIV & AIDS HIV, the Human Immunodeficiency Virus, develops into AIDS, Acquired Immune Deficiency Syndrome, which is a fatal disease. HIV is a major problem in many countries.

Any exposure to blood, blood products or body fluids may put the individual at risk. The disease is often transmitted through sexual contact or dirty needles – vaccinations, acupuncture, tattooing and body piercing can be potentially as dangerous as intravenous drug use.

Fear of HIV infection should never preclude treatment for serious medical conditions.

Cuts, Bites & Stings

Insect Bites & Stings Bee and wasp stings are usually painful rather than dangerous. However in people who are allergic

to them severe breathing difficulties may occur and require urgent medical care. Calamine lotion or Stingose spray will give relief and ice packs will reduce the pain and swelling.

Ticks You should always check all over your body if you have been walking through a potentially tick-infested area, as ticks can cause skin infections and other more serious diseases.

If a tick is found attached, press down around the tick's head with tweezers, grab the head and gently pull upwards. Avoid pulling the rear of the body as this may squeeze the tick's gut contents through the attached mouth parts into the skin, increasing the risk of infection and disease. Smearing chemicals on the tick will not make it let go and is not recommended.

Snakes To minimise your chances of being bitten always wear boots, socks and long trousers when walking through undergrowth where snakes may be present. Don't put your hands into holes and crevices, and be careful when collecting firewood.

Snake bites do not cause instantaneous death and antivenenes are usually available. Immediately wrap the bitten limb tightly, as you would for a sprained ankle, and then attach a splint to immobilise it. Keep the victim still and seek medical help. Try to observe the markings of the snake, as this can be of help when administering antivenenes.

Don't attempt to catch the snake if there is a possibility of being bitten again. Remember that more people get bitten trying to kill snakes than by any other activity related to them; the best thing to do is to try to observe the markings.

Also note that tourniquets and sucking out the poison are now comprehensively discredited.

Women's Health

Gynaecological Problems Sexually transmitted diseases are a major cause of vaginal problems. Symptoms include an odorous discharge, painful intercourse and sometimes a burning sensation when urinating. Male sexual partners must also be treated. Medical attention should be sought. Besides abstinence, the best thing is to practice safe sex using condoms.

Antibiotic use, synthetic underwear, sweating and contraceptive pills can lead to fungal vaginal infections when travelling in hot climates. Maintaining good personal hygiene, and loose-fitting clothes and cotton underwear will help prevent these infections.

Fungal infections, characterised by a rash, itch and discharge, can be treated with a vinegar or lemon-juice douche, or with yoghurt. Nystatin, miconazole or clotrimazole pessaries or vaginal cream are the usual treatment.

WOMEN TRAVELLERS

Women face no special danger in Croatia and can often extract many small favours and concessions from Croatian men who are generally interested in appearing gallant and courteous. Women on their own may occasionally be harassed and followed in large coastal cities however, and some of the local bars and cafés can seem like private men's clubs – a woman alone is likely to be greeted with sudden silence and cold stares. It's important to be careful about being alone with an unfamiliar man since 'date rape' is not likely to be taken very seriously.

Feminism has not gained much of a foothold yet in Croatia. There are few women in leadership positions and you will notice a surfeit of women in low-paid menial jobs. Women usually shoulder the bulk of housework and child care responsibility even though the current economic situation is pushing more of them into the work force.

Croatian women place a high priority on good grooming and try to buy the most fashionable clothes they can afford. Topless sunbathing is considered acceptable; judging from the ubiquitous photos of topless women in tourist brochures it seems almost obligatory.

GAY & LESBIAN TRAVELLERS

Homosexuality has been legal in Croatia since 1977 and is generally tolerated, if not welcomed with open arms. Public displays of affection between members of the same sex may meet with hostility however, especially outside major cities. A small lesbian and gay community is developing in Zagreb but not to the extent of many western European cities. For further information contact LIGMA (Lesbian and Gay Men Action, ☎ 01-276 188, PO Box 488, 10001 Zagreb).

DISABLED TRAVELLERS

Because of the number of wounded war veterans, more attention is being paid to the needs of disabled travellers. Public toilets at bus stations, train stations, airports, and large public venues are usually wheelchair accessible. Large hotels and student dorms are wheelchair accessible. Bus and train stations in major cities such as Zagreb, Rijeka, Split and Dubrovnik are wheelchair accessible but the Jadrolinija coastal and local ferries do not have ramps. In Zagreb ZET (Zagrebački Električni Tramva) Electric Tram Company offers a service for the disabled that would otherwise find it difficult to get around the city. Call ☎ 01 66 00 443 Monday to Friday from 7.45 am to 2 pm and reserve a special vehicle for transport between addresses; The service is free for the disabled and the accompanying person pays the cost of a tram ticket. They do not help transporting the disabled person to the vehicle. You should try to order two days in advance but sometimes it can be organised immediately. For further information regarding help for the disabled, contact Savez Organizacija Invalida Hrvatske (Association of Organisations of Disabled Persons in Croatia, ☎/fax 01-48 29 394) Savska cesta 3, Zagreb 10000.

LEGAL MATTERS

Although it is highly unlikely that you'll be hassled by the police, you should keep identification with you at all times as the police have the right to stop you and demand ID.

By international treaty, you have the right to notify your consular official if arrested. Consulates normally can refer you to English-speaking lawyers although they will not pay for one.

BUSINESS HOURS

Official office hours are from 8 am to 4 pm. Banking hours vary but generally are from 8 am to 5 pm weekdays (sometimes with a lunch break), and 8 am to noon Saturday. Post offices keep long hours, Monday through Saturday, generally from 7 am to 9 pm. Many shops open from 8 am to 7 pm weekdays, 8 am to 2 pm Saturday. Croats are early risers and by 7 am there will be lots of people on the street and many places already open.

Along the coast, life is more relaxed; shops and offices frequently close around 1 pm for an afternoon break.

Working hours of travel agencies and tourist offices depend on the season. In July and August, offices are open from early in the morning until late at night without a break. Hours in the shoulder season of June and September are somewhat shorter and off season you can only count on offices being open in the morning. Restaurants keep long hours and you can get a meal any time of day.

PUBLIC HOLIDAYS & SPECIAL EVENTS

The public holidays of Croatia are:

New Year's Day
    1 January
Easter Monday
    March/April
Labour Day
    1 May
Bleiburg and Way of the Cross Victims Day
    15 May
Statehood Day (marks the anniversary of 1991 declaration of independence)
    30 May
Day of Antifascist Struggle (marks the outbreak of resistance in 1941)
    22 June

Homeland Thanksgiving Day
    5 August
Feast of the Assumption
    15 August
All Saints' Day
    1 November
Christmas
    25 and 26 December

Traditional Croat culture has been celebrated and promoted since independence with an emphasis on traditional dances, songs and festivals. The best place to see traditional festivals is along the coast and the best time is during the summer. The weekend closest to Assumption (August 15) is the scene of a festival celebrating the victory of the region of Sinj over the Ottoman Turks. Held in Sinj, the highlight of the festival is the competition where local 'knights' try to get a lance through a ring while rushing by on a galloping horse. On July 27, the town of Rab holds its traditional crossbow competition where men dress up in Renaissance tunics and plumed hats, and shoot arrows at a bullseye.

Many revived traditions centre on religious holidays, especially Lent and Easter. Carnival celebrations that mark the beginning of Lent are gaining in popularity each year with attendant parades and festivities. Although each town has their Carnival, the most elaborate festival is in Rijeka where the town business stops for seven days of partying. Samobor, outside of Zagreb, is also known for its Carnival, which attracts several hundred thousand visitors for parades, music and dancing. In and around Dubrovnik, palm or olive twigs are decorated with flowers, blessed and placed in homes on Palm Sunday. Holy Week preceding Easter is celebrated in Hvar, Brač and Korčula with processions. Central Croatia celebrates Holy Week with bonfires (*krijes*) and painted eggs are given as Easter gifts.

ACTIVITIES
Yachting

There's no better way to appreciate the Croatian Adriatic than by boat. The long, rugged islands off Croatia's mountainous coast all the way from Istria to Dubrovnik make this a yachting paradise. Fine, deep channels with abundant anchorage and steady winds attract yachties from around the world. Throughout the region there are quaint little ports where you can get provisions, and yachts can tie up right in the middle of everything.

There are 40 marinas along the coast, some with more facilities than others. Every coastal town mentioned in this book has a marina, from little Sali on Dugi Otok to the large marinas in Opatija, Zadar, Split and Dubrovnik. Most marinas are open throughout the year but its best to check first. A good source of information is Hrvatska Udruga Marina (Croatian Marinas Association, ☎ 051-209 147, fax 051-216 033), Bulevar Oslobođenja 23, 51000 Rijeka, which represents all Croatian marinas. You might also try the ACI Club in Opatija (☎ 051-271 288, fax 051-271 824) which represents about half the marinas.

Although you can row, motor or sail any vessel up to 3m long without authorisation, for larger boats you'll need to get authorisation from the harbour master at your port of entry, which will be at any harbour open to international traffic. Come equipped with a boat certificate, documents proving your sailing qualifications, insurance documents and money. A one year authorisation costs anywhere from 360KN for a five metre boat to 1440KN for a 20m boat.

Atlas travel agency has a small fleet of yachts for rental that cost US$2990 a week plus an extra US$100 a day for a skipper. The boat is a 13m ALAN 431. Boats are available from mid-April to mid-October and are less expensive outside the main June to September season. You can pick up the boat in Dubrovnik, Split or Pula. The only local operator with a US representative is Kiriacoulis in Pula who works with Le Boat (☎ 877-453 2628, fax 508-540 7802), PO Box 627, West Falmouth, Massachusetts 02574. They have yachts available in all sizes that start at US$1740 for a 9m class two boat and run to US$5220 for a 14m class five boat. The 9m will sleep four people comfortably; six is possible, but a squeeze. You can pick up the boat in Pula, Zadar or Split and a skipper is an extra US$100 a day.

Kayaking

There are countless possibilities for anyone carrying a folding sea kayak, especially among the Elafiti Islands (take the daily ferry from Dubrovnik to Lopud) and the Kornati Islands (take the ferry from Zadar to Sali). See Organised Tours in the Getting Around section for information on sailing and kayaking tours.

Hiking

The steep gorges and beech forests of Paklenica National Park, 40km north-east of Zadar, offer excellent hiking. Stari Grad, the main access town for the park, is well connected by hourly buses from Zadar. Hotels and private accommodation are available in Stari Grad, as well as a camping ground, *Paklenica* (☎ 023-369 236), open May to September.

Risnjak National Park at Crni Lug, 12km west of Delnice between Zagreb and Rijeka, is a good hiking area in summer. Buses run from Delnice to Crni Lug near the park entrance about three times a day, and there's a small *park-operated hotel* (☎ 051-836 133) at Crni Lug, with rooms at around 120KN per person including breakfast. Because of the likelihood of heavy snowfalls, hiking is only advisable from late spring to early autumn. It's a 9km, 2½-hour climb from the park entrance at Bijela Vodica to Veliki Risnjak (1528m).

For a great view of the barren coastal mountains, climb Mt Ilija (961m) above Orebić, opposite Korčula or Sveti Jure (1762m) from Makarska.

Scuba Diving

The varied underwater topography of the Croatian coast has spurred a growing diving industry. From Istria to Dubrovnik, nearly every coastal resort has a diving centre, usually German-owned. If you're not certified, a short 'Introduction to Diving' course at about 550KN will give you a taste of underwater life. If you want to become certified, a PADI or CMAS certification will cost from 1550 to 2100KN. If you're already certified, one dive with rented equipment runs from 225 to 275KN. Bring a wetsuit or you'll need to rent one, since the 25°C surface water temperature cools down dramatically as you descend.

In order to dive, you must get permission papers, which is easy to do. Go to the harbour captain in any port with your passport, certification card and 70KN. If you dive with a company, they will usually take care of the permission papers for you, for an extra fee. Permission is valid for a year in any dive spot throughout the country and the fee is slated for the preservation of underwater life.

Although there's a little bit of everything along the coast, the primary attractions are shipwrecks and caves. The porous karstic stone that forms the coastal mountains has

Responsible Diving

The popularity of diving is placing immense pressure on many sites. Please consider the following tips when diving and help preserve the ecology and beauty of reefs:
• Do not use anchors on the reef, and take care not to ground boats on coral. Encourage dive operators and regulatory bodies to establish permanent moorings at popular dive sites.
• Avoid touching living marine organisms with your body or dragging anything across the reef. Polyps can be damaged by even the gentlest contact. Never stand on corals, even if they look solid and robust. If you must secure yourself to the reef, only hold fast to exposed rock or dead coral.
• Be conscious of your flippers (fins). Even without contact the surge from heavy flipper strokes near the reef can damage delicate organisms. When treading water in shallow reef areas, take care not to kick up clouds of sand. Settling sand can easily smother the delicate organisms of the reef.
• Practise and maintain proper buoyancy control. Major damage can be done by divers descending too fast and colliding with the reef. Make sure you are correctly weighted and that your weight belt is positioned so that you stay horizontal. If you have not dived for a while, have a practice dive in a pool before taking to the reef. Be aware that buoyancy can change over the period of an extended trip: initially you may breathe harder and need more weighting; a few days later you may breathe more easily and need less weight.
• Take great care in underwater caves. Spend as little time within them as possible as your air bubbles may be caught within the roof and thereby leave previously submerged organisms high and dry. Taking turns to inspect the interior of a small cave will lessen the chances of damaging contact.
• Resist the temptation to collect or buy corals or shells. Aside from the ecological damage, taking home marine souvenirs depletes the beauty of a site and spoils the enjoyment of others.
• The same goes for marine archaeological sites (mainly shipwrecks). Respect their integrity; Croatian law protects shipwrecks and archaeological sites, and fines are stiff.
• Ensure that you take home all your rubbish, and any litter you may find as well. Plastics in particular are a serious threat to marine life. Turtles will mistake plastic for jellyfish and eat it.
• Resist the temptation to feed fish. You may disturb their normal eating habits, encourage aggressive behaviour or feed them food that is detrimental to their health.

created an astonishing variety of underwater caves all along the coast, but especially in the Kornati Islands.

Shipwrecks are also a common sight, most notoriously the Baron Gautsch wreck near Rovinj. Remains of Roman wrecks with 1st century amphorae can be found within reach of Dubrovnik, but special permission is necessary since they are protected cultural monuments. Diving from Lošinj island offers a good mixture of sights – sea walls, caves and wrecks.

The marine life is not as rich as the Red Sea or the Caribbean, for example, but you'll regularly see groper, eels, sardines and snails. Sponges and sea fans are common sea flora but coral reefs tend to lie in deep water – around 40m – since the shallower coral has already been plundered. The waters around Vis island are richest in marine life because the island was an off-limits military base for many years and the sea was not over-fished.

Rock Climbing

The karstic stone of Croatia's coast provides excellent climbing opportunities. Paklenica National Park has the widest range of routes – nearly 400 – for all levels of experience. Spring, summer or autumn are good seasons but in winter you'll be fighting the fierce *bura* wind. Other popular climbing spots include the rocks surrounding Baška on Krk island that can be climbed year-round; although if you come in summer you can combine climbing with a beach holiday. Brela on the Makarska Riviera also allows climbing and beach-bumming but in winter there's a strong bura. Also on the Makarska Riviera, is the wall from Baška Voda to Makarska on Biokovo Mountain with 200 to 400m routes. For more information contact the Croatian Climbing Federation, (☎/fax 01-448 774) Kozaričeva 22 Zagreb 10000. There's also plenty of extremely useful information, maps and pictures to be found at the *'Free Climbing in Croatia'* Web site (http://public.srce.hr/hpd–zeljeznicar/AO/climbing.htm).

Windsurfing

Although most coastal resorts offer windsurfing courses and board rentals, serious windsurfers gravitate to the town of Bol on Brač island. The strong, steady *maestral* blows from April to October and the wide bay catches the wind perfectly. The best windsurfing is at the end of May, beginning of June and at the end of July, beginning of August. The wind generally reaches its peak in early afternoon and then dies down at the end of the day.

COURSES

The Croatian Heritage Foundation (Hrvatska matica iseljenika), Trg Stjepana Radića 3, 10000 Zagreb (☎ 01-61 15 116, fax 01-45 50 700, nives@matis.hr) runs a series of programs on Croatian language and culture during July and August (exact dates become known the preceding February). Though designed for people of Croatian descent living abroad, everyone is welcome. For more information see www.matis.hr/odjeli.htm.

On the island of Badija near Korčula a 10 day program explores Croatian folk dances and Croatian folk music. The cost is US$110 tuition plus US$17 daily board. Two 14 day 'Croaticum' programs are offered at Supetar on Brač island (in association with the National University of Split), costing 1244DM with tuition, full board and an excursion to a nearby historical city included.

The Faculty of Arts at the University of Zagreb (founded in 1669) organises a more intensive, academically oriented four or five-week course (US$720/900 school fees plus US$250 registration). Room and board (sharing a twin room) at a student dormitory is US$14 per person per day. Contact the Croatian Heritage Foundation in Zagreb for application information or Professor Luka Budak (☎ 02-9850 7040, fax 02-9850 8890, lbudak@ocs1.ocs.mq.edu.au), at the Croatian Studies Department, Macquarie University, Sydney, NSW 2109, Australia; Dr Vinko Grubišić (☎ /fax 519-746 5243), Faculty of Arts, University of Waterloo, Waterloo, ON N2L 3G1 Canada, or Ms Susan MacNally

(☎ 913-864 3742, fax 913 864 5040, sumac@ukans.edu), Study Abroad Programs, University of Kansas, Lawrence, KS 66045 USA. Also ask about regular semester courses offered throughout the academic year.

For the ecologically minded, Svanimir (Croatian Society for the Protection of Natural and Cultural Heritage) runs three week programs to protect Croatia's natural environment. Volunteers may work on protecting the griffon vulture or saving small marshes on the island of Cres. The cost is 350DM per week and 12DM a day for food. Contact Svanimir (☎ 01 530 205), Ilirski trg 9, 10000 Zagreb.

These courses are an excellent way to learn about Croatian culture and meet a lot of interesting people, while providing a productive anchor for a Mediterranean holiday – highly recommended.

WORK

Unemployment is high in Croatia and job opportunities are scarce. In order to obtain a valid work permit, you must have either a permanent residence permit or an employment contract based upon a particular expertise that could not readily be found in Croatia. So far, there's little market for English teachers. The best way to work in Croatia is to participate in an organised program.

The Croatian Heritage Foundation organises summer 'task forces' of young people from around the world, often of Croatian descent, who gather to assist in war reconstruction. Often these programs have an ecological or archaeological slant such as repairing the bridges in Plitvice National Park, restoring a damaged church or excavating an archaeological site. The work day ends at 2 pm, leaving plenty of free time for swimming and sports as well as various excursions to cultural heritage sites. Applicants must be from 17 to 30 years old and present two references, one from a Croatian person or association within their community. Costs of accommodation and meals for successful applicants are covered by the foundation. For details, contact the Croatian Heritage Foundation in Zagreb or Sylvia Hrkač (☎ 905-270 2672, fax 905-270 3325), c/o C.I.Y.C., 19 Dundas Str, Suite 203 Mississauga, Ontario Canada, or Edi Živković, Croatian Information Centre, PO Box 73 O'Connor, ACT 2602 Australia.

Suncokret (☎ 01-211 104, fax 01-222 715, suncokret@public.srce.com), at Seferova 10, 10000 Zagreb, is a non-profit organisation founded in 1992 to deal with the humanitarian wreckage of the recent war. They accept summer volunteers to do unpaid relief work among women, children and the elderly traumatised by the war in Croatia. Preference is given to teachers, social workers, counsellors and applicants with prior experience in the welfare professions. Camps are in Pula, Varaždin, Knin and Topusko (near Zagreb) and volunteers are expected to pay 200 to 300DM for food, accommodation and organisational expenses.

ACCOMMODATION

Along the coast, accommodation is priced according to three seasons, which vary from place to place. Generally April, May and October are the cheapest months, June and September are medium, but in July and August count on paying top price, especially in the peak period that starts in mid-July and lasts till mid-August. Prices quoted in this book are for the peak period and do not include 'residence tax' of 7.60KN in peak season, 5KN in the shoulder season, and 4.30KN in the off season. Deduct about 20% if you come in the shoulder season – June, the beginning of July and September. Deduct about 30% for May and October and about 40% for all other times. Prices for accommodation in Zagreb are constant all year.

Accommodation is generally cheaper in Dalmatia than in Kvarner or Istria but in July and August you should make arrangements in advance wherever you go.

This book provides the phone numbers of most accommodation facilities. Once you know your itinerary it pays to go to a post office, buy a telephone card and start calling around to check prices, availability etc. Most receptionists speak English.

Camping

Nearly 100 camping grounds are scattered along the Croatian coast. Most operate from mid-May to September only, although a few are open in April and October. In May and late September, call ahead to make sure that the camping ground is open before beginning the long trek out. Don't go by the opening and closing dates you read in travel brochures or this book, as these can change. Even local tourist offices can be wrong.

Most camping grounds have a per person charge that runs from 12 to 20KN. The tent charge is sometimes included or it's an extra 12 to 20KN. If you come in a caravan you'll pay from 18 to 25KN.

Although small, family-owned camping grounds are starting to pop up, most camps are gigantic 'autocamps' with restaurants, shops and row upon row of caravans. If you want a more intimate environment, the town tourist office should be able to refer you to smaller camping grounds, but you may have to insist upon it. Nudist camping grounds (marked FKK) are among the best because their secluded locations ensure peace and quiet. Freelance camping is officially prohibited.

Hostels

The Croatian YHA (☎ 01-422 953, fax 01-48 41 269, hfhs-cms@alf.tel.hr) at Dežmanova 9, 10000 Zagreb, operates summer youth hostels in Dubrovnik, Šibenik and Zadar, and year-round hostels at Zagreb and Pula. Bed and breakfast at these is about 65KN for YHA members in the low season (May, June, September and October) and 75KN for members in July and August. Non-members pay an additional 12KN per person daily for a welcome card; six stamps on the card then entitles you to a membership. The Zagreb hostel has higher prices. For more information see www.nncomp.com/hfhs/hfhs.html.

In November 1998, Croatia became a member of the European Youth Card Asso-ciation, and all Youth Card holders (Euro<26) can now use their cards at around 300 places of interest in Croatia.

Private Rooms

The best accommodation in Croatia is private rooms in local homes, the equivalent of small private guesthouses in other countries. Not only is it cheaper than staying in hotels, but interacting with your host will provide invaluable insight into the local culture. Such rooms can be arranged by travel agencies but they add a lot of taxes and commission to your bill, so you'll almost always do better dealing directly with proprietors you meet on the street or by knocking on the doors of houses with *sobe* or *zimmer* signs. This way you avoid the residence tax and four-night minimum stay, but you also forgo the agency's quality control.

Language barriers can also make negotiation difficult since proprietors are likely to speak only Croatian, German or Italian. If you choose the knocking-on-doors approach, start early in the day since proprietors may be out on errands in the afternoon. You'll be more comfortable and in a better position to negotiate a price if you leave your luggage in a left-luggage office before trudging around town.

Proprietors will sometimes check coastal bus stations and ferry terminals for potential customers, so if you're struggling to find a room you may find something there. Town cafés are also a good source of accommodation leads, but remember to exercise the usual caution.

If the price asked is too high, bargain. Be sure to clarify whether the price agreed upon is per person or for the room. Tell the proprietor in advance how long you plan to stay or they may try to add a surprise 'supplement' when you leave after a night or two. At the agencies, singles are expensive and scarce, but on the street, *sobe* prices are usually per person, which favours the single traveller. Showers are always included but breakfast often is not, so ask about the breakfast charge.

It may be worthwhile to take half-board. Most families on the coast have a garden, a vineyard and access to the sea. You could begin with a home-made aperitif, and progress on to garden-fresh salad, home-grown potatoes and grilled fresh fish, washed down with your host's very own wine.

Although renting an unofficial room is common practice along the Adriatic coast, be discreet, as technically you're breaking the law by not registering with the police. Don't brag to travel agencies about the low rate you got, for example.

If you stay less than four nights, the agencies add a 20 to 30% surcharge. Travel agencies have been classifying the rooms according to categories I, II or III, which is in the process of changing to a star system. The most expensive rooms will be three star and include a private bathroom. In a two star room, the bathroom is shared with one other room and in a one star room, the bathroom is shared with two other rooms. Studios with cooking facilities can be a good deal, costing little more than a double room and if you're travelling in a small group, it may be worthwhile to get an apartment.

At the time of writing, accommodation rates were fixed with little variance from agency to agency but that system is changing and, by the time of your trip, it may be worthwhile to compare prices. Also note that the prices quoted in the following chapters could leap dramatically if there's a scarcity of accommodation and a surfeit of tourists.

Hotels

Tourism in Croatia (then part of Yugoslavia) really started to take off in the 1970s and 1980s, which was when most of the hotels along the coast were built. At the time, the idea was to market the coast to package tourists and then pack them off to 'tourist settlements', usually far from town and along a stretch of beach. Since they were all state-owned and built at the same time with the same idea, it's unsurprising that they all look alike. There is nothing

particularly Istrian or even Croatian in an Istrian hotel complex to distinguish it from a Dalmatian or Spanish hotel complex. The advantage of this approach is that it left the historic old towns more or less alone, free of a lot of the tourist trappings that would have been present if tourists had commandeered the town for the summer. From a visitors point of view, the disadvantage is the lack of small family-owned hotels where the owner's taste and personality is reflected in the rooms. For a more personal experience, you have to stay in private accommodation.

There are some exceptions. Zagreb and other big cities have at least one grand old hotel built in the 19th century when the railway came through. Opatija was a popular resort in the Austro-Hungarian empire and has a conglomeration of elegant, European-style hotels that retain a certain faded splendour. Other old hotels on the coast were often the ones used to house refugees during the recent war and need a large infusion of cash before they can re-open.

Privatisation may change the hotel picture. Although most of the state-owned hotels wound up in the hands of wealthy tycoons who invest as little as possible in their property, there are some signs here and there of local entrepreneurs taking over a hotel. If you can find them, these places usually offer a good deal – competitive prices in a freshly renovated space.

Croatian hotels may not charm you, but they are clean, serviceable and fairly efficient. Double rooms, if not singles, are a good size and nearly all rooms in Croatian hotels have private bathrooms, even modest pensions. The vast majority of hotels in Croatia fall into the moderate range – around 400KN a double in the summer along the coast dropping to around 250KN in late spring or early autumn. At that price you can get a pleasant, clean but unexceptional room equipped with a bathroom, a telephone and sometimes a TV with a satellite hook-up. Since there's usually no surcharge for a short stay, hotels can be a better deal than private accommodation if you're only staying a night or two.

Most hotels offer the option of taking half-board. In a 'tourist settlement' far from town, half-board may be the only dining possibility within reach. Sometimes half-board is only a marginal increase over the bed & breakfast rate, making it worth considering even if you only plan to take a few meals at the hotel. Except in luxury establishments, the meals centre on cheaper cuts of meat although some hotels are starting to offer a vegetarian menu.

In the past, hotels have been rated in categories from A to D with A being the most deluxe establishments and D the most basic. Most hotels fall into the B-category but you'll find a few deluxe hotels in Zagreb and in major coastal cities. C and D category hotels are rare.

FOOD

Croatian cuisine reflects the cultures that have influenced the country over the course of its history. Thus, there's a sharp divide between the Italian-style cuisine on the coast and the Hungarian, Viennese and Turkish-style cuisine in the interior. Each region has its own specialty, but wherever you go you'll be surprised by the generally good quality food, made from fresh, seasonal ingredients.

Zagreb and north-western Croatia favour the kind of hearty meat dishes you might find in Vienna. Juicy spit-roasted meat (*pečenje*), lamb (*janje*), pork (*svinjetina*) and duck (*patka*) are real favourites around Zagreb and north-western Croatia, often accompanied by baked noodles (*mlinci*) or roast potatoes (*prženi krumpir*). Turkey (*puran*) with (*mlinci*) is practically an institution on Zagreb menus along with steak *a la Zagreb* (veal stuffed with ham and cheese, then fried in breadcrumbs) – another calorie-ridden specialty. Hungarian influence is found in the goulash (*gulaš*) and *palačinka* – thin pancakes filled with jam and topped with chocolate – you'll find on many menus. Vegetarians have a tough time of it in northern Croatia but you can

begin with a hearty soup such as *manistra od bobića* (beans and fresh maize soup) or *juha od krumpira na zagorski način* (Zagorje potato soup) and follow with *štrukli* (baked cheese dumplings) or *blitva* (a leafy vegetable cooked with potatoes and garlic).

Cuisine in Eastern Slavonia is spicier than in other regions, using liberal amounts of paprika and garlic. The nearby Drava River provides fresh fish such as carp and pike that is stewed in a paprika sauce and served with home-made noodles (*riblji paprikaš*). Their sausages are also renowned, especially *kulen*, a paprika flavoured sausage served with cottage cheese, peppers, tomatoes and pickled vegetables (*turšija*). Cakes stuffed with walnuts, poppyseeds and plum jam make a delicious dessert.

Coastal cuisine is typically Mediterranean using a lot of olive oil, garlic, fish and herbs. Meals often begin with a first course of pasta such as spaghetti or risotto (*rizot*) topped with seafood (*prstaci*). In Istria you may see *menestra*, which is a vegetable and bean soup similar to Italian minestrone soup. If you see risotto or pasta with *tartufe*, grab it – these wild truffles are a real delicacy in Istria. Thin slices of smoked Istrian or Dalmatian ham are often on the appetiser list. It's expensive because of the long hours and personal attention involved in smoking the meat, but it does acquire a unique flavour. For a special non-meat appetiser, try Pag cheese, a pungent hard cheese from Pag island that's served with olives. Dalmatian *brodet* (mixed fish stewed with rice) is another regional treat but it's often only available in two-person portions.

Dalmatian *pašticada* (beef stuffed with lard and roasted in wine and spices) appears more on menus in the interior than it does along the coast but makes a hearty winter dish.

For inexpensive, quick meals, you'll find that pizza is often astonishingly good wherever you go and costs about half of what you'd pay in Western Europe. The spaghetti and risotto listed as an appetiser can make a filling meal especially if you soak up the sauce with heaps of bread. For fast food, you can usually snack on *čevapčići* (spicy beef or pork meatballs), *ražnjiči* (shish kebab) or *burek* (a heavy pastry stuffed with meat or cheese). Along the coast, look for lightly breaded and fried squid (*lignje*) as a main course.

Self-service cafeterias are quick, easy and inexpensive, though the quality of the food varies. If the samples behind glass look cold or dried out, ask them to dish out a fresh plate for you. Better restaurants aren't that much more expensive if you choose carefully and pizzerias are often cheaper.

A restaurant (restauracija) or pub may also be called a gostionica or a konoba, and a café is a kavana. Restaurants in Croatia can be a hassle because they rarely post their menus outside, so to find out what they offer and the price range you have to walk in and ask to see the menu. Then if you don't like what you see, you must walk back out and appear rude.

The price and quality of meals varies little as there is an upper limit to what the local crowd can afford to pay, and a bottom line to what they'll find acceptable. With the current economic situation, Croats have little money for dining out, but when they do they expect the food to be worth it, which it usually is. Restaurants cluster in the middle of the range – very few are unbelievably cheap and even fewer are exorbitantly expensive. In a good, moderate restaurant expect to pay about 25KN for a starter and 60 to 70KN for a main course. Bread usually costs extra and a few restaurants tack on a service charge, which is supposed to be indicated on the menu. Fish and shellfish are more expensive and usually charged by the kilogram. An average portion is about 250g but sometimes you'll be expected to choose a whole fish from a selection, making it more difficult to estimate the final cost.

Breakfast is difficult in Croatia as all you can get easily is coffee. For eggs, toast and jam you'll have to go somewhere expensive, otherwise you can buy some bread, cheese and milk at a supermarket and picnic somewhere. Throughout ex-Yugoslavia the breakfast of the people is *burek*, a greasy layered pie made with meat *(mesa)* or cheese *(sira)* and cut on a huge metal tray.

A load of fruit and vegetables from the local market can make a healthy, cheap picnic lunch. There are plenty of supermarkets in Croatia – cheese, bread, ham and milk are readily available and fairly cheap. The person behind the meat counter at supermarkets will make a big cheese or bologna sandwich for you upon request and you only pay the regular price of the ingredients.

DRINKS

It's customary to have a small glass of brandy before a meal. Croatia is famous for its plum brandies *(šljivovica)*, herbal brandies *(travarica)*, cognacs *(vinjak)* and liqueurs such as *maraschino*, a cherry liqueur made in Zadar, *prosecco*, a sweet dessert wine or herbal *pelinkovac*.

Zagreb's Ožujsko beer *(pivo)* is very good but Karlovačko beer from Karlovac is better. You'll want to practice saying the word *živjeli!* (cheers!).

Wine is an important part of Croatian meals but oenophiles will be dismayed to see Croats diluting their wine with water. It's hardly necessary. Although not on a world-class level, Croatian wines are eminently drinkable and occasionally distinguished.

Virtually every region produces its own wine. The Istria and Kvarner regions are known for *Žlahtina* of Vrbnik on Krk island, *Cabernet* from Poreč and *Terrano* from Buzet. Dalmatia has the oldest wine-producing tradition. Look for *Pošip* and *Grk* on Korčula, *Dingač* and *Postup* from the Pelješac Peninsula, *Plavac* from Brač island and *Malmsy* from Dubrovnik. Eastern Slavonia produces excellent white wines such as Kutjevačka Graševina, Kutjevo Chardonnay, Rhine Riesling and Krauthaker Graševina.

Strong brewed espresso served in tiny cups is popular throughout Croatia. You can have it diluted with milk or order cappuccino, regular or decaf. Herbal teas are widely available but regular tea is apt to be too weak for aficionados.

ENTERTAINMENT

Culture was heavily subsidised by the communists, and admission to operas, operettas and concerts is still reasonable. The main theatres offering musical programs are listed herein, so note the location and drop by some time during the day to see what's on and purchase tickets.

In the interior cities, winter is the best time to enjoy the theatres and concert halls. The main season at the opera houses of Rijeka, Split and Zagreb runs from October to May. These close for holidays in summer and the cultural scene shifts to the many summer festivals. Pula's impressive Roman amphitheatre is attracting first-rate international musicians and opera companies all year round. Dubrovnik's summer festival in July and August intersperses local and national artists with international guest conductors and singers. Ask municipal tourist offices about cultural events in their area.

Discos operate in summer in the coastal resorts and all year in the interior cities, but the best way to mix with the local population is to enjoy a leisurely coffee or ice cream in a café. With the first hint of mild weather, Croatians head for an outdoor terrace to drink, smoke and watch the passing parade.

'Terrace dancing' is a summer tradition along the coast. At least one hotel in every coastal resort hires a couple of musicians to play for dance music evenings on their terrace. The play list usually includes a smattering of local tunes along with international favourites. You won't meet many Croats but it can be a pleasant evening out for the price of a drink.

The cheapest entertainment in Croatia is a movie at a *kino* (cinema). Admission fees are always low and the soundtracks are in the original language. The selection leans towards popular American blockbusters and the last film of the day is usually hardcore pornography. Check the time on your ticket carefully, as admission is not allowed once the film has started.

Croatian international footballer Davor Suker scored more goals than any other player at the 1998 World Cup in France. Football is a popular spectator sport in Croatia.

SPECTATOR SPORTS

Basketball and tennis both draw crowds and Croatia has contributed a number of world-class players in both sports.

But by far the most popular spectator sport in Croatia is football (soccer). The national team performed outstandingly to finish third in the 1998 World Cup in France, following stunning victories over teams of the calibre of Germany and Holland.

In addition, Davor Suker won the prestigious 'Golden Boot' award for being the tournament's leading goal scorer with six goals.

SHOPPING

The finest artisans' product from Croatia is the intricate lace from Pag island, part of a centuries-old tradition that's still going strong. Although you'll sometimes see it in handicraft shops in Zagreb and Dubrovnik, it's more fun to take a trip out to Pag where you can buy the patches of lace directly from the ladies that make them.

Embroidered fabrics are also featured in many souvenir shops. Croatian embroidery is distinguished by the cheerful red geometric patterns set against a white background that you'll see on tablecloths, pillowcases and blouses.

Lavender and other fragrant herbs made into scented sachets or transmuted into oils, are popular and inexpensive gifts. You can find them on most central Dalmatian islands, but especially on Hvar island, known for its lavender fields.

Brač island is known for its lustrous stone. Ashtrays, vases, candlestick holders and other small, but heavy items carved from Brač stone are on sale throughout the island.

Samples of local food, wine and spirits can also make great gifts or souvenirs. If you're in Samobor, pick up some mustard or Bermet liquor; in Pag you can buy savoury home-made cheese, but be aware that customs regulations in many countries forbid the importation of unwrapped cheese; *Cukarini* pastries from Korčula island keep a while if wrapped in cellophane; local brandies, often with herbs inside the bottle, can conjure up the scents and flavours of each region, since it seems that almost every town produces its own special brandy.

Getting There & Away

The information in this chapter is particularly vulnerable to change: prices for international travel are volatile, routes are introduced and cancelled, schedules change, special deals come and go, and rules and visa requirements are amended. Airlines, boat companies and governments seem to take a perverse pleasure in making price structures and regulations as complicated as possible. You should check directly with the airline, boat company or a travel agent to make sure you understand how a fare (and ticket you may buy) works. In addition, the travel industry is highly competitive and there are many lurks and perks.

The upshot of this is that you should get opinions, quotes and advice from as many companies and travel agents as possible before you part with your hard-earned cash. The details given in this chapter should be regarded as pointers and are not a substitute for your own careful, up-to-date research.

AIR
Airports & Airlines

Croatia Airlines (☎ 01-45 51 340 or ☎ 01-45 51 244), Zrinjevac 17, Zagreb 10000, is the national carrier. Although they have no planes for long-haul flights, they work with other carriers to provide services from Zagreb to Amsterdam, Berlin, Brussels, Copenhagen, Dublin, Düsseldorf, Frankfurt, London, Moscow, Mostar, Munich, Paris, Prague, Rome, Sarajevo, Skopje, Stuttgart, Tirana, Vienna and Zürich. Note that all batteries must be removed from checked luggage for flights departing from any airport in Croatia.

Buying Tickets

The plane ticket will probably be the single most expensive item in your budget, and buying it can be an intimidating business. There is likely to be a multitude of airlines and travel agents hoping to separate you from your money, and it is always worth putting aside a few hours to research the current state of the market. Start early: some of the cheapest tickets have to be bought months in advance, and some popular flights sell out early. Talk to other recent travellers – they may be able to stop you making some of the same old mistakes. Look at the ads in newspapers and magazines (not forgetting the press of the ethnic group whose country you plan to visit), consult reference books and watch for special offers. Then phone around travel agents for bargains. (Airlines can supply information on routes and timetables; however, except at times of inter-airline war they do not supply the cheapest tickets.) Find out the fare, the route, the duration of the journey and any restrictions on the ticket. Then sit back and decide which is best for you.

You may discover that those impossibly cheap flights are 'fully booked, but we have another one that costs a bit more ...' Or the flight is on an airline notorious for its poor safety standards and leaves you in the world's least favourite airport in mid-journey for 14 hours. Or they claim only to have the last two seats available for that country for the whole of July, which they will hold for you for a maximum of two hours. Don't panic – keep ringing around.

Use the fares quoted in this book as a guide only. They are approximate and based on the rates advertised by travel agents at the time of going to press. Quoted air fares do not necessarily constitute a recommendation for the carrier. If you are travelling from the UK or the USA, you will probably find that the cheapest flights are being advertised by obscure bucket shops whose names haven't yet reached the telephone directory. Many such firms are honest and solvent, but there are a few rogues who will take your money and disappear, to reopen elsewhere a month or two later under a new name. If you feel suspicious about a firm, don't give them all the

Air Travel Glossary

Baggage Allowance This will be written on your ticket and usually includes one 20kg item to go in the hold, plus one item of hand luggage.

Bucket Shops These are unbonded travel agencies specialising in discounted airline tickets.

Bumped Just because you have a confirmed seat doesn't mean you're going to get on the plane (see Overbooking).

Cancellation Penalties If you have to cancel or change a discounted ticket, there are often heavy penalties involved; insurance can sometimes be taken out against these penalties. Some airlines impose penalties on regular tickets as well, particularly against 'no-show' passengers.

Check-In Airlines ask you to check in a certain time ahead of the flight departure (usually one to two hours on international flights). If you fail to check in on time and the flight is overbooked, the airline can cancel your booking and give your seat to somebody else.

Confirmation Having a ticket written out with the flight and date you want doesn't mean you have a seat until the agent has checked with the airline that your status is 'OK' or confirmed. Meanwhile you could just be 'on request'.

Courier Fares Businesses often need to send urgent documents or freight securely and quickly. Courier companies hire people to accompany the package through customs and, in return, offer a discount ticket which is sometimes a phenomenal bargain. In effect, what the companies do is ship their freight as your luggage on regular commercial flights. This is a legitimate operation, but there are two shortcomings - the short turnaround time of the ticket (usually not longer than a month) and the limitation on your luggage allowance. You may have to surrender all your allowance and take only carry-on luggage.

Full Fares Airlines traditionally offer 1st class (coded F), business class (coded J) and economy class (coded Y) tickets. These days there are so many promotional and discounted fares available that few passengers pay full economy fare.

ITX An ITX, or 'independent inclusive tour excursion', is often available on tickets to popular holiday destinations. Officially it's a package deal combined with hotel accommodation, but many agents will sell you one of these for the flight only and give you phoney hotel vouchers in the unlikely event that you're challenged at the airport.

Lost Tickets If you lose your airline ticket an airline will usually treat it like a travellers cheque and, after inquiries, issue you with another one. Legally, however, an airline is entitled to treat it like cash and if you lose it then it's gone forever. Take good care of your tickets.

MCO An MCO, or 'miscellaneous charge order', is a voucher that looks like an airline ticket but carries no destination or date. It can be exchanged through any International Association of Travel Agents (IATA) airline for a ticket on a specific flight. It's a useful alternative to an onward ticket in those countries that demand one, and is more flexible than an ordinary ticket if you're unsure of your route.

No-Shows No-shows are passengers who fail to show up for their flight. Full-fare passengers who fail to turn up are sometimes entitled to travel on a later flight. The rest are penalised (see Cancellation Penalties).

On Request This is an unconfirmed booking for a flight.

Air Travel Glossary

Onward Tickets An entry requirement for many countries is that you have a ticket out of the country. If you're unsure of your next move, the easiest solution is to buy the cheapest onward ticket to a neighbouring country or a ticket from a reliable airline which can later be refunded if you do not use it.

Open Jaw Tickets These are return tickets where you fly out to one place but return from another. If available, this can save you backtracking to your arrival point.

Overbooking Airlines hate to fly empty seats and since every flight has some passengers who fail to show up, airlines often book more passengers than they have seats. Usually excess passengers make up for the no-shows, but occasionally somebody gets bumped. Guess who it is most likely to be? The passengers who check in late.

Point-to-Point Tickets These are discount tickets that can be bought on some routes in return for passengers waiving their rights to a stopover.

Promotional Fares These are officially discounted fares, available from travel agencies or direct from the airline.

Reconfirmation At least 72 hours prior to departure time of an onward or return flight, you must contact the airline and 'reconfirm' that you intend to be on the flight. If you don't do this the airline can delete your name from the passenger list and you could lose your seat.

Restrictions Discounted tickets often have various restrictions on them - such as needing to be paid for in advance and incurring a penalty to be altered. Others are restrictions on the minimum and maximum period you must be away, such as a minimum of 14 days or a maximum of one year.

Round-the-World Tickets RTW tickets give you a limited period (usually a year) in which to circumnavigate the globe. You can go anywhere the carrying airlines go, as long as you don't backtrack. The number of stopovers or total number of separate flights is decided before you set off and they usually cost a bit more than a basic return flight.

Stand-by This is a discounted ticket where you only fly if there is a seat free at the last moment. Stand-by fares are usually available only on domestic routes.

Travel Agencies Travel agencies vary widely and you should choose one that suits your needs. Some simply handle tours, while full-services agencies handle everything from tours and tickets to car rental and hotel bookings. If all you want is a ticket at the lowest possible price, then go to an agency specialising in discounted tickets.

Transferred Tickets Airline tickets cannot be transferred from one person to another. Travellers sometimes try to sell the return half of their ticket, but officials can ask you to prove that you are the person named on the ticket. This is less likely to happen on domestic flights, but on an international flight tickets are compared with passports.

Travel Periods Ticket prices vary with the time of year. There is a low (off-peak) season and a high (peak) season, and often a low-shoulder season and a high-shoulder season as well. Usually the fare depends on your outward flight - if you depart in the high season and return in the low season, you pay the high-season fare.

money at once – leave a deposit of 20% or so and pay the balance when you get the ticket. If they insist on cash in advance, go somewhere else. And once you have the ticket, ring the airline to confirm that you are actually booked on the flight.

You may decide to pay more than the rock-bottom fare by opting for the safety of a better-known travel agent. Firms such as STA Travel, which has offices worldwide, Council Travel in the USA or Travel CUTS in Canada are not going to disappear overnight, leaving you clutching a receipt for a nonexistent ticket, but they do offer good prices to most destinations.

Once you have your ticket, write down its number, together with the flight number and other details, and keep the information somewhere separate. If the ticket is lost or stolen, this will help you get a replacement. It's sensible to buy travel insurance as early as possible. If you buy it the week before you fly, you may find, for example, that you're not covered for delays to your flight caused by industrial action.

Travellers with Special Needs

If you have special needs of any sort – you've broken a leg, you're vegetarian, travelling in a wheelchair, taking the baby, terrified of flying – you should let the airline know as soon as possible so that they can make arrangements accordingly. You should remind them when you reconfirm your booking (at least 72 hours before departure) and again when you check in at the airport. It may also be worth ringing round the airlines before you make your booking to find out how they can handle your particular needs.

Airports and airlines can be surprisingly helpful, but they do need advance warning. Most international airports will provide escorts from check-in desk to plane where needed, and there should be ramps, lifts, accessible toilets and reachable phones. Aircraft toilets, on the other hand, are likely to present a problem; travellers should discuss this with the airline at an early stage and, if necessary, with their doctor.

Guide dogs for the blind will often have to travel in a specially pressurised baggage compartment with other animals, away from their owner; smaller guide dogs may be admitted to the cabin. All guide dogs will be subject to the same quarantine laws (six months in isolation etc) as any other animal when entering or returning to countries free of rabies such as Australia.

Deaf travellers can ask for airport and inflight announcements to be written down for them.

Children aged under two travel for 10% of the standard fare (or free, on some airlines), as long as they don't occupy a seat. They don't get a baggage allowance either. 'Skycots' should be provided by the airline if requested in advance; these will take a child weighing up to about 10kg. Children aged between two and 12 can usually occupy a seat for half to two-thirds of the full fare and do get a baggage allowance. Push chairs can often be taken as hand luggage.

Departure Tax

Croatia has a departure tax of 37KN that is normally included in the price of your ticket.

The USA

The *New York Times*, the *LA Times*, the *Chicago Tribune* and the *San Francisco Examiner* all produce weekly travel sections in which you'll find any number of travel agents' ads. Council Travel and STA Travel have offices in major cities nationwide. The magazine *Travel Unlimited* (PO Box 1058, Allston, Mass 02134) publishes details of the cheapest air fares and courier possibilities for destinations all over the world from the USA.

Canada

Travel CUTS has offices in all major cities. The Toronto *Globe & Mail* and the *Vancouver Sun* carry travel agents' ads. The magazine *Great Expeditions* (PO Box 8000-411, Abbotsford BC V2S 6H1) is useful.

JON DAVISON

JEANNE OLIVER

Harbourside at Rovinj

Around town in Rovinj

Australia

STA Travel and Flight Centres International are major dealers in cheap air fares. Check the travel agents' ads in the Yellow Pages and ring around.

New Zealand

As in Australia, STA Travel and Flight Centres International are popular travel agents.

The UK

Trailfinders in west London produce a lavishly illustrated brochure that includes air fare details.

STA Travel also has branches in the UK. Look in the Sunday papers and *Exchange & Mart* for ads.

Also look out for the free magazines widely available in London – start by looking outside the main train stations.

Most British travel agents are registered with ABTA (Association of British Travel Agents). If you have bought your ticket from an ABTA-registered agent that then goes out of business, ABTA will guarantee a refund or an alternative. Unregistered bucket shops are riskier but also sometimes cheaper.

The Globetrotters Club (BCM Roving, London WC1N 3XX) publishes a newsletter called *Globe* that covers obscure destinations and can help in finding travelling companions.

Continental Europe

In Amsterdam, NBBS is a popular travel agent.

Asia

Although most Asian countries are now offering fairly competitive air fare deals, Bangkok, Singapore and Hong Kong are still the best places to shop around for discount tickets. Hong Kong's travel market can be unpredictable, but some excellent bargains are available if you are lucky.

STA Travel, which is reliable, has branches in Hong Kong, Tokyo, Singapore, Bangkok and Kuala Lumpur.

LAND

Bus

Austria Eurolines (☎ 01-712 0453), Landstrasser Hauptstrasse 1b, A-1030 Vienna, runs two buses a week from Vienna to Rijeka, Split and Zadar (312KN) and a daily bus to Zagreb (157KN). There's also a twice-weekly bus between Vienna and Osijek (203KN). For more information see www.eurolines.at/eurolines.

Bosnia-Hercegovina From Dubrovnik there are connections to Mostar (three hours, three daily, 70KN) and Sarajevo (six hours, two daily, 155KN). From Split there are seven daily buses to Međugorje (3½ hours, 60KN), 11 to Mostar (four hours, 53KN) and six to Sarajevo (seven hours, 129KN). Zadar is connected with Mostar (seven hours, four daily, 148KN) and Sarajevo (11 hours, twice daily, 185KN). From Makarska there's a daily bus to Sarajevo (5½ hours, 109KN).

Hungary There are frequent connections between Zagreb and Nagykanizsa (four hours, twice daily, 55KN) and Zagreb and Barcs (four hours, five daily, 30KN), going on to Pécs. From Barcs there are frequent trains to Pécs and then less-frequent buses to Szeged, where there are trains and buses to Subotica in Vojvodina (Yugoslavia).

Varaždin is well connected to Hungary with a daily early morning bus to Nagykanizsa (three hours, 29KN). Nagykanizsa is more convenient if you're travelling to/from Budapest. From Osijek there are three daily buses to Pećs (2½ hours, 42KN) and a daily bus to Mohaćs, Hungary (1½ hours, 24KN).

Yugoslavia Buses leave every hour from 5 am to 1 pm from Zagreb to Belgrade (six hours, 180KN). At Bajakovo on the border, a Yugoslav bus takes you on to Belgrade.

Germany Because Croatia is a prime destination for Germans on vacation and Germany is a prime destination for Croatian workers, bus service is good. All buses are handled by Deutsche Touring GmbH (☎ 069-79 03 50), Am Romerhof 17, Frankfurt, and are cheaper than the train. For more information see www.deutsche-touring.com. There are buses from Berlin, Cologne, Dortmund, Frankfurt/Main, Mannheim, Munich, Nuremberg and Stuttgart; buses depart five times a week from Berlin, and daily from the others. There's a weekly bus to Istria from Frankfurt and two buses a week from Munich.

The Dalmatian coast is also served by daily buses from German cities and there's a twice weekly bus direct from Berlin to Rijeka and on to Split. Baggage is DM5 extra per piece. Information is available at bus stations in the cities just mentioned.

Benelux Budget Bus/Eurolines (☎ 020-520 8787, Rokin 10, Amsterdam) offers a weekly bus all year to Zagreb (26 hours, 781KN one way and 1218KN return) and another bus to Rijeka and Split with an added weekly bus to both destinations during the summer. All buses change at Frankfurt. Reductions are available for children under 13, but not for students or seniors. For more information see www.eurolines.nl.

Eurolines (☎ 02-203 0707), rue du Progres 80, 1210 Brussels, operates a twice weekly service all year from Brussels (Belgium) to Zagreb, changing in Munich, and another twice weekly bus to Rijeka and the Dalmatian coast, changing in Frankfurt. On all of the Dutch and Belgian services you will be charged DM5 per piece for luggage. An advance reservation (19KN) is recommended.

Train

Since most international trains originate or terminate in Zagreb, it's useful to consult the Zagreb train station (☎ 9830) for the latest schedules. For information see www.tel.hr.

Italy Railway fares in Italy are relatively cheap, so if you can get across the Italian border from France or Switzerland, it won't cost an arm and a leg to take a train on to

Trieste, where there are frequent bus connections to Croatia via Koper. Between Venice and Zagreb there are the *Simplon* and *Venezia* express trains via Trieste and Ljubljana (seven hours, twice daily, 226KN). Between Trieste and Zagreb, there's the daily *Kras* via Ljubljana (five hours, 174KN).

Germany InterCity 296/297 goes overnight daily from Munich to Zagreb (nine hours, 443KN) via Salzburg and Ljubljana. Reservations are required southbound but not northbound. The EuroCity *Mimara* between Berlin and Zagreb (17 hours, once daily, 1110KN), stopping at Leipzig and Munich, travels by day.

Austria The *Ljubljana* express travels daily from Vienna to Rijeka (eight hours, 284KN), via Ljubljana, and the EuroCity *Croatia* from Vienna to Zagreb (6½ hours, once daily, 304KN) both travel via Maribor.

Hungary To go from Budapest to Zagreb (seven hours, 181KN) you have a choice of four trains daily. Curiously, you pay the same price whether your ticket is one way or return. A daily train links Zagreb to Pécs (four hours, 105KN), leaving Pécs in the early morning and Zagreb in the afternoon, connecting through Osijek. As well as the international express trains, there are unreserved local trains between Gyékényes (Hungary) and Koprivnica (20 minutes, 26KN) three times a day, with connections in Gyékényes to/from Nagykanizsa, Pécs and Kaposvár. Two unreserved trains a day travel between Varaždin and Nagykanizsa (1½ hours, 39KN).

Romania There are no direct trains between Bucharest and Zagreb but there are two daily trains that connect in Budapest with trains to Zagreb (18 to 26 hours, 670KN).

Yugoslavia Two trains a day connect Zagreb with Belgrade (6½ hours, 220KN).

Car & Motorcycle

The main highway entry/exit points between Croatia and Hungary are Goričan (between Nagykanizsa and Varaždin), Gola (23km east of Koprivnica), Terezino Polje (opposite Barcs) and Donji Miholjac (7km south of Harkány). There are 29 crossing points to/from Slovenia, too many to list here. There are 23 border crossings into Bosnia-Hercegovina and ten into Yugoslavia including the main Zagreb to Belgrade highway. Major destinations in Bosnia-Hercegovina such as Sarajevo, Mostar and Međugorje are accessible from Zagreb, Split and Dubrovnik.

SEA

Regular boats connect Croatia with Italy and Greece. The Croatian Jadrolinija (☎ 051-211 444, fax 051-211 485, Riva 16, Rijeka 5100, www.tel.hr/jadrolinija/english/menux.htm), the Italian Adriatica Navigazione (☎ 041-781 611, fax 041-781 894, Zattere, 1411 Venezia, www.adriatica.it) and the Croatian company Lošinjska Plovidba (☎ 231 077, fax 231 611, Riva Lošinjskih Kapetana 8 Mali Lošinj 51550) all serve the Adriatic coast. There are five or six Jadrolinija ferries a week all year round between Ancona and Split (10 hours, 249KN), stopping twice a week in July and August at Stari Grad on Hvar island. Adriatica Navigazione connects Ancona and Split three times a week in the summer for about the same price and twice a week in the winter.

Other Jadrolinija lines in the summer from Ancona stop at Zadar (four times a week, 224KN), Šibenik, Vis island, and Vela Luka on Korčula island (weekly, 249KN).

From Bari, Adriatica Navigazione runs a ferry to Dubrovnik once a week all year and Jadrolinija connects the two cities four times a week in the summer and once a week in the winter. The eight hour trip costs about 249KN.

Both Adriatica Navigazione and Lošinjska Plovidba connect Italy with the Istrian coast in summer. From May to September Adriatica Navigazione runs the *Marconi* between Trieste and Rovinj (3½ hours, 30,000 Lire), stopping at the Brijuni Islands six times a week and stopping twice a week in July and August at Poreč. In Trieste, contact Agemar (☎ 040-363 737), Piazza Duca degli Abruzzi, 1a. Lošinjska Plovidba's *Marina* connects Venice with Zadar (14½ hours, 89,000 Lire) twice a week from late June to September, stopping at Pula and Mali Lošinj. In Venice, contact Agenzia Favret (☎ 041-257 3511), Via Appia 20. Payment must be made in Italian lire and the prices include departure tax.

From May to September, Atlas travel agency runs a fast boat between Zadar and Ancona (three hours, 340KN) and there's a new Croatian company, SEM (☎ 021-589 433, www.sem.hr/marina/english.html), that runs a daily boat between Split, Trieste, and Ancona for 234KN.

During the summer, Jadrolinija runs a ferry twice a week between Dubrovnik and Igoumenitsa, stopping in Bari (17½ hours, 265KN). Unless the ferry service to Albania resumes, there is no choice but to connect via Ancona or Bari. Both the Jadrolinija line to Bari and the Adriatica Navigazione line to Ancona connect well to other Adriatica Navigazione ferries to Durrës. From Ancona and Bari it is also possible to catch the Anek Lines boats to Igoumenitsa, Patrasso and Corfu.

Prices given above are for deck passage in the summer season. Prices are about 10% less off-season and there's a 25% reduction for a return ticket on Jadrolinija ferries. A couchette on an overnight boat costs about an extra 90 to 100KN. There is no port tax if you are leaving the country by boat.

Getting Around

AIR

Croatia Airlines is the only carrier operating domestic flights. Zagreb is the hub with daily flights to Pula (414KN), Split (556KN) and Dubrovnik (620KN). These summer rates – from June to August – are discounted the rest of the year. Young people between the ages of 12 and 25 are eligible for reductions of 35% on domestic routes and over 50% on international routes. Even at their cheapest, however, the prices are high compared to buses and trains.

Croatia Airlines has offices wherever there are flights, as well as in other major towns. The head office is in Zagreb (☎ 01-45 51 340 or ☎ 01-45 51 244) at Zrinjevac 17. The airline accepts Diners Club, American Express, MasterCard, Eurocard and Visa. Note that all batteries must be removed from checked luggage before check-in.

BUS

Bus services in Croatia are excellent. Express buses go everywhere, often with several services per day, and they'll stop to pick up passengers at designated stops along the route.

Prices vary slightly among companies and depend on the route. Because the price is per kilometre, it's possible to pay more for a slow local bus than an express. Luggage stowed in the baggage compartment under the bus is extra, costing 5KN apiece including insurance.

At large stations, bus tickets must be purchased at the office, not from drivers; try to book ahead to be sure of a seat. Departure lists over the various windows at the bus stations tell you which one sells tickets for your bus. Tickets for buses that arrive from elsewhere are usually purchased from the conductor. On Croatian bus schedules, *vozi svaki dan* means 'every day' and *ne vozi nedjeljom ni praznikom* means 'no service Sundays and public holidays'.

Some buses travel overnight, allowing you to save a night's accommodation – but don't expect to get much sleep, the inside lights will be on and music will be blasting the whole night. Take care not to be left behind at meal or rest stops and beware of buses leaving 10 minutes early.

TRAIN

Zagreb is the hub for Croatia's less-than-extensive train system. Because the network was put in place in the 19th century when Croatia was still part of the Austro-Hungarian empire, the main routes were designed to link Croatia with its former overlords rather than to link Croatian cities with each other. You'll notice that no trains run along the coast and only a few coastal cities are connected with Zagreb. For travellers, the main lines of interest run from Zagreb to Rijeka and Pula; Zagreb to Zadar, Šibenik and Split; Zagreb to Varaždin and Koprivnica and Zagreb to Osijek. Before the recent war, trains connected the coastal cities with Belgrade via Bosnia-Hercegovina but it is unlikely that service will be restored in the near future.

Trains are slower and less frequent than buses but cheaper and more comfortable. Domestic trains are either 'express' or 'passenger'. Express trains have smoking and non-smoking as well as first and second class cars. A reservation is advisable and they are more expensive than passenger trains which offer only unreserved second-class seating. There are no couchettes available on any domestic services but there are sleeping cars on the overnight trains between Zagreb and Split. Baggage is free on trains and most train stations have left-luggage offices charging about 10KN apiece per day (passport required). EU residents who hold an InterRail pass can use it in Croatia for free travel but it is unlikely that you would take enough trains in the country to justify the cost.

For further information about the train network contact Croatian Railways (Hrvatske Zeljeznice, ☎ 01-45 77 111, Mihanovićeva 12, Zagreb 10000, www.tel.hr/hz).

Train travel is about 15% cheaper than bus travel and often more comfortable, if slower. Local trains usually have only unreserved 2nd-class seats but they're rarely crowded. Reservations may be required on express trains.

'Executive' trains have only 1st-class seats and are 40% more expensive than local trains. No couchettes are available on any domestic services. Most train stations have left-luggage offices charging about 10KN apiece (passport required).

There are at least two daily trains from Zagreb to Zadar and Split stopping at Knin where you can change to Šibenik. Other trains include Zagreb to Osijek (288km, five hours), Koprivnica (92km, 1½ hours, local), Varaždin (110km, three hours, local), Ljubljana (160km, three hours, local), Rijeka (243km, five hours, local) and Pula. There are also trains from Rijeka to Ljubljana (155km, 2½ hours, local).

On posted timetables at train stations, the word for arrivals is *dolazak*, and for departures it's *odlazak* or *polazak*. Other terms you may encounter include *poslovni* (executive train), *brzi* or *ubrazni* (fast train), *putnički* (local train), *rezerviranje mjesta obvezatno* (compulsory seat reservation), *presjedanje* (change of trains), *ne vozi nedjeljom i blagdanom* (no service Sunday and holidays) and *svako-dnevno* (daily).

BOAT
Coastal Ferries

Ferries are a lot more comfortable than buses, though considerably more expensive. All year-round big white and blue international Jadrolinija car ferries operate along the Rijeka to Dubrovnik (152KN) coastal route, stopping at Dugi Otok (116KN), Zadar (116KN), Split (116KN), and the islands Rab, Hvar (Stari Grad 128KN), Vis (128KN), Korčula (140KN), and Mljet (152KN). For more information, call Jadrolinija on ☎ 51-211 444.

Although you can take the big coastal ferry for short routes, for example Split to Stari Grad, it's substantially more expensive than taking a local car ferry.

The above prices are at least 10% cheaper from October to May and on certain boats there is a surcharge of 10% on weekends to and from Rijeka. There is a 25% reduction if you buy a return ticket. Children under four travel free and there's a 50% reduction for kids aged between four and 12. Service is almost daily to the big cities during summer but is greatly reduced in winter. The most scenic section is Split to Dubrovnik, which all of the Jadrolinija ferries cover during the day. Rijeka to Split (13 hours) is usually an overnight trip in either direction.

With a through ticket, deck passengers can stop at any port for up to a week, provided you notify the purser beforehand and have your ticket validated. This is much cheaper than buying individual sector tickets. Cabins should be booked a week ahead, but deck space is usually available on all sailings.

Deck passage on Jadrolinija is just that: reclining seats (*poltrone*) are about 26KN extra and four-berth cabins (if available) begin at 329KN (Rijeka-Dubrovnik). Cabins can be arranged at the reservation counter aboard ship, but advance bookings are recommended if you want to be sure of a place. Deck space is fine for passages during daylight hours and when you can stretch out a sleeping bag on the upper deck in good weather, but if it's rainy you could end up sitting in the smoky cafeteria which stays open all night. During the crowded midsummer season, deck class can be unpleasant in wet weather.

Meals in the restaurants aboard Jadrolinija ships are about 80KN for a fixed-price menu of somewhat mediocre food. All the cafeteria offers is ham and cheese sandwiches for 18KN. Coffee is cheap in the cafeteria but wine and spirits tend to be expensive. Breakfast in the restaurant is about 30KN. It's best to bring some food and drink with you.

Local Ferries

Local ferries connect the bigger offshore islands with each other and with the mainland. The most important Jadrolinija car ferry routes are Baška on Krk island to Lopar on Rab island (twice daily, May-September), Zadar to Preko on Ugljan island (nine daily), Split to Stari Grad on Hvar island (three daily), Zadar to Mali Lošinj (three times weekly, June-September), Zadar to Dugi Otok (twice daily), Split to Stari Grad (six daily), Split to Rogač (five daily), Split to Vis (daily) Split to Vela Luka on Korčula island via Hvar (daily), Orebić to Korčula island (ten daily) and Dubrovnik to Sobra on Mljet island (twice daily). On most lines, service is less frequent from October to April. Tickets must be bought in advance – there are no ticket sales on board.

Taking a bicycle on these services incurs a small charge and taking a vehicle aboard incurs a large charge. The car charge is calculated according to the size of your vehicle and begins at about four times the price of a passenger ticket. In the summer season ferries to the islands fill up fast, so you should reserve as far in advance as possible if you're bringing your car. On some of the shorter routes such as Jablanac to Mišnjak or Drvenik to Sućuraj, the ferries run non-stop in the summer and an advance reservation is unnecessary. If there's no Jadrolinija office in town, you can buy the ticket at a stall near the ferry stop that usually opens 30 minutes before departure. In summer you'll be told to arrive one to two hours in advance for ferries to the more popular islands even if you've already bought your ticket. Foot passengers and cyclists should have no problem getting on.

Extra passenger boats are added in the summer which are usually faster, more comfortable and more expensive than the car ferries. The most important passenger line is Jadrolinija's *Adriana* boat that connects Split with Bol (Brač island, one hour, 45KN), Hvar (45 minutes, 50KN), Vis (1¼ hours, 60KN), Korčula (two hours, 70KN) and Lastovo (2½ hours, 70KN) from June to September. Service is daily to Hvar but only Thursday through Sunday to Brač and Korčula.

In the summer, Dalmacijaturist (☎ 021-345 166 or ☎ 021-345 078) operates a fast passenger boat daily (except Sunday) between Split and Jelsa (1¾ hours, 45KN) on the island of Hvar stopping at Bol (1¼ hours, 45KN), and Milna (30 minutes, 30KN) on the island of Brač. There's also a twice daily service to Rogač (30 minutes, 15KN).

Travel agencies such as Atlas run fast hydrofoils up and down the coast in the summer, especially between Rijeka and Zadar (3½ hours, 210KN), with Rab and Hvar also served. Stop in at any Atlas office and ask for the summer schedule.

CAR & MOTORCYCLE

Motorists require vehicle registration papers and the green insurance card to enter Croatia (the Green Card is internationally recognized proof of auto insurance; most UK motor insurance policies automatically provide this for EU countries but you should check to make sure that Croatia is listed on the card). Two-way amateur radios built into cars are no problem but must be reported at the border.

Petrol is either leaded super, unleaded (*bezolovni*), or diesel which is the cheapest. You have to pay tolls on the motorways around Zagreb, to use the Učka tunnel between Rijeka and Istria, and for the bridge to Krk island.

Along the coast, the spectacular Adriatic highway from Italy to Albania hugs the steep slopes of the coastal range, with abrupt drops to the sea and a curve a minute. You can drive as far south as Vitaljina, 56km south-east of Dubrovnik, but the border to Montenegro is closed. Following is a table of road distances between major towns:

from	to	distance
Zagreb	Dubrovnik	572km
Zagreb	Zadar	288km
Zagreb	Osijek	280km

Zagreb	Rijeka	182km
Zagreb	Split	365km
Split	Dubrovnik	216km
Split	Rijeka	393km
Split	Zadar	168km
Rijeka	Dubrovnik	601km
Rijeka	Pula	110km
Rijeka	Zadar	224km

Motorists can turn to the Croatian Automobile Club – Hrvatski Autoklub (HAK) – for help or advice. Addresses of local HAK offices are provided in this book and the HAK's nationwide road assistance (*vučna služba*) number is ☎ 987. See their Web site at www.hak.hr for more information.

Road Rules

Unless otherwise posted, the speed limits for cars and motorcycles are 60km/h in built-up areas, 90km/h on main highways and 130km/h on motorways. Police systematically fine motorists exceeding these limits. On any of Croatia's winding two-lane highways, it's illegal to pass long military convoys or a whole line of cars caught behind a slow-moving truck. Drive defensively, since speeding, reckless overtaking and tailgating are practically national sports in Croatia.

Rental

The large car-rental chains represented in Croatia are Avis, Budget, Europcar and Hertz, with Budget (offices in Opatija, Split and Zagreb) generally the cheapest and Hertz the most expensive. Avis, Budget and Hertz have offices at Zagreb and Split airports. Throughout Croatia, Avis is allied with Autotehna, while Hertz is often represented by Kompas.

Independent local companies are often much less expensive than the international chains, but Avis, Budget, Europcar and Hertz have the big advantage of offering one-way rentals which allow you to drop the car off at any one of their many stations in Croatia at no extra charge. Some local companies also offer this service but have fewer stations. Phone numbers for the major firms are:

Budget Rent-a-Car ☎ 01-45 54 936
Europcar ☎ 01-65 54 003
Avis Autotehna ☎ 01-48 36 296
Hertz ☎ 01-48 47 222

The cheapest cars include the Renault 5, Peugeot 106, Opel Corsa and Fiat Uno. Prices at local companies begin at around 80KN a day plus 80KN per kilometre (100km minimum), or 225KN a day with unlimited kilometres. Shop around as deals vary widely and 'special' discounts and weekend rates are often available.

Third-party public liability insurance is included by law, but make sure your quoted price includes full collision insurance, known as a collision damage waiver (CDW). Otherwise your responsibility for damage done to the vehicle is usually determined as a percentage of the car's value beginning at around 1000KN. Full CDW begins at 45KN extra a day (compulsory for those aged under 25), theft insurance at 15KN a day, and personal accident insurance is another 10KN a day. Add 22% value-added tax to all charges.

The minimum age to rent a car is 21 and some companies require that you have had a driver's licence for at least a year. If you're paying by cash the amount of the cash deposit is usually based upon the type of car and the length of the rental.

Sometimes you can get a lower rate by booking the car from abroad. Tour companies in western Europe often have fly-drive packages which include a flight to Croatia and a car (two-person minimum).

BICYCLE

Bicycling can be a great way to explore the islands and bicycles are easy to rent. Relatively flat islands such as Mljet and Mali Lošinj offer the most relaxed biking but the winding hilly roads on other islands offer spectacular views. Some tourist offices have maps of suggested routes. Bicycling along the coast or on the mainland isn't advisable as most roads are busy two-lane highways without bicycle lanes.

0 44

HITCHING

Hitchhiking is never entirely safe in any country in the world, and we don't recommend it. Travellers who decide to hitch should understand that they are taking a small but potentially serious risk. People who do choose to hitch will be safer if they travel in pairs and let someone know where they are planning to go.

Hitching in Croatia is a gamble. You'll have better luck on the islands but in the interior you'll notice that cars are small and usually full. Tourists never stop. Unfortunately, the image many Croats have of this activity is based on violent movies like *Hitchhiker*.

LOCAL TRANSPORT

Zagreb and Osijek have a well-developed tram system as well as local buses but in the rest of the country you'll only find buses. Buses in major cities such as Rijeka, Split, Zadar and Dubrovnik run about once every 20 minutes and less on Sunday. A ride is usually five or six kuna, with a small discount if you buy the ticket at a *tisak* (kiosk). Small medieval towns along the coast are generally closed to traffic and have infrequent links to outlying suburbs. Bus transportation within the islands is spotty since most people have their own cars. Whatever transportation exists is scheduled for the workday needs of the inhabitants, not the holiday needs of tourists. To get out and see the island, you'll need to rent a bike, boat, motorcycle or car.

ORGANISED TOURS

Atlas travel agency offers 'adventure' tours which feature birdwatching, canoeing, caving, cycling, diving, fishing, hiking, riding, sailing, sea kayaking and white-water rafting in both Croatia and Slovenia. The eight-day tours run from about US$700-$900 all-inclusive and you join the group in Croatia. Atlas' head office in Croatia is in Dubrovnik at Miha Klaica 2 (☎ 20-442 222, fax 20-411 100, atlasdbk@atlas.tel.hr). Travel agents in North America can book through Atlas Ambassador of Dubrovnik (☎ 202-483 8919, fax 202-462 7160, npw21@aol.com), 1601 18th St NW, Washington D.C. 20009.

In Britain, the Croatian owned Dalmatian and Istrian Travel (☎ 081-749 5255 or ☎ 020-8749 5255, fax 081-740 4432 or fax 020-8740 4432), 21 Sawley Rd, London W12 0LG, offers independent accommodation packages ranging from luxury hotels to camping as well as discounts on boat travel and outdoor activities. A typical package that includes a London/Dubrovnik return air fare and a week's stay in private accommodation during the high season will cost about £320.

Experiencing the coast by boat is the best way to appreciate the natural features of the landscape and visit otherwise inaccessible coves. Katarina Line (☎ 051-272 110, fax 051-271 372), Hotel Admiral 51410 Opatija, offers weeklong cruises from Opatija to Krk, Rab, Pag, Mali Lošinj and Cres on an attractive wooden ship. Prices start at 1800KN a week including half-board, but can be higher depending on the boat. Adriana Travel (☎ 051-272 088, fax 051-271 164), Obala Maršala Tita 158/1 51410 Opatija, offers a similar program including full board beginning at 2160KN a week in high season (from June to September), and beginning at 1440KN in low season. There are one and two-week excursions from Rijeka and one-week excursions from Split that visit Central Dalmatia and the Kornati Islands.

Zagreb

• pop 810,000 ☎ 01

As the political, economic and cultural capital of Croatia, Zagreb throbs with the energy you would expect from a major city. At the same time, it has retained a good deal of Old World graciousness. It's Croatia's largest city, the seat of government, and headquarters for most of Croatia's international companies. Yet the city's sober and industrious mood is lightened by the stately 19th century buildings in Zagreb's commercial centre and the intimate streets of the city's old quarter.

Zagreb is not a city that dazzles you with its charms at first glance – it requires time to appreciate. Begin with a walk through town and notice the beautifully crafted façades that may remind you of Vienna or Budapest. Stroll through the landscaped park promenade that extends from the train station to the town centre, freshening the city with an expanse of greenery. Linger in a sidewalk café on bohemian Tkalčića ulica or stop for an impromptu street concert on Trg Petra Preradovića and a pleasure-loving side of the city emerges. Take in one of the many fine museums or galleries and you'll see that Zagreb is not all business but a lively cultural centre as well.

Beyond the central core, the architecture dwindles into dreary apartment blocks but several large parks relieve the monotony. North-east of the city centre, Maksimir Park is a romantic oasis of shady walks and placid ponds. Jarun Lake in the south-west is less alluring but there's swimming and boating in the summer. When Zagreb residents head for the hills, they don't have far to go: Medvednica Mountain is only a tram ride away and offers hiking, skiing and great views over the city.

The main disadvantage of the city is a shortage of moderately-priced hotels and a total lack of budget hotels. Even the higher-priced establishments can fill up during important fairs, making accommodation a

HIGHLIGHTS

- Visiting the Mimara Museum
- Wandering the streets of Zagreb's hilly Gradec and Kaptol quarter
- Seeing Meštrović's masterful sculpture, *The Well of Life*, in front of the Croatian National Theatre
- Contemplating the meaning of it all in Mirogoj cemetery
- Spending a Saturday night on Tkalčićeva
- Visiting the castles of Varaždin and Trakošćan
- Imagining Tito with a hoe in his hand at Kumrovec
- Relaxing with a Bermet and a slice of custard pie on Samobor's main square
- Going back to medieval times at the Medvedgrad monument at Mount Medvednica

traveller's biggest problem in Zagreb. Once you get your room straightened out though, you'll find there's plenty to see and do within the city and in the surrounding region.

History

Zagreb's story begins with two hills, Gradec and Kaptol. Little is known about Zagreb's early history but it appears that Slavs may have built forts and churches on the hills as early as the eighth or ninth centuries. In 1094 the Hungarian King Ladislas established the Zagreb diocese on Kaptol hill and a canonical settlement developed soon after, north of the Cathedral. Another small settlement was developing on Gradec hill, but both settlements were devastated by the Mongol invasion of 1242. Legend has it that the Mongols even stabled their horses in Zagreb Cathedral.

The Mongols swept across the country to Trogir and then abruptly left, leaving a trail of destruction. In order to attract foreign artisans (mostly Germans) to the wasteland, King Bela issued a 'Golden Bull' proclaiming Gradec and other towns autonomous royal cities, subject to no one but the king, which freed its residents from many costly and onerous obligations. As an added inducement, he ordered that walls be built around his city, protecting it from any future armies on the rampage. Kaptol remained under the church's jurisdiction, however, which sowed the seeds of a ruinous rivalry between the two towns.

During the 14th and 15th centuries the two warring hilltop administrations created havoc as they each sought to protect their economic and political interests. The bishops of Kaptol would excommunicate the entire town of Gradec, which would respond by looting and burning Kaptol. The two communities put aside their quarrels only when their commercial interests united them, such as during the annual fairs that brought merchants and money to the neighbourhood. Unfortunately there were only three big fairs a year – Kermis, St Margaret and St Mark – lasting two weeks each.

In the middle of the 15th century the Turks began making inroads into the region, prompting the bishop to begin fortifying Kaptol in 1478. Thick towers and walls were built around the town virtually under the eyes of the Turks who were camped only a few kilometres south on the Sava River. The walls were finished in 1520 and by the mid-16th century the Turks had taken much surrounding territory, but not the two hill towns. The bishopric at Kaptol lost a number of estates to the Turks however, which cut into its revenue. When a 1609 statute was passed limiting the privileges of Gradec citizens, the two diminished and perhaps chastened communities gradually merged and became known as Zagreb.

Although Zagreb emerged as the capital of the Croatian state in the 16th century, there was very little left of Croatia that hadn't fallen to the Turks. The commercial life of the city stagnated during the ensuing two centuries of warfare. It was compounded by fires (in 1645, 1674, 1706 and 1731) and plague (in 1647 and 1682). In 1756 the seat of Croatian government fled from Zagreb to Varaždin, where it remained until 1776. By the end of the 18th century there were a mere 2800 residents, of whom the majority was German or Hungarian.

Meanwhile, the plain below the fortified hill towns began to attract settlers. In 1641, municipal authorities decided to move the annual fairs to a larger space outside the city walls. The space now known as Trg Josip Jelačić was chosen for its proximity to both Kaptol and Gradec as well as a source of fresh water – the Manduševac stream (later paved over). The new marketplace spurred construction around its edges that increased as the Turkish threat receded in the 18th century. The straight streets running south of Trg Josip Jelačić provided an important link between Zagreb and other villages on and beyond the Sava River.

In the 19th century, Zagreb finally matured politically and economically. The population expanded with the development of a prosperous clothing trade in the city followed by a steam mill and a tannery.

Zagreb became the centre for the Pan-Slavic Illyrian movement that was pressing for south-Slavic unification, greater autonomy within the Austro-Hungarian Empire, and recognition of the Slavic language. Count Janko Drašković, lord of Trakošćan castle, published a manifesto in *Illyrian* in 1832 and his call for national revival resounded throughout Croatia.

The city's cultural and educational life also blossomed. The Music Institute opened in 1826, the first theatre opened in 1834, the first opera in Croatian (*Ljubavi zloba* by Vatroslav Lisinski) was performed in 1846, the Yugoslav (now Croatian) Academy of Arts and Sciences opened in 1866 and the University of Zagreb was founded in 1874 with a Chair in Illyrian studies.

Transportation improved. In 1862, a rail link was built to Slovenia that connected with Vienna, and in 1870 Zagreb was linked with Gyekenyes in Hungary that connected with Budapest. The first public transportation in Zagreb was the horse-drawn tram that appeared in 1891, followed by the electric tram in 1910.

By 1910 Zagreb had more than 100 industrial companies, primarily machine-building, textiles, food processing and printing companies. The population had reached 60,000 fuelling a demand for residences and public buildings. Most of the grand old houses you'll see in the Lower Town were built in the last decades of the 19th century in a variety of styles. Among the outstanding public buildings, note the Croatian Academy of Sciences and Arts by the Viennese architect F. Schmidt (1884) in a Tuscan Renaissance style, the Arts and Crafts Museum designed by Herman Bollé (1891) in German Renaissance style and the Art Pavilion (1898) and the Croatian National Theatre (1895) both designed by the Viennese architectural team of Hellmer and Fellner. The 'horseshoe' of squares and parks that runs from the train station to the town centre was laid out from 1865 to 1887 as a public promenade.

Croatia and its capital joined the Kingdom of Serbs, Croats and Slovenes after WWI.

Between the two world wars, working-class neighbourhoods emerged between the railway and the Sava River and new residential quarters were built on the southern slope of Medvednica Mountain. In April 1941, the Germans invaded Yugoslavia and entered Zagreb without resistance. Ante Pavelić and the Ustashe moved quickly to proclaim the establishment of the Independent State of Croatia (Nezavisna Država Harvatska) with Zagreb as its capital. Although Pavelić ran his fascist state from Zagreb until 1944, he never enjoyed a great deal of support within the capital, which maintained support for Tito's Partisans.

In postwar Yugoslavia, Zagreb clearly took second place to Belgrade but the city continued expanding. The area south of the Sava River developed into a new district, Novi Zagreb, with residential blocks, Pleso airport and the Zagreb fairgrounds. Zagreb has been capital of Croatia since 1991, when the country became independent.

Orientation

Lying between the southern slopes of the Medvednica Mountain and the Sava River, Zagreb covers 631 sq km but most of the city's highlights lie within the Upper Town (Gornji Grad) that includes Gradec and Kaptol and the Lower Town (Donji Grad) that runs between the Upper Town and the train station. The majestic central square of the Lower Town is Trg bana Josip Jelačića (commonly known as Trg Jelačića) which is the hub for most of Zagreb's trams. Radiating west from Trg Jelačića is Ilica, the main commercial street lined with offices, shops and a department store. North of the square is the Cathedral and the medieval Gradec and Kaptol neighbourhoods. Many streets in the Upper and Lower Towns are closed to cars, which makes driving a nightmare but brings a measure of peace to the city's centre.

The train station is in the southern part of the city just a few blocks north of the Sava River. Novi Zagreb is south of the train station, across the Sava River, and is the only substantial development on the south

ZAGREB

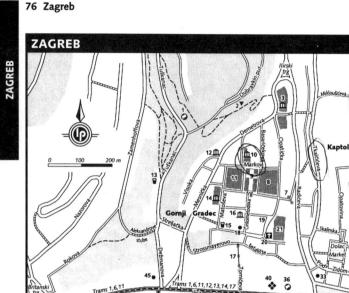
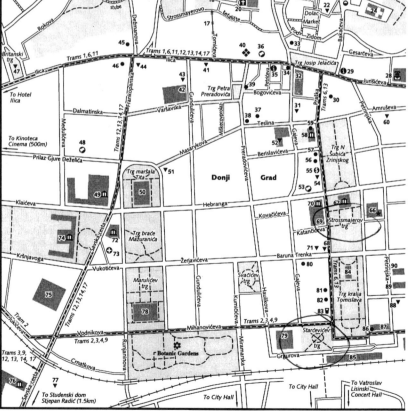

0   100   200 m

Ilirski trg

Mikloušićeva

Demetrova

Basaričekova

Opatička

Kaptol

Park

Ribnjak

12 10
Markov

Kaptol

Opatovina

11   8

Radićeva

Gornji Gradec

Matoševa

14

Streljačka

16   19

Ćirilometodska

15
18   20   21

Skalinska

Dolac
Market

23   22   24

Aleksandrove stube

Dežmanova

Strossmayerovo

17   Šetalište

Zidom

Baščaršija

Rokova

Gesarčeva

45

Britanski trg
47

Trams 1,6,11   Ilica

40   36

33

Trg Josip Jelačića
29

Jurišićeva
28

To Hotel
Ilica

Ilica

46   44

43

41

35   34   32

Gajeva

30

Trams 6, 13

Petrinjska

Amruševa

60

Dalmatinska

Frankopanska

Varšavska

42   Trg Petra
Preradovića
39

Bogovićeva

Praška

To Kinoteca
Cinema (500m)

Gundulićeva

Mesničavoveljaka

31

38   37

Teslina

59

58

57   56   55   54   53

Trg N
Šubića
Zrinjskog

48

Prilaz Gjure Deželića

Medulićeva

Trams 12,13,14,17

Masarykova

Preradovićeva

Berislavićeva

52

Trg maršala
Tita

51

Donji   Grad

Klaićeva

49   50

Hebranga

Kovačićeva

70   67   66

Savska cesta

69
Strossmayerov
trg

Katančićeva

74   72   73

Trg braće
Mažuranića

Žerjavićeva

Baruna Trenka

71   68

80

Vukotićeva

Gundulićeva

Marulićev
trg

Svačićev
trg

81   82

Trg kralja
Tomislava

84   90   89   88

75

78

83

86   87

Vodnikova
Trams 2,3,4,9

Trams 12,13,14,17

Mihanovićeva   Trams 2,3,4,9

79   Starčevićev
trg

85

Trams 2

Rumanjinova

Miramarska

Crnatkova

Grgurova

Botanic Gardens

Trams 3,9,
12,13,14,17

Savska cesta

76   77

To Studenski dom
Stjepan Radić (1.5km)

To City Hall

To City Hall

To Vatroslav
Lisinski
Concert Hall

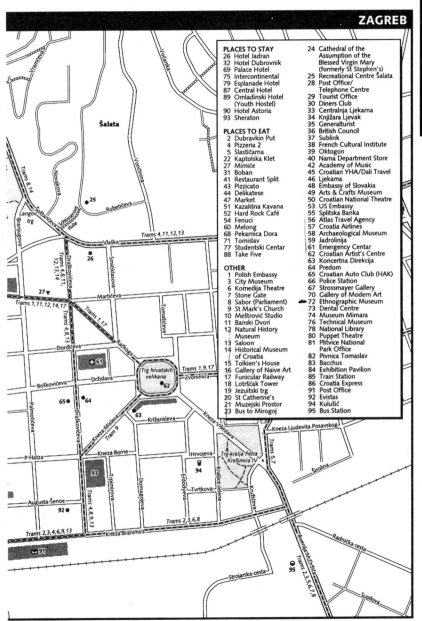

PLACES TO STAY
26 Hotel Jadran
32 Hotel Dubrovnik
69 Palace Hotel
75 Intercontinental
79 Esplanade Hotel
87 Central Hotel
89 Omladinski Hotel
   (Youth Hostel)
90 Hotel Astoria
93 Sheraton

PLACES TO EAT
2 Dubravkin Put
4 Pizzeria 2
5 Slastičarna
22 Kaptolska Klet
27 Mimice
31 Boban
41 Restaurant Split
43 Pizzicato
44 Delikatese
47 Market
51 Kazališna Kavana
52 Hard Rock Café
54 Fenuci
60 Melong
68 Pekarnica Dora
71 Tomislav
77 Studentski Centar
88 Take Five

OTHER
1 Polish Embassy
3 City Museum
6 Komedija Theatre
7 Stone Gate
8 Sabor (Parliament)
9 St Mark's Church
10 Meštrović Studio
11 Banski Dvori
12 Natural History
   Museum
13 Saloon
14 Historical Museum
   of Croatia
15 Tolkien's House
16 Gallery of Naive Art
17 Funicular Railway
18 Lotrščak Tower
19 Jezuitski trg
20 St Catherine's
21 Muzejski Prostor
23 Bus to Mirogoj

24 Cathedral of the
   Assumption of the
   Blessed Virgin Mary
   (formerly St Stephen's)
25 Recreational Centre Šalata
28 Post Office/
   Telephone Centre
29 Tourist Office
30 Diners Club
33 Centralnja Ljekarna
34 Knjižara Ljevak
35 Generalturist
36 British Council
37 Sublink
38 French Cultural Institute
39 Oktogon
40 Nama Department Store
42 Academy of Music
45 Croatian YHA/Dali Travel
46 Ljekama
48 Embassy of Slovakia
49 Arts & Crafts Museum
50 Croatian National Theatre
53 US Embassy
55 Splitska Banka
56 Atlas Travel Agency
57 Croatia Airlines
58 Archaeological Museum
59 Jadrolinija
61 Emergency Centar
62 Croatian Artist's Centre
63 Koncertna Direkcija
64 Predom
65 Croatian Auto Club (HAK)
66 Police Station
67 Strossmayer Gallery
70 Gallery of Modern Art
72 Ethnographic Museum
73 Dental Centre
74 Museum Mimara
76 Technical Museum
78 National Library
80 Puppet Theatre
81 Plitvice National
   Park Office
82 Pivnica Tomaslav
83 Bacchus
84 Exhibition Pavilion
85 Train Station
86 Croatia Express
91 Post Office
92 Evistas
94 Kulušić
95 Bus Station

side of the river. As you come out of the train station, you'll see a series of parks and pavilions directly in front of you which lead into the centre of town.

The bus station is 1km east of the train station. Tram Nos 2, 3 and 6 run from the bus station to the train station, with No 6 continuing to Trg Jelačića.

Information

Tourist Offices The tourist office (☎ 48 14 051), Trg Jelačića 11, is open weekdays from 8.30 am to 8 pm, Saturday from 10 am to 6 pm and Sunday from 10 am to 2 pm. The free *City Walks* leaflet provides a good introduction to Zagreb's sights. The monthly leaflet *Events and Performances* is an essential source of information about concerts, exhibitions, festivals and sporting events. There's a smaller office (☎ 45 52 869) at Trg Nikole Šubića Zrinsko 14 which has the same opening hours.

The Croatian Auto Club (HAK) has two travel offices in Zagreb: a smaller office (☎ 431 142) at Draškovićeva ulica 46 and a main information centre (☎ 46 40 800) six blocks east at Derenčinova 20.

Plitvice National Park maintains an information office (☎ 46 13 586) at Trg Tomislava 19. Open Monday to Friday from 8 am to 4 pm, it also has information on other national parks around Croatia.

Jadrolinija (☎ 421 777), Zrinjevac 20, has information about the boats and ferries that ply the coast. It's open from Monday to Friday from 8 am to 7 pm and weekends 8 am to 1 pm. There's a handy computer screen on the window that allows you to get boat information at all hours and in three languages.

For information about flights and to reserve tickets, head to the Croatia Airlines office (☎ 45 51 340 or ☎ 45 51 244), Zrinjevac 17, which is open Monday to Friday from 8 am to 7 pm, Saturday 8 am to 3 pm.

Money There are government change offices and private exchange offices which are recognisable by the name of the owner outside. Most offices are government operated and offer the same rate as the banks. They charge 1.5% commission and accept travellers cheques. You will get a slightly better rate at private exchange offices. If you have cash, try the two offices in the Importanne shopping center next to the train station. They are open Monday to Saturday from 7 am to 9 pm and Sunday 8 am to 7 pm. If you need to change money outside of business hours head to the change offices in the train station (open daily 7 am to 9 pm) or the bus station (6 am to 8 pm).

ATMs You can withdraw cash using Eurocard, MasterCard or Cirrus at any Zagrebačka Banka as well as other locations. Look for the BANKOMAT sign.

Credit Cards American Express cardholders can withdraw cash at the Lastovska 23 branch or on Zrinjevac 17.

Visa cardholders who need to withdraw cash can go to Splitska Banka (☎ 48 14 410) at Zrinskog 16 Monday to Friday between 9 am and 3 pm. There is also an ATM machine there.

Post & Communications The main post office, at Jurisćeva 13, is open Monday to Friday from 7 am to 9 pm, Saturday 7 am to 7 pm and Sunday 8 am to 2 pm. Posterestante mail is held (for one month) in the post office on the east side of the train station at Branimirova 4, which is open 24 hours from Monday to Saturday and 1 pm to midnight on Sunday. Have your letters addressed to Poste Restante, 10000 Zagreb, Croatia.

The best place to send packages abroad is from the post office at Branimirova 4 which offers packing services. The maximum weight per parcel is limited to 15 kilograms and there's a customs counter for information on duties as well as handling refunds of the VAT.

You can make long-distance telephone calls or send faxes from either post office.

Public telephones in Zagreb use phonecards and the postcode for Zagreb is 10000.

Email & Internet Access Zagreb's first and only cybercafé is Sublink (☎ 48 11 329, sublink@sublink.hr) Teslina 12, open Monday to Friday noon to 10 pm and weekends 3 to 10 pm. A lifetime 'membership' with an email address and 30 minutes of Internet time costs 10KN. Internet time then costs 20KN per half-hour or 50KN for 200 minutes The connection is fast and the casual staff are friendly and willing to help out with any difficulties.

Travel Agencies Dali Travel (☎ 422 953), Dežmanova 9, the travel branch of the Croatian YHA, can provide information on HI hostels throughout Croatia and make advance bookings. It also issues ISIC student cards (40KN), requiring proof of attendance at an educational institution. It's open weekdays from 8 am to 4 pm but don't expect much help from the unfriendly staff.

Generalturist (☎ 48 10 033), Ilica 1 has branches throughout Croatia and books excursions to the coast, cruises and plane tickets. It's open Monday to Friday from 8 am to 8 pm and Saturday 8 am to 2 pm. Dalmacijaturist (☎ 427 611), Zrinskog 16, next to the tourist office, specialises in the Dalmatian coast, also books excursions and air tickets and is a good source of information on boat and ferry routes along the coast. Croatia Express (☎ 45 77 752), Branimirova 1, is across from the railway station and makes train reservations, changes money, rents cars, sells air tickets and books hotels around the country.

The American Express representative is Atlas travel agency (☎ 61 24 389), Trg Zrinjskoga 17, Zagreb 10000. It will hold clients' mail.

Bookshops Algoritam in the Hotel Dubrovnik, Gajeva 1, has the widest selection of English language books in Zagreb. You'll find everything from science fiction to best sellers to special interest non-fiction. They also carry English translations of Croatian writers such as Miroslav Krleža and Ivo Antić. The bookshop is downstairs while the upstairs level carries a wide se-

lection of English language magazines and a few German, French and Italian periodicals. It's open Monday to Friday from 9 am to 9 pm and Saturday 9 am to 3 pm. The Knjižara Ljevak bookstore at Ilica 1 has an excellent selection of maps as well as informational pamphlets on Croatia and destinations around the country. It's open Monday to Friday from 9 am to 7 pm and Saturday 9 am to 3 pm. Antikvarijat, next to Atlas travel agency, has good deals on 19th century novels in English.

Libraries The British Council (☎ 424 733), Ilica 12, has a library open Monday, Tuesday and Thursday from 10.30 am to 4 pm, Wednesday 1.30 to 6.30 pm and Friday 10.30 am to 4 pm where you can read British and American newspapers, books and periodicals, watch BBC news and borrow books and videotapes (30KN membership for borrowing privileges). They also have a selection of brochures on Croatia and sponsor occasional plays, concerts and exhibits. The French Cultural Institute (☎ 45 58 111) on Preradovićeva also has a reading room and media centre. Enter at No 5 to listen to French tapes or watch French news in the Mediateque, open Monday to Friday from 1 to 7 pm and Saturday 10 am to noon. The library has a selection of French books, magazines and newspapers and is open Monday to Friday from 10 am to 5 pm (40KN for borrowing privileges). Both libraries are closed for five or six weeks in the summer.

Laundry Predom, across the street from HAK on Draškovića 31, is open Saturday mornings and weekdays from 7 am to 7 pm. Jeans and shirts cost 6KN each to wash and press. Underwear and socks are washed for 1KN each.

Left Luggage Left-luggage offices in both the bus and train stations are open 24 hours. The price posted at the left-luggage office in the bus station is 1.20KN *per hour*, so be careful. At the train station you pay a fixed price of about 10KN per day.

Medical Services If you need to see a doctor, your best bet is the Emergency Centar (☎ 46 00 911), Draskovićeva 19. It's open all the time and costs 200KN for an examination. There are several round-the-clock pharmacies (*ljekarna*): try Centralna ljekarna (☎ 276 305), Trg Jalačića 3 or the ljekarna at Ilica 43 (☎ 48 48 450). For dental emergencies, call the dental centre (☎ 48 28 488) at Perkovčeva 3.

If you need to extend your visa, head to the police station (☎ 456 311) at Petrinjska 30, which has an office to handle visa matters. It's open Monday to Friday from 8 am to 2 pm.

Things to See

The best way to see Zagreb is to take a stroll around town. You can pick up a copy of *City Walks* free from the tourist office which suggests two walking tours around the town centre, one exploring the Upper Town and the other exploring the Lower Town. As the oldest part of Zagreb, the Upper Town offers landmark buildings and churches from the earlier centuries of Zagreb's history. The Lower Town has the city's most interesting art museums and fine examples of 19th and 20th century architecture.

Upper Town Walking Tour The natural starting point for any tour of the city is **Trg bana J Jelačića** (the square is also known simply as Trg Jelačića), as it is the spiritual if not the geographic heart of the city. Ban Jelačić was the 19th century *ban* or viceroy who led Croatian troops into an unsuccessful battle with Hungary in the hope of winning more autonomy for his people. The statue of Jelačić in the centre stood in the square from 1866 until 1947, when Tito ordered its removal because it was too closely linked with Croat nationalism. One of the first acts of the new government in 1990 was to dig the statue out of storage and return it to the square. Most of the buildings date from the 19th century but note the reliefs by sculptor Ivan Meštrović at No 4. At the south-eastern corner of the square go uphill on Bakača to **Kaptol** square.

Most of the baroque buildings on the square date from the end of the 17th century. Notice the canonical residences at Nos 8, 13, 28 and the mansions at Nos 14 and 26. Kaptol is dominated by the **Cathedral of the Assumption of the Blessed Virgin Mary** (Katedrala marijina Uznesenja), formerly known as St Stephen's, whose twin spires soar over the city. Built on the site of an earlier Romanesque cathedral, destroyed by the Tatar invasion in 1242, construction of this cathedral began in the second half of the 13th century following the prototype of the church of St Urban in Troyes, France. Although the cathedral's original Gothic structure has been transformed many times over, the sacristy still contains a cycle of frescoes that date from the second half of the 13th century. As the last outpost of Christianity in the 15th century, the cathedral was surrounded by walls with towers, one of which is still visible on the eastern side. An earthquake in 1880 badly damaged the cathedral and reconstruction in a neogothic style began around the turn of this century.

Despite the travails suffered by the structure, there is much to admire on the inside. Notice the triptych by Albrecht Dürer on the side altar, Baroque marble altars, statues and a pulpit as well as the tomb of Cardinal Alojzije Stepinac by Ivan Meštrović. To the north of the cathedral an **Archbishop's Palace** was built in the 18th century in a baroque style but little remains. Under the north-east wing of the cathedral is a 19th century park with a sculpture of a female nude by Antun Augustinčić.

The Kaptol neighbourhood stretches up Kaptol ulica but turn left from the cathedral into a narrow passage that leads to **Dolac**, Zagreb's colourful fruit and vegetable market that functions daily, with especially large gatherings on Friday and Saturday. Leave the market at the north end and pass through Opatovina ulica, the site of a flower market, with the statue of Petrica Kerempuh, a legendary folk hero shown playing music beside a hanged man. Many of the one, two and three-storey town houses were

Ban Josip Jelačić

Croatia's most beloved hero was born in 1801 near Novi Sad in what is now the Vojvodina region of Serbia. Educated in Vienna, the young Jelačić entered military service under the Habsburgs, stationed first in Italy and then in the Krajina region. A daring raid against the Turks who were periodically attacking the region won him the respect and even adoration of his troops.

Although uninvolved in the political changes sweeping 19th century Croatia, the popular officer was drafted by the Illyrian party in 1848 to become the next *ban* or viceroy of Croatia. Sworn in as ban by Catholic and Orthodox bishops, Jelačić seemed destined to herald in the long-awaited unification of south-Slavic peoples. He implemented the Illyrian programme calling for the union of Dalmatia and the Krajina region with Croatia, which was an historical milestone. For the first time the *Sabor* (Parliament) allowed the participation of elected as well as hereditary representatives. Feudalism was finally abolished although the peasants remained grindingly poor for many more years.

His refusal to take the customary oath of loyalty to Hungary led to a charge of treason by the Hungarian government but before he could travel to Hungary to answer the charge, more pressing events occurred. Hungary was shaken by a revolutionary movement demanding independence from Habsburg rule. Jelačić led an army of 40,000 Krajina soldiers prepared to intervene on behalf of the Habsburgs in exchange for greater autonomy for Croatia.

The military operation was not wholly successful because Jelačić was forced to send part of his army to Vienna to defend the Habsburgs from another revolutionary uprising in Vienna. Having successfully quelled the uprising, Jelačić and the Croatians expected that their demands for greater self-rule would be met by a grateful Austria. It was not the case. A new reactionary government in Vienna clamped down viciously on Croatia, closing the Sabor and suspending the constitution.

Jelačić was embittered by the realisation that he had achieved nothing for Croatia, although he continued as *ban* with greatly diminished influence in Vienna. The disappointments in his professional life were compounded by the tragic loss of his only child. His health broke under the strain and he died in 1859.

Plans to erect a monument in his honour began almost immediately after his death but it was several years before the money was raised and the statue was cast. Finally, in November 1866 his statue was placed on Trg Jelačića in a splendid ceremony. Tens of thousands of people crowded the square. As the cannons boomed, the crowd shouted over and over 'Slava mu!' – hail him!

The Controversial Cardinal Stepinac

When Pope John Paul travelled to Croatia in October 1998 to beatify Cardinal Alojzije Stepinac he re-opened one of the more controversial chapters in Croatian history. Cardinal Stepinac was archbishop of Zagreb from 1934 to 1946 and thus presided over the rise and fall of Ante Pavelić and his fascist Independent State of Croatia. When Tito took power in 1945, he attempted to persuade the archbishop to separate the Croatian Catholic Church from Rome and set up a new church that would more closely resemble the Orthodox Church. The archbishop refused. He was tried and convicted of treason for collaborating with the Nazi puppet regime, then sentenced to 16 years of prison, of which he served five years. He left prison in 1951 and spent the remainder of his life under house arrest in his native Krašic. His health deteriorated badly and he died in 1960 at the age of 62, possibly of poisoning.

To the Croats, Cardinal Stepinac was a martyr to the cause of Croatian self-determination who chose to remain in Croatia and suffer an unjust punishment when he could have fled. To the Serbs, he was the highest representative of a Church that participated in the forced conversion and massacres of tens of thousands of Serbs. To the Catholic Church, he was persecuted for maintaining the integrity of the Church against Tito's hostile, atheist regime.

Stepinac's supporters point to numerous letters and speeches during the Pavelić years when the archbishop unequivocally deplored the persecution of Jews, Serbs and Gypsies. 'Every nation and every race on the earth has the right to a life worthy of a person and to treatment worthy of a person. All without differentiation, whether members of the Gypsy race or any others, whether black or distinguished Europeans, despised Jews or haughty Aryans, have the same right to say: "Our Father who art in Heaven!"' said the archbishop in 1942. The Jewish community of Zagreb has credited Stepinac with saving several hundred Jewish lives during the war.

Opponents of Stepinac's beatification note that his determination to see a Croatian state led him to embrace the Pavelić government too early and distance himself from it too late. They argue that he supported the forced conversions of hundreds of thousands of Serbs and failed to take strong, effective measures against priests who were personally supervising the massacre of the Serbian population. His supporters counter that he only supported conversion as a measure to save Serbian lives and spoke out against the massacres when he became aware of them.

Although Stepinac's wartime actions may have been ambiguous, his decision to stay in Croatia at a time when the Ustashe were scattering to the four corners of the world to escape retribution indicates that he, at least, believed he had nothing to hide. The possibility of a comfortable exile was repeatedly dangled before him, yet he rejected any easy escape from his plight and steadfastly refused to compromise with Tito's regime. He believed in the Catholic Church, he believed in an independent Croatia and his life is a source of profound inspiration in a country that has suffered for the same principles.

built in the 18th century on the left defensive wall of medieval Kaptol. Turn left onto Skalinska ulica and then left on Tkalčića, a street of lively cafés and restaurants. A short passage takes you to the parallel Radić ulica, which used to house German cobblers. About 100m up the street a passage to your left takes you to the Stone Gate – the eastern gate to the medieval Gradec town, now a shrine. According to legend, a great fire in 1731 destroyed every part of the wooden gate except for the painting of the

Virgin and Child by an unknown 17th century artist. People believe that the painting possesses magical powers and come regularly to pray before it and leave flowers. On the west façade of the Stone Gate you'll see a statue of Dora, the heroine of an 18th century historical novel who lived with her father next to the Stone Gate.

Turn right and proceed up Opatička ulica to the **City Museum**, housed in the 17th century Convent of St Clair built along the eastern wall of the town. Since 1907 it has housed a historical museum presenting the history of Zagreb in documents, artwork and crafts. Most interesting is a scale model of old Gradec. Summaries of the exhibits are posted in English and German of each room. It's open Tuesday through Friday from 10 am to 6 pm, Saturday and Sunday 10 am to 1 pm.

From the museum go downhill along Demetrova and bear left on Mletačka to the **Meštrović Studio** at No 8. From 1922 to 1942, Meštrović lived and worked in this 17th century house which now presents an excellent collection of some 100 sculptures, drawings, lithographs and furniture from the first four decades of his artistic life. The museums reflect the artists preoccupations with philosophical and religious themes as well as nudes, portraits and self-portraits. It's open Monday to Friday from 9 am to 2 pm.

Return to Demetrova and continue downhill to the **Museum of Natural Science**, Demetrova 1, which has a collection of prehistoric tools and bones excavated from the Krapina cave plus exhibits showing the evolution of animal and plant life in Croatia. Temporary exhibits often focus on specific regions, such as the island of Mljet. The museum is open Tuesday to Friday from 10 am to 5 pm, Saturday and Sunday 10 am to 1 pm.

Continue down Demetrova, turn left on Brezov and continue downhill on Matoševa to the **Croatian Historical Museum** at No 9 which currently only presents temporary exhibitions on Croatian history. It's open Monday to Friday from 10 am to 5 pm, Saturday and Sunday 10 am to 1 pm.

Continue down Mletačka, cross the street and continue downhill to Trg Svetog Marka, the square around **St Mark's Church** (Crkva Sveti Marka), with its unique tiled roof constructed in 1880. The tiles on the left side depict the medieval coat of arms of Croatia, Dalmatia and Slavonia, while the emblem of Zagreb is on the right side. The 13th century church was named for the annual St Mark's fair, which was held in Gradec at the time, and retains a 13th century Romanesque window on the south side. The Gothic portal composed of 15 figures in shallow niches was sculpted in the 14th century. The present belltower replaces an earlier one that was destroyed by an earthquake in 1502. The interior contains sculptures by Meštrović but the church is only open for Mass twice a day weekdays and four times a day Sunday.

The eastern side of the square is taken up by the Croatian **Sabor** (Parliament), built in 1910 on the site of baroque 17th and 18th century townhouses. The neo-classical style seems incongruous here but the secession of Croatia from the Austro-Hungarian Monarchy was proclaimed from its balcony in 1918 and it is still the centre of Croatian politics. On the opposite side of the square is the **Ban's Palace** (Banski dvori), which was once the seat of Croatian viceroys and is now the presidential palace. The building is composed of two baroque mansions and houses courts, archives and other government offices. In October 1991 the palace was bombed by the federal army, in what some believe to have been an assassination attempt on President Franjo Tudjman. From April to September there is a guard changing ceremony every Saturday and Sunday at noon. Leaving the square by Čirilometodska ulica, named after the Slav apostles Cyril and Methodius, you'll come across a sculpted stone head representing Matija Gubec, the leader of a celebrated peasant rebellion who was allegedly beheaded in St Mark's Square. At No 5 is the Old City Hall, where municipal assembly meetings are held and. At No 3 is the **Gallery of Naive Art**. The most important artists in Croatia's long tradition of naive art are represented here including Generalić, Mraz, Virius and Smaljić, as well as international artists working in the same style. There are over 1000 works, mainly paintings and drawings, and the museum is open Tuesday to Saturday from 10 am to 6 pm and Sunday 10 am to 1 pm.

Continuing along the same street leads you down to Jezuitski trg named after the Jesuit monastery that once stood here. On the east side of Jezuitski trg is the **City Art Gallery** (MGC Klovićevi Dvori), Jezuitski trg 4, housed in the former Jesuit monastery. The space is the most prestigious exhibition space for modern Croatian art which is presented in a series of changing exhibitions. Recent exhibitions include *Treasure of the Zagreb Cathedral, Ivan Meštrović, The ancient Chinese Culture* and *The Golden Eral of Dubrovnik*. The gallery is open Tuesday to Sunday from 10 am to 6 pm. Opposite the City Art Gallery is the 18th century Dverce mansion restored in the 19th century and now used for official receptions. Before leaving the square, note the fountain with the statue *Fisherman with Snake* created by Simeon Roksandić in 1908.

South of Jezuitski trg you'll come to Katarina trg with the **Jesuit Church of St Catherine** (Crkva Sveti Katarine) built between 1620 and 1632. Although battered by fire and earthquake, the Baroque facade still gleams and the interior contains a fine altar from 1762. The interior stucco work dates from 1720 and there are 18th century medallions depicting the life of St Catherine on the ceiling of the nave.

Take the Dverce passage in the south of the square which leads to the **Lotrščak Tower**, built in the middle of the 13th century in order to protect the southern city gate. For the last hundred years a cannon has been fired every day at noon commemorating a legendary event from Zagreb's history. According to the legend, a cannon was fired at noon one day at the Turks camped across the Sava River. On its way across the river, the cannonball happened to hit a rooster. The rooster was blown to bits and, the story goes, that's why the Turks

became so demoralised they failed to attack the city. The tower may be climbed for a sweeping 360° view of the city (closed Sunday). From the tower take a walk on the Strossmayerov promenade before taking the funicular down to the Lower Town.

Lower Town Museums Zagreb is a city of museums, and many of them are in the lower town. Zagreb's finest art gallery is the **Museum Mimara** at Rooseveltov trg 5. Housed in a neo-Renaissance former school building (1883), this diverse collection shows the loving hand of Ante Topić Mimara, a private collector who donated over 3750 priceless objects to his native Zagreb, even though he spent much of his life in Salzburg, Austria. The collection spans a wide range of periods and regions. There is an archaeological collection with 200 items from Egypt, Mesopotamia, Persia, Greece, Rome and early-medieval Europe, exhibits of ancient Far Eastern artworks, a glass, textile and furniture collection that spans centuries and one thousand European art objects. In painting, Italian artists Raphael, Veronese, Caravaggeio and Canaletto are represented. Dutch artists Rembrandt and Ruidael are also present, and there are Flemish paintings from Bosch, Rubens and Van Dyck. Spanish painters Vasquez, Murillo and Goya, German and English painters and French masters de la Tour, Boucher, Delacroix, Corot, Manet, Renoir and Degas are also in the collection. The museum is open Tuesday, Wednesday, Friday and Saturday from 10 am to 5 pm, and Thursday 10 am to 2 pm.

The **Strossmayer Gallery of Old Masters**, Trg Zrinjskog 11, is another fine art museum exhibiting the collection of the illustrious Bishop Strossmayer, which he donated in 1884. The original collection was extended by subsequent donations from private collectors. Housed on the second floor of the 19th century neo-Renaissance Croatian Academy of Sciences and Arts, the museum includes Italian masters from the 14th to 18th centuries such as G Bellini,

Veronese and Tiepolo; Dutch and Flemish painters such as J Bruegel the Younger, and French artists Proudhon and Carpeaux as well as classic Croatian artists Medulić and Benković. The interior courtyard contains the Baška slab (Baščanska Ploča), a stone tablet from the Krk island which contains the oldest example of Glagolitic script, dating from 1102 (see illustration, page 31).

Note the statue of Bishop Strossmayer by Ivan Meštrović. The museum is open Tuesday to Sunday from 10 am to 5 pm.

Also in the park but further south is the yellow **exhibition pavilion** which presents changing exhibitions of contemporary art. Constructed in 1897 in stunning art nouveau style, the pavilion is the only space that was specifically designed to host large

Bishop Strossmayer

Robert William Seton-Watson, the English scholar of Yugoslavia, once wrote about Strossmayer, 'As the patron and inspirer of thought and culture, his influence upon Croatia and the southern Slavs cannot be exaggerated. As Jelačić typifies the military prowess and loyalty of the Croat, so Strossmayer stands for those qualities of faith and romantic idealism for which the best sons of the race have been distinguished.' Like Jelačić, Bishop Josip Strossmayer believed in the unity of Catholic and Orthodox Croatians but unlike Jelačić he distrusted the Habsburgs and detested Hungary. Brilliant, cultivated and charismatic, Strossmayer seemed able to rise above political disappointments in a way that eluded the tortured *ban*.

Born in Osijek in 1815 of mixed Croatian, German and Austrian stock, Josip Strossmayer was educated at a prestigious seminary in Vienna. His outstanding intellect fuelled a meteoric rise through the church hierarchy and he was appointed bishop of his home diocese at the relatively tender age of 34. By 1860 he had become the de facto leader of the National Party which had replaced the former Illyrian party. The great question facing the reconstituted *Sabor* at the time was whether it should take part in the new Austro-Hungarian parliament. Strossmayer argued that Croatian demands for greater autonomy must be met before it participated in the parliament but his strategy was unsuccessful. The birth of the Dual Monarchy in 1867 placed Croatia squarely within Hungarian control and Strossmayer's party was voted out of the Sabor. Although he returned to the Sabor briefly, in 1873 he retired from active political life.

Politics was only part of Strossmayer's life, however. As bishop of Slavonia, he oversaw the construction of a magnificent new cathedral in Đakovo. His art collection became the foundation of the Strossmayer Gallery in Zagreb. In 1866 he founded the Yugoslav Academy of Art & Science in Zagreb as an intellectual centre for scholarship and debate. It took 15 years, but he finally forced Vienna to accept the establishment of the University of Zagreb, the first university in the southern Slav lands.

Along the way, Strossmayer managed to alienate any and all authorities. Espousing the reconciliation of the Catholic and Orthodox Churches put him on a collision course with the Catholic Church. His outspoken demands for Croatian autonomy infuriated the Austro-Hungarian emperor. His continued campaign for Croat-Serb unification cost him the support of the Croat population who were turning towards the nationalist ideology of Ante Starčević. When he died in 1905, his dream of south-Slavic unity seemed for a time to expire with him though it would take another 85 years for it to be completely buried. The great Bishop Strossmayer is interred in the cathedral of Đakovo.

exhibits. It's open Monday to Saturday from 11 am to 7 pm, Sunday 10 am to 1 pm.

West of the Strossmayer Gallery is the **Gallery of Contemporary Art**, Hebranga 1, which shows works by 19th and 20th century Croatian artists such as Bukovac, Mihanović, Račić and others. Although the holdings of paintings, sculpture, graphics and tapestries number about 10,000, the gallery has been closed since the recent war.

The **Archaeological Museum** at Trg Nikole Zrinjskog 19 has also not re-opened since the war, although it used to display prehistoric to medieval artefacts, as well as Egyptian mummies. The coin collection is one of the most important in Europe containing some 260,000 coins, medals, medallions and decorations. The courtyard has a collection of Roman monuments dating from the 5th to 4th century BC and is now an open-air café.

The **Ethnographic Museum,** Mažuranićev trg 14, is also worthwhile. Housed in a domed building from 1903, the museum houses the ethnographic heritage of Croatia which amounts to some 70,000 items. Only about 2750 exhibits are on display including ceramics, jewellery, musical instruments, tools and weapons as well as Croatian folk costumes, lace from the island of Pag and gold-embroidered scarves from Slavonia. Thanks to donations from the Croatian explorers Mirko and Stevo Seljan, there are also exhibits from South America, the Congo, Ethiopia, China, Japan, New Guinea and Australia. The museum is open Tuesday, Wednesday and Thursday from 10 am to 6 pm, Friday, Saturday and Sunday from 10 am to 1 pm.

Nearby is the **Arts and Crafts Museum**, Trg Maršala Tita 10, built between 1882 and 1892. The museum exhibits furniture, textiles, metal, ceramic and glass from the middle ages to the 20th century. You can see Gothic and baroque sculptures from northern Croatia as well as paintings, prints, bells, stoves, rings, clocks, bound books, toys, photos and industrial designs. The museum also contains an important library and there are frequent temporary exhibitions. It's open Tuesday to Friday from 10 am to 6 pm, Saturday and Sunday from 10 am to 1 pm.

Also on Trg Maršala Tita is the neo-baroque **Croatian National Theatre** (1895), with Ivan Meštrović's sculpture *Fountain of Life* (1905) standing in front. The theatre was designed in 1894 by Herman Helmer and Ferdinand Fellner, the same team that built the Art Pavilion.

Kids usually like the **Technical Museum,** Savska 18, which has a planetarium, steam engine locomotives, scale models of satellites and space ships, and a replica of a mine within the building, as well as departments of agriculture, geology, energy and transportation. It's open Tuesday to Friday from 9 am to 5 pm, and Saturday and Sunday 9 am to 1 pm.

It may be slightly out-of-the way but the unusual architecture makes it worth the walk. The **Croatian Artist's Centre** (Dom Hrvatskih Likovnih Umjetnika) on Trg velikana is one of the few architectural works by the sculptor Ivan Meštrović. It was built as an exhibition pavilion, and then transformed into a mosque before finally becoming a showplace for contemporary Croatian artists. It's open Tuesday to Sunday from 11 am to 7 pm, Monday 2 to 7 pm.

For a change from museums and galleries, relax in the lovely **Botanical Garden** on ulica Mihanovićeva (closed Monday, free admission), laid out in 1890. In addition to 10,000 species of plants, including 1,800 tropical flora specimens, the landscaping has created restful paths and corners that seem a world away from bustling Zagreb.

North of the Centre A 20 minute ride north on bus No 106 from the cathedral takes you to **Mirogoj**, one of the most beautiful cemeteries in Europe. One wag commented that the people here are better housed in death than they ever were in life. The cemetery was designed in 1876 by one of Croatia's finest architects, Herman Bollé who also created numerous buildings around Zagreb. In Mirogoj he built a majestic arcade topped by a string of cupolas, that looks like a fortress from the outside but is calm and graceful from the inside. The cemetery is lushly green and the paths are interspersed with sculpture and artfully designed tombs. Highlights include the graves of poet Petar Preradović, the political leader Stjepan Radić, the bust of Vladimir Becić by Ivan Meštrović and the sculpture by Mihanović for the Mayer family.

The medieval fortress of **Medvedgrad** on the southern side of Mount Medvednica just above Zagreb, is the most important medieval monument in Zagreb. Built from 1249 to 1254, it was erected to protect the city from Tatar invasions and is well protected by high rocks. The fortress was owned by a succession of aristocratic families but fell into ruin from earthquake and general neglect. Restoration began in 1979, but was pursued with greater enthusiasm in 1993 and 1994 when the country was looking to honour monuments from its past. Today you can see the rebuilt thick walls and towers, a small chapel with frescoes and especially the Shrine of the Homeland which pays homage to those who have died for a free Croatia. On a clear day, it also offers a beautiful view of Zagreb and surroundings.

East of the Centre Maksimir is a peaceful wooded enclave covering 18 hectares and easily accessible by tram Nos 4, 7, 11 and 12. Opened to the public in 1794, it was the first public promenade in south-eastern Europe and is landscaped like an English garden-style park with alleys, lawns, and artificial lakes. The most photographed structure in the park is the exquisite Bellevue Pavilion which was constructed in 1843, but there is also the Echo Pavilion and a house built to resemble a rustic Swiss cottage.

Activities

The **Sports Park Mladost** (☎ 323 011), Jarunska cesta 5, has outdoor and indoor Olympic-size swimming pools, as well as smaller pools for children, and a gym. It's open Monday to Friday from 6.30 am to 9 am and 1 pm to 8 pm, weekends 8 am to 8 pm. Admission is 15KN for adults and 10KN for children.

The **Sports and Recreational Centre** Šalata (☎ 46 16 300), Schlosserove stube 2, offers outdoor and indoor tennis courts, a gym and a winter ice skating rink as well as two outdoor swimming pools which are open Monday to Friday from 11 am to 6 pm and weekends 11 am to 7 pm. There's also an indoor ice skating rink which rents skates. Admission is 20KN on weekdays and 25KN on weekends.

Although Zagreb is not normally associated with winter sports, if the snow lasts long enough you can **ski** right outside town at Sljeme, the main peak of Medvednica Mountain. It has four ski-runs, three ski-lifts and a triple chair lift; call the ski centre (☎ 45 55 827) for information on snow conditions.

Jarun Lake in south Zagreb is a popular getaway for residents any time of year but especially in the summer when the clear waters are ideal for **swimming**. Although part of the lake is marked off for boating competitions, there is more than enough space to enjoy a leisurely swim. Take tram No 5 or 17 to the last stop and follow signs to the lake (*jezero*). When you come to the lake you can head left to Malo Jezero for swimming and canoe or pedalboat rental or right to Veliko Jezero, which also has a pebble beach and **windsurfing**. Call ☎ 316 689 for further information.

Medvednica Mountain to the north of Zagreb offers excellent **hiking** opportunities. There are two popular routes: you can take tram No 14 to the last stop and then change to tram No 15 and take it to the last stop. You will be near the funicular that goes to the top of the mountain and next to the funicular there is a clearly marked footpath that goes to the top. Or you can take bus No 102 from Trg Britanski to the church in Šestine and take the hiking route from there. Allow about three hours for each of these hikes and remember that this is a heavily wooded mountain with ample opportunities to become completely lost. Take warm clothes, water and make sure to return before sundown. There is also a danger of disease-carrying ticks in the summer. Wear trousers and long sleeves and examine your body carefully after the hike for ticks (see the Facts for the Visitor section for more information on tick-borne infections).

Organised Tours

The tourist office organises walking tours for 45KN per person (minimum four people) and minibus tours. They leave on Wednesday mornings at 10 am from the Intercontinental Hotel or the Esplanade Hotel. Tickets are 75KN; sign up at the tourist office a day in advance.

Special Events

With the first breath of warm air, Zagreb residents start dreaming of their getaway on the coast and by mid-July the city becomes almost bucolic. Even though some museums and galleries shut their doors, the city's cultural life bubbles along in the popular Zagreb Summer Festival. From the beginning of July until mid-August, national and international orchestras and soloists stage concerts in venues around the city. The atrium of MGC Klovićevi dvori on Jezuiti trg, St Catherine's church, St Mark's church and the Zagreb cathedral are often used and sometimes the concerts are held in squares in the Upper Town. Open-air events are free but admission is usually charged for the indoor concerts. Prices depend upon the concert, but tickets can be purchased from the organisers, Koncertna direkcija Zagreb (☎ 46 11 808) Kneza Mislava 18.

The International Folklore Festival has been taking place in Zagreb for over 30 years, usually for six days in July. As one of the more colourful events in Zagreb, the program includes folk dancers and singers from Croatia and other European countries dressed in traditional costumes. There are processions and performances from Trg Jalačića to the Upper Town and you are free

to join workshops in dance, music and art designed to introduce you to Croatian folk culture.

In September, there's the International Autumn Zagreb Fair – a trade show of science, technology, crafts and agricultural exhibits that takes place at the Zagreb Fair grounds. In odd-numbered years in April there's the Zagreb Biennial of Contemporary Music, Croatia's most important music event since 1961. Zagreb also hosts a festival of animated films every even-numbered year in June.

Places to Stay

If you can't arrange a morning arrival and afternoon departure to avoid spending the night in Zagreb, be prepared to bite the bullet and pay a lot more for a place to sleep than you would elsewhere in Croatia. Budget accommodation is in short supply in Zagreb. An early arrival is recommended, since private room-finding agencies are an attractive alternative and usually refuse telephone bookings. The only easy escape is to book an overnight bus to Split or Dubrovnik.

Camping There's a camping area outside the *Motel Plitvice* (☎ 65 30 444) which is not in Plitvice at all but near the town of Lučko on the Obilazinica Highway. The motel sometimes runs a minibus from Savski Most. Call to find out if and when their service is operating. Otherwise, take tram No 7 or 14 to Savski Most and then the Lučko bus to Lučko village from which the motel/camp site is about a 10 minute walk. The price is 23KN per person and 20KN per tent; there's a lake and a sports centre nearby.

Hostels The noisy 215-bed *Omladinski Hotel* (☎ 48 41 261, fax 48 41 269, Petrinjska 77), actually near a youth hostel, near the train station is open all year and costs 210KN for a double without bath, 280KN with bath, including tax (no singles). Some of the six-bed dormitories here (at 73KN per person) may still be occupied by war refugees but most rooms remain available.

The 5KN YHA discount is only available to persons under 27 sleeping in the dormitory. You must check out by 9 am and you can't occupy the room until 2 pm.

The *Studenthotel Cvjetno Naselje* (☎ 61 91 240), off Slavonska avenija in the south of the city, charges 219/287KN for a single/double, breakfast included. The rooms are good, each with private bath, and the staff are friendly. There's no student discount, although showing your ISIC and pleading poverty occasionally works. There's a self-service student restaurant here where a filling meal with a Coke will cost 30KN. The Cvjetno Naselje is available to visitors from mid-July to the end of September only – the rest of the year it's a student dormitory. Take tram No 4, 5, 14, 16 or 17 south-west on Savska cesta to 'Vjesnik'. Opposite the stop is a tall building marked 'Vjesnik'. The student complex is just behind it.

In July and August make straight for the *Studentski dom Stjepan Radić* (☎ 334 255, *Jarunska ulica 3*) off Horvaćanska ulica in the south-west of the city near the Sava River (tram No 5 or 17). Rooms in this huge student complex cost 200/250KN for a single/double and one of Zagreb's more popular discos, The Best, is across the street.

Private Rooms Try not to arrive on Sunday if you intend to stay in a private apartment, since most of the agencies are closed. You'll notice that prices are surprisingly high but little of the money actually goes to your host. Taxes bite off a big chunk and the agency takes nearly half the money, leaving barely a quarter for the proprietor.

The *Turističko Društvo Novi Zagreb* (☎ 65 52 047, fax 65 21 523, Trnsko 15e) has private rooms in apartment buildings in the Novi Zagreb neighbourhood south of the Sava River for 200/260KN a single/double, plus tax, with a 30% surcharge for one-night stays. The office is open weekdays from 8 am to 6 pm and Saturday 9 am to 1 pm. Tram Nos 7, 14 or 16 will take you to Trnsko, near the apartments.

Just south of the town centre is *Lina Gabino* (☎ 39 21 27), 28 Petračićeva, who rents both two-bedroom apartments 400/420KN a single/double and private rooms for 265/350KN a single/double plus tax. Prices are about 10% cheaper if you stay more than one night. Her office is open weekdays from 9 am to 5 pm, Saturday 9 am to 2 pm.

Evistas (☎ 429 974 or 48 19 133, fax 431 987, Šenoina 28), between the bus and train station, also rents apartments beginning at 350KN for two people and rising to 675KN for five with a minimum stay of three nights. Private rooms are also available in the town centre for 170/230KN a single/double (145/190KN for people under 25). The office is open weekdays from 9 am to 1.30 pm and 5 to 8 pm, and Saturday 9.30 am to 5 pm.

If you're new to Croatia, don't be put off by these high prices. Along the coast, especially from Rab south, private rooms cost less than half as much.

Hotels There aren't any cheap hotels in Zagreb. In the former Yugoslavia, hotels were state-run with standardised prices and service. The idea of private hotels is new to Zagreb but a few are starting to spring up – although none are real budget places. You will find clean modern rooms with private baths and breakfast but very little in the way of personalised decoration except in a few of the top category establishments. Prices stay the same in all seasons but be prepared for a 20% surcharge if you arrive during a festival, especially the Autumn Fair.

Hotels – Budget The best deal in the town centre is the brand new and friendly *Hotel Ilica* (☎ 37 77 522, fax 37 77 722, Ilica 102). The hotel is set back from the street, which insures a quiet night's sleep and most rooms are shaded from the sun, leaving them cool during the day. Two stops from Trg Jelačića just after Britanski trg, the 12 pleasant rooms with bath and breakfast cost 251/380KN a single/double and 441KN for a double with two beds.

If you don't mind staying out of town, you can try **Tomislavov Dom** (☎ 45 55 833, fax 45 55 834, Sljemenska cesta bb) on the Sljeme peak of Medvenica Mountain. You'll need to take two trams (Nos 14 and 21) and a funicular to get up there, but the setting is tranquil and the prices cheap for Zagreb – only 200/300KN a single/double.

Also out the town centre, south-east of the bus station is the relatively inexpensive hotel **Park** (☎ 23 33 422, fax 220 820, Ivanićgradska 52), which is adequate if not luxurious. There are 136 simply furnished doubles, a terrace, casino and restaurant. Expect to pay 280/320KN for a single/double with breakfast.

Hotels – Mid-Range Opposite the train station, the 110-room **Central Hotel** (☎ 484 11 22, fax 48 41 304, Branimirova 3) is bland but convenient to tram lines for getting around the city. Prices are 308/446KN a single/double including breakfast. Each room is equipped with satellite TV and some rooms have minibars and hair dryers.

The six-storey **Hotel Jadran** (☎ 45 53 777, fax 46 12 151, Vlaška 50) has a superb location only minutes from Trg Jelačića. There are 48 rooms that are clean but unmemorable. Prices are 362/432KN with shower and breakfast.

For a little more you could stay at the **Hotel Astoria** (☎ 48 41 222, fax 48 41 304, Petrinjska 71), but it is not as centrally located. There is a good Chinese restaurant on the premises and the hotel is close to the bus and train stations. Prices are 390/550KN.

To be near the 'beach' try the **Hotel Lido** (☎ 331 315, fax 332 179, Malo Jarunsko jezero bb) on Jarun Lake. The air is fresh and there are plenty of day activities and nightlife nearby. Prices are 366/439KN a single/double.

Hotels – Top End **Hotel International** (☎ 61 08 800, fax 61 59 459, Miramarska 24) is south of the train station and still houses war refugees in a portion of its 370 rooms. Although it would never win any

prizes for charm, it has the facilities of most big-city hotels, including a restaurant, bar, casino and conference rooms. Prices begin at 457/515KN for a single/double but there are large and more expensive rooms available.

For that price, you might as well pay a little more and stay downtown at the **Hotel Dubrovnik** (☎ 45 55 155, fax 424 451, Gajeva 1) which is convenient to almost anything you want to do in Zagreb. It's on a pedestrian street, however, which means that you will have to walk about 25m with your luggage in order to access the hotel. There are 262 well-maintained rooms in this modern, glass-fronted tower. Prices are 520/700 a single/double.

For a memorable splurge, stay at the top-category **Hotel Esplanade** (☎ 45 66 666, fax 45 77 907) next to the train station (890/1200KN a single/double). Built in 1925 when Zagreb was a stop on the Orient Express, this six-storey, 215-room hotel epitomises old-world refinement. The lobby décor is a study of Art Deco chic with swirling marble and subdued lighting and the hotel restaurant is one of the best in town. There's a 30% discount for weekend stays.

Every big city with aspirations must have a modern chain hotel and Zagreb is no exception to the rule. The 17-storey **Hotel Inter-Continental** (☎ 45 53 411, fax 444 431, Kršnjavoga 1) has 414 rooms, all with air-con, as well as 40 apartments and two presidential suites. Rooms have satellite TV, minibars, and hair dryers, and the hotel has a rooftop restaurant and two other restaurants as well as parking facilities. You'll pay 1140/1380KN a single/double.

The new **Sheraton** (☎ 45 53 535, fax 45 53 035, Kneza Borne 2) is also in the deluxe category with two restaurants, a café, piano bar and health and fitness club with an indoor pool, sauna, and sundeck. The rooms begin at 1024/1259KN a single/double and are every bit as luxurious as you would expect.

Places to Eat
Town Centre The main shopping street, Ilica, is lined with fast food joints and inex-

pensive snack bars. **Delikatese** *(Ilica 39)* is a good place to pick up cheese, fruit, bread, yoghurt, and cold meat for a picnic. Next door is the **Konzum** grocery store that sells whole roasted chicken and an assortment of prepared salads. Further along Ilica at Trg Britanski, there's a daily fruit and vegetable **market** every day until 3 pm which sells farm fresh produce. There's also the fruit and vegetable **market** at Dolac. Don't hesitate to bargain. A new bakery close to the train station, **Pekarnica Dora** *(Stross-mayerova 7),* is open 24 hours for those late-night pastry needs and you can fill up on burek at **Slastičarna** *(Kaptol 25).*

You can't get much cheaper than **Mimiće** *(Jurišićeva 21)* which has been a local favourite for decades, turning out plates of fried fish that begin at 9KN for ten sardines and a hunk of bread. The fish is sure to be fresh because turnover is heavy, especially at noontime when workers in the offices around Trg Jelačić turn out in droves for their lunch. It's open Monday through Friday from 7 am to 10 pm and Saturday till 6 pm.

Pizza is a popular dish for budget-minded Croatians (which includes just about the entire country) and the pies at **Pizzicato** *(Gundilićeva 4)* in the Academy of Music are excellent. The copious topping and the freshly-made pastry are in perfect balance, making a hearty and delicious meal. Prices start at a mere 18KN and the menu is translated into English. It's open Monday to Friday from 11 am to 10 pm and Saturday till 4 pm. Another contender for best pizza is the slightly more upscale **Pizzeria 2** *(Novi Ves 2)* in upper Kaptol which also turns out a variety of pasta dishes as well. Pizza and pasta run from about 25 to 35KN and the restaurant is open Monday to Saturday from 9 am to 11 pm. **Boban** *(Gajeva 9)* offers sophisticated Italian food at reasonable prices. There's an outdoor terrace on pedestrian Gajeva ulica and an indoor lounge and terrace that is popular with Zagreb yuppies. Imaginative pasta dishes, pizza and a variety of salads are served in the spacious cellar restaurant ranging from 25KN to

40KN. The restaurant is open daily from 10 am to midnight.

Even non-vegetarians will enjoy the vegie meals at **Melong** *(Petrinjska 9)* near Ilica with its simple cheerful decor. The menu is in Croatian and the staff speaks limited English, but there are pictures on the menu to help you decide. Whatever you order is bound to be tasty. The daily specialty may run about 40KN but you can get soup for 10KN and a main course for 25KN. It's open daily from 7 am to 11 pm.

Near the train station, a good place for local dishes is **Tomislav** *(Trenkova 2)* which is informal and reasonably priced; it's open daily from 8 am to 11 pm. **Fenuci** *(Zrinskog 16)* is a slick new restaurant/bar with a modern, upscale look that would fit it into any international capital. You can get a sophisticated plate of noodles for 45KN but the meaty main courses begin at 55KN. It's open Monday to Saturday from 8 am to 11 pm.

Foreign food hasn't yet made great inroads in Zagreb. You can get decent Chinese-Szechuan food at **Asia** in the Hotel Astoria, but it's not cheap. Plan on spending 55KN to 65KN for a main dish with rice. It's open Monday to Saturday from noon to midnight, and Sunday 6 pm to midnight. South of the centre near Slavonska avenija, there's an Indian restaurant, **Tandor**, which serves fairly authentic Indian food Tuesday to Sunday from noon to 11 pm.

Kaptolska Klet *(Kaptol 5)* across from the Cathedral serves local specialties in a semi-enclosed indoor terrace furnished in bright tablecloths and wicker chairs. There are a variety of grilled meats including spit-roasted lamb, duck, pork and veal as well as homemade sausages and a couple of fish dishes. Vegetarians can stick with pasta dishes or a vegetable-bean plate. The menu is in English and prices are moderate, starting at 54KN for roast turkey with noodles and running about 70KN for other meat dishes. It's open daily from 10 am to midnight.

Fish tends to be expensive in Zagreb but is trucked in daily from the coast, guaranteeing good quality. **Split** *(Ilica 19)* serves good fresh seafood in pleasant, relaxed surroundings accompanied by light, local white wines. The cod is especially good. It's open Monday to Saturday from 6 am to midnight.

One of the most elegant places in town is undoubtedly the *Paviljon (Trg Tomislava 22)* in the yellow exhibition pavilion across the park from the train station. The spacious, glossy dining room is a favourite of local businesspeople trying to impress their clients. The food has an Italian accent and is beautifully presented. Main courses average about 70KN but you can get an excellent plate of pasta for 40KN. There's an outdoor terrace and the restaurant is open Monday to Saturday from 10 am to midnight.

The trendiest spot is the upscale refurbished *Dubravkin Put (Dubravkin put 2)* in a woodsy area north-west of the town centre. The decor is light, pleasant and modern with pine floors and ceiling lights but it is the outstanding fish specialties that are attracting Zagreb's fashionable crowd. The owner is from Dubrovnik and the cuisine is inspired by his native Dalmatia, with risottos as starters and main courses of perfectly grilled fish. The restaurant is not cheap – starters begin at about 50KN – but makes a fine evening out. It's open daily from 11 am to midnight.

Out of Town *Okrugljak (Mlinjovi 28)* is a popular spot on Medvenica Mountain for city people celebrating a special occasion. Dining is casual; you can sit at wood tables in carved out wine barrels or on the terrace. There is usually music on weekends and the occasional wedding reception can make the ambience more than lively. The spit-roasted meat, especially lamb or duck, is unusually juicy and served with delicious *mlinci* baked noodles. The restaurant is open daily from 11 am to 1 am.

Also on Medvenica Mountain, surrounded by foliage and a bubbling brook, is a cheaper local dining spot, *Gračanka (Gračanska cesta 48)*. Although the emphasis is on meat dishes such as goose liver, brains, and grilled veal, vegetarians will enjoy specialties such as cheese fried in breadcrumbs and a variety of mushrooms, grilled, stewed or fried. The restaurant is open Tuesday to Saturday from 11 am to 11 pm and Sunday noon to 5 pm.

Cafés & Bars The narrow streets in the Upper Town are lined with outdoor cafés and restaurants that attract crowds of strollers and sightseers especially on summer evenings. The liveliest scene is along Tkalčićeva, north off Trg Jelačića, where crowds spill out of cafés onto the street, drinks in hand.

Farther up on Kozarska ulica the city's young people cluster shoulder to shoulder. Trg Petra Preradovića, Zagreb's flower-market square attracts street performers in mild weather and occasional bands. Zagreb's most pretentious cafés are *Gradska Kavana* on Trg Jelačića and *Kazališna Kavana* on Trg Maršala Tita opposite the Croatian National Theatre. *Models* café next door to *Kazališna Kavana* is adorned with photos of the superstar models the café is evidently trying (and, so far, failing) to attract.

The most unusual bar is *Tolkien's House* on the corner of Matoševa and Vranic just up the street from Lotrščak Tower. This tiny mustard-colored café is decorated in the style of Tolkien's famous books and has a cosy enclosed terrace where you can drink the best hot chocolate in Zagreb. It's open daily from 9 am to midnight.

The *Rock Forum Café (Gajeva ulica 13)* occupies the rear sculpture garden of the Archaeological Museum (open in summer only) and across the street is the *Hard Rock Café*, full of 1950s and 1960s memorabilia. Farther back in the passageway from Hard Rock is the *Art Café Thalia* which really tries to live up to its name. A couple of other cafés and music shops share this lively complex at the corner of Teslina and Gajeva streets. Check out the *BP Club* in the complex basement for jazz, blues and rock bands.

The *Pivnica Tomislav (Trg Tomislava 18)* facing the park in front of the train station, is a good local bar with inexpensive draught beer and light meals.

Gays are generally welcome in Zagreb's bars and discos but the city's only exclusively gay bar is **Bacchus** bar on Tomislava near the train station. At the moment the bar attracts mostly men with a sprinkling of women. *Gjuro (Medveščak 58)* in north Kaptol is a disco that attracts a gay and straight crowd.

Entertainment

Zagreb is a happening city. Its theatres and concert halls present a great variety of programs throughout the year. Many (but not all) are listed in the monthly brochure *Zagreb Events & Performances*, which is usually available from the tourist office.

It's worth your while making the rounds of the theatres in person to check out the calendars. Tickets are usually available, even for the most in-demand shows. A small office marked 'Kazalište Komedija' (look for the posters) in the Oktogon also sells theatre tickets; it's in a passage connecting Trg Petra Preradovića to Ilica near Trg Jelačića.

Theatre The neo-baroque *Croatian National Theatre (☎ 48 28 532, Trg Maršala Tita 15)* was established in 1895. It stages opera and ballet performances and the box office is open weekdays from 10 am to 1 pm and 5 to 7.30 pm, and Saturday 10 am to 1 pm as well as 30 minutes before performances on Sundays. You have a choice of orchestra (*parket*), lodge (*lože*) or balcony (*balkon*) seats.

The **Komedija Theatre** *(☎ 433 209, Kaptol 9)* near the cathedral, stages operettas and musicals. The ticket office of the *Vatroslav Lisinski Concert Hall (☎ 61 21 166)* just south of the train station, is open weekdays from 9 am to 8 pm, Saturday 9 am to 2 pm. Concerts also take place at the *Croatian Music Institute (☎ 424 533, Gundulićeva 6a)* off Ilica. There are performances at the **Puppet Theatre** *(ulica Baruna Trenka 3)* Saturday at 5 pm and Sunday at noon.

Discos *Kulušić (Hrvojeva 6)*, near the Sheraton Hotel (open Thursday to Sunday from 10 pm to 4 am), is a casual, funky disco that offers occasional live bands, fashion shows and record promos as well as standard disco fare.

Sokol klub, across the street from the Ethnographic Museum (open Wednesday to Sunday from 10 pm to 4 am) is more polished and admits women free before midnight. Live rock concerts are presented every Sunday.

The recently re-opened *Saloon (Tuškanac 1a)* deliberately tries to attract all ages during the week but at last report admitted only the over-25 crowd on weekends. It's open Tuesday to Saturday from 10 pm to 4 am.

The Best at the Sports Centre 'Mladost', Horvaćanski zavoj, is near the student dorm Stjepan Radić and is one of the hottest spots in town (open Wednesday to Sunday from 10 pm to 4 am). Take tram 5 or 17 to the Studenski Dom stop. *Aquarius* is on Jarun Lake and is open Monday to Saturday from 9 am to 4 am. Entry is about 30KN at all of the above discos.

Cinemas There are 18 cinemas in Zagreb which show foreign movies in their original language with subtitles. Posters around town advertise the programs. *Kinoteca (Kordunska 1)* shows classic foreign movies weekdays at 6.30 pm.

Spectator Sports

Basketball is popular in Zagreb, and from October to April games take place at the Cibona Centar, Savska cesta 30 opposite the Technical Museum, usually on Saturday at 7.30 pm. Tickets are available at the door.

Football matches are held on Sunday afternoon at the Maksimir Stadium, Maksimirska 128 on the east side of Zagreb (tram No 4, 7, 11 or 12 to Bukovačka). If you arrive too early for the game, Zagreb's zoo is just across the street.

Jarun Lake hosts competitions in rowing, kayaking, and canoeing in the summer and there's a racetrack in south Zagreb, across the Sava River.

Shopping

Ilica is Zagreb's main shopping street. Get in touch with Croatian consumerism at the Nama department store on Ilica near Trg Jelačića.

Folk-music CDs are available from Fonoteca at Nama. Rokotvorine, Trg Jelačića 7, sells traditional Croatian handicrafts such as red and white embroidered tablecloths, dolls and pottery.

The shops, fast food outlets and grocery stores in the Importanne mall under the tracks beside the train station have long opening hours.

Getting There & Away

Bus Zagreb's big, modern bus station has a large, enclosed waiting room where you can stretch out while waiting for your bus (but be warned – there's no heating in winter).

Buy most international tickets at window Nos 11 and 12, and change money (including travellers cheques) at A Tours, open seven days a week from 6 am to 8 pm. The left-luggage office is always open, but take care – they charge a massive 1.20KN *per hour*. Call ☎ 060 313 333 for all bus information.

Buses depart from Zagreb for most of Croatia, Slovenia and places beyond. Buy an advance ticket at the station if you're planning on travelling far.

The following domestic buses depart from Zagreb:

destination	distance	frequency	cost
Dubrovnik	713km	8 daily	140KN
Krk	229km	3 daily	95KN
Ljubljana	135km	5 daily	60KN
Plitvice	140km	19 daily	40KN
Poreč	264km	6 daily	65KN
Pula	283km	13 daily	100KN
Rab	211km	1 daily	60KN
Rijeka	173km	21 daily	70KN
Rovinj	278km	8 daily	110KN
Split	478km	27 daily	100KN
Varaždin	77km	20 daily	43KN
Mali Lošinj	298km	1 daily	120KN
Zadar	320km	20 daily	80KN

Bus service has resumed to Yugoslavia. From 5 am to 1 pm there are hourly buses to Belgrade, changing at the border town, Bajakovo, for a local bus. The six hour trip costs 180KN. There are two buses a day to Sarajevo (417km, 362KN) and four to Međugorje (420km, 153KN).

To Hungary, there's Zagreb-Nagykanizsa (145km, twice daily, 55KN), five daily Zagreb-Barcs buses (202km, 90KN). Nagykanizsa is preferable if you're bound for Budapest or Lake Balaton, Barcs for Pécs or Yugoslavia. Other international buses worth knowing about are Zagreb to Vienna (twice daily, 157KN), Munich (576km, twice daily, 285KN) and Berlin (twice daily, DM190, payment in Deutschmarks only). Luggage is DM5 per piece.

Train The *Venezia* and *Maestral* express trains depart from Zagreb for Budapest (412km, seven hours, 181KN) every morning. The *Avas* leaves early afternoon and the *Kvarner* late afternoon. A ticket from Zagreb to Nagykanizsa, the first main junction inside Hungary, is 72KN. A useful daily train runs between Zagreb and Pécs, Hungary (267km, five hours, 105KN).

Zagreb is on both the Munich-Ljubljana and Vienna-Maribor main lines. There are trains twice a day between Munich and Zagreb (613km, nine hours, 443KN) via Salzburg. Two trains a day arrive from Venice (seven hours, 226KN).

The following domestic trains depart from Zagreb:

destination	distance	frequency	time	cost
Osijek	288km	4 daily	4½ hrs	73KN
Koprivnica	92km	6 daily	2 hrs	29KN
Varaždin	110km	13 daily	3 hrs	33KN
Ljubljana	160km	7 daily	3 hrs	62KN
Rijeka	243km	4 daily	5 hrs	58KN
Pula	418km	2 daily	5½ hrs	145KN
Split	535km	4 daily	9 hrs	91KN
Zadar	311km	2 daily	11 hrs	80KN

Trains to Zadar stop at Knin.
Reservations are required on some trains.

For train information call ☎ 9830.

Getting Around

Public transport is based on an efficient but overcrowded network of trams, although the city centre is compact enough to make them unnecessary.

Zagreb has recently installed welcome tram maps at most stations making the system easier to navigate. Tram Nos 3 and 8 don't run on weekends. Buy tickets (4.50KN) at newspaper kiosks. You can use your ticket for transfers within 90 minutes, but only in one direction.

A day ticket (*dnevna karta*), valid on all public transport until 4 am the next morning, is available for 12KN at most Vjesnik or Tisak news outlets.

To/From the Airport The Croatia Airlines bus to Pleso Airport, 17km south-east of Zagreb, leaves from the bus station every half-hour or hour from about 4 am to 8.30 pm depending on flights and returns from the airport on about the same schedule (20KN).

Taxi Zagreb's taxis all have meters which begin at a whopping 15KN and then ring up 6KN per kilometre. On Sunday and nights from 10 pm to 5 am there's a 20% surcharge. Waiting time is 40KN an hour. The baggage surcharge is 2KN per suitcase. At those rates, you'll have no trouble finding idle taxis, usually at blue-marked taxi signs or you can call ☎ 970 to reserve a taxi.

Car Of the major car rental companies, Budget Rent-a-Car (☎ 45 54 936) in the Hotel Sheraton often has the lowest rates (325KN a day including unlimited kilometres). Other companies are Europcar (☎ 65 54 003) at the airport, Avis Autotehna (☎ 48 36 296) at the Intercontinental Hotel, and Hertz (☎ 48 47 222), Kačićeva 9a, on the western side of the Intercontinental Hotel.

Local companies usually have lower rates, so shop around. Try Niva Rent-a-Car (☎ 61 59 280), Miramarska 22 near the Hotel Esplanade, and, at the airport, Mack (☎ 442 222) and Uni Rent (☎ 65 25 006).

Around Zagreb

HRVATSKO ZAGORJE

Too-often ignored by travellers making a bee-line for the coast, the 'Croatian Zagorje' north-west of Zagreb offers green, rolling hills dotted with bucolic villages, medieval castles, and thermal springs. The region begins north of Medvednica Mountain outside of Zagreb and extends west to the Slovenian border, east to the E71 highway and almost as far north as Varaždin. Over 40% of the surface is covered with forests, mostly beech, oak, chestnut and fir trees. The sandy soil is generally unreceptive to cultivation but you'll see some vineyards, orchards and an occasional corn or wheat field. Besides the landscape, the main attractions of the region are castles, museums and a taste of small-town life in the Croatian interior.

The Zagorje region has been inhabited since the Paleolithic age. On Hušnjakovo hill, near **Krapina**, archaeological excavations revealed human and animal bones from a Neanderthal tribe that lived in the cave from 100,000 to 35,000 BC. Some 650 bones belonging to 80 Neanderthals were found along with tools and weapons, making the site one of the most significant in Europe.

Although the bones and artefacts are now displayed in the Museum of Natural Sciences in Zagreb, there's a park on the hill with sculpted life-size models of Neanderthals in everyday activities such as wielding clubs and throwing stones. The nearby Museum of Evolution, Šetalište V Sluge bb, has a few prehistoric artefacts and other exhibits tracing the history and geology of the region. It's open daily from 8 am to 6 pm.

The town of Krapina is unremarkable but you can take a look at the baroque Franciscan monastery and church with a 17th century altar and 18th century paintings. Next to the church is an 18th century column dedicated to the Virgin Mary. There's also a City Art Gallery, Magistratska 25, which is open Monday to Saturday

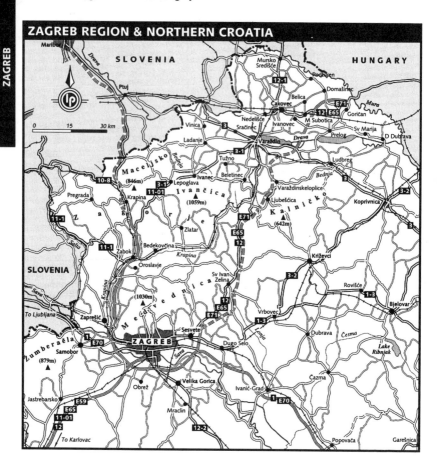

ZAGREB REGION & NORTHERN CROATIA

from 10 am to 1 pm. If you're around at the beginning of September, check out the Festival of Kajkavian Songs which includes regional folklore concerts, poetry readings and a lot of delicious Zagorje food in street stalls.

The Croatian aristocracy began building fortified castles in the region to stave off the Turkish threat at the end of the 16th century. **Veliki Tabor**, 57km north-west of Zagreb,

was built in the early 16th century and restored several times. Strategically perched on top of a hill, the fortress-mansion has everything a medieval master could want – towers, turrets, and holes in the walls for pouring tar and hot oil on the enemy. It later belonged to the venerable Ratkaj family, then the painter Iveković and is now used as an exhibition space while restoration work continues. It's open daily from 10 am to 5 pm.

The most impressive castle in Croatia is **Trakošćan Castle**, 83km north-west of Zagreb. Although the exact date of its construction is unknown, it retains classical 12th and 13th century features and was occupied by the aristocratic Draškovićs from the end of the 16th century. Unlike Veliki Tabor, the interior is furnished with original pieces from the Drašković family who occupied the castle until the early 20th century. When the castle was restored in 1860 the surrounding grounds were landscaped and turned into an attractive park with exotic trees and an artificial lake. If you wonder what the Draškovićs looked like, there are plenty of family portraits throughout the castle as well as an armaments collection, cavalry flats, a kitchen and library. Note the unusual exterior heating system that allowed servants to stoke the fires without entering the family rooms. The castle is open daily from 9 am to 6 pm.

The Zagorje region was also the birthplace of several celebrated Croats, most notably Maršal Tito, born as Josip Broz in **Kumrovec**. The entire village has been transformed into a recreation of a 19th century village. About 40 houses and barns made of pressed earth and wood have been preserved and filled with tools, furniture, and mannequins in order to evoke their original function. There are toys in the toymaker's hut, a wine press in the winemaker's hut, a blacksmith's hut with tools and so forth. Lying on a slope beside the Sutla River with a stream bubbling through the bucolic setting, this open-air museum presents an idyllic view of village life (if villages were this pleasant, no one would ever have left) but the thoughtful exhibits and captions in English give a vivid glimpse of traditional peasant life. It's open daily from 8 am to 4 pm, and on weekends from May to September there are demonstrations of traditional blacksmithing, pottery, and weaving.

The sculptor Antun Augustinčić (1900-79), who created the Monument to Peace in front of the United Nations building in New York, was another notable from Zagorje.

His hometown, **Klanjec**, has a museum devoted to his work, including his memorial to fallen Partisans. The small town makes a pleasant stroll and there's a 17th century baroque church. The museum is open Monday to Saturday from 9 am to 4 pm.

The largest pilgrimage centre in Croatia is in Zagorje at **Marija Bistrica**, a village on the northern slopes of Medvednica Mountain. The focus of attention is the Marija Bistrica church which contains a wooden Gothic statue of the Madonna created in the 16th century. The statue's alleged miraculous power dates back to the 16th century Turkish invasions when the statue was saved from destruction. The church attracts 600,000 visitors a year and is reached by the 'Way of the Cross', adorned with works by Croatian sculptors.

Getting There & Away

The best way to experience Zagorje is by car, as it allows you to visit all of the above sights in a day trip. However, there are regular buses to most destinations. There are nine buses a day from Zagreb to Krapina (61km) on weekdays and four on weekends. There are two daily buses to Kumrovec (49km) that stop in Klanjec (43km) and six daily buses to Desinić (60km) which is 3km west of Veliki Tabor. There are no buses from Zagreb to Trakošćan but there are hourly buses from Varaždin (40km). There are 15 buses a day to Marija Bistrica (32km) from Monday to Saturday and eight on Sunday.

BANIJA-KORDUN REGION

Lying south of Zagreb and bounded by the Sava River basin in the north, the Una and Kupa rivers in the east and west, and Mala Kapela Mountain in the south, the Banija-Kordun region had little tourism before the recent war and now has nearly none. The large Serbian majority made it a tempting target for Serbian expansion in the early days of the recent war and large parts of the region remained under Serbian control until 1995. Before the war, the region's many rivers were popular with local anglers and

ZAGREB

Josip Broz Tito

Josip Broz was born in Kumvrovec in 1892, to a Croat father and Slovene mother. When WWI broke out, Tito was drafted into the Austro-Hungarian army and was taken prisoner by the Russians. He escaped just before the 1917 revolution, became a communist and joined the Red Army, where he served with distinction. He returned to Croatia in 1920 and became a union organiser while working as a metalworker.

As secretary of the Zagreb committee of the outlawed Communist Party, he worked hard to unify the party and managed to dramatically increase its membership by the end of the 1930s. When the Nazis invaded Yugoslavia in 1941 he adopted the name Tito, after the 18th century Croat writer Tito Brezovački, and organised small bands of guerrillas called partisans. His successful campaign against the Germans, Italians and Chetniks attracted military support from the British and Americans but Russia repeatedly rebuffed his requests for aid, perhaps setting the stage for the later rift between Yugoslavia and the Soviet Union.

In 1945, he became Premier of a reconstituted Yugoslavia. Although loyal to Moscow, Tito had a pronounced streak of independence that led him to clash sharply with Stalin. In 1948 he was effectively banished from the Cominform (the Communist Information Bureau, established in 1947 to exchange information between European communist parties) and thereafter adopted a conciliatory policy towards the west which nevertheless continued to consider Yugoslavia as a Soviet satellite state.

Yugoslavia's rival nationalities were Tito's biggest headache which he dealt with by suppressing all dissent and trying to ensure a rough equality of representation at the upper echelons of government. Although he was half-Croat, he manifested no particular favouritism towards Croat interests and resided in Belgrade. None of his wives or mistresses were Croat (in fact two were Serb) and Tito never publicly referred to himself as a Croat. As a committed communist, he viewed ethnic disputes as unwelcome deviations from the common pursuit of the common good.

Yet Tito was well aware of the ethnic tensions that simmered just below the surface of Yugoslavia. Preparations for his succession began in the early 1970s as he aimed to create a balance of power among the ethnic groups of Yugoslavia. He set up a collective presidency that was to rotate annually among representatives of each of the six republics plus Serbia's two autonomous provinces of Kosovo and Vojvodina. The system proved unworkable. Later events revealed how dependent Yugoslavia was on their wily, charismatic leader.

When Tito died in May 1980, his body was carried from Ljubljana to Belgrade in a blue train. Thousands of mourners flocked the streets to pay respects to the man who had united a difficult country for 35 years. It was the last common outpouring of emotion that all Yugoslavia's fractious nationalities were able to share.

hunters combed the woods for prey. The many mines laid in the countryside around Karlovac and Sisak have ended sporting activities and, outside of the main towns, the region is unsafe to visit. If you travel through Banija-Kordun, it's important not to stray from the main roads. Karlovac, Sisak and most small villages were badly damaged during the recent war and are undergoing reconstruction.

Karlovac lies on the main road that links Zagreb with Rijeka at the confluence of four rivers – the Kupa, the Korana, the Mrežnica and the Dobra. The town was constructed in 1579 as a military stronghold against the Turks and it's historical centre is shaped in the form of a six-point star, divided into 24 almost rectangular blocks. Although only the moats remain from the original fortification, the town centre retains its tidy geometrical streets of baroque buildings that radiate out from the central square, Trg Jelačića. The 17th century Church of the Holy Trinity, with its black marble altar and the adjacent Franciscan Monastery, are the highlights of Trg Jelačića. The north-western part of the old town contains a semicircular baroque-style square built in the 18th century that features the town museum. Housed in an early baroque palace, the museum has a collection of archaeological and historical exhibits as well as displays of local handicrafts. Swimming and fishing are popular activities in the nearby rivers.

Sisak lies at the confluence of the Kupa and Sava rivers and is Croatia's largest river port. The highlight of the town is the unusual 16th century triangular fortress that was built as a defence against the Turks and was the scene of an important victory by Croatian forces in 1593. The well-preserved fortress has three massive cylindrical towers that were restored after WWII. Now turned into a museum, the fortress is well worth a visit if only for the tranquil views over the Kupa River. Other town highlights include several baroque palaces and the brick Old Bridge (Stari Most) over the Kupa River.

Getting There & Away

Karlovac and Sisak are well linked to Zagreb by train and bus, making them easy day trips. There are 11 daily passenger trains making the 40 minute trip to Sisak, and buses run about every 30 minutes (57km). There are four express trains to Karlovac a day that take 40 minutes, and 11 regular trains taking one hour as well as buses every 30 minutes (55km).

SAMOBOR

Samobor is a picture-perfect little town 20km west of Zagreb that is a favourite retreat for big-city folk taking a breather from Zagreb's noise and bustle. A shallow stream stocked with trout curves through a town centre composed of trim pastel houses and several old churches. The town has conserved its culture as well as its architecture. The small family businesses involved in handicrafts, restaurants, and the production of mustard and 'spirits' have survived well, seemingly untouched by the political fads sweeping through the rest of the country. The literary and musical tradition that produced the poet Stanko Vraz and the composer Ferdo Livadić is reflected in a number of annual festivals, most famously the Samobor Carnival (fašnik) on the eve of Lent which attracts some 300,000 visitors.

Orientation & Information

The bus stop (no left-luggage office) is on Šmidheva, about 100m uphill from the town, which centres on Trg Kralja Tomislava. The Turistički Ured (☎/fax 780 044, fax 780 054), Trg Kralja Tomislava 5 is open Monday to Friday from 8 am to 3 pm, Saturday 8.30 am to noon and Sunday from 3 to 8 pm but they have little information. The postcode for Samobor is 10430.

Things to See & Do

The hills surrounding Samobor offer great hiking opportunities. From the town centre you can see the ruins of the old medieval fort perched on a hill west of town. You'll find the footpath by following the stream west and it only takes about 40 minutes to reach the top. Other peaks include Plešivica (780m) and Oštrc (753m). The tourist office has maps of the surrounding hills.

Places to Eat

The main thing to do in Samobor is eat and walk and then maybe eat again. The town is renowned for its cuisine which is the main draw for its bustling tourist business. Meals tend to be more expensive than in Zagreb but well worth it. *Pri Staroj Vuri (Giznik 2)* is about 50m uphill from the town square, Trg Kralja Tomislava, and serves traditional family dishes in a homey cottage. The restaurant sometimes hosts poetry readings. The specialties of the house are *Hrvatska pisanica* (beefsteak in a spicy mushroom, onion, tomato and red wine sauce) and *Šruklova Juha* (soup with štrukli). A two-course meal runs from 70 to 100KN and the restaurant is open Monday to Saturday from 10 am to 11 pm, Sunday 10 am to 5 pm.

For a less expensive meal, try *Samoborska Pivnica (Šmidhena 3)* on the edge of the parking lot which also serves well-prepared dishes for 30KN to 55KN. It's open Sunday to Thursday from 9 am to 11 pm, Friday and Saturday 9 am to midnight. The best *kremšnite* (custard slice) in town is served on the main square at *U Prolazu (Trg Kralja Tomislava 5),* open daily from 8 am to midnight.

Shopping

The local aperitif is a delicious, woody red drink called *Bermet* that Samobor has been producing for centuries according to a top-secret recipe. It's not for every taste so try it in town first with lemon and ice before deciding to buy a bottle which will cost about 80KN. *Samoborska Muštarda,* Samobor mustard, is from another age-old recipe. 40KN may seem expensive for mustard, but it comes in attractive (and re-usable) clay pots.

Getting There & Away

Samobor is easy to reach. Local buses leave from the Central bus station in Zagreb every half hour or so for the price of a local ride.

VARAŽDIN

Varaždin, 81kms north of Zagreb, is a useful transit point on the way to/from Hungary and a pleasant town in which to pass the day. As the centre of Varaždin county, the city is known mainly for its castle and baroque buildings but it also played an important role in Croatia's history.

At the intersection of several Roman roads, the town of Garestine, now Varaždin, became a local administrative centre in 1181 under King Bela III. It was later raised to the status of a free royal borough and given its own seal and coat of arms.

When Croatia was under siege by the Turks, Varaždin was the most powerful stronghold on the Slavonian frontier and the residence of choice for generals. As the threat receded Varaždin prospered and the cultural, political and commercial centre of Croatia and was made the capital in 1756, a position it held until 1776.

The town's position near northern Europe and it's prosperity facilitated the development of baroque architecture that was flourishing in Europe during this period. Top artisans and builders gravitated to the town, designing mansions, churches and public buildings in the new style. After the disastrous fire of 1776, the Croatian Ban moved his administration to Zagreb and the town was left to rebuild.

Today the town is a centre for textiles, shoes, furniture and agricultural products. The town has an army base that had belonged to the former Yugoslav army but the town was left unscathed by the recent war and remains relatively prosperous. Accommodation is less expensive than in Zagreb and offers better value so you may wish to spend a night here on your way to or from the capital.

Orientation

The bus and train station are at opposite ends of town, about 2km apart and not linked by public transportation. The town centre lies between them and to the north. The main commercial street lined with Varaždin's famous baroque buildings is

Gundulića; it leads to the main square, Trg Kralja Tomislava. The left-luggage office at the bus station is open daily from 6 am to 10 pm and costs 5KN per day. The left-luggage office at the train station is open 24 hours and costs 10KN.

Information

At the bus station, Autobus Promet is open Monday to Saturday from 8 am to 8.30 pm, Sunday 1 pm to 8.30 pm to change money and sell international bus tickets. Croatia Express at the train station is open Monday to Friday from 8 am to 6 pm, and Saturday from 8 am to 3 pm to change money and sell rail tickets.

The Turistički Ured (☎ 210 987), Padovčeva 3, is open Monday to Friday from 8 am to 4 pm.

T-Tours (☎ 210 989, fax 210 990), Gundulićeva 2, finds private accommodation and is a good source of information on town events. Atlas travel agency (☎ 320 718), Pavlinska 5, is open Monday to Friday from 8 am to 8 pm, Saturday 8 am to 1 pm.

The main post office, at Trg Sloboda 9, is open Monday to Saturday from 7 am to 9 pm, and 9 am to noon on Sunday. The postcode for Varaždin is 42000.

You can change money at the bus or train station, the post office or at any bank. All branches of Varaždinska Banka have ATM machines where you can withdraw cash using Cirrus, MasterCard or Eurocard. There is a branch close to the bus station at Zagrebačka 12.

Things to See

The town is justifiably proud of its **Castle**, Strossmera 7, which is really a fortress and a beautifully preserved example of medieval defensive architecture. Construction began in the 14th century but it was the Earl of Celje who turned it into a strong fortress in the 15th century, adding the rounded towers that typify Gothic architecture in northern Croatia.

By the early 16th century, it was the chief regional fortification against the encroaching Ottoman Turks. It remained in private

hands until 1925 when it was turned into the town museum.

Today, it houses furniture, paintings, decorative objects and weapons amassed during the course of Varaždin's history. The museum is open Tuesday to Friday from 10 am to 5 pm, Saturday and Sunday from 10 am to 1 pm. Admission is 12KN (8KN for students). The architecture alone is worth the price and the exhibits are interesting. The town also has an art gallery, the **Gallery of Old and Modern Masters**, Trg Staričića 3, which exhibits portraits and landscapes from Italian, Dutch, German and Flemish schools. It's open Tuesday to Friday from 10 am to 5 pm, Saturday and Sunday 10 am to 1 pm. Admission is 12KN (8KN for students).

Special Events

Varaždin is famous for its baroque music festival *Varaždin Baroque Evenings* that takes place for three to four weeks each September. Local and international orchestras play baroque music in churches and theatres around the city for prices that range from 10 to 100KN, depending on the program. There's also a Summer Cultural Festival in July and August of music, dance and theatre; it's often held in the city's squares and parks.

What's Free

The best sight in Varaždin is the town centre, composed of baroque buildings ornamented with pastel stucco. Trg Kralja Tomislava is the central square dominated by the Town Council building with a tower that makes it resemble a church. The old streets radiate from the square in a large pedestrian zone of attractive 18th century buildings. There's a guard-changing ceremony in front of the Town Council building every Saturday from 10 am to noon.

ZAGREB

Places to Stay

Camping Since the recent war there has been no camping grounds between the Hungarian border and Zagreb but that is changing. There is a hotel/camping ground opening about 8km south of Varaždin on the road to Zagreb. No information was available at the time this book was printed, but ask about Camp Varaždin Breg at the tourist office or the T-Tours agency.

Private Rooms The only agency in town that finds rooms is T-Tours, which has top end singles/doubles for 100/170KN and mid-range rooms for 85KN/140KN. There is no supplement for a single night stay and prices stay the same year-round. There aren't many rooms available, but then there also aren't many people asking for them either.

Hotels Hotels in Varaždin are clean, well-maintained and offer good value for money. Their clientele is mostly made up of visiting business people from Zagreb and neighbouring countries – this means they are likely to be full during the week and empty on weekends. The cheapest place in town is *Pansion Maltar* (☎ 55 111, fax 211 190, Pre*šernova 1*), across from the bus station. This cheerful little pansion has only 10 rooms so book in advance. Rooms are in excellent condition and have satellite TV but no telephones. Prices are 180/354KN a single/double. *Garestin* hotel (☎/fax 214 314, Zagrebačka 34) is the newest establishment with a glossy modern decor that usually indicates high prices. Yet, rooms with phones, TV and minibar cost a reasonable 250/360KN a single/double and the hotel is only a short walk from the bus station. At the higher end of the range, there is the *Hotel Turist* (☎ 105 105, Kralja Zvonimira 1) which has simple rooms for 257/378KN and renovated 'business class' rooms for 357/588KN.

Places to Eat

One of the newer additions to the restaurant scene is *Tempio* (*Prešlernova 3*), which offers fine local specialties such as *husarska pečenka* (steak with onions and bacon) for

55KN and fried or baked vegetable platters for 29KN, in a modern mirrored interior or on an attractive terrace. Prices will probably rise along with the restaurant's popularity but right now it's a steal. It's open Monday to Thursday from 11 am to 10 pm, Friday and Saturday 11 am to 11 pm. *Park (Habdelić 6)* overlooks a leafy park and offers grilled meat or chicken for 38KN to 55KN and a salad buffet for 20KN. It's open daily from 8 am to 11 pm. *The 'Raj' Club (Gundulića 11)* is in the centre of town and offers local dishes such as venison goulash for about 25KN and pizza for 15KN. It's open Monday to Saturday from 9 am to 11 pm. There's a daily market at Bana Jelačića trg until 2 pm and many bakeries sell Varaždin's special finger-shaped bread, *klipići*.

Getting There & Away

Varaždin is a major transportation hub in north Croatia with bus and train lines running in all directions. For long-haul buses to Germany and northern Europe, see the Getting There & Away section for Zagreb, since all buses originate there, stop at Varaždin and cost the same whether you buy the ticket in Zagreb or Varaždin. There are also daily buses to Split (10½ hours, 125KN), Rijeka (five hours, 96KN), Pula (seven hours, 128KN) and Dubrovnik (14 hours, 270KN – this service stops in Bosnia at Mostar and Međugorje). Four buses a day go to Zadar (seven hours, 99KN) in the summer, dropping to one a day from September to May. There's a daily early morning bus to Nagykanizsa, Hungary (three hours, 29KN), and a daily bus to Graz, Austria (three hours, 54KN). There are buses to Trakošćan about every hour (one hour, 16KN) and buses to Zagreb every half-hour to hour (two hours, 43KN).

There's a daily train to Rijeka (seven hours, 80KN) and Zadar in the summer (11 hours, 117KN). There are two trains a day to Budapest (155KN) that stop at Nagykanizsa and an additional unreserved train to Nagykanizsa (40KN). The only train to Vienna takes 11 hours (280KN), making a direct train from Zagreb a better bet.

Slavonia

Slavonia is a fertile region that stretches from the Ilova River in the west, over the Sava and Drava basins to the Hungarian border in the north, to the border of Bosnia-Hercegovina in the south and the Yugoslav border in the east. It includes the counties of Osijek-Baranja, Vukovar-Srijem, and part of Brodsko-Posavska.

The land is the most productive in Croatia, yielding wheat, corn, sugar beets, sunflowers, alfalfa and clover, as well as oil and gas. In contrast to the rugged Croatian coastline, the terrain is pancake-flat; as locals say, 'The highest mountain is a cabba.

The region had been prosperous until the recent war destroyed the economy, and once had splendid cities of baroque buildings and castles – until they were torn apart by Serbian artillery.

Before the 1991 war displaced tens of thousands of inhabitants, Slavonia contained one of the most ethnically diverse populations in Europe. Settled by Slavic tribes in the 7th century, the region was conquered by the Turks in the 16th century. Catholic residents fled and Serbian Orthodox settlers, who were better received by the Turks, arrived en masse.

In 1690, Serb supporters of Vienna, in their battles with the Turks, left Kosovo and settled in the Srijem region around Vukovar. The Turks ceded the land to Austria in 1699 and the Habsburgs turned a large part of the region into a Military Frontier (Vojna Krajina).

The Muslim population fled but more Serbs arrived, joined by German merchants, Hungarian, Slovak and Ukrainian peasants, Catholic Albanians and Jews. Much land was sold to German and Hungarian aristocrats who built huge baroque and classical mansions around Osijek, Vukovar, Ilok and other towns.

Many Germans were killed or expelled after WWI and WWII and their home-

HIGHLIGHTS

- Swimming in the Drava River
- Sampling the spicy fish stew, *riblji paprikaš*
- Strolling the riverside promenade

HUNGARY

YUGO-
SLAVIA

Osijek p106

BOSNIA-HERCEGOVINA

SLAVONIA

steads occupied by Serbs and Montenegrins from southern Yugoslavia.

The large Serbian minority prompted Serbian president Slobodan Milošević's attempt to incorporate the region into 'Greater Serbia'. This assault began with the destruction of Vukovar and the shelling of Osijek in 1991. A cease-fire prevailed in 1992, but it wasn't until January 1998 that the region was returned to Croatia as part of the Dayton peace agreement.

Large parts of the region's eastern portion were mined during the occupation, and land mine clearance operations are not

SLAVONIA

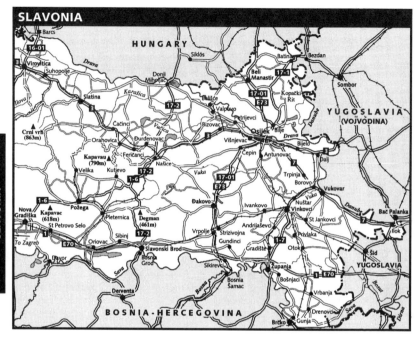

yet complete. Housing is a major problem as displaced Serbs and Croats return to their ruined villages.

Outside of Osijek, the largest city in Slavonia, there is little accommodation available for visitors and, until the land mines are removed, the countryside is extremely unsafe to visit.

OSIJEK

• pop 104,760   ☎ 031

Photographs of Osijek before the recent war reveal a relaxed river city of wide avenues, leafy parks and stately 19th century Viennese architecture. The avenues and parks are still there, but the fine old mansions were badly scarred by the shells that fell on the town as part of the 1991 Yugoslav offensive.

Although many major buildings along the avenue were patched up and restored to their former lustre, the pits and pockmarks on other buildings are grim reminders of the war that ravaged Eastern Slavonia in the early 1990s.

Nevertheless, through the general aura of decay, you can still perceive the resilient spirit of the city. A severe shortage of accommodation makes a visit here problematic and expensive but if you're willing to put up with the hassle, there's a pleasant waterfront promenade, swimming in the Drava River and an imposing 18th century fortress on the hill.

Osijek's excellent location on the Drava River, near its junction with the Danube, has made it strategically important for more than two millenia. After the Illyrians, the Romans arrived in the 1st century and built a military colony; these buildings were destroyed in the Barbarian invasions of the 6th century.

It was the Slav settlers that gave Osijek its name and by the 12th century it was a thriving market town owned by the Cistercian abbey. When the Turks conquered Osijek in 1529, they made it an important administrative centre and the town became predominantly Muslim.

The Austrians finally chased the Turks out in 1687, the Muslims fled into Bosnia and the city was repopulated with Serbs, Croats, Germans and Hungarians. The new settlers erased all remnants of Turkish rule and demolished the mosques, erecting churches on the ruins.

Still wary of Turkish attacks, the Austrians made Osijek the capital of the Slavonian Military Frontier and in the early 18th century, built the fortress, Tvrđa, that still dominates the town.

Osijek prospered during the 18th and 19th centuries and remained part of the Austro-Hungarian empire until 1918 when it joined the Kingdom of Serbs, Croats and Slovenes. Until the recent war, Osijek was a powerful industrial centre producing matches, beer, refined sugar, chemicals, textiles, shoes and agricultural machinery.

When war broke out in 1991 following Croatia's declaration of independence, the federal Yugoslav army and Serbian paramilitary units overran the Baranja region north of Osijek.

The first shells began falling in July 1991 from Serbian positions across the Drava River and continued into the autumn. When Vukovar fell in November of that year, federal and Serbian forces made Osijek the object of their undivided attention, pounding the city with artillery as thousands of terrified residents poured out of the city. By that time, Serbian President Milošević was committing Yugoslavia to a peace-keeping operation, and the expected destruction of Osijek never materialised, but the shelling continued until May 1992.

The city is now struggling to recover, but the economy has been badly hurt by the cost of reconstruction, housing refugees and the loss of markets for its products.

Orientation

Stretching along the southern bank of the Drava River, Osijek is composed of three settlements: the Upper Town, the Lower Town and the 18th century fortress, Tvrđa. The bus station and train station are adjacent in the southern part of the Upper Town, and you'll find most sights, hotels, cafés and shopping between the train and bus station and the river. There is no left-luggage office in the train station but there is one in the bus station which is open Monday to Saturday from 7 am to 8 pm and Sunday 7 am to 4 pm.

The main shopping street is Kapucinska which becomes Europska Avenija in the east, bordered by three parks planted with chestnut and linden trees. A promenade stretches along the riverbanks till the city's outskirts.

Information

Tourist Offices The Turistički Ured (☎ 23 755, fax 23 947, grad-osijek@os.tel.hr), Županijska 2, has a good set of brochures and maps and is open Monday to Friday from 7 am to 8 pm and Saturday 8 am to noon.

Money Croatia Express, in the train station, changes money. It's open Monday to Friday from 7 am to 7.30 pm and Saturday 7 am to 5 pm.

In town, you can change money at Zagrebačka Banka, Strossmayera 1. It's open Monday to Friday from 7.30 am to 7 pm and Saturday 7.30 am to noon, as well as at other banks in the town centre. There is also an ATM at Zagrebačka Banka which accepts Cirrus and MasterCard.

Post & Communications The main post office is at Alojzija Stepinca 17 and is open Monday to Saturday from 7 am to 8 pm, and on Sunday from 8 am to noon and 4 to 9 pm.

You can change money, make phone calls and get cash on MasterCard. The postcode for Osijek is 31000.

SLAVONIA

Travel Agencies Panturist (☎ 23 388), Kapucinska 19, is the largest travel agency in Slavonia and runs buses to the coast as well as Germany, Switzerland and Bosnia-Hercegovina. It sells bus and air tickets and arranges accommodation along the Adriatic coast. Opening times are Monday to Friday from 8 am to 8 pm and Saturday 8 am to 1 pm.

Generalturist (☎ 211 500), Kapucinska 41, sells air tickets and package tours to European destinations.

Dangers & Annoyances Osijek and the surrounding region was heavily laid with land mines during the recent war. Although the city and the outskirts along the main road have been de-mined and are completely safe, it would be unwise to set out into the swampland north of the Drava River that leads to Kopački Rit.

In summer, the mosquitoes are bloodthirsty little devils, chewing through every bit of flesh they can find. Wear long sleeves and trousers or slather on a lot of repellent after dark.

Things to See & Do

Tvrđa Built under Habsburg rule as a defence against Turkish attacks, this 18th century fortress was relatively undamaged during the recent war, leaving its baroque architecture intact. Because most of it was designed solely by the Austrian architect Maximilian de Gosseau between 1712 and 1721, the buildings present a remarkable architectural unity.

The main square, Trg Svetog Trojstva, is marked by the elaborate **Holy Trinity Monument**, erected in 1729 to commemorate the victims of the 15th century plague that swept through the city.

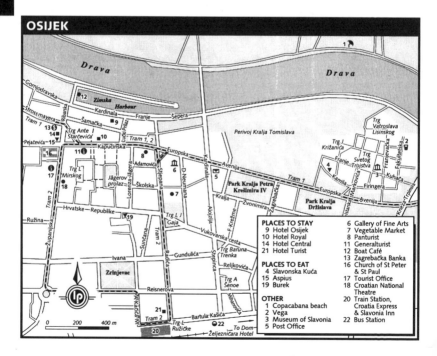

The **Museum of Slavonia,** Trg sv. Trojstva 6, on the east side of the square is housed in the former Magistrate Building of 1702. Open daily from 10 am to 1 pm, the museum traces Slavonia's long history beginning with Bronze Age implements and displays of coins, pottery, sculpture and utensils from the Roman occupation.

Upper Town The towering **Church of Saint Peter and Paul** looms over Trg Ante Starčeća. The 90m-high tower is the second highest in Croatia, surpassed only by the cathedral in Zagreb. Although often referred to as the 'Cathedral' because of its size and majesty, in fact this brick neogothic structure is a parish church built at the end of the 19th century. The style is Viennese, from the overall design to the 40 stained glass windows inside as well as the stonework from the Viennese sculptor Eduard Hauser. The wall paintings have long been attributed to Croatian painter, Mirko Rački, but recent scholarship indicates that they were in fact executed by one of his disciples.

The **Gallery of Fine Arts,** Europska avenija 9, is housed in an elegant 19th century mansion and contains a collection of paintings by Slavonian artists and some contemporary Croatian works. It's open Monday to Friday from 9 am to 1 pm.

Swimming The Drava River is clean and you can take a refreshing dip on a muggy summer day. The current can be strong but there is a safe roped off area on the north bank called the 'Copacabana' directly across from Tvrđa.

Places to Stay

Hotels in Osijek are a rip-off and unfortunately there are no alternative places to stay. The private accommodation that existed before the war is now occupied by refugees and there are no camping grounds or hostels.

As there have been virtually no tourists since the outbreak of war in 1991, hotels have not had the revenue to perform the most basic maintenance. Their solution to this problem has been to jack up the prices and extract whatever money they can from the few visitors that wander into town.

The cheapest place to stay is the *Hotel Royal* (☎ 26 033, fax 24 628, Kapucinska 34), but at last report all rooms were occupied by refugees. The *Hotel Turist* (☎ 127 622, fax 23 636, Radića 58) has basic, poorly maintained rooms for 174/268KN for singles/doubles including breakfast. Only about 20% of the rooms are available for tourists, the rest are occupied by refugees.

Dom Željezničara (☎ 127 987, fax 27 599, Kašića 2) has rooms for 240/400KN. *Hotel Central* (☎ 126 188, fax 126 770, Trg Ante Starčevića 6) has the most character of any of the hotels with a stunning Art Deco lobby and café. It has rooms for 266/408KN.

The *Osijek* (☎ 125 333, fax 32 135, Šamačka 4) has rooms for 290/444KN without TV and minibar, and 370/568KN for renovated rooms with TV and minibar, some of which overlook the Drava but none of which are worth the price.

Places to Eat

Food is the strong point of Osijek and offers much better value for money than accommodation. The cuisine is spicy and strongly influenced by neighbouring Hungary, although Slavonia does produce its own brand of hot paprika. As elsewhere in Croatia, there is a strong emphasis on meat but you can also find freshwater fish, often served in a delicious stew called *riblji paprikaš* with noodles.

One of the best places to try the fish stew as well as other regional specialties is *Slavonska Kuća (Firingera 26, Tvrđa)*, in an appealingly rustic old house with wooden booths and lace curtains. You can get a main course for under 50KN and starters for 25KN. Wash it down with *Krauthaker*, a fruity white Grašenina wine. It's open daily from 9 am to midnight.

The Siege of Vukovar

Until 1991, Vukovar was a bustling town of elegant baroque mansions, art galleries and museums. It was one of the prettiest towns on the Danube with roots that stretched back to the 10th century.

Now it lies in charred ruins. The museums, galleries and library have been plundered, the mansions and churches reduced to rubble. The economy is destroyed and the mixed Serb-Croat population is just beginning to drift back to their rebuilt houses. What happened?

Vukovar is cursed with an unfortunate geography that placed it just across the river from the Vojvodina region of Serbia. As the gateway city to fertile, oil-rich eastern Slavonia, Vukovar had to be captured by the Serbs to realise their territorial ambitions in Croatia once former Yugoslavia disintegrated.

The military build-up around Vukovar began in July 1991 after the Serbs, supported by the federal Yugoslav forces, had already gained a foothold around Osijek. By August the city was surrounded by 600 tanks and 40,000 to 60,000 soldiers.

The sporadic shelling of July grew into a full-scale artillery and infantry assault on 25 August as the federal army attempted to seize the town. Although pitifully outnumbered, the town's defenders managed to repel the attack but by the end of August all but 15,000 of the Vukovar's original 50,000 inhabitants had fled.

On 14 September, the Serbs launched another attack on the city that stalled after about a week in the face of fierce resistance. The army changed its tactics and began an unremitting air and artillery assault. When the last land route out of the city fell to Serb-Yugoslav forces in October, the possibility of escape was virtually eliminated. The remaining Croat and Serb residents cowered in bomb-proof cellars, living on tinned food and rationed water while bodies piled up in the streets above them.

Still the city held out. Morale in the federal Yugoslav army crumbled as soldiers deserted or simply refused to fight while the heroism of the town's thousand or so defenders was broadcast nightly across Croatia. Appeals for international help went unheeded because, by that time, the world's attention was focused on Dubrovnik.

Although the assault on Vukovar was immeasurably more brutal than that launched upon Dubrovnik, the Adriatic city's renowned architectural heritage triumphed in the great global media sweepstakes and Vukovar was left to fend for itself.

The situation could not continue. After three weeks of hand-to-hand fighting, the town finally surrendered on 17 November. Thin, pale, mostly elderly civilians emerged from their cellars and trudged out of the city with whatever they could carry. But the agony of Vukovar had not yet ended.

On 19 November, Serb-Yugoslav soldiers entered Vukovar's hospital complex deliberately ahead of international monitors and massacred all but 60 of the 420 patients, dumping their bodies in a mass grave outside town. At the time of writing, this act was the subject of a war crimes investigation.

It's estimated that 1700 people – including 1100 civilians – were killed in the defence of Vukovar. There were 4000 wounded and several thousand who disappeared. The remains of the 'disappeared' are now reappearing in mass graves around the town.

Reconstruction of Vukovar has begun but it is estimated that it would cost US$2.5 billion to fully restore the town.

In the Upper Town, try **Aspius** (*Ribarska 2*), which also serves good regional food for about the same price, although the setting is bland. It's open Monday to Saturday from 10 am to 11 pm, and Sunday from noon to 10 pm.

The **Slavonia Inn** at the railway station is surprisingly pleasant and serves main courses for an unbelievably cheap 15KN. The high turnover ensures that the fish is fresh – it's open 24 hours. There's a **burek place** at Republike 15 and a daily **vegetable market** open until mid-afternoon at Trg Gaja.

Entertainment

The **Croatian National Theatre** (*Županijska 9*) was designed in 1866 and is a fine example of historicist style. In a strange paradox, local pride prompted a painstaking restoration of the building after it had been damaged by shells, only to see a McDonald's open on the ground floor. The theatre has a regular program of drama and opera from September to May.

In summer, everyone heads out to outdoor cafés, usually near the river. Ribarska ulica has a cluster of cafés and there's a boat docked at Zimska Harbour with a 'bar' on deck. It's open daily from 8 am to 1 am. In winter, the Art Deco *café* in the Central Hotel is popular.

There are five discos in town. Try **Vega** (*Fakultetska 2, Tvrđa*), open Friday, Saturday and Sunday from 10 pm to 5 am.

Getting There & Away

Osijek is well connected to Hungary, Germany and Zagreb by both rail and bus. There are two trains a day in either direction between Pećs and Osijek (2½ hours, 60KN). The trains from Osijek connect to Budapest (six hours, 162KN).

There are five trains a day between Osijek and Zagreb (three to four hours, 79KN), and from June to September the evening train to Zagreb goes on to Rijeka (10 hours, 132KN), arriving early in the morning.

There are three daily buses to Pećs (2½ hours, 42KN) and a daily bus to Mohaćs in Hungary (1½ hours, 24KN), seven daily buses to Zagreb (4-4½ hours, 80KN) and a twice weekly bus to Vienna (10 hours, 203KN).

Panturist runs a bus on Monday and Tuesday to Tuzla in Bosnia-Hercegovina (3½ hours, 89KN) and many buses to Germany. Among the larger towns serviced, there's a daily bus to Munich (12 hours, 324KN), and two weekly buses to Dresden (16 hours, 576KN) and Berlin (19 hours, 684KN). There are also two weekend buses to Zurich (19½ hours, 600KN), and a daily overnight bus to Zagreb (4¾ hours, 80KN) that goes on to Rijeka (8¾ hours, 134KN) and Umag (11 hours, 183KN). There are also two other daily buses to Zagreb and an overnight bus to Split that leaves each evening at 6 pm and arrives in Split at 5 am (200KN).

You can drive to the coast through Bosnia-Hercegovina but the area is still unstable and there have been reports of spontaneous police 'checkpoints' where you must come up with some cash to pass through.

Getting Around

Osijek has a tram line that dates from 1884 and makes transportation within the city easy. The fare is 6KN each way if you buy from the driver but you get two trips for 10KN if you buy at a *tisak* (kiosk).

For visitors, the most useful tram lines are the No 2, which connects the train and bus station with Trg Ante Starčevića in the town centre and the No 1, which connects the town centre with Tvrđa.

AROUND OSIJEK

Đakovo is an easy day trip from Osijek and has a 19th century brick cathedral commissioned by Bishop Strossmayer. Đakovo's main event is the yearly *Đakovačvki Vezovi* (Đakovo Embroidery) which takes place at the beginning of July, a folklore show that includes folk costumes, folklore dancing and traditional songs from the entire region.

Slavonski Brod on the Sava River has an 18th century fortress and a spacious baroque church. In mid-June, there's a folklore festival, the Brod Round Dance, and a festival of patriotic folk songs in May.

Požega, in the Požega Valley, has a picturesque main square lined by rows of 18th and 19th century townhouses. On St Gregory's Day, March 12, there's a traditional show of cannons and mortars which commemorates the victory over the Turks on nearby **Sokolovac Hill** in 1688.

Kopački Rit

Before the war, Osijek made a good base to arrange a visit to the Kopački Rit marshes and bird sanctuary. An important nesting ground for domestic and migratory species, the 10,510 hectare wetlands has been a nature reserve since 1984. Unfortunately, the reserve fell squarely within the disputed eastern Slavonia region and was heavily mined during the recent war. At last report, de-mining operations were continuing and no regular tours were scheduled to visit the park; that should change. Ask the tourist office in Osijek for the latest information.

Kvarner Region

The Kvarner (Italian: Quarnero) coast and its offshore islands are a microcosm of the many influences that have formed Croatian culture. Rijeka, Croatia's third largest city, owes its architecture to Hungary, which ruled the city in the late 19th century. The opening of a rail link to Vienna in 1857 made Opatija the resort of choice for the Austrian aristocracy. Venetian influence pervades the islands of Cres, Lošinj and Rab, while Krk was the seat of Croatia's native nobility, the Frankopan dukes.

Today, tourism is shaping the region, transforming it into a summer playground for sun and sea seekers. The vacation experiences on offer are diverse. Rijeka makes a good base from which to connect to the 19th century elegance of Opatija or Baška's sandy beach on Krk island. You can explore the colourful old towns of Krk, Rab, Mali Lošinj and Cres, or take a boat to the remote coves of these large islands. The clear sea is ideal for swimming or scuba diving and inland there are plenty of trails for hiking or biking.

The region's mild climate has played an important part in the growth of tourism. The Kvarner Gulf is protected from harsh weather by the mountain range running from Mt Učka in the north-west to Gorski Kotor in the east and the Velebit Range in the south-east. Summers are long and cooled by the *maestral* from the west, and although the *bura* brings sudden rushes of cold air in winter, temperatures rarely drop below freezing. The weather patterns explain the region's rich variety of vegetation: Cres, Lošinj and Krk number some 1300 plant species; Rab is known for its evergreen forests; and the luxuriant greenery around Opatija helped establish its reputation as a health resort.

Although the islands are well connected to Rijeka, transportation between them can be inconvenient. Unless you have your

HIGHLIGHTS

- Taking a stroll on the Lungomare promenade in Opatija

- Enjoying the view from Rijeka's Trsat Castle on a clear day

- Exploring the coves of Valun

- Sipping Žlahtina wine in Vrbnik

- Viewing the modern sculpture in ancient Osor

own car, you may have to backtrack to Rijeka to get from one island to another. Krk is the largest island, but it's overrun with tourists in July and August. Mali Lošinj also gets loads of visitors but you're within easy reach of unspoiled Cres. Rab has the most picturesque old town and enough coves and bays for you to easily escape the shoulder-to-shoulder crowds in the summer.

KVARNER

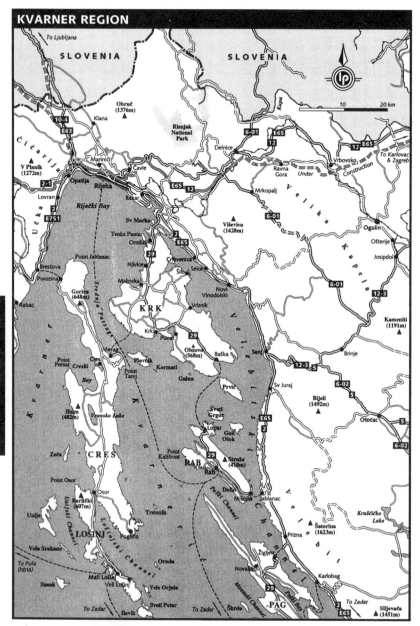

KVARNER REGION

Rijeka

- **pop 167,964** ☎ 051

Rijeka (Italian: Fiume), 126km south of Ljubljana in Slovenia, is such an important transportation hub that it's almost impossible to avoid. The network of buses, trains and ferries connecting Istria and Dalmatia with Zagreb and points beyond all seem to pass through the city. Croatia's largest port, Rijeka is full of boats, cargo, fumes, cranes and the kind of seedy energy that characterises most port cities. However, because there's no beach, resources for visitors are scarce. The assumption seems to be that everyone will either leave the area as fast as possible or base themselves in Opatija.

Although Rijeka is hardly a 'must see' destination, it does have a few saving graces, such as the pedestrian mall (Korzo) and a tree-lined promenade along the harbour. Despite some unfortunate postwar architectural ventures, much of the cityscape contains the sort of ornate, imposing public buildings you would expect to find in Vienna or Budapest, evidence of the strong Austro-Hungarian influence exerted on the city's cultural and economic life in the 19th century.

HISTORY

Following their successful conquest of the indigenous Illyrian Liburnian tribe, the Romans built a settlement here called Tarsaticae. Excavations have revealed the foundations of ancient walls under the Korzo, a gate and a necropolis.

The Slavic tribes that migrated to the region in the 7th century built a new settlement within the old Roman walls, attracted by the port and the abundance of drinking water from the nearby Rječina River.

Although initially under the jurisdiction of the bishop in Pula, Rijeka developed more autonomy in the 13th century under the feudal authority of German nobility. After briefly passing into the hands of the Frankopan dukes of Krk, the town changed feudal masters a few times before becoming part of the Austrian empire at the end of the 15th century.

Rijeka was an important outlet to the sea for the Austrians and a new road was built in 1725 connecting Vienna with the Kvarner coast at Kraljevica, south of the city. The new road spurred economic development, especially shipbuilding. The first modern shipyard in the region opened in Kraljevica in 1729 and the industry has remained the centrepiece of Rijeka's economy ever since. In the 19th century Rijeka modernised its harbour and successfully managed the transition to the building of steamships.

With the birth of the Austro-Hungarian dual monarchy in 1867, Rijeka was given over to the jurisdiction of the Hungarian government, with the support of a pro-Hungarian faction in Rijeka.

The urban landscape acquired a new look as Hungarian architects descended upon the city to erect municipal buildings. A new railway was built linking the city to Zagreb, Budapest and Vienna, further assisting shipbuilding and bringing the first tourists to the Kvarner Gulf.

In 1918 Italian troops seized Rijeka along with Istria and in the 1920 Treaty of Rapallo between Yugoslavia and Italy, Rijeka became an independent state under the trusteeship of the League of Nations. Independence didn't last long. As part of the 1924 Treaty of Rome, Rijeka west of the Rječina River became part of Italy while the Sušak region east of the river became part of the Kingdom of Serbs, Croats and Slovenes. The Italian part of Rijeka was liberated from Fascist control in 1942 by the Partisans and became part of postwar Yugoslavia. Rijeka retains a sizeable and well-organised Italian minority who have their own newspaper, *La Voce del Popolo*.

ORIENTATION

The bus station is on Trg Žabica below the Capuchin Church in the centre of town. If the left-luggage office in the bus station (open daily from 5.30 am to 10.30 pm) is full, there's a larger *garderoba* (cloakroom)

KVARNER

in the train station (open from 7.30 am to 9 pm), a seven minute walk west on ulica Krešimirova. The Jadrolinija ferry wharf (no left-luggage) is just a few minutes walk east of the bus station. Korzo runs east through the city centre towards the fast-moving Rječina River.

INFORMATION
Tourist Offices

The Turistički Ured (☎ 335 882, fax 214 706), Užarska 14, is a good source of maps, brochures and information on concerts and other events. It's open Monday to Saturday from 8 am to 8 pm.

Jadroagent (☎ 211 276, fax 335 172), at Trg Ivana Koblera 2, is an excellent source of information on all ferry sailings from Croatia. Jadrolinija (☎ 211 444, fax 211 485) at Riva 16 is the ferry company's head office and the final authority on its ever-changing schedule. The Auto-Klub Rijeka (☎ 621 824), Preluk 6 on the road to Opatija, assists motorists.

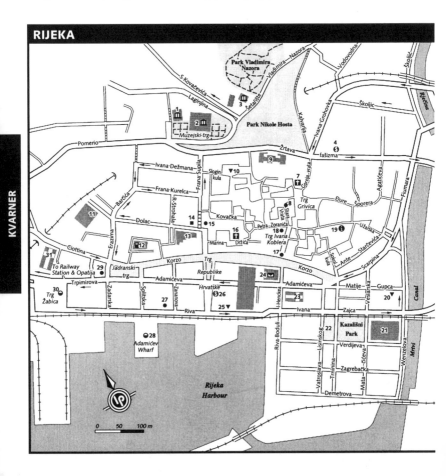

Money

Money can be changed at the Croatia Express office, which is located on Platform No 1 at the train station. It's open Monday to Friday from 8 am to 9 pm; weekend hours are from 9 am to 1 pm and 5 to 9 pm.

There's an automatic change machine at Kaptol Banka, Riva 8, where you can get money out round the clock. You can also withdraw money from an ATM that accepts MasterCard at Zagrebačka Banka, Žrtava fašizma 10.

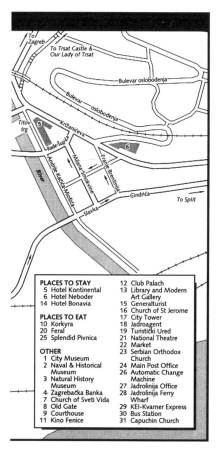

PLACES TO STAY
5 Hotel Kontinental
6 Hotel Neboder
14 Hotel Bonavia

PLACES TO EAT
10 Korkyra
20 Feral
25 Splendid Pivnica

OTHER
1 City Museum
2 Naval & Historical Museum
3 Natural History Museum
4 Zagrebačka Banka
7 Church of Sveti Vida
8 Old Gate
9 Courthouse
11 Kino Fenice
12 Club Palach
13 Library and Modern Art Gallery
15 Generalturist
16 Church of St Jerome
17 City Tower
18 Jadroagent
19 Turistički Ured
21 National Theatre
22 Market
23 Serbian Orthodox Church
24 Main Post Office
26 Automatic Change Machine
27 Jadrolinija Office
28 Jadrolinija Ferry Wharf
29 KEI-Kvarner Express
30 Bus Station
31 Capuchin Church

Post & Communications

The main post office on Korzo is open from 7 am to 9 pm daily. There's a telephone centre, a change counter and you can send foreign packages from here. You can also withdraw money on MasterCard or Diners Club. The postcode for Rijeka is 51000.

For surfing the Net or checking email, go to the Library at Dolac 1. It's open daily from 10 am to noon and an Internet connection is only 5KN a day.

Travel Agencies

KEI-Kvarner Express (☎ 213 808, fax 213 352), Jadranski trg 3, near the bus station, finds private accommodation, changes money and books excursions. It's open daily from 8 am to noon and 2 to 7 pm. Generalturist (☎ 212 900), Trg Republike Hrvatske 8a, changes money and books excursions.

THINGS TO SEE
Monuments

Rijeka was struck by a devastating earthquake in 1750 and the city was almost entirely rebuilt. The pedestrian street **Korzo** was built as a wide commercial avenue on the site of the demolished town walls. The **City Tower** was originally one of the main gates to the city and one of the few monuments to have survived the earthquake. The portal with reliefs of emperors was added soon after the disaster and in 1873 a clock was mounted on the tower, which is still functioning. The tower was reconstructed again in 1890 and a new dome added.

Passing under the City Tower and continuing through Trg Ivana Koblera, you'll find the oldest architectural monument in Rijeka, the **Roman Gate** at the end of Stara Vrata. The lack of decoration indicates that it was probably the entrance to a Roman fortification.

Churches

It would be hard to miss the **Capuchin Church of Our Lady of Lourdes** (Gospe Lurdske), with its ornate neogothic façade looming over the bus station. The Capuchin

KVARNER

sponsors of the project ran into financing problems midway through the construction and enlisted the aid of a 'St Johanca', who allegedly sweated blood in front of the credulous masses. Gifts and money poured into the coffers and the building was finally completed in 1929. ('St Johanca' was arrested for fraud in 1913). The ceiling is decorated with frescoes of angels by a prominent local artist, Romulo Venucci, but the church is only open for mass.

Another prominent church is **St Vito** (Sveti Vida) at Grivica 11. St Vito is the patron saint of Rijeka and construction of this building was begun in 1638 on the site of an older church dedicated to the saint. The Jesuit order supervised the project which lasted several hundred years. Massive pillars support the central dome and surround chapels with multicoloured baroque marble altars. The main altar has a 13th century Gothic crucifix that belonged to the older church. According to legend, someone threw a stone at the crucifix in 1296 and blood began to flow from Christ's body, which is still held in an ampoule. The church is open for visits daily from 6.30 am to noon and 5 to 7 pm.

Also of note is **St Jerome** (Sveti Jeronima) on Trg Riječke Rezolucije. The church was part of a 14th century Augustinian monastery complex that once dominated this square and was financed by the Counts of Duino, the feudal lords of Rijeka at the time. Construction lasted from 1315 to 1408 and the church sanctuary houses the tombs of the financing families. Little of the original Gothic structure remains due to the 1750 earthquake. The church was rebuilt in a baroque style in 1768 and contains tombs of captains, noblemen and patricians from Rijeka. The church is only open for mass.

The most renowned church in Rijeka is **Our Lady of Trsat** (Gospe Trsatske) on Trsat Hill, a centuries-old magnet for believers. According to legend, angels carrying the house in which the Annunciation took place rested in Trsat before depositing the building in Italy. A chapel erected on the site attracted some pilgrims, but numbers were increased in the 14th century when the local nobility petitioned the Pope for the donation of a 'miraculous' icon of Mary thought to have been painted by St Luke. A bigger church was soon needed, and in 1453 the Frankopan Prince Martin built a single-nave church to house the painting and a Franciscan monastery next door.

The monastery was rebuilt in 1691 after a fire and a new nave was added to the church in 1644.

The famous painting is on the main altar and the church also contains tombs of the Frankopans and other notables. A magnificent wrought-iron gate separates the sanctuary from the nave, and the treasury of the Franciscan monastery contains a valuable art collection, open by appointment only. The church is open daily.

Museums

The **Naval & Historical Museum**, Muzejski trg 1, was founded in 1876 at the height of Rijeka's shipbuilding years. Part of the museum traces the development of sailing, with models and paintings of ships and portraits of captains. There are also various archaeological finds, weapons and documents, as well as furniture from the 17th to 20th centuries.

The museum is housed in the imposing Governor's palace and some of the rooms are decorated in period style. The Governor's palace was the residence of the Hungarian governor after a Hungarian provisional government was established here in 1869. The building was intended to show off the best of Hungarian architecture and to impress the populace with the power of Hungarian rule. The Budapest architect, Alayos Hauszmann, took full advantage of his prestigious assignment to create a glittering showpiece of white stone. The museum is open Tuesday to Sunday from 9 am to 1 pm.

Next door is the **City Museum** (formerly the National Revolution Museum) which is currently open only for temporary exhibits on Rijeka's history.

The **Natural History Museum**, Lorenzov prolaz 1, just above Muzejski trg, is devoted to the geology and botany of the region. There are also exhibits on the sea life and vertebrates of the region. The museum is open Monday to Friday from 9 am to 7 pm, Saturday from 9 am to 2 pm.

Trsat Castle

High on a hill overlooking Rijeka and the Rječina River gorge, this 13th century fort occupies a position of immense strategic importance. There may have been a Liburnian hill fort here but it was the Frankopan dukes of Krk who built the present castle to protect their holdings in Vinodol, further east. The **Konak**, an enclosed yard with a cistern, is the best preserved part of the original structure. From the 13th to the 15th century, Trsat belonged to the Frankopans or their relatives but it was seized by the Habsburgs at the end of the 15th century.

As threats from Venice and the Ottoman Empire receded in the 17th century, the castle fell into decay and its decline was accelerated by the earthquake of 1750. In 1826 the fortress was purchased by the Austrian vice-marshal Laval Nugent, who had it restored in a neogothic style and built a mausoleum adorned with the coat of arms of the Nugent family.

The fortress is a popular venue for concerts and plays during the summer, and art galleries open on site from 9 am to 1 pm and 6 to 9 pm. The castle is open daily from 9 am to midnight.

The No 1 bus takes you to Trsat Castle or you can climb the **Petar Kružić Stairway** from Križanićeva ulica. Captain Petar Kružić built the lower part of the stairway in 1531 and it was expanded later to number 538 steps. The chapels along the staircase are dedicated to saints and were used as rest stops for the pilgrims on their way to pay homage to Our Lady of Trsat.

SPECIAL EVENTS

The Rijeka Carnival in February is the largest and most elaborate in Croatia, with seven days of partying. Balls are by invitation only but there are plenty of parades and street dances that are open to everyone.

PLACES TO STAY
Camping

The closest camping ground is listed in the following Opatija section.

Private Rooms

Kvarner Express (☎ 213 808), Jadranski trg 3, can organise private rooms for 100/140KN a single/double but only in the summer. Singles are seldom available and frequently all rooms are full.

Hotels

Prices stay the same all year round in Rijeka except at carnival time, when you can expect to pay a surcharge. You should also book far in advance if you want a room during this time.

The modern *Hotel Neboder* (☎ 217 355, fax 216 592, Strossmayerova 1) and cheaper and older *Hotel Kontinental* (☎ 216 477, fax 216 495, A.K.Miošića 1) are a few blocks apart in an uninspiring neighbourhood north-east of the town centre. Single/double rooms with bath cost 249/311KN at the Neboder and 271/333KN at the Kontinental.

About 1km east of the town centre are two hotels on the water. *Hotel Park* (☎ 216 155, fax 216 592, Šetalište divizije 68) has seen better days but you can swim from the rocks in front of it. Rooms are 216/266KN with breakfast.

The *Hotel Jadran* (☎ 216 600, fax 217 667, Šetalište divizije 46) is in better condition and lies further from town so the water is likely to be cleaner. Rooms are 255/362KN.

The top-end place to stay is the *Hotel Bonavia* (☎ 333 744, Dolac 4), centrally located with rooms with bath for 348/476KN.

PLACES TO EAT

Korkyra (*Slogin kula 5*) is one of the finest restaurants in the region and not excessively expensive, especially considering the quality. The cosy restaurant has an appealingly casual ambience and serves up risotto (35KN), grilled calamari (27KN) and an assortment of specialties such as *brodetto* (fish stew), *bakalar* (codfish stew) and various pastas. If you come between 9 am and 1 pm you can get hot dishes for 18KN to 20KN. The restaurant is open Monday to Saturday from 9 am to 10 pm.

Feral (*M Gupca 6*) has a marine-theme décor which complements the many fish specialties on offer. It's open Monday to Saturday from 10 am to midnight, and occasionally presents piano players in the evening.

Splendid Pivnica (*Riva 6*) is a comfortable place for a drink as well as a bite to eat, with reasonable prices and modern surroundings. You can get risotto for 24KN, an omelette for 25KN and main meals from 50KN to 65KN. It's open daily from 7 am to 10 pm.

Restoran Index (*ulica Krešimirova 18*), between the bus and train stations, has a good self-service section (*samoposluzi*), open daily from 7 am to 9 pm. *Express* (*14 Riva*), near the Jadrolinija office, is another self-service place open every day from 7 am to 9 pm.

For self-caterers, there's a large **supermarket** between the bus and train station on ulica Krešimirova.

ENTERTAINMENT

Performances at the *Ivan Zajc National Theatre* (1885) are mostly dramas in Croatian, though opera and ballet are sometimes offered. The ticket office is open weekdays.

Club Palach, in the back alley accessible through a small passageway off Trg Jadranski, opens at 8 pm daily. It's a good, low-key place to drink and dance.

SHOPPING

Look for the traditional Rijeka design known as Morčić, a ceramic jewellery piece of a moor in a turban. The jewellery made from specially prepared enamel has traditionally been manufactured on Užarska ulica, where you can still buy the pieces at Mala Galerija, Užarska 12.

GETTING THERE & AWAY
Bus

There are 13 buses a day between Rijeka and Krk (56km, 1½ hours, 27KN), using the huge Krk Bridge. Buses to Krk are overcrowded and a seat reservation in no way guarantees you a seat. Don't worry — the bus empties fairly fast so you won't be standing for long.

destination	distance	frequency
Baška	76km	6 daily
Dubrovnik	639km	3 daily
Koper	86km	1 daily
Ljubljana	128km	1 daily
Mali Lošinj	122km	4 daily
Poreč	91km	9 daily
Pula	110km	17 daily
Rab	115km	2 daily
Rovinj	105km	7 daily
Split	404km	18 daily
Trieste	70km	5 daily
Zadar	228km	14 daily
Zagreb	173km	23 daily

note: seven of the 18 buses to Split run express

There's a bus to Vienna every Sunday evening, buses twice a week to Zürich (801km) and Berlin, and daily buses to Frankfurt, Munich (571km) and Stuttgart (786km). A bus to Amsterdam (740KN) leaves every Sunday. Luggage is DM5 per piece on all international services (Deutschmarks in cash required).

Train

There's a train on Saturday and Sunday to Budapest (595km, 11 hours, 296KN) and an evening train to Munich (439KN) and Salzburg (283KN).

Four trains a day run to Zagreb (243km, five hours, 58KN). Several of the seven daily services to Ljubljana (155km, three hours, US$7) require a change of trains at the Slovenian border and again at Postojna. The *poslovni* (executive) trains have 1st-class seats only and reservations are compulsory.

Morčići

The *morčići* or *moretto* is a traditional symbol of Rijeka. The image of a black person topped with a colourful turban is made into ceramic brooches and earrings, and is a popular disguise at the Rijeka carnival. In 1991 it was proclaimed the official mascot of Rijeka.

Two legends explain its emergence as the Rijeka's most recognisable symbol. One story places its origin in the 16th century Turkish invasions. According to this version, the men were waging a losing battle against the Turks while the women and children were praying for a rain of stones to bury their enemy. Finally one of their arrows struck the Turkish Pasha in the temple, killing him. The Turks scattered and – lo and behold! – the skies opened and a hail of stones buried the Turks. The men were so grateful for their wives' assistance that they presented them with not a pot or a broom but colourful moretto earrings.

Another version has it that an Italian baroness was so fond of her black slave that she granted the woman her freedom and had earrings made in her image.

More mundanely, it appears that the morčići was a spin-off of the Venetian moretto design that was part of a 17th and 18th century fad for the Orient. The gem-encrusted Venetian moor was simplified by Rijekan jewellers and sold to poorer women as simple black and white ceramic earrings. Men picked up on the fashion. A single earring was worn by only sons, sailors and fishermen for good luck. There was a male morčić with a turban and a female one with a straw hat, although today's morčić is fairly androgynous.

In the second half of the 19th century, Rijekan jewellers improved the quality of the artisanship and branched out into rings, brooches and necklaces. Upper-class women snatched up the pieces and, with a display at the Vienna International Exhibition of 1873, morčići became popular throughout Europe. After WWII, many of the jewellers emigrated and the morčići dropped out of sight but in the recent back-to-basics trend in Croatian culture, this endearing figure has regained the prominence it deserves.

KVARNER

Car

ATR Rent a Car (☎ 337 544), Riva 20, near the bus station, has rental cars from 480KN a day with unlimited kilometres. On a weekly basis it's 1980KN with unlimited kilometres. You can also try Kompas Hertz (☎ 215 425), Zagrebačka 21.

Boat

Jadrolinija has tickets for the large coastal ferries that run all year between Rijeka and Dubrovnik. Southbound ferries depart from Rijeka at 6 pm daily.

Fares are 116KN to Split (13 hours), 140KN to Korčula (18 hours) and 152KN to Dubrovnik (17 to 24 hours). Fares are lower in winter and higher on summer weekends. Berths to Dubrovnik are 329KN per person in a four-bed cabin,

399KN in a double or 479KN in a double with private bath.

Since the Jadrolinija ferries travel between Rijeka and Split at night you don't get to see a lot, so it's probably better to go from Rijeka to Split by bus and enjoy excellent views of the Adriatic coast. In contrast, the ferry trip from Split to Dubrovnik is highly recommended.

Opatija

• pop 9073   ☎ 051

Just 13km south-west of Rijeka, Opatija was *the* fashionable seaside resort of the Austro-Hungarian empire until WWI. The grand residences of the wealthy are now hotels that offer a healthy dose of the elegance and sophistication of a bygone age. This is a good place to splurge on a hotel since you have virtually no chance of landing in one of the concrete boxes that litter so many coastal resorts. The façades are painted in fresh pastels and the interiors offer spacious halls and chandeliers. The stunning coastline can be appreciated from a waterfront promenade that stretches for 12km along the gulf of Kvarner. West of Opatija rises Mt Učka (1396m), the highest point on the Istrian Peninsula.

The town sprung up around St Jacob's church, which was built on the foundations of a Benedictine abbey. (The word 'abbey' translates as *opatija* in Croatian.) Until 1844, the town was a humble fishing village with 35 houses and a church, but the arrival of wealthy Iginio Scarpa from Rijeka turned the town around. He built the villa Angiolina (named after his wife) on the shore and surrounded it with species of exotic plants from Japan, China, South America and Australia. The villa hosted some of the European aristocracy's finest, including the Austrian queen Maria Anna, wife of Ferdinand. The town's reputation as a retreat for the elite was born.

Opatija's development was also assisted by the construction of a rail link on the Vienna-Trieste line from Pivka in Slovenia to Rijeka in 1873. Construction of Opatija's first hotel, the Quarnero (today the Hotel Kvarner), began and wealthy visitors arrived en masse. Between 1884 and 1895, they tried to outdo each other in building elaborate mansions, hiring the finest architects they could find – or afford. Doctors were quick to proclaim the climate healthy, thus providing a perfect excuse for a long vacation for those who could afford it.

It seemed everyone who was anyone was compelled to visit Opatija, including kings from Romania and Sweden, Russian tsars and the celebrities of the day such as Isadora Duncan, Gustav Mahler, Puccini, Mascagni, Chekov, Franz Lehar and Beniamino Gigli, who came to rehabilitate his vocal cords.

The outbreak of WWI put an end to the Austro-Hungarian empire and an aristocracy that could frolic by the sea, but Opatija has never really lost its popularity.

Although Opatija has never acquired the glitter of the French Riviera, it has its devotees who return every year including a sizeable number of elderly Austrians who come in the winter to nibble on cakes in the Hotel Kvarner and take a healthy promenade by the sea.

ORIENTATION

Opatija sits on a narrow strip of land sandwiched between the sea and the foothills of Mt Učka. Obala Maršala Tita is the main road that runs through town and where you'll find travel agencies, restaurants, shops and hotels. The bus from Rijeka stops first at the Hotel Belvedere, then in front of the Hotel Agava and finally at the bus station at the foot of the town on Trg Vladimira Gortana. If you're looking for private accommodation, it's better to get off at the second stop and walk downhill to the travel agencies rather than walking uphill from the bus station. There's no left-luggage facility at the bus station but Autotrans Agency at the station will usually watch luggage.

INFORMATION
Tourist Offices

The Turistički Ured (☎ 271 310) is at Maršala Tita 101 and is open daily June to September from 8 am to 8 pm. Off season it's open Monday to Friday from 9 am to 4 pm and on Saturday from 9 am to 3 pm. It has a supply of brochures and maps to Opatija and surrounding areas.

Money

You can change money at any travel agency and at the post office, as well as at Zagrebačka Banka, Maršala Tita 153, which is open Monday to Friday from 8 am to 1 pm, Saturday from 8 to 11.30 am. There's an ATM outside where you can get cash on your MasterCard. There's another ATM next to KEI-Kvarner Express where you can get cash on Diners Club and American Express.

Post & Communications

The main post office, at Eugena Kumičiča 2 behind the market *(tržnica)*, is open Monday to Saturday from 8 am to 7 pm and on Sunday from 9 am to noon. You can withdraw cash on MasterCard and Diners Club. The postcode for Opatija is 51410.

Travel Agencies

All the travel agencies in Opatija are on Obala Maršala Tita. The American Express representative is Atlas travel agency (☎ 271 032) at No 116; KEI-Kvarner Express (☎ 711 070) is at No 128; Generalturist (☎ 271 613, fax 271 345) is next to the Hotel Paris at Nazora bb; and GIT (☎/fax 271 967) is at No 65. They all work long hours from June to September – daily from 8 am to about 9 pm – but close earlier and on Sunday in the off season.

ACTIVITIES

The 12km Lungomare is a coastal parade that winds along the sea, passing a number of **swimming** spots including the town's concrete 'beach'. Marked **hiking** trails lead up to Učka, including the one from the Hotel Palace up to Poklon (3¼ hours) and from the market to Orljak (two hours). The sightseeing tower on Vojak (the highest point at 1396m) is also used as a mountaineering shelter. There's a natural halfway mark at 700m where the chestnut and oak trees stop and the beech forests begin.

PLACES TO STAY

Preluk Autokamp (☎ 621 913), beside the busy highway between Rijeka and Opatija, is open from May to September. City bus No 32 stops nearby. *Medveja* (☎ 2291 191) is past Opatija on the road to Pula, located on a pretty cove.

For private rooms, try Kvarner Express, Generalturist and GIT. All have rooms for 70KN per person plus a 50% surcharge for single-room occupancy, a 30% surcharge for stays less than four nights and 20KN for breakfast.

There are no cheap hotels in Opatija but the most reasonable are the elegant *Hotel Paris* (☎ 271 911, fax 711 823, Nazorova bb) and the sprawling *Jadran* (☎ 271 700, fax 271 519, Obala Maršala Tita 193) on the sea. Both have rooms for 252/468KN a single/double for a four-night stay in high season, including bath and breakfast.

Hotel-Restaurant Ika (☎ 291 777, fax 292 044, Obala Maršala Tita 16) is in Ičići, 7km south of Opatija, but it offers a good deal in a small, family-run environment. Rooms with telephone and television are 260/432KN in high season, with breakfast, and the hotel is on a rocky beach. Half-board is a worthwhile investment at an additional 54KN per person.

Stay in the *Hotel Kvarner* (☎ 271 233, fax 271 202, Park 1), and you'll feel like European royalty – pampered in an indoor swimming pool, walking through plush hallways, reclining on antique furniture in high-ceilinged rooms. The hotel's proudest feature is the eye-popping Crystal Ballroom, now used for conventions and banquets. They don't build them like that any more. Rooms are 468/792KN a single/double in high season with half-board.

PLACES TO EAT

Obala Maršala Tita is lined with serviceable restaurants offering pizza, grilled meat and fish, but the better restaurants are out of town. *Restaurant Bevanda* at No 62 is an excellent fish restaurant on the eastern edge of town, where you can get the usual specialties such as scampi, grilled calamari and freshly grilled fish at about 220KN a kilogram. It's open daily from noon to midnight.

Hidden away near the Hotel Kvarner, the *Madonnina Pizzeria* (*Pava Tomašiča 3*) has a long menu of delicious pizza and pasta dishes at a reasonable price. It's open daily from 10 am to midnight. The terrace of the *Imperial Hotel* is where James Joyce used to take his coffee, and it's still an excellent spot for people-watching.

For self-caterers there's a *supermarket/deli* (*Maršala Tita 80*) and a *burek stand* down the stairs next to No 55 on Stubište Tomaševac.

GETTING THERE & AWAY

Bus No 32 stops in front of the train station in Rijeka (11km, 11KN) and runs right along the Opatija Riviera west from Rijeka to Lovran every 20 minutes until late in the evening.

AROUND OPATIJA
Volosko

Two kilometres east of Opatija town, Volosko is a little fishing village with appealing Mediterranean features such as narrow alleyways, stone cottages and balconies dripping with flowers. Its small harbour recalls the days when tuna fishing was the main source of income in the bay. The town's quiet allure makes it irresistible to tourists, but it is still a relatively quiet retreat from Opatija when the summer crowds descend in force. The coastal promenade from Opatija ends in Volosko, making it an easy walk past bay trees, palms, figs and oaks, behind which you can glimpse a number of villas dating from the end of the 19th century.

Whilst in Volosko, try **Restaurant Amfora** (*Crinkovica bb*), which serves fish and Croatian dishes in a great location overlooking the sea. The restaurant is open daily from 10 am to midnight.

Lošinj & Cres Islands

These two serpentine islands in the Kvarner archipelago are separated by only an 11m-wide canal, and are thus often treated as a single entity. Although their topography is different, the island's identities are also blurred by a shared history and close transportation links. On Lošinj (Italian: Lussino), the fishing villages of Mali Lošinj and Veli Lošinj attract hordes of tourists in the summer, especially from Italy, which is linked to Mali Lošinj from Venice. Cres (Italian: Crepsa) is more deserted, especially outside Cres town, and you can still find many remote camp sites and pristine beaches. Both islands are criss-crossed by hiking and biking trails.

Cres is the longer island, stretching 68km from tip to tip. About half the island is covered with fields and rocks, with large pine and oak forests in the north. The western coast is more settled than the steeper eastern coast which is home to the griffon vulture. Lošinj is 31km long and has a more indented coastline than Cres especially in the south. The towns of Mali Lošinj and Veli Lošinj are ringed by natural pine forests interspersed with tall Aleppo pines, planted last century.

Excavations indicate that a prehistoric culture spread out over both islands from the Stone Age to the Bronze Age. The first recorded settlements sprang up on Cres island where the Liburnian tribe used the natural harbours of Cres town and Osor, and built hilltop fortresses at Merag, Porozina and Lubenice. The ancient Greeks called both islands the Apsirtides and they were conquered by the Romans in the 1st century BC. After the division of the Roman Empire, the islands spent a few centuries under Byzantine rule and were settled by Slavic tribes in the 6th and 7th centuries. In the 6th century a bishopric was established in Osor, on the southern tip of Cres, that controlled both Cres and the largely unpopulated Lošinj throughout the early Middle Ages. From 1000 to 1358, the islands were under the rule of Venice, followed by that of the Croatian-Hungarian kings, and returning to Venice from 1409 to 1797.

The islands stagnated under Venetian rule. All maritime was suppressed as the Venetians were fearful of rivalry from the substantial fleet at Osor. Male residents were pressed into service as galley slaves on Venetian ships. The final blow to Osor's importance came in the 15th century when a malaria epidemic chased people out of the town to the safer settlements at Cres, Mali Lošinj and Veli Lošinj.

By the time Venice fell in 1797, Veli and Mali Lošinj had become important maritime centres while Cres devoted its attention to vineyards and olive production. During the 19th century shipbuilding flourished in Lošinj but the advent of steam ships at the end of the century caused an irreversible decline in the maritime business. Meanwhile, Cres had its own problems in the form of a phylloxera epidemic that wiped out its vineyards. Both islands were poor when they were annexed to Italy as part of the 1920 Treaty of Rapallo. They became part of Yugoslavia in 1945.

Today, there is a small shipyard in Nerezine in north Lošinj and olive cultivation in Cres. There's some sheep breeding on Cres, and fishermen regularly ply the waters, but the main activity on both islands is now tourism.

GETTING THERE & AWAY
Boat
The main maritime port of entry for the islands is Mali Lošinj, which is connected to Pula, Zadar and Venice in the summer. Jadrolinija runs a weekly ferry year round between Zadar and Mali Lošinj (4½ hours, 31KN). From June through September there are two additional Jadrolinija ferries as well as the car ferry *Marina*, operated four times a week by Lošinska Plovidba and running from Zadar and Pula to Mali Lošinj (four hours, 50KN), going on to Venice (11 hours, L82000 payable in Italian lire). From late June to early September Lošinska Plovidba runs the passenger boat *Poreč* three times a week from Mali Lošinj to Susak (45 minutes, 18KN), Cres (4½ hours, 28KN) and Rijeka (6½ hours, 63KN).

Bus
All buses travelling to and from the islands originate in Veli Lošinj and stop in Mali Lošinj before continuing to Cres and the mainland. There are eight daily buses from Veli Lošinj to Cres town (1½ hours, 21KN), four daily buses to Merag (two hours, 27KN), four buses a day to Valbiska on Krk island (2½ hours, 46KN), two daily buses to Porozina (2½ hours, 35KN), two daily buses to Brestova in Istria (three hours, 54KN), five buses a day to Rijeka (3½ hours, 67KN), three buses a day to Zagreb (6½ hours, 136KN) and one daily bus to Ljubljana (six hours, 123KN).

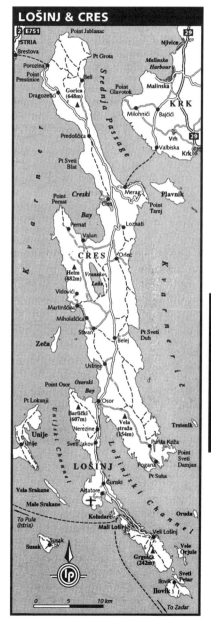

KVARNER

LOŠINJ ISLAND
Mali Lošinj
* pop 6500   ☎ 051

Mali Lošinj sits at the foot of a protected harbour on the south-eastern coast of Lošinj island. Its 19th century-prosperity is evident in the stately sea captain's houses lined up along the north-east harbour, but its 20th century affluence rests upon the large hotels leading up from the south-west harbour. In the late 19th century, as shipbuilding was dying out, the wealthy citizens of Vienna and Budapest gravitated to the 'healthy air' of Mali Lošinj, building villas and luxurious hotels on Čikat cove behind the south-west harbour.

Although most of the current hotels are modern developments, they blend in fairly well with the dense pine forests that blanket the cove. During the summer, Mali Lošinj may not be the most relaxed place, but it's a good base for excursions around Lošinj and Cres or to the small islands of Susak and Ilovik.

Orientation The Jadrolinija dock for all the large boats is on the north-eastern part of town, a 500m walk along the harbour to the town centre. The bus station is on the edge of Riva Lošinjskih Kapetana, the road that runs along the harbour. (The left-luggage office at the bus station is open from 6 am to midnight.)

Most stores, travel agencies, and cafés are along the stretch of Riva Lošinjskih Kapetana that runs from the tourist office to the Trg Republike Hrvatske and its new fountain. When you cross over to the other end of the harbour, roads take you to the hotels and beaches of Čikat cove.

Information The Turistički Ured (☎/fax 231 884, tzg-mali-losinj@ri.tel.hr), Riva Lošinjskih Kapetana 29, has useful brochures, maps and information. It's open daily in the summer from 8 am to 8 pm, and off-season hours are Monday to Saturday from 8 am to 3 pm.

The Jadrolinija office (☎ 231 765), Riva Lošinjskih Kapetana 20, is open on Monday, Tuesday, Friday and Saturday from 7 am to 2.30 pm, on Wednesday and Thursday from 7 am to 3.30 pm and on Sunday from 10 am to 1 pm and 3 to 5 pm.

There are no ATMs in the town or on the island. For a cash infusion, go to the post office if you have MasterCard or Istarska Banka Trg Republike Hrvatske if you have a Visa card. It's open Monday to Friday from 7.30 am to 8 pm, Saturday 8 am to noon. You can change money there, at the post office or at any travel agency. Riječka Banka, Riva Lošinjskih Kapetana 4, also changes money and is open Monday to Friday from 8 am to 2 pm and 6 to 8 pm, Saturday 8 am to 12.30 pm. Most banks and agencies on the island charge 1.5% commission.

Like everything else, the post office is on the harbour. It's open Monday to Saturday from 7 am to 9 pm, and is overwhelmed by tourists in the summer. The postal code for Lošinj is 51550.

With the town's long history of tourism there is no shortage of travel agencies to arrange private accommodation, handle air tickets, change money and book excursions. KEI Kvarner Express (☎ 231 831), Vladimira Gortana 20, is open Monday to Saturday from 8.30 am to 1.30 pm and 6 to 8 pm, Sunday from 9 am to noon, and mornings only Monday to Saturday off season.

In addition to the above activities, Lošinska Plovidba (☎ 231 077, fax 231 611), Riva Lošinjskih Kapetana 8, sells tickets for its boats connecting Mali Lošinj to Venice and other islands. In summer the office is open Monday to Saturday from 8 am to 10 pm, Sunday from 9 am to 1 pm and 6 to 9 pm, but it keeps much shorter hours off season. There's a small Lošinska Plovidba ticket office near the marina, open half an hour before each sailing.

Things to See The main attraction of Mali Lošinj is the attractive port and the greenery of the surrounding hills dipping into the sea but there are a few sights that recall the island's history. In the **graveyard** around the Church of St Martin are the tombs of

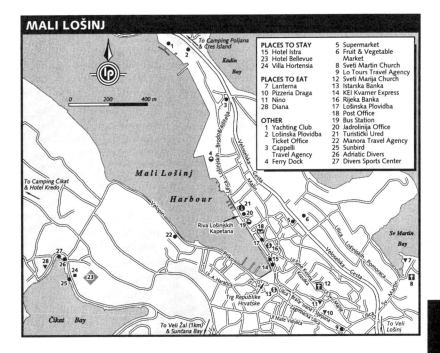

MALI LOŠINJ

PLACES TO STAY
15 Hotel Istra
23 Hotel Bellevue
24 Villa Hortensia

PLACES TO EAT
7 Lanterna
10 Pizzeria Draga
11 Nino
28 Diana

OTHER
1 Yachting Club
2 Lošinska Plovidba
   Ticket Office
3 Cappelli
   Travel Agency
4 Ferry Dock

5 Supermarket
6 Fruit & Vegetable
   Market
8 Sveti Martin Church
9 Lo Tours Travel Agency
12 Sveti Marija Church
13 Istarska Banka
14 KEI Kvarner Express
16 Rijeka Banka
17 Lošinska Plovidba
18 Post Office
19 Bus Station
20 Jadrolinija Office
21 Turistički Ured
22 Manora Travel Agency
25 Sunbird
26 Adriatic Divers
27 Divers Sports Center

earlier inhabitants of Mali Lošinj – sailors, fortune seekers from Italy and Austria, Italian royalty and 19th century Austrian children sent here in the hopes that the mild climate would cure their tuberculosis or respiratory problems.

In the town centre, peek in the church of **Sveti Marija** either before or after mass. Built from 1696 to 1757, the baroque façade overlooks a paved square that used to be the central meeting place for the town. Inside there are some notable artworks, including a painting of the Nativity of the Blessed Virgin by an 18th century Venetian artist, a marble Crucifixion by the sculptor Bartolomeo Ferrari and a painting of the saints on the northern altar that shows the church neighbourhood in the 18th century.

Organised Tours Kvarner Express and other travel agencies book day trips to the nearby islands of Susak and Ilovik for 59/99KN a half/whole day but check out the ferry schedule first since it's much cheaper.

Activities Čikat Bay offers the best **swimming**, with its long, narrow pebble beach and tiny sandy beach.

GOF (☎ 231 170), Lošinjskih Kapetana 34, rents small **motorboats** for 300KN a day, which is a splendid way to discover the island. Experienced sailors can contact the Yachting Club (☎ 231 626) at the marina and charter a 9m yacht for 6840KN a week.

The gentle hills and many paths on the island are great for **cycling**. You can rent a mountain bike at Sunbird (☎ 231 222) on Čikat Bay near the Hotel Bellevue for 15KN an hour or 65KN for eight hours. You can also zip around the island on a motorbike for 170KN a day, available at Manora travel agency (☎ 233 391), Velopin 2, on Čikat Bay.

Čikat Bay is the best spot for **windsurfing** and the best months are April to May and mid-August through September. Sunbird rents boards for 47KN an hour or 366KN for 10 hours and also offers windsurfing courses.

The waters surrounding Lošinj island offer good opportunities for **scuba diving**. There's a wreck dating from 1917, a large, relatively shallow cave suitable for beginners and a reef off the island of Susak. Although it can't be guaranteed that you'll see one, the waters off Lošinj and Cres host a protected colony of 150 dolphins. The two leading dive operations are on Čikat Bay. Adriatic Divers (☎/fax 232 918) offers one boat dive for 133KN with discounts for repeated dives and a one-week dive package including accommodation for 1440KN (not available in July and August). Divers Sport Center (☎ 233 900) offers one boat dive for 155KN with discounts for repeated dives.

There are stables (☎ 235 112) on the road to the airport in Ćunski offering **horse riding** for 72KN an hour and a day trip that includes a beach lunch for 366KN.

Places to Stay – Camping *Camping Čikat* (☎ 232 125, fax 231 708) is a large camping ground on Čikat Bay, close to the beach. It is open from the end of April to mid-October. *Poljana* (☎ 231 726, fax 231 524) is a smaller, quieter and more remote camping ground about 5km north of town. Although there is no local bus, you can take any Rijeka-bound bus and ask to be dropped off at the site. It is open from around mid-April to mid-October. Also on the road to Rijeka is the camping ground *Lopari* (☎ 237 128), open from May through August.

Places to Stay – Private Rooms Agencies finding rooms and apartments are plentiful in Mali Lošinj. In addition to the travel agencies noted above, try Cappelli (☎ 231 582), Kadin bb; Manora (☎ 233 391), Velopin 2; or Lo Tours (☎/fax 231 618), Braće Vidulić 50a. Prices are more or less the same. Expect to pay 112/172KN a single/double for a good room and 86/137KN for a cheaper one with shared bath, not including residence tax or breakfast. There are also studios available for 227KN daily and two-room apartments for 263KN daily.

Places to Stay – Hotels Most hotels are in the pine forest on the hill over Čikat Bay, but the cheapest is the bottom-end *Hotel Istra* (☎ 232 151, Lošinjskih Kapetana 1) in the town centre. Rooms are simple but clean and freshly renovated with showers and toilets in the hall. You'll pay 133/254KN for a single/double with half-board which is only a few kuna more than a room with breakfast only.

The hotel resorts around Čikat Bay are the usual tourist developments and nearly indistinguishable, at least from the outside. The best and most expensive is the *Hotel Bellevue* (☎ 231 222), only steps from the bay and with an indoor swimming pool. Rooms are 263/475KN a single/double. There's a lower-priced annex, *Villa Hortensia*, which is an attractive 19th century residence right on the beach. Singles/doubles are 226/425KN or you can rent a two-person apartment for 432KN a night.

Hotel Kredo (☎ 233 595) is a 19th century residence that was recently purchased by investors and totally overhauled. It's on a quiet cove and the rooms have aircon as well as satellite TV and minibars. You'll pay for the luxuries however, to the tune of 310/496KN a single/double. To get there, take the road to Camping Čikat and continue along the path for about 200m.

Places to Eat Catering to the tremendous influx of Italian tourists in the summer has lent the island's cuisine a decidedly Italian flavour. As on many islands, there is not a wide variety in price or quality and the menus tend to be more or less the same with an accent on seafood, grilled fish, pasta and risotto. Fish runs from 180 to 220KN a kilogram and a pasta starter costs from 25KN to 40KN. You'll generally eat better away from the main harbour area. Most restaurants close for a month or two in winter.

Diana is beautifully located on Čikat Bay and offers delicious grilled fish that costs about 220KN a kilogram. It's open all year from 11 am to 11 pm. *Veli Žal* is cooled by the sea breezes of Sunčana Bay. It's a terrace restaurant specialising in fish, near the Hotel Aurora, open from 10 am to midnight in summer and 10 am to 10 pm in winter. On a small boat harbour near Sveti Martin church, *Lanterna* serves up a tangy octopus salad for 35KN as well as the usual fish, pasta and grilled-meat main courses. It's off the tourist track and apt to attract boating and fishing types. It's open daily from 10 am to midnight.

There are plenty of pizza places but *Pizzeria Draga* (*Braće Vidulića 77*) seems to make a special effort. It's open from 9 am to midnight in the summer but closes a little earlier off season.

Self-caterers can head to the daily fruit and vegetable *market* on Trg Zagazinjine and the large *supermarket* across the street.

Entertainment On summer evenings many of the large hotels in Čikat have 'terrace dancing'; that is, a couple of musicians with an electronic keyboard play an assortment of local or international tunes, according to their mood.

Getting There & Away There are nine buses a day between Mali Lošinj and Veli Lošinj (10 minutes, 8KN). The camping grounds and hotels on Čikat Bay are easily reachable in the summer by a local bus that leaves from the bus station hourly. For other bus and boat connections see Getting There & Away in the introduction to this section.

Around Mali Lošinj

The nearby islands of Susak and Ilovik are the most popular day trips from Mali Lošinj. Tiny **Susak island** (pop 188, 3.8 sq km) is unique for the thick layer of fine sand that blankets the underlying limestone and creates delightful beaches. The island culture is also unusual. You can still see the

local women outfitted in traditional multi-coloured skirts and red leggings. Islanders speak their own dialect that is nearly incomprehensible to other Croats. When you see the old stone houses on the island, consider that each stone had to be brought over from Mali Lošinj and hand carried to its destination. No wonder that the island has steadily lost its population, with many of its citizens heading to the USA – Hoboken, New Jersey, to be precise.

In contrast to flat Susak, **Ilovik** (pop 145, 5.8 sq km) is a hilly island that's a popular destination for boaters. There are some secluded swimming coves and nearly every house has oleanders, roses and other flowers growing around it.

Getting There & Away Many travel agencies sell excursions to Susak and Ilovik but it's easy enough to get there on your own. Jadrolinija makes a circuit from Mali Lošinj to Susak (one hour), Ilovik (50 minutes), Unije, Vela Srakane and back to Mali Lošinj twice a day in the early morning and late afternoon, which can make a pleasant day trip.

Veli Lošinj

Veli Lošinj retains much more of its fishing village character than busy Mali Lošinj, only 4km north-west, and it's smaller, quieter and somewhat less crowded. Pastel-coloured baroque houses cluster around a narrow bay that protrudes like a thumb into the south-eastern coastline of Lošinj. Hilly, cobblestoned streets lead from the central square past cottages buried in foliage to the rocky coast. The absence of cars in the town centre is also a refreshing change of pace but the town can be uncomfortably crowded from mid-July to the end of August.

Like Mali Lošinj, Veli Lošinj had its share of rich sea captains who built villas and surrounded them with gardens of exotic plants they brought back from their travels. You can glimpse these villas on a walk up the steep, narrow streets. Sea captains also furnished the churches in town, most notably Sveti Antun on the harbour.

KVARNER

Orientation The bus station (no left-luggage facility) is on a hill over the harbour. Ulica Vladimira Nazora takes you down to the harbour, which is the town centre. The bank, post offices, tourist agencies and a number of cafés are on Obala Maršala Tita which wraps around the bay. A coastal route leads north up to the Hotel Punta beach and east to the Rovenska Bay beach.

Information There is no municipal tourist office but the Val tourist agency (☎/fax 236 352), Obala Maršala Tita 34 on the harbour, finds private accommodation and changes money. It's open daily from 9 am to noon and 5 to 10 pm in the summer but is only open Monday to Friday from 9 am to noon in the winter. The nearby tourist biro (☎ 236 256) on Obala Maršala Tita 17 is smaller but also finds private accommodation and changes money.

The post office, Obala Maršala Tita 33, is open Monday to Saturday from 7 am to 9 pm. Riječka Banka on Obala Maršala Tita has a foreign exchange counter and is open Monday to Friday from 8 to 11.30 am and 6 to 8 pm, Saturday 8 to 11 am.

Things to See You can't miss the hulking St Anthony's church (Sveti Antun) on the harbour with its tall bell tower. Built in 1774 on the site of an older church, St Anthony's contains an impressive collection of Italian paintings thanks to generous sea captains. The captains also saw that the old wooden altars were replaced by seven baroque marble altars that they bought second-hand in Italy. The church is open during the morning only in July and August.

Places to Stay Both travel agencies will find you private accommodation for 111/173KN a single/double for a room with private bathroom.

Hotel Saturn (☎ 236 102) is a pretty pink and white renovated villa on Obala Maršala Tita across from the church. It has rooms with minibars for 126KN per person including breakfast. Front rooms on the harbour are apt to be noisy on summer evenings when crowds fill the downstairs terrace restaurant.

Hotel Punta (☎ 662 000) offers a standard resort experience on a hill overlooking the harbour with easy access to a swimming cove. There are singles/doubles with sea views and balconies for 234/424KN but some of the singles are ridiculously small.

Places to Eat *Bistro Sirius* (*Rovenska 4*) is a good escape from the open-air restaurants that sprawl over the harbour in the summer. On quiet Rovenska Bay east of the town centre, the exceptionally fresh fish makes the restaurant popular with a local crowd. It's open daily from 11 am to midnight. *Veli Deli* (*obala Maršala Tita 27*) was opened by a couple from New York to fill the need for good, inexpensive food you can eat on the run any time of day. The pizza and sandwiches are good and the pasta salads are a bargain at 7KN a portion. It opens daily from June to September, between 10 am to 1 am.

Entertainment There's terrace dancing nightly at the *Hotel Punta* in the summer and there's also a disco inside.

CRES ISLAND
Cres Town
• pop 2234   ☎ 051

Cres town so resembles an Italian fishing village you might wonder if you had strayed across a border somewhere. Pastel terrace houses crowd around the harbour-within-a-harbour (Mandrać) glinting in the afternoon sun. Even at the height of the tourist season, when the harbour is crowded with boats, it's a lazy sun-drenched town.

The Italian influence dates from the 15th century Venetians who relocated their headquarters to Cres town after Osor fell victim to plague and pestilence. Public buildings and patricians' palaces were built along the harbour and in the 16th century the Venetian administration built a town wall. As you stroll the streets you'll notice reminders of

Venetian rule including coats of arms of powerful Venetian families. You may hear as much Italian spoken as Croatian since the port is a popular destination for Italian boaters.

Orientation The bus stop (no left-luggage facility) is on the south-eastern side of Mandrać harbour next to the tourist office and bank. The old town stretches from the harbour promenade, Riva Creskih Kapetana, inland to Aprila XX Šetalište. You'll find most monuments and churches within this area. If you continue around the harbour to Lungomare Sveti Mikula you'll come to the rocky beaches around the Hotel Kimen and Autocamp Kovačine after about 1km.

Information The helpful Turistički Ured (☎ 571 133), Cons 11, is a good source of information for maps and brochures; the staff can also arrange private accommodation and change money. In summer it's open daily from 7.30 am to 10 pm, but off season it closes at noon on Sunday.

The post office is across the square from the tourist office and is open Monday to Saturday from 7 am to 9 pm, Sunday 9 am to noon. The postal code for Cres island is 51557.

Riječka Banka, Cons 8, is open Monday to Friday from 8 am to 2 pm.

Things to See At the end of Riva Creskih Kapetana is Trg F Petrica and the graceful 16th century **Loggia**, scene of public announcements and judgments, financial transactions and festivals under Venetian rule. On the central pillar in front of the loggia you can see signs of the chain that used to bind lawbreakers to the column for public ridicule. Now the loggia is the scene of a morning fruit and vegetable market.

Behind the loggia is the 16th century **Main Gate**. The niche above the gate used to hold the Venetian lion but after the fall of Venice in 1797 the lion was removed and thrown into the sea while the townspeople cheered.

The church on Pod Urom inside the gate is **St Mary of the Snow** (Sveti Marija Snježne).

The façade is notable for the Renaissance portal with a relief of the Virgin and Child and above the double-sided pilasters are statues of the Archangel Gabriel and the Virgin. Although the church is only open for mass, it's worth arriving half an hour before or after the mass to see the serene interior. The bottom part of the altarpiece on the right altar shows a panorama of Cres town in the 18th century and the left altar has a lovely carved wooden *Pietà* from the 15th century (now under protective glass).

Behind the Hotel Cres on Riva Creskih Kapetana is the **Town Museum** with a selection of amphorae from the 2nd century BC, a collection of stone monuments and medieval sculptures. It's housed in the 15th century Petrić family palace, a fine example of late-Gothic architecture with light, lacy windows. Locals refer to it as the 'Arsan' because the town arsenal used to be stored here. It's open daily from 9 to 11 am and 7 to 9 pm but may be closed off season.

Activities The best **swimming** is around the Hotel Kimen. Diving Cres (☎/fax 571 706 or ☎ 571 161) is in the Autocamp Kovačine and offers **scuba diving** for 86KN a boat dive, 126KN for wreck diving and equipment rental of 180KN.

Special Events The patron saint of the town is St Mary of the Snow and on her feast day, 5 August, there's an outdoor bazaar on the main square where stalls sell a selection of the island's offerings – olive oil, honey, herbs, fruits and vegetables.

Places to Stay – Camping *Autocamp Kovačine* (☎ *571 423*) is about 1km out of town and is open from April to October. It costs 43KN per person daily but there's no tent charge.

Places to Stay – Private Rooms The tourist office can find private rooms for 151/200KN or 97/130KN (bottom-end) plus a 30% surcharge for stays less than four nights. You can also rent a studio for 260KN.

KVARNER

Places to Stay – Hotels The *Hotel Cres* (☎/fax 571 535, Riva Creskih Kapetana 10) is an omelette- yellow restored building on the waterfront. Rooms are simple without telephone or TV but some overlook the harbour. In July and August a room with shared bath and breakfast is 242/324KN a single/double but about a third less the rest of the year.

The only other hotel is the *Kimen* (☎ 571 322, fax 571 513) on the road to the auto-camp. It's a large development but right near beaches for swimming. Rooms are 252/432KN a single/double in high season with private bath and breakfast.

Places to Eat *Restaurant Riva* (*Obala Creskih Kapetana 13*) has an attractive terrace on the harbour and serves fish at about 220KN a kilogram and pasta from 30KN. It's open daily from 10 am to mid-night. *Belona Gostionica* (*Šetalište XX Aprila 24*) is a favourite when the locals want to enjoy a night out. Fish is the spe-cialty but you can also get meat and pasta dishes. It's open daily from noon to mid-night. The *supermarket* across from the loggia is open Monday to Saturday from 6.30 am to 9 pm, Sunday 7 am to noon.

Getting There & Away In summer the *Poreč* boat runs three times a week from Cres town to Martinšćica (1½ hours, 15KN), Rijeka (two hours, 41KN) and Susak (3½ hours, 27KN). See the Getting There & Away information at the begin-ning of this section for other services.

Osor

• pop 80   ☎ 051

When crossing from Lošinj to Osor, you may have to wait at the drawbridge spanning the canal, as the bridge is raised twice a day to allow boats to move from the Lošinski canal to the Gulf of Kvarner and back. It's a treat to watch the yachts, sailboats and motorboats file through the narrow canal that separates the two islands. Usually the bridge opens at 9 am and then again in the evening.

The canal is thought to have been dug by the Romans, and because of it Osor was able to control a key navigational route through-out the Middle Ages. Until the 15th century, Osor was a strong commercial, religious and political presence in the region, but a com-bination of plague, malaria and new sea routes devastated the town's economy and it slowly decayed. Now it's gaining a new life as a museum-town of churches and country lanes that meander off from a traditional 15th century town centre.

There's been an obvious investment in bringing the village back to life, even though practically no one lives here. The town square and a few other smaller squares display modern sculpture of an astonishing-ly high quality. The Music Evenings of Osor in July and August draw fine musicians from around the country to perform in the church-es. Osor is an easy day trip from Mali Lošinj and Cres town, and should not be missed. Bring a bathing suit, as there are swimming coves outside of town past the Franciscan monastery.

Things to See Entering through the gate on the canal, you walk right into the centre of one of the most delightful towns in the northern Adriatic. First you'll pass the remains of an old castle and then on your left there's the **Bishop's Palace** behind a small garden. The palace has been turned into a museum with a collection of stone fragments and reliefs from the Roman and early Christian periods. Eighth to 11th century *pleter* (braided) ornamentation is also on display. The museum has recently been restored and there are plans for more exhibits recalling the town's proud history. The museum is open in July and August daily from 9 am to noon and 7 to 9 pm but it's closed in winter. Admission is 10KN and includes a guided visit in Croatian, German or Italian. If you admit to speaking any of these languages, the enthusiastic guide will keep you in the museum for hours, explaining every exhibit. The ex-hibits are well captioned in English and give a good overview of Osor's history.

Your admission ticket to the Bishop's Palace also includes entrance to the **cathedral** across the street on the main square. Built in the late 15th century, the façade has a rich Renaissance portal and inside there's a baroque altar from the 17th century as well as paintings by Venetian artists from the 16th to 18th centuries. On the western side of the cathedral, notice the altar picture of St Gaudencius with a snake at his feet.

According to local legend, Gaudencius was born in the 11th century in nearby Tržic and became a bishop. As a bishop, he took it upon himself to castigate the townspeople for their sins and corruption for which he was expelled from town. The bitter bishop became a hermit in a cave and put a curse upon all the poisonous snakes on the island.

Less interesting is the **Archaeological Museum** across the square in the old town hall which contains a collection of poorly captioned stone monuments, prehistoric vessels and grave artefacts. It's open in July and August from 9 am to 1 pm.

Before leaving the square notice the Meštrović statue *Daleki Akordi* (Distant Chords), one of many sculptures on a musical theme scattered throughout the town.

Take the road between the town hall and the bell tower heading away from the canal, and on the remains of the eastern town gate you'll notice **St Mark's lion**, the Venetian reminder of who built the 15th century walls. Continue past the walls and follow the lane down to the cove where you'll find the remains of a **Franciscan monastery**, with Glagolitic inscriptions on the stone jamb of the monastery and on the bell tower of the church. The monastery was taken over by the Franciscans in 1460 and abandoned in 1841.

Special Events The Musical Evenings of Osor take place from the middle of July to the middle of August and attract a range of high-calibre classical artists from around the country. Information about the concerts is posted around town or you can inquire at the tourist offices in Mali Lošinj and Cres town.

Places to Stay Near Osor, there's *Preko Mosta* (☎ 237 350) overlooking the bridge to Mali Lošinj, open from May through August, and *Bijar* (☎ 237 027) near Nerezine on Mali Lošinj.

Getting There & Away All buses travelling between Cres and Mali Lošinj buses stop at Osor (12KN).

Valun
• pop 68   ☎ 051

In a country with many idyllic coves, Valun is a standout. The little hamlet, 15km southwest of Cres town, is buried at the foot of steep cliffs and surrounded by shingle beaches. It's a long descent by car, and then you leave the car on top of the hill and go down steep steps to the old town that drops to the cove. The relative inaccessibility means that the narrow cove is rarely crowded and there are no souvenir stalls blocking your view of the old stone town clinging to the hills. There are a few restaurants along the harbour that serve up seafood and pasta dishes on wooden tables as you gaze out at the tranquil cove.

The town was founded by villagers from Bućevo, further up the hill above the parking lot, who gradually moved down to the coast. The main sight is the 11th century **Glagolitic tablet** in Valun's parish church. The tablet is a tombstone that was originally found in St Mark's church in Bućevo. It's inscribed in both Glagolitic and Latin, reflecting the ethnic composition of the island which was inhabited by Roman descendants and newcomers who spoke Croatian.

The main attraction of Valun is the **beaches**. To the right of the harbour a path leads to a beach and camp site. West of the hamlet, about 700m further on, there's another lovely pebble beach bordered by pines.

The tourist office (☎ 525 050 or ☎ 525 084, fax 525 085) is in the town centre up a few steps from the harbour and will book private accommodation. The office is only open in July and August from 8 am to 10 pm; at other times of year you can send a fax requesting a room. Private accommodation is scarce in Valun (it's a tiny town) and usually reserved long in advance. Expect to pay the same price as for private accommodation in Cres town.

Camping *Zdovice* (☎ *535 050, fax 535 085*) is a small camping ground on the eastern cove that costs 40KN per person in July and August. It's open from May to September and reservations should be made in advance.

Getting There & Away The long, steep hill that leads down to the cove would make hiking or biking back from Valun a long, exhausting struggle. Unless you have your own wheels, the best way to come is on a Monday or Wednesday bus that leaves Cres town at 5 am and returns at 5 pm. There's also a Friday bus that leaves Cres at 7 pm. It's a 30 minute ride.

Krk Island

• **pop 16,402**   ☎ **051**

Croatia's largest island, 409 sq km Krk (Italian: Veglia) is also one of the busiest in the summer as Germans and Austrians stream over the Krk bridge to its holiday houses, autocamps and hotels. Krk's booming tourist industry managed to weather the storm in ex-Yugoslavia, helped by its proximity to the mainland and distance from the fighting. It may not be the lushest or most beautiful island in Croatia but its decades of experience in tourism make it an easy place to visit, with good transportation connections and a well-organised tourism infrastructure.

The north-western coast of the island is rocky and steep with few settlements, probably because of the fierce bura wind that whips the coast in winter. The climate is milder in the south, with more vegetation and beaches, coves and inlets. The forests that account for 31% of the island are mainly found on the south-western coast, along with the major towns – Krk, Punat and Baška.

The town of Krk is centrally located and makes a good base for exploring the island.

From Punat, you're within easy reach of the unique Košljun island and monastery, and Baška is on a wide sandy bay at the foot of a scenic mountain range. On the south-eastern coast, the main town is Vrbnik, a clifftop medieval village known for its fine Žlahtina wine.

The oldest known inhabitants of Krk were the Illyrian Liburnian tribe, followed by the Romans. Taking advantage of the island's position on an important maritime route through the Adriatic, the Romans settled near Omišalj on the northern coast. In 49 BC a naval battle between Octavian and Mark Antony was waged near the island. With the decline of the Roman Empirse, Krk was incorporated into the Byzantine empire, then passed between Venice and the Croatian-Hungarian kings.

In the 11th century Krk became the centre of the Glagolitic language – the old Slavic language put into writing by the Greek missionaries Cyril and Methodius. The oldest preserved example of the script was found in a former Benedictine abbey in Krk town. A later tablet with the script was found near Baška and is now exhibited in Zagreb. The script was used on the island up to the first decades of the 19th century.

In 1358 Venice granted rule over the island to the Dukes of Krk, later known as the Frankopans, who became one of the richest and most powerful families in Croatia. Although vassals of Venice, they ruled with a measure of independence until 1480 when the last member of the line put the island under the protection of Venice. Venetian rule was painful for the island, its male residents forced into service as oarsmen on Venetian galleys and its oak trees felled to build Venetian ships.

After the fall of Venice, Krk's history followed that of the rest of the coast – falling to the Austrians, the French and then the Austrians again before becoming part of the Kingdom of Serbs, Croats and Slovenes.

Although tourism is the dominant activity on the island, there are two shipyards in Punat and Krk for small-ship repairs and some agriculture and fishing. Vineyards

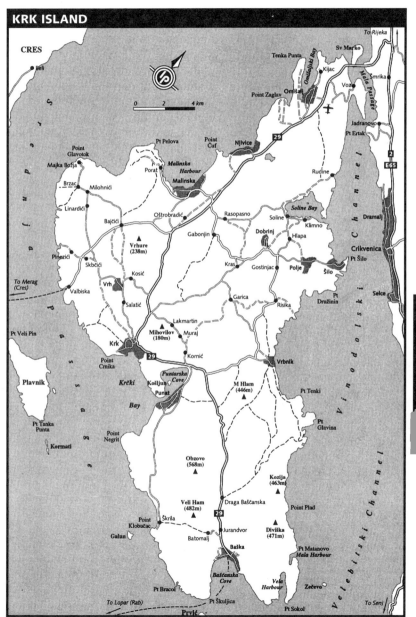

KRK ISLAND

KVARNER

surround Vrbnik and lamb from the island's sheep is especially tasty. Fishermen still ply the sea and olive oil production has recently been stepped up, taking advantage of the groves around Punat, Krk, Malinska and Njivice.

GETTING THERE & AWAY
Bus
About 14 buses a day travel between Rijeka and Krk town (1½ hours, 24KN), stopping at Omišalj, Njivice, Malinska and Punat. Eleven continue on to Baška (20km, one hour) and two to Vrbnik (15 minutes). There are five daily buses from Zagreb (4¾ hours, 82KN) that make most of the same stops as the Rijeka bus. To go from Krk to the islands of Cres and Lošinj, change buses at Malinska for the Lošinj-bound bus that comes from Rijeka, but check the times carefully as the connection only works once or twice a day.

Boat
The ferry between Baška and Lopar (23KN) on Rab island operates from June through September two to five times a day, but between October and May there's no service.

Car
The Krk bridge links the northern part of the island with the mainland and a regular car ferry links Valbiska with Merag on Cres island.

GETTING AROUND
Bus
Bus connections between towns are frequent because the many buses to and from Rijeka pick up passengers in all the island's main towns.

KRK TOWN
On the south-western coast of the island is the town of Krk on Krčki Bay. The medieval walled town has expanded to include a port, beaches, camp sites and hotels around the surrounding coves and hills. The harbour can get crowded in the summer but the real attraction is the web of narrow streets that weave around the Romanesque cathedral and a 15th century castle.

Already settled by the time of the Roman occupation, the Romans built walls around the town and baths with an underground heating system called a hypocaust. A few of the walls are still visible but the baths were later covered with the cathedral and are inaccessible.

You won't need more than a couple of hours to see the sights in town but, from a base in Krk town, it's easy to hop on a bus to other island towns or take a boat trip around the island.

Orientation
The bus station (no left-luggage facility) is along the harbour, only a few minutes walk north to the historic town centre which is the nucleus of a modern residential district. Most hotels are east of the town centre past Dražica cove's small sandy beach and pine forest.

Information
Tourist Offices The Turistička Zajednica municipal tourist office (☎/fax 221 414), Velika Placa 1, is in the city wall's Guard Tower and is open Monday to Friday from 8 am to 3 pm, Saturday from 8 am to 2 pm. Although it has some brochures, the travel agencies will have more specific practical information about accommodation, excursions etc.

Money You can change money at any travel agency, at the post office or at Riječka Banka on Trg Josip Jelačića, open Monday to Friday from 8 am to 1 pm and 2.30 to 8 pm, Saturday from 8 am to 12.30 pm. There are no ATMs in town.

Post & Communications The post office, on Ognjana Price, is open Monday to Saturday from 7 am to 9 pm. You can change money and get cash on your MasterCard and Diners Club card. The postcode for Krk town is 51500.

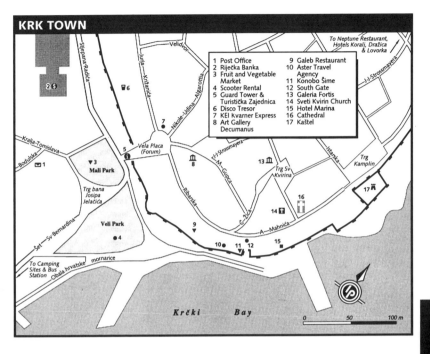

KRK TOWN

1 Post Office
2 Riječka Banka
3 Fruit and Vegetable Market
4 Scooter Rental
5 Guard Tower & Turistička Zajednica
6 Disco Tresor
7 KEI Kvarner Express
8 Art Gallery Decumanus
9 Galeb Restaurant
10 Aster Travel Agency
11 Konobo Šime
12 South Gate
13 Galeria Fortis
14 Sveti Kvirin Church
15 Hotel Marina
16 Cathedral
17 Kaštel

KVARNER

Travel Agencies Aster (☎/fax 222 500), Obala hrvatske mornarice 3, is open in the summer only, from 9 am to 1 pm and 6 to 10 pm every day. KEI Kvarner Express (☎ 221 403, ☎/fax 221 035), Križanića 5 on the main square, is open daily in summer from 8 am to 8 pm and Monday to Saturday off season from 8 am to noon. Both places change money, find private accommodation and book excursions. In addition to those services, Autotrans (☎ 221 111) in the bus station sells international bus tickets and is a good source of transportation information.

Things to See

On the site of a 6th century early Christian basilica, the present **Krk Cathedral** was begun in the 13th century and finished with a 16th century bell tower. The cathedral's early Christian origins are apparent in a carving of two birds eating a fish on the first

column next to the apse (the fish is an early Christian symbol of Christ and Christians were often represented as birds). The left nave features the Frankopan Chapel from the 15th century with the coats of arms of the Frankopan princes. In the chapel at the end of the right nave, notice *The Entombment* by Pordenone.

Although the cathedral is only open for mass, you can enter the adjoining **St Quirinus** (Sveti Kvirin) from a side entrance which looks out over the cathedral. The church museum has a collection of Italian paintings from the 16th and 17th centuries and a silver altarpiece of the Madonna from 1477. The museum is open daily from 9 am to 1 pm.

The fortified **Kaštel** on the edge of town, with a round tower and three gates, is a Venetian structure from around the 15th or 16th century. The castle is now used as an open-air theatre for summer concerts. The

Franciscan monastery north-west of the harbour is closed to the public but nearby you can see remains of the Roman walls. Other interesting sites include the **Galeria Fortis** at Vrizeća 1, with its small collection of objects from the Roman era including amphorae, pottery, tools and tablet. It's open daily from 9.30 am to 1 pm and 6 to 11 pm. **Art Gallery Decumanus** on Gupca is worth visiting for its changing exhibitions of contemporary Croatian artists. It's open daily from 9 am to noon and 7 to 10 pm.

Activities

A number of outfits organise **scuba-diving** trips around the island and especially to the nearby island of Plavnik. Near the bus station, try the Correct Diving Club (☎ 221 091), Braće Juras 3, or Krk Dive Center (☎ 222 563), Lukobran bb. The price runs from around 144KN for a boat dive and 126KN for a shore dive. Equipment rental is 180KN. Popular dive sites include a sunken Greek cargo vessel, an underwater cave near Vrbnik and, in particular, the red coral on the vertical walls around Plavnik island.

You can rent a small motorboat at the Aster travel agency for 300KN a day and seek out your own coves along the coast, or rent one of the scooters arrayed outside in Veli Park for 350KN a day.

Organised Tours

The most popular excursion in Krk is a 'fish picnic', usually an all-day boat excursion in which you catch your fish in the morning, make a swim stop or two around the island, have your fish lunch on the boat or onshore and swim again in the afternoon before arriving back in town. Favourite stops include Plavnik island, Sveti Grgur island, Stara Baška and Pinezići. It costs about 150KN, including lunch, and you can book them through Aster or KEI Kvarner Express, or directly from the boats that line up in front of the Hotel Marina. Aster also offers two-hour glass-bottom boat trips for 70KN, and boat trips to Rab, Grgur and Goli (Seagull) islands for 250KN, including lunch.

Special Events

In July and August the Krk Summer Festival presents concerts, plays and dances in the Kaštel. The fourth of July is the day of the town's patron saint, Sveti Kvirin, and is celebrated with music and processions.

Places to Stay

There is a range of accommodation options in and around Krk, but many places only open for the summer.

Camping There are three camping grounds. The closest is *Autocamp Ježevac* (☎ 221 081) on the coast, a 10 minute walk south-west of Krk town. The rocky soil makes it nearly impossible to use tent pegs, but there are lots of stones to anchor your lines. There's good shade and places to swim, and its open from May to October.

Camping Bor (☎ 221 581) is on a hill inland from Ježevac and is open year round. *Politin FKK* (☎ 221 351) is a naturist camp south-east of Krk, just beyond the large resort hotels, open from May to September.

Private Rooms KEI-Kvarner Express (☎ 221 403, fax 221 035) has private rooms for 90/130KN a single/double plus a 30% surcharge for stays of less than four nights. Similar rooms can be booked from Autotrans (☎ 221 111) at the bus station and Adriatours (☎ 222 666) in the old town. Prices are about 10% cheaper in May and June, and about 20% cheaper outside high season. Ask for the brochure with pictures of accommodation available.

Hotels The cheapest place is the *Hotel Lovorka* (☎/fax 221 022), which has singles/doubles for 216/288KN in peak season (the third week in July to the third week in August). There's no telephone or TV but the beach is not far away. Nearby in the same development east of town is the slightly more expensive *Dražica* (☎ 221 022), with a café and restaurant but similarly basic rooms for 223/306KN in high season.

The two best hotels are the *Marina* (☎/fax 221 128) in the town centre, with views over the harbour, and the **Koralj** (*☎/fax 221 044*), a glossy, modern hotel, north-east of town on a cove. Prices are about the same at 252/ 396KN a single/double, including breakfast.

Places to Eat

The **Hotel Neptune** is in a lovely setting overlooking a cove and serves up fish, seafood and pasta dishes ranging from 80 to 100KN. It's open daily from 10 am to midnight. **Konobo Nono** (*Krčkih iseljenika 8*), behind the Neptune restaurant, offers a range of local specialties such as *šurlice*, home-made noodles topped with goulash, as well as grilled fish and meat dishes. Main courses are from 30KN to 50KN and the restaurant is open daily from 9 am to midnight. **Galeb** is a popular and inexpensive pizzeria with a large open-air terrace on the harbour. It's a great place to linger and people-watch. It's open daily from 10 am to midnight.

For a quick bite, go to the popular **Konoba Šime** on the harbour, with a medieval, cave-like interior and a selection of drinks and snacks. It's open daily from 11 am to 3 pm and 6 to 11 pm. There's a daily fruit and vegetable **market** outside the west walls that also sells bread, pastry, pizza, fast food and roast chicken. You can pick up picnic supplies at the large, modern **supermarket** across from the bus station, open daily from 7 am to 9 pm, or at the **supermarket** in the old town on Strossmayera, open Monday to Saturday from 7 am to 9 pm, Sunday from 7 to 11 am.

Entertainment

Disco Trezor is the only disco in town, open daily from 10 pm in summer but weekends only off season.

AROUND KRK TOWN
Vrbnik

This enchanting medieval village of steep, arched streets is perched on a cliff overlooking the sea. It was once the centre of the Glagolitic language and repository for many Glagolitic manuscripts. The language was kept alive by priests, who were always plentiful in the town since many young men entered the priesthood to avoid serving on Venetian galleys.

Now the town is a good place to sample the Žlahtina wine produced in the surrounding region. Try **Restaurant Nada** (*Glavača 22*), which has a bar for wine-tasting as well as a cosy cave-like restaurant to sample excellent seafood specialties. It's open March to November from noon to 11 pm. After strolling the streets and admiring the view you can descend to the town beach for some swimming.

Only two buses a day travel the 12km to Vrbnik, making it tricky to organise as a day trip unless you have your own wheels.

BAŠKA

At the southern end of Krk island, Baška is a popular resort with a 2km-long pebbly beach set below a high ridge. The swimming and scenery are better than at Krk, and there are a number of trails leading up to the surrounding mountains.

Dating back to the Roman era, the original settlement was erected on a hill overlooking the north-east corner of town, now the site of the Sveti Ivan church. The old settlement was burned in 1380 by the Venetians in the course of a battle. In 1525 a new settlement was begun closer to the sea, marked today by rows of houses with interconnected façades. These 16th century houses are well preserved despite the shops and small businesses installed in many of the ground floors. Although crowded in summer, the old town and harbour make a pleasant stroll and there's always that splendid beach.

Orientation

The town lies at the north end of Baška Draga Bay, encircled by a dramatic, barren range of mountains. The bus from Krk stops at the top of a hill on the edge of the old town, between the beach and the harbour (no left-luggage facility). The main street is Zvonimirova, overlooking the harbour, and the beach begins at the west end of the harbour, continuing south past the tourist development around the Hotel Corinthia.

KVARNER

Information

Tourist Offices The tourist office (☎ 856 817, fax 856 336, tz-baska@ri.tel.hr) is at Zvonimirova 114, just down the street from the bus stop.

Post & Communications The post office is on the corner of Prilaz Kupalistu and Zdenke Čermakove on the way to the Hotel Corinthia. You can withdraw cash on MasterCard and Diners Club. It's open Monday to Saturday from 7 am to 9 pm, Sunday from 9 am to noon. The postcode for Baška is 51523.

Travel Agencies The main travel agencies are Guliver (☎ 656 004) and Primaturist (☎ 856 132, fax 856 971), both at Zvonimirova 98 in the town centre. At the Hotel Corinthia, there's KEI-Kvarner Express (☎/fax 856 895), Kompas (☎ 856 460) and Ara (☎ 856 298).

Activities

The tourist office provides a good free map of marked **hiking** trails throughout the southern tip of the island. Several popular trails begin around Camping Zablaće, including an 8km walk to Stara Baška, a restful little village on a bay surrounded by stark, salt-washed limestone hills.

Another short 2.5km route leads to **St Lucy** (Sveti Lucija) church, where the 11th century Baška tablet was found that is now in the Archaeology Museum in Zagreb. The church was built at the end of the 9th century by Benedictine monks on the site of a Roman villa. In addition to a great view, you'll see ruins of the former monastery which was abandoned at the end of the 15th century.

A trail from the naturist camp leads east to the remains of the ancient Illyrian settlement of Bosar (Corinthia) between the Vela luka and Mala luka bays.

You can also arrange **scuba diving** at the Delfin Agency (☎ 656 126) on the beach behind the Hotel Corinthia, which will take you down for 137KN a dive plus equipment rental of 180KN per day.

Places to Stay

During July and August, it is essential to arrange accommodation well in advance since the town is swarming with Austrian, German and Czech tourists. Hotel space is booked solid for the summer season by late spring, and accommodation is tight in the shoulder season as well.

Camping There are two camping options at Baška. *Camping Zablaće* (☎ 856 909), open from May to September, is on the beach south-west of the bus stop (look for the rows of caravans). In heavy rain you risk getting flooded here.

A better bet is *FKK Camp Bunculuka* (☎ 856 806), open from May to September. This quiet and shady naturist camping ground is a 15 minute walk over the hill east of the harbour.

Private Rooms All of the travel agencies listed above arrange for private accommodation. Expect to pay at least 88/126KN a single/double for basic rooms, 126/158KN for better rooms and 217KN for a studio, plus a 30% surcharge for stays of less than four nights and 28KN for breakfast.

If you come in July or August, you may find it impossible to rent a room for less than four nights, impossible to rent a single room or to rent a room near town – or just plain impossible. Plan ahead.

Hotels All hotels are in the 'tourist settlement', about 1km south-west of town. The modern complex wreaked havoc on the pine forest but there's still a tree-lined promenade along the beach. The cheapest rooms are at the *Hotel Zvonimir* or *Adria*, where you can find singles/doubles for 234/396KN. The simple rooms with bath are adequate but short on decor. Next up in price is the *Corinthia II*, which has rooms for 277/486KN. Head of the pack is the *Hotel Corinthia* (☎ 656 111, fax 856 584), with rooms in good condition with telephones and TV for 366/612KN. Bookings for all four places are made through the Hotel Corinthia.

PUNAT

Eight kilometres south-east of Krk town, Punat has replaced its traditional shipbuilding industry with the task of tending to the many yachts that descend upon the port each summer. Although the town is not as attractive as Krk or Baška, the presence of several camp sites and a youth hostel makes it a good alternative place to stay.

Orientation & Information

The bus drops you off on the south end of town (no left-luggage office) close to several hotels. The tourist office (☎/fax 854 970) is on Obala 72 and is a good source of free town maps and brochures. During the summer it's open daily from 8 am to 9 pm but off season it's open mornings only Monday to Saturday. The post office is nearby on Obala and is open Monday to Saturday from 7 am to 9 pm. You can withdraw cash using Diners Club. The postal code for Punat is 51521. You can change money at Marina Tours travel agency (☎ 854 375), Obala 81, or Punat Tours travel agency (☎ 854 104), Obala 94.

Places to Stay

Camping *Camping Pila* (☎ 854 122) occupies a large area just south of the town centre, only a few minutes walk from the bus stop. It's open from Easter to the end of September. There's also the naturist camp *FKK Konobe* (☎ 854 036), in the same direction about 3km down the coast. It's open from May to September.

Hostel From mid-June to September youth hostel accommodation is available at the *Ljetovalište Ferialnog Saveza* (☎ 854 037, fax 434 962), just up from the harbour on Novi Put. You can get a bed for 75KN plus 12KN for breakfast but you're close enough to town to grab some coffee and pastry in a local café.

Private Rooms Punat Tours travel agency (☎ 854 104, fax 854 101), Obala 94, arranges private accommodation for 126/158KN a single/double in high season plus a 30% surcharge for stays less than three nights. Breakfast is another 30KN.

Hotels The *Park* (☎ 854 024), *Park II* (☎ 854 044) and *Dependance Kvarner* (☎ 854 044) hotels offer roughly comparable rooms at the same rates at 201/353KN a single/double in high season. They are all clustered on the southern end of town near the bus station and the beach.

AROUND PUNAT
Košljun Island Monastery

Perhaps the best reason to pay a visit to Punat is the monastery on Košljun island. Only a 20 minute boat ride from Punat, the tiny island contains a 16th century Franciscan monastery built on the site of a 12th century Benedictine abbey. The monastery church contains a large, appropriately chilling *Last Judgment*, painted in 1653, as well as several other religious paintings.

The monastery also contains a museum displaying other paintings, an ethnographic collection and a rare copy of Ptolemy's *Atlas* printed in Venice in the late 16th century. Concerts are sometimes held in the summer during the Krk Summer Festival. After visiting the monastery, take time to stroll around the forested island. Although agencies in Krk town organise excursions to Košljun, it's cheaper to take one of the frequent buses to Punat and then one of the taxi boats from the harbour that leave six times a day and cost 20KN return.

Rab Island

Rab (Italian: Arbe), near the centre of the Kvarner island group, is one of the most enticing islands in the Adriatic. The more densely populated south-west is green with pine forests and dotted with sandy beaches and coves. High mountains protect Rab's interior from cold north and east winds, allowing olives, grapes and vegetables to be cultivated. The Lopar peninsula in the north-east corner is a fertile oasis that offers the island's best beaches along its two wide bays. The north-west peninsula that emerges from Supetarska Draga is fringed with coves and lagoons that continue on to the Kalifront peninsula and the Suha Punta resort.

The cultural and historical centre of the island is Rab town, characterised by four elegant bell towers rising from the ancient stone streets. The island has a strong tourist business but outside of July and August you'll find it lively without being overrun with visitors.

Like much of the Adriatic, Rab was first inhabited by the Illyrian Liburnian tribe before it was occupied by the Romans in the 2nd century BC. Defensive towers and walls protected the settlement and the Romans built country villas and naval bases. With the division of the Roman Empire, Rab came under Byzantine rule in the 9th century.

In the 10th century, Byzantium made a deal with the Croatian king Tomislav that ac-knowledged Croatian sovereignty over the island, but the rising power of Venice forced Byzantium and then the Croat-Hungarian kings to gradually allow increasing Venetian influence in Rab.

In 1409 Rab was sold to Venice along with Dalmatia and remained under Venetian rule until 1797. Farming, fishing, vineyards and salt production were the economic mainstays but most income from these activities ended up in Venice. The inhabitants succeeded in wresting some political autonomy from Venice but class divisions prevented the islanders from fighting their way out of poverty. Two plague epidemics in the 15th century nearly wiped out the population and brought the economy to a standstill. The Turkish penetration of Bosnia in the 15th century forced many Slavs to migrate to Rab which placed further economic pressure on the island and increased

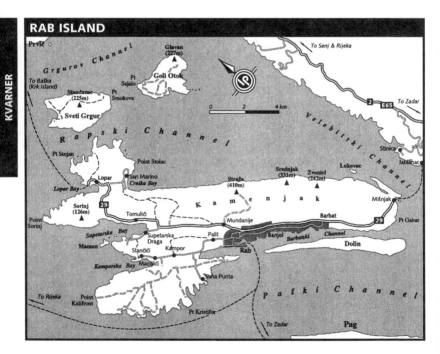

the division between the Italianised elite and Slav commoners.

When Venice fell, there was a short period of Austrian rule until the French arrived in 1805. After the fall of Napoleon in 1813, Rab became part of the Austrian territories. The Austrians favoured the Italianised elite and it was not until 1897 that Croatian was made an 'official' language. After the fall of Austria in 1918, Rab eventually became part of the Kingdom of Yugoslavia. The island was occupied by Italian troops in 1941 and by the Germans in 1944, and it was liberated in 1945.

The tourism industry that began gearing up at the turn of the 20th century was a godsend for the impoverished island. Even during the recent war, Rab managed to hold on to its German tourists, which is not surprising considering the hospitality of the people and the beauty of the island. Rab would be the perfect stepping stone between Krk and Zadar if only the boat transportation connections were more convenient.

GETTING THERE & AWAY
Bus
The most reliable way to come and go is on one of the two daily buses between Rab and Rijeka (115km, 62KN). In the tourist season there are two direct buses from Zagreb to Rab (211km, five hours). These services can fill up, so book ahead if possible. There's no direct bus from Rab to Zadar but there are two daily buses that connect at Senj with Rijeka buses travelling to Zadar (five hours, 94KN). In order to avoid backtracking from Senj to Jablanac, and also to save some kuna, you can take the bus to the highway at Jablanac, wait for about 1½ hours and catch the Rijeka bus as it heads to Zadar.

Boat
The ferry between Baška on Krk island and Lopar (23KN) operates June through September from two to five times daily, but between October and May there's no service. There's a weekly Jadrolinija ferry to Rab town but for passengers only, not cars, and

the boat *Ivan Zajc* doesn't call in at Rab at all.

Car
If you have your own car, there are nonstop ferries in July and August from Jablanac on the mainland to Mišnjak on the south-east corner of Rab and frequent ferries throughout the year.

GETTING AROUND
Bus
From Lopar to Rab town (12km) there are nine buses daily in either direction; some are timed to meet the Baška-Lopar ferry. There are eight daily buses from Rab town to Kampor (2.5km), eight to Barbat (3km) and five to Suha Punta (5km).

Boat
In addition to island tours operated from Rab town, there's a water-taxi service between Rab town and Suha Punta resort that operates four times a day in July and August (8KN), leaving from in front of the Hotel Istra and the Hotel Padova.

RAB TOWN
• pop 592   ☎ 051
Medieval Rab town is built on a narrow peninsula between the bay of St Euphemija (Svet Fumija), and the port, Gradska Harbour. The oldest part of town is Kaldanac on the south-east tip of the peninsula, which was settled before the Roman conquest.In the 14th and 15th centuries the town expanded to include the Varoš section, further north, and, as an important military outpost for the Venetians, it became surrounded by defensive walls, some of which are still visible. Trg Municipium Arba divides the two sections and you'll notice a difference in architectural styles. Besides the old stone buildings and streets, the town has richly endowed churches that often host concerts and art exhibitions. When you get 'churched-out', there are excursion boats to whisk you off to beaches and coves around the island.

Orientation

The old town lies directly across the bay from the marina. Narrow side-streets climb up from the main north-south streets – Donja, Srednja and Gornja ulica, or lower, middle and upper roads. The large Jadrolinija ferries tie up on the south-eastern tip of the peninsula and the small boat harbour is on the north-western side.

A five minute walk north of the old town is the new commercial centre with the Merkur department store, some travel agencies and the bus station. Despite a sign at the bus station advertising a *garderoba* (left-luggage office), it's not operational because the station is only open limited hours. The north-west portion of the peninsula is given over to the 100-year-old Komrčar Park, bordered by the town beaches. There are also beaches around the hotel and autocamp Padova but you'll find better swimming further from town.

Information

Tourist Offices There are two municipal tourist offices. The Turistički Ured (☎ 771 111) with the most information and the longest hours is around the corner from the bus station, opposite the Merkur department store. The office is open daily in summer from 7 am to 10 pm and off season Monday to Saturday from 8 am to 2 pm. The other office is on Arba Municipium, and is open daily in summer from 8 am to noon and 7 to 9 pm. Off season it's open Monday to Saturday mornings only.

Money Any post office or travel agency can change money for you. It can also be changed at Riječka Banka, located in Rab's commercial centre. The bank is open Monday to Friday from 8 am to 12.30 pm and from 2.30 to 8 pm. There are no ATMs in town.

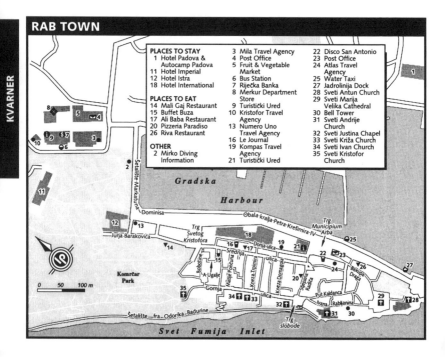

RAB TOWN

KVARNER

PLACES TO STAY
1 Hotel Padova & Autocamp Padova
11 Hotel Imperial
12 Hotel Istra
18 Hotel International

PLACES TO EAT
14 Mali Gaj Restaurant
15 Buffet Buza
17 Ali Baba Restaurant
20 Pizzeria Paradiso
26 Riva Restaurant

OTHER
2 Mirko Diving Information

3 Mila Travel Agency
4 Post Office
5 Fruit & Vegetable Market
6 Bus Station
7 Riječka Banka
8 Merkur Department Store
9 Turistički Ured
10 Kristofor Travel Agency
13 Numero Uno Travel Agency
16 Le Journal
19 Kompas Travel Agency
21 Turistički Ured

22 Disco San Antonio
23 Post Office
24 Atlas Travel Agency
25 Water Taxi
27 Jadrolinija Dock
28 Sveti Antun Church
29 Sveti Marija Velika Cathedral
30 Bell Tower
31 Sveti Andrije Church
32 Sveti Justina Chapel
33 Sveti Križa Church
34 Sveti Ivan Church
35 Sveti Kristofor Church

Post & Communications There is a post office in the commercial centre and another on Arba Municipium. The one in the commercial centre is open Monday to Saturday from 7 am to 9 pm. The other office is open Monday to Saturday from 8 am to noon and 7 to 9 pm. You can get cash on your MasterCard or Diners Club card at either branch. The postal code for Rab island is 51280.

Travel Agencies Atlas travel agency (☎ 724 585) is on Arba Municipium, opposite the post office. In summer it's open daily from 8 am to 10 pm but in winter it's open Monday to Saturday from 8 am to 1 pm. Numero Uno (☎/fax 724 688) is opposite the Hotel Istra and is open daily in summer from 7.30 am to midnight. In winter it's open daily from 8 am to noon and 5 to 8 pm. Turist biro Mila (☎ 725 499), on the south-east corner of the bus station, and Turist biro Kristofor (☎ 725 543, kristofor@ri.tel.hr), next to the bus station, keep roughly similar hours.

Kompas (☎ 724 939) is on Donja Ulica 4, and opens in summer Monday to Saturday from 10 am to midnight and Sunday from noon to midnight. Off-season hours are shorter.

Things to See

Most of Rab's famous churches and towers are along Gornja ulica, the upper road that continues on as Ivana Rablianina in the Kaldanac section. Start your walk from Trg Svetog Kristofora near the harbour. In the centre of the square is a fountain with sculptures of the two legendary figures Kalifront and Draga. According to the story, the passionate Kalifront attempted to seduce the shepherdess Draga, who had taken a vow of chastity. The goddess to whom Draga had pledged chastity turned her into stone to save her from the seducer.

Go up Bobotine and pause at the corner of Srednja ulica to admire the **Dominis Palace** on the left. Built at the end of the 15th century for a prominent patrician family, the façade has decorated Renaissance windows and a striking portal decorated with the family coat of arms. Continue to the top and the **St Christopher** (Sveti Kristofor) church which was part of the highest tower of the ramparts. Next to it is a **lapidarium**, open daily from 9 am to 1 pm and 6 to 8 pm. From the tower a passage leads to Komrčar Park.

Continuing south along Gornja ulica, you'll come to the ruins of the church of **Sveti Ivan** (St John), which probably dates to the beginning of the 7th century. Little survives but the 13th century **bell tower** next to it which can be climbed. The church was part of a monastery that was occupied by Benedictine nuns in the 11th century, Franciscans from 1298 to 1783 and was later converted into a Bishop's Residence. Next to the bell tower is the 16th century **Sveti Križa** (Holy Cross) church, which was briefly called the Church of the Weeping Cross after a legend circulated that Christ wept on the church's cross because of the immorality of the town's residents. While the cathedral is undergoing renovation, Sveti Križa is the town church and displays sacred objects from the cathedral. It's open for visits in July and August from 10 am to noon and 4 to 6 pm, and in June and September from 9 am to noon and 3 to 5 pm.

Further along Gornja ulica is **St Justine** (Sveti Justina) church, with a bell tower dating from 1572. Today the church hosts a collection of religious artefacts, including a portable altar donated to the town by King Koloman, fragments of the illuminated evangelistary from the 11th century and the silver-plated reliquary for the head of St Christopher. There's also a polyptych by Paolo Veneziano and a Renaissance terracotta of the Madonna from the 15th century. In July and August it's open from 9 am to noon and 6 to 8 pm and in June and September from 7.30 to 9 pm.

Pass Trg slobode bearing right and on your right you'll see the Romanesque bell tower of **Sveti Andrije** (St Andrew) which dates from 1181. The biggest tower is coming up on the right. The cathedral of **Sveti Marija Velika** (St Mary the Great) and its bell tower were built in the 12th century. The 25m tall tower stands on the remains of Roman buildings and is divided into four floors, terminating in an octagonal pyramid surrounded by a Romanesque balustrade. The pyramid is topped by a cross with five small globes and reliquaries of several saints were placed in the highest globe. The symmetrical arrangement of windows and arches creates a wonderful sense of lightness and harmony that makes the tower one of the most beautiful on the Croatian coast. You can climb it for a small fee. The cathedral is closed for renovation and is due to reopen in the year 2000.

The extreme end of the cape accommodates a monastery of Franciscan nuns and the baroque **St Anthony** (Sveti Antun) church built in 1675. The altar is decorated with 17th century inlaid marble and a painting of St Anthony.

Activities

Numero Uno travel agency rents **bicycles** for 50KN a day and scooters for 120KN a day. Kristofor travel agency rents small boats for 350KN a day and small motorcycles for 170KN a day.

You can arrange to **scuba dive** from the Mirko Diving information office in town but the company's boats leave from its main office in Barbat (☎/fax 721 154). It offers two dives for 252KN plus an additional 208KN for equipment rental. You can also contact the Rabeko Diving Center (☎ 776 272) in Kampor which offers dives at the same price and can arrange private accommodation as well.

From behind the Hotel Istra, there's a marked **hiking** trail that leads north-east to the top of Sveti Ilija (100m). It only takes about 30 minutes and the view is great.

Organised Tours

Atlas and other travel agencies offer day tours of the island by boat for 120KN that include plenty of swim stops around the island and at nearby Sveti Grgur island. In summer, tourist agencies offer day excursions to Lošinj (130KN return) or Pag island (70KN return) once or twice a week.

Special Events

Rab has recently revived the crossbow competitions that date from its early history. Residents are becoming increasingly practised at the skill and are proud to demonstrate it on several national and local holidays – they don't even seem to mind dressing up in tunics, plumed hats and tights for the occasion. Sveti Kristofor Day is 27 July, when the town's patron saint is celebrated with crossbow competitions and local dances.

The 15 August Assumption celebration is another good opportunity to see the crossbow competitors, and they make another appearance on the Croatian National Day, 29 May. Rab Music Evenings take place from June to September and revolve around the Wednesday-night concerts in Sveti Križa church at 9 pm. Tickets are from 30KN to 50KN depending on the artist.

Places To Stay

Everything from camping to expensive hotels can be found in and around Rab town.

Camping To sleep cheap, carry your tent around the bay and walk south along the waterfront for about 25 minutes to *Autocamp Padova* (☎ 724 355) at Banjol (14KN per person, 13KN per tent). It's open from April to October.

There's also a small camping ground further out of town at Kampor on a large cove. Called *Halović* (☎ 776 087), it's run by an elderly couple.

Private Rooms The travel agencies can organise private rooms, with prices beginning at 90/103KN a single/double, rising to 108/144KN, plus 21KN for breakfast and a 30% surcharge for stays less than three nights. You can also rent a studio for 234KN a night in addition to the 30% surcharge for stays less than three nights. Some agencies forgo the surcharges when things are slow.

Hotels The *Hotel International* (☎ *711 266, fax 724 206, Obala kralja Petra Krešimira IV*), facing the harbour, has the cheapest rooms at 259/432KN a single/ double with half-board in peak season with an 18KN deduction per person for bed and breakfast only. It's a pleasant place to stay, but for a few extra kuna, you're better off at the *Hotel Imperial* (☎ *724 522, fax 724 126*), set back from the town in a wooded park. It has rooms for 277/468KN in high season including half pension, and there is an 18KN deduction per person for bed and breakfast only.

Hotel Istra (☎ *724 134, fax 724 050, hotelistra@hotmail.com, M de Dominisa bb*) offers rooms for 248/460KN a single/double in high season including bed and breakfast, with an extra 10KN for half pension plus a 30% surcharge for stays less than three nights. It's a cheery yellow building right on the edge of town with newly decorated rooms. Across the bay, the oversized concrete *Hotel Padova* (☎ *724 444, fax 724 418*) offers rooms with half-board for 302/518KN.

Places to Eat

Rab cuisine revolves around fresh fish, seafood and pasta. The quality and prices are generally uniform – you'll pay 80 to 100KN for a complete meal. One of the few restaurants in Rab which posts a menu outside is *Ali Baba* (*Srednja ulica 30*), in the old town. It's not cheap but it does have a good selection of seafood and a pleasant garden-terrace. It's open Monday to Saturday from noon to 3 pm and 5.30 pm to midnight.

Pizzeria Paradiso (*ulica Radića 2*) serves pizza for 40KN in a touristy but attractive enclosed terrace. It's open daily from 10 am to 3 pm and 5.30 pm to midnight. *Riva Restaurant* (*Obala kralja Petra Krešimira IV*) has a particularly atmospheric stone interior and a terrace with a sea view. *Mali Gaj* is another popular seafood/pasta place on the edge of Komrčar park. For fast food, head to *Buffet Buza* (*ulica Ugalje*), near Arba Municipium, where you can eat a plate of fried squid for 20KN.

There's a good *supermarket* in the basement of the Merkur department store for picnic supplies.

Entertainment *Disco San Antonio*, behind Trg Municipium Arba, is the most popular disco in town, open daily in summer but weekends only in winter. There are also discos in the Hotel International and the Hotel Padova. *Le Journal* is a popular club, bar and hang-out open daily year round.

LOPAR

The ferry from Baška lands at Lopar but the ferry stop is the least attractive part of the peninsula, which is marked by beautiful coves, bays and hamlets. There are 22 sandy beaches bordered by pine groves around Lopar, and the shallow sea makes them perfect for small children. Lopar Bay is on one side of the peninsula and Crnika Bay is on the other. The north-eastern part of the peninsula is steep and barren, with many naturist beaches. The 1500m-long **Paradise Beach** (Rajska Plaža) lies 3km south of the ferry landing on Crnika Bay. The road between the ferry landing and the San Marino hotel and autocamp on Crnika Bay passes a small commercial centre and several restaurants. The postal code for Lopar is 51281.

Places to Stay

Camping San Marino (☎ *775 133*) is in the midst of pine groves on a wide swath of sandy beach. It's large (3600 places) and can get crowded in the summer but the setting is unbeatable. It's open from the beginning of April to the end of October. Prices are about 20KN per person and 16KN per tent.

For private accommodation go to Dedan Tours (☎ *775 105*) in the commercial centre, which is open from 8 am to 9 pm in summer but closed in winter. Rooms are 54KN to 72KN per person in high season plus a 29KN surcharge for a single room. There are also some houses with *sobe* signs along the road.

KVARNER

San Marino and San Marino

You've probably been asking yourself: 'San Marino the tiny, independent tourist village on the northern coast of Rab, and San Marino the tiny, independent republic on the north-east coast of Italy – what's the connection?' There is a connection, at least according to the residents of Lopar.

According to legend, the founder of San Marino was born in Lopar: once upon a time, back in the 3rd century, the sculptor Marin (Marinus) left Lopar to work on the fortifications around Ariminum (now Rimini) in Italy. Marin was a Christian and, at the time, Emperor Diocletian was ferociously persecuting Christians up and down the Adriatic coast. Marin was forced to secrete himself in a cave in nearby Mt Titano, where he became a hermit. He developed a coterie of followers who erected a church and monastery on the slopes of Mount Titano that grew into the town and state of San Marino. Marin became a saint and San Marino (the republic) became a 'twin town' of Lopar, whose inhabitants named a tourist settlement and hotel after their illustrious ancestor.

The *San Marino Hotel* (☎ 775 149, fax 775 128) offers singles/doubles for 248/410KN. It has the usual package-tour ambience but the location on Paradise Beach makes up for the dreary architecture.

BARBAT

Barbat is the southernmost village on Rab island, sprawling along the Barbatski Channel that separates Rab from Dolin island. It's 3km south-east of Rab town on a coastal plateau covered with vineyards and vegetable gardens. Although the tiny town centre is nowhere near as interesting as Rab town, it has a 3km coast lined with houses offering private accommodation. Boating facilities have taken over a good part of the coast but there are several attractive gravel beaches close to town.

There are 15 buses a day between Rab town and Barbat that drop you off on the main road overlooking the coast.

The tourist agency (☎ 721 227) is a few metres from the bus stop and has rooms for 70KN per person with a 35KN single supplement and a 30% surcharge for stays less than three nights. In summer it's open daily from 7.30 am to 9.30 pm but off-season hours are Monday to Saturday from 8 am to noon and 5 to 7 pm.

From the main road about 1km north-west of the bus stop, marked trails lead to the ruins of **Sveti Damjana** church and the remains of what may have been a Greek military fortress. You'll also have a great view of the coast down to Mali Lošinj on a clear day.

SUHA PUNTA

The Suha Punta resort is on the south-eastern side of the forested Kalifront peninsula overlooking a spectacular bay. The hotel complex is integrated into the surrounding pine forest, leaving the natural beauty of the setting more or less intact. The beaches are rocky but a shady coastal path leads east through the pines to other coves and naturist beaches. Another pleasant walk leads north-west to the village of Kampor and the sandy Bay of Kampor. There's a supermarket and a couple of restaurants as well as tennis and miniature golf at the resort. As far as tourist developments go, this is one of the least objectionable and it makes an easy day trip from Rab town.

There is no camping or private accommodation, and the cheapest place to stay is in the simple bungalows at the *Suha Punta Tourist Village* (☎ 724 060), which cost 230/374KN a single/double including half-board. It also has studios for 342KN.

The *Hotel Eva* (☎ 724 233) offers singles/doubles at 288/490KN per day with half-board. The most expensive hotel is the *Hotel Carolina* (☎ 724 133, fax 724 133), which is in a great location overlooking the cove. There's an outdoor terrace and a swimming pool. Singles/doubles are 309/532KN a day with half-board.

Istria

The largest peninsula in the Adriatic (3160 sq km), Istria (Italian: Istra) is blessed with a 430km indented shoreline and an interior of green rolling hills, drowned valleys and fertile plains. The northern part of the peninsula belongs to Slovenia while the Dinaric mountain range in the north-east corner separates Istria from the continental mainland. Most of the resorts are on the highly developed west coast. The scenic interior is less visited by tourists but contains several medieval hill towns offering panoramic views of the region. Pazin, in the interior, is the administrative capital of the region while Pula, with its thriving shipyard, is the economic centre.

Flat and over-endowed with bland, sprawling tourist complexes, the Istrian coast is not the most beautiful in Croatia but its culture is unique. With borders that have changed five times in the last century, it's unsurprising that Istria is the most tolerant and cosmopolitan region in Croatia. In a 1991 census, nearly 20% of the inhabitants declared their nationality as Istrian rather than Croatian, which is why the Istrian National Party repeatedly trounces the ruling HDZ at the polls. Although only 8% of the population is ethnic Italian, many Istrians have Italian passports enabling them to work in Italy and receive Italian pensions.

Istria's proximity and close economic links with Italy have given the coastal cities a strong Italian flavour. Virtually all Istrians speak Italian fluently and you'll notice more Italian than Croatian specialties on local menus. If you come in July and August, the streets will be thronged with Italian visitors who are the mainstay of the Istrian tourist industry since the recent war disrupted the flow of English and Dutch tourists. Outside the main season, tourism quiets down considerably, leaving you free to enjoy the Roman ruins, old Venetian ports, beaches, forests, vineyards and hill towns of this fascinating region.

HIGHLIGHTS

- Visiting the Euphrasian Basilica in Poreč, a World Heritage site
- Taking in a concert at Pula's Roman amphitheatre
- Watching fishermen pull in their catch in Rovinj
- Browsing the craft shops in Motovun
- Listening to musicians practise in Grožnjan

History

Archaeological excavations near Pula reveal that the Istrian peninsula has been settled since the Paleolithic era, between 2,500,000 and 800,000 years BC. Towards the end of the second millennium BC, the Illyrian Histrian tribe settled the region and built fortified villages on top of the region's coastal and interior hills. Ancient Greek

ISTRIA

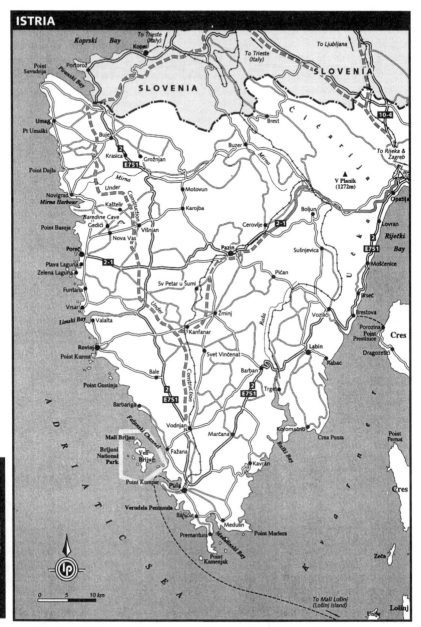

ISTRIA

chroniclers indicated that the region was on an important trade route – the Amber Route – through which Greek ships passed on trading missions from the Aegean.

The Romans swept into Istria in the 3rd century BC and, after fierce resistance, managed to subdue the region in the 2nd century BC. After the conquest, the Romans began building roads and fortified towns. Pola (Pula) and Parentium (Poreč) were Illyrian hill forts that the Romans chose as highly fortified strongholds because of their well-sheltered bays and strategic positions overlooking the lowlands. The best preserved Roman ruins are in Pula and date from the reign of Augustus (63 BC to 14 AD).

In the 4th and 5th centuries, Rome and Istria came under assault from Huns and Visigoths and the empire began to crumble. The Byzantine empire crushed the Ostrogoths in the 6th century and Istria remained under Byzantine rule from 539 to 751. The most impressive remnant of Byzantine culture is the Basilica of Euphrasius in Poreč, with its stunning mosaics.

Slavic tribes moved into the region in the 6th and 7th centuries and enjoyed some autonomy before Charlemagne's conquest of Istria in 788. The ensuing centuries brought more turbulence as the Franks were supplanted by a succession of German rulers that lasted until the death of Friedrich II in 1250.

An increasingly powerful Venice wrested control of the Istrian coast from German rulers in the early 13th century, forcing the rulers of continental Istria to turn to the Habsburgs for protection. Treaties signed in 1374 and 1466 gave continental Istria to the Habsburgs. Istrian coastal cities, under threat from southern Dalmatian pirates, were willing to become vassals of Venice in exchange for Venetian protection of their trade routes.

Istrian coastal towns became important way stations for the repair and maintenance of Venetian ships, but the Venetian embrace brought other problems in the form of devastating attacks by Venice's rival, the Genoans. Misery, famine and warfare haunted the peninsula. Bubonic plague first broke out in 1371 and regularly ravaged Istrian cities until the 17th century. Malaria was endemic. Although the Turks never reached Istria, the peninsula lay in the path of the fearsome Uskoks from Senj who repeatedly attacked Venice's Istrian cities throughout the 16th and 17th centuries.

With the fall of Venice in 1797, Istria fell under Austrian rule, followed by the French (1809-1813), and again the Austrians. During the 19th and early 20th century, most of Istria was little more than a neglected outpost of the Austro-Hungarian empire, which concentrated on developing the port of Trieste. The economy of the coastal cities was badly affected by the decline in sailing ships although the construction of a naval port and shipyard in Pula in the late 19th century gave the region a boost. The Slavic farmers in the interior of the peninsula continued to cultivate the land and raise cattle.

When the Austro-Hungarian empire disintegrated at the end of WWI, Italy moved quickly to secure Istria. Italian troops occupied Pula in November 1918, and, in the 1920 Treaty of Rapallo, the Kingdom of Serbs, Croats and Slovenes ceded Istria along with Zadar and several islands to Italy as a reward for joining the Allied powers in WWI. A massive population shift followed as 30,000 to 40,000 Italians arrived from Mussolini's Italy and many Croats left, fearing fascism. Their fears were not misplaced as Istria's Italian masters attempted to consolidate their hold by banning Slavic speech, printing, education and cultural activities. Italy retained the region until its defeat in WWII when Istria became part of Yugoslavia, causing another mass exodus as Italians and many Croats fled Tito's communists. Trieste and the north-western tip of the peninsula was a point of contention between Italy and Yugoslavia until 1954 when it was finally awarded to Italy. As a result of Tito's reorganisation of Yugoslavia, the northern part of the peninsula was incorporated into Slovenia, where it has remained.

ISTRIA

Roman Architecture

The Roman heritage in Croatia spans six centuries, beginning with 1st century BC constructions in Istria and ending with 5th century basilicas in Salona. Travelling from Istria south to Split provides an almost chronological record of the evolution of Roman style from the classical period to late antiquity. The confidence of the young empire as shown in Istria slowly erodes as foreign and early Christian influences begin to make themselves felt in Split and Salona.

Istria has excellent examples of buildings constructed during the classical, Augustan period when Hellenistic views of proportion and harmony permeated the architecture. The most outstanding example is the 1st century Triumphal Arch of Sergius in Pula with its harmonious proportions, fine reliefs and Corinthian capitals. Artists and architects from Michelangelo to Robert Adam studied and sketched this exceptionally well preserved monument. The Temple of Augustus also reflects the purity of classical style while the amphitheatre shows the transition to more monumental architecture.

Streets are also laid out according to Hellenistic principles. In Pula and Trogir you'll see that the Romans retained the oval ground-plan and radial streets of older settlements but in Poreč and Zadar the streets intersect at neat right angles in the typical Roman layout. As in any Roman city, the centre is cut into four parcels by two perpendicular streets, the Cardo and the Decumanus.

In the ruins of Salona, the first stirrings of Christianity can be glimpsed. In the necropolises of Marusinac and Manastirine, monumental basilicas were raised in the 5th century around the graves of the 4th century Christian martyrs Domnius (St Dujam) and Anastasius (St Staš). The aisled basilica of St Staš at Marusinac with its open nave is a rare example of a roofless basilica in which open-air funeral rites were performed. The unusual width of the nave recalls the Peristyle of Diocletian's Palace in Split.

The vast 4th century palace built by Emperor Diocletian in Split is the largest Roman monument in Croatia. The symmetrical layout of the structure with its two intersecting streets is classical but most of the palace reflects the eclecticism of late antiquity. Part imperial villa and part fortified camp, the palace is remarkable for the diversity of forms that include the octagonal domed mausoleum, the rectangular Temple of Jupiter, the cruciform lower level of the Vestibule, and circular temples to Cybele and Venus. The vast Roman Empire of late antiquity easily absorbed foreign influences, apparent in the Egyptian sphinxes outside the Temple of Jupiter and the mausoleum. Poised between the classical and the medieval Christian civilisation, Diocletian's palace is a compendium of all the styles that preceded it.

The Temple of Augustus in Pula

PULA

• pop 62,378   ☎ 052

Pula (the Roman Polensium) is a large regional centre with some industry, a big naval base and a busy commercial harbour. An important base for the Romans, the city contains a wealth of Roman ruins topped by a remarkably well preserved amphitheatre which is now the centre of Pula's lively summer cultural scene. Although there are no beaches within the city, a short bus ride takes you south to the resorts on the Verudela Peninsula. The scenery around Pula is undramatic, as the region is relatively flat and its original oak forests have been replaced with shrubs and pine groves. The landscape is also marred by a crush of residential and holiday development, but the indented coastline south of the city that extends to the Premantura peninsula is studded with rocky bays and coves.

In the 1st century BC, the Illyrian Pola was conquered by the Romans and used as their administrative headquarters for the region that stretched from the Lim Fjord to the Raša River. The Romans cleverly exploited Pula's terrain, using Kaštel Hill, which now contains the Citadel, as a vantage point to protect the bay. The ancient town developed in concentric circles around Kaštel Hill, with the amphitheatre placed outside the fortified town centre. Pula joined the powerful Venetian empire in 1150 to protect itself against piracy, but the city suffered badly under Venetian rule. First subjected to ruinous assaults by Genoa, the city was then repeatedly invaded by Venice's rivals – the Patriarch of Aquilea, the Croatian-Hungarian kings and the Habsburgs. Plague and malaria had nearly wiped out the population by the 17th century. The fall of Venice in 1797 brought in the Habsburgs as the new rulers. Pula continued to stagnate until the Austro-Hungarian monarchy chose Pula as the empire's main naval port in 1853. The construction of its naval port and the 1886 opening of its large shipyard unleashed a demographic and economic expansion that transformed Pula into a military and industrial powerhouse. The city fell into decline once again under Italian fascist rule which lasted from 1918 to 1943, when the city was occupied by the Germans. At the end of WWII, Pula was administered by Anglo-American forces until it became part of postwar Yugoslavia in 1947. Pula's industrial base weathered the recent war relatively well and the city remains an important centre for shipbuilding, textiles, metals and glass.

Orientation

The oldest part of the city follows the ancient Roman street plan of streets, circling around the central citadel, while the city's newer portions follow a rectangular grid pattern. The bus station is on ulica Carrarina in the centre of town and one block south is Giardini, the central hub. Most shops, agencies and businesses are clustered in and around the old town as well as on Giardini, ulica Carrarina, Istarska ulica and Riva, which runs along the harbour. The train station is near the water about 1km north of town. The bus station's left-luggage office is open daily from 5 am to 10 pm, except for two half-hour breaks, and the train station's left-luggage office is open Monday to Saturday from 9 am to 4 pm. Hotels, restaurants and beaches are 3km south of the city on the Verudela Peninsula and can be reached by walking south on Arsenalska ulica and then ulica Veruda.

Information

Tourist Offices The official Tourist Information Centre (☎ 33 557), Istarska 11, publishes a useful city guide and will have the latest city map. It's open weekdays from 9 am to 1 pm and 5 to 8 pm. Jadroagent (☎ 22 568), Riva 14, sells ferry tickets. It's open Monday to Saturday from 7 am to 3 pm in summer but is closed Saturday off season. Croatia Airlines (☎ 23 322), Carrarina 8, is across the street from the bus station. It's open Monday to Friday from 8 am to 7 pm, Saturday 8 am to noon. Motorists can turn to the HAK Auto Klub (☎ 540 987), Štiglićeva 34.

ISTRIA

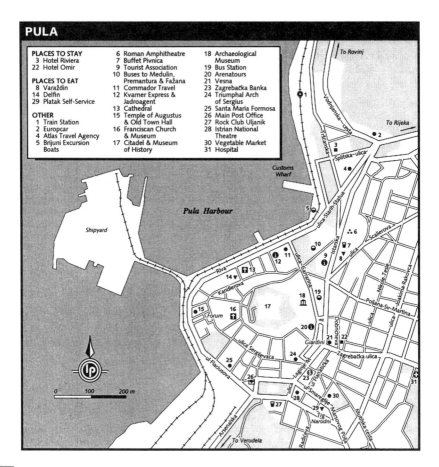

PULA

PLACES TO STAY	6 Roman Amphitheatre	18 Archaeological
3 Hotel Riviera	7 Buffet Pivnica	Museum
22 Hotel Omir	9 Tourist Association	19 Bus Station
	10 Buses to Medulin,	20 Arenatours
PLACES TO EAT	Premantura & Fažana	21 Vesna
8 Varaždin	11 Commador Travel	23 Zagrebačka Banka
14 Delfin	12 Kvarner Express &	24 Triumphal Arch
29 Platak Self-Service	Jadroagent	of Sergius
	13 Cathedral	25 Santa Maria Formosa
OTHER	15 Temple of Augustus	26 Main Post Office
1 Train Station	& Old Town Hall	27 Rock Club Uljanik
2 Europcar	16 Franciscan Church	28 Istrian National
4 Atlas Travel Agency	& Museum	Theatre
5 Brijuni Excursion	17 Citadel & Museum	30 Vegetable Market
Boats	of History	31 Hospital

Money You can change money at the post office, travel agencies and at Zagrebačka Banka, M. Laginje 1, which also has an ATM where you can withdraw cash on MasterCard. The bank is open Monday to Friday from 8 am to 12.30 pm and 6 to 8.30 pm, Saturday 8 am to noon. There's also an ATM outside Commodore Travel, Riva 14.

Post & Communications The main post office is at Danteov Trg 4. It's open Monday to Saturday from 7 am to 9 pm, Sunday 9 am to noon. The postcode for Pula is 52100.

Travel Agencies Kvarner Express (☎ 22 519), Riva 14, sells ferry tickets, excursions and finds private accommodation. The American Express representative is Atlas travel agency (☎ 214 172), Starih Statuta 1. There's also Arenatours (☎ 34 355), Giardini 4, a block south of the bus station, which represents most of the hotels in Pula; Brijuni

Turist Biro (☎ 22 477), ulica Istarska 3, beside the bus station; and Generalturist (☎ 22 777), Giardini 2, which handles air tickets.

Things to See

Roman Ruins Pula's most imposing sight is the 1st century **Roman amphitheatre** overlooking the harbour north-east of the old town. Built entirely from local limestone, the amphitheatre was designed to host gladiatorial contests and could accommodate up to 20,000 spectators. The 30m-high outer wall is almost intact and contains two rows of 72 arches but the stone spectator seats were removed for building materials in the Middle Ages. On the top of the walls is a gutter which collected rain water and you can still see the slabs used to secure the fabric canopy that protected spectators from the sun. Around the end of July a Croatian film festival is held in the amphitheatre, and there are also pop and classical concerts all summer. The amphitheatre is open daily from 9 am to 9 pm (4.30 pm off season) and admission is 14KN.

Along the street facing the bus station are **Roman walls** which mark the east boundary of old Pula. Follow these walls south and continue down Giardini to the **Triumphal Arch of Sergius**. This majestic arch was erected in 27 BC to commemorate three members of the Sergius family who achieved distinction in Pula. The outer side is lavishly ornamented with columns and friezes while the inner side that led to the old town is simpler. Until the 19th century the arch was backed by the city gate and surrounded by walls that were pulled down to allow the city to expand beyond the old town.

The pedestrian street beyond the arch, ulica Sergijevaca, winds right around old Pula. Follow it to where you'll find the ancient **forum**, the town's central meeting place from antiquity through the Middle Ages. It used to contain temples and public buildings, but today the only visible remnant from the Roman era is the **Temple of Augustus**, erected from 2 BC to 14 AD.

Pula's amphitheatre, designed for gladiatorial contests, held 20,000 bloodthirsty spectators

When the Romans left, the temple became a church and then a grain warehouse. The building suffered a direct hit when Pula was bombed in 1944, and it was almost totally destroyed. It was reconstructed in 1947. Also in the forum, notice the **old town hall** which was built in 1296 as the seat of Pula's municipal authorities. The building underwent a number of reconstructions over the centuries, which is apparent in the mixture of architectural styles – from Romanesque to Renaissance. It's still the seat of Pula's mayor.

Churches The **Cathedral** on Kandlerova ulica traces its origins back to the 5th century. The main altar is even older, being a Roman sarcophagus from the 3rd century, and the floor reveals fragments of 5th and 6th century mosaics. The church was reconstructed following a fire in 1242 and again in the 15th century when the Renaissance south portal was added. The late-Renaissance façade was added in the early 16th century and the 17th century bell tower was made of stones from the amphitheatre.

ISTRIA

The **Chapel of St Mary of Formosa** (Kapela Marije Formoze) on ulica Flaciusova is all that remains of the 6th century Benedictine abbey that once stood here. This Byzantine structure was adorned with mosaics which are now in the Archaeological Museum.

Museums The **Archaeological Museum**, ulica Carrarina 3, opposite the bus station, presents archaeological finds from all over Istria. The permanent exhibits cover Prehistory to the Middle Ages, but the accent is on the period from the 2nd century BC to the 6th century AD. In the summer the museum is open daily from 9 am to 7 pm and off-season hours are Monday to Friday from 9 am to 2.30 pm. Even if you don't visit the museum be sure to visit the large sculpture garden around it, and the **Roman Theatre** behind. The garden is entered through 2nd century twin gates.

The **Museum of History** (open daily) is in the 17th century Venetian citadel on a hill in the centre of the old town. The meagre exhibits deal mostly with the maritime history of Pula but the views of Pula from the citadel walls are good.

Activities

At the Sports Center Verudela (☎ 34 777), on Verudela Peninsula near the Hotel Brioni, there's **water-skiing** and **parasailing**, and you can rent rowboats, canoes and jet skis. **Scuba diving** is handled by Abyss Diving School (☎ 098-219 106) in the Autocamp Stoja.

Organised Tours

Most excursions are operated by Atlas travel agency, which offers a day trip to the Brijuni Islands for 200KN, a 'fish picnic' for 145KN and a tour of the Istrian interior for 180KN.

Places to Stay

Pula's main season runs from the second week of July to the end of August. During this period, it's wise to make advance reservations.

Camping The closest camping ground to Pula is *Autocamp Stoja* (☎ 24 144), 3km south-west of the centre (take bus No 1 to the terminus at Stoja). Open mid-April to mid-October, there's lots of space on the shady promontory, with swimming possible off the rocks. The two restaurants at the camping ground are good. *Autocamp Ribarska Koliba* (☎ 22 966) is a small camping ground on the coast of the Verudela Peninsula, 3km south of Pula. It's open from June through August.

Hostels The *Ljetovalište Ferijalnog Saveza Youth Hostel* (☎ 210 002, fax 212 394) is 3km south of central Pula in a great location overlooking a clean pebble beach. Take the No 2 or No 7 Verudela bus to the 'Piramida' stop and walk back to the first street, turn left and look for the sign. Bed and breakfast is 75KN per person, and camping is allowed for 56KN including breakfast. The hostel is now heated and open all year. You can sit and sip cold beer on the terrace, where a rock band plays on some summer evenings.

Private Rooms Arenatours, Kvarner Express, Brijuni Turist Biro and Atlas travel agency have basic private rooms for 54/86KN for a single/double, rising to 90/144KN, with an additional 50% surcharge for one night stays and 25% surcharge if you stay less than four nights. These high-season rates drop by about 40% from mid-September to mid-May.

Hotels There are no cheap hotels in town, but for a little luxury try the elegant, old *Hotel Riviera* (☎ 211 166, fax 211 166, Splitska ulica 1), overlooking the harbour. Erected in 1908, it offers large, comfortable rooms for 195/330KN a single/double with shared bath, 220/370KN with private bath, breakfast included. From October to May prices are about 25% lower. Compare the price of a room with half and full-board when you check in. *Hotel Omir* (☎ 22 019, Dobricheva 6), just off Zagrebačka ulica near Giardini, is a private hotel with 11 rooms for 235/375KN single/double with bath and breakfast. If you're willing to pay that, you're better off at the Riviera.

The tip of the Verudela Peninsula, 6km south-west of the city centre, has been turned into a vast tourist complex replete with hotels and tourist apartments. It's not especially attractive but there are beaches, restaurants and lots of watersports. The best and most expensive of the five hotels is the *Histria* (☎ *590 000, fax 214 175*), with an indoor and outdoor swimming pool, casino, disco and sauna. The well-appointed rooms have satellite TV and air-con. Rooms start at 370/660KN a single/double in high season. For information and reservations for the other hotels contact Arenatours in Pula.

For a more personal experience try *Valsabbion* (☎/fax 22 991, *Pješčana Uvala IX/26*), 2km south of the city centre. This small, family-owned hotel is a welcome addition to the accommodation scene in Pula, offering 15 attractively decorated rooms in a villa by the sea. There's a rooftop fitness centre with a pool and the restaurant is now considered to be the finest in Croatia. The hotel is open all year and has rooms in July and August for 396KN (612KN for a room with a sea view and air-con) not including breakfast, which is an extra 50KN per person. Half-board starts at a steep 392KN per person but the food is worth it. Prices are only about 10% lower off season. Bus No 6 will drop you off in Pješčana Uvala.

Places to Eat

Town Centre For grilled meats and local dishes such as goulash, smoked ham and squid risotto, try *Varaždin* (*Istarska 30*). It's a little expensive but manageable if you order carefully, and it's open daily from 11 am to midnight. *Delfin* (*Kandlerova 17*) has a pleasant terrace and an excellent selection of Istrian dishes, especially fish, seafood and *manestra*, similar to Italian minestrone soup. Both restaurants are moderately priced with two-course meals running to about 100KN.

Locals rave about the home cooking at *Vodnjanka* (*Vitežića 4*). It's cheap and

casual but open for lunch only Monday to Friday. The small menu concentrates on simple Istrian dishes which means that vegetarians will not be pleased. To get there, walk south on Radićeva to Vitežića.

Konoba Taj (*Škokovica 3*) is another inexpensive local favourite that leans heavily toward meat dishes. The specialty is young donkey, but you'll also find sausages and cabbage, smoked ham and pork chops. Expect to pay about 80KN for a two-course meal. It's open Monday to Saturday from 11 am to 11 pm.

Platak Self-Service (*Narodni trg 5*), opposite the vegetable market, is easy since you see what you're getting and pay at the end of the line. It's open daily from 9.30 am to 8.45 pm.

The people at the cheese counter in *Vesna*, next to Kino Istra on Giardini, prepare healthy sandwiches while you wait. Vesna is open Monday to Saturday from 6.30 am to 8 pm.

South of Town The best dining is out of town on and around the Verudela Peninsula. *Villa Borghese* (*Monte Paradiso 25*) has a devoted following of Italian residents and tourists who appreciate the fine pasta starters and fresh fish. The restaurant is in a freshly renovated country villa with an elegant, upmarket ambience. A two-course meal will cost from 120 to 150KN and the restaurant is open Tuesday to Sunday from 11 am to midnight.

Valsabbion (see Places to Stay) was recently voted the best restaurant in Croatia by a panel of experts. The menu has a variety of international dishes and the culinary style reflects the imaginative flavours of nouvelle cuisine. Starters begin at 70KN, so it's not cheap, but the quality is outstanding. The restaurant is open daily from noon to midnight.

Entertainment

Posters around Pula advertise live performances and you should definitely try to catch a concert in the spectacular amphitheatre; the tourist office will have the details.

ISTRIA

An Istrian Feast

Istrian cuisine closely resembles that of its Italian neighbour but with a few distinctive touches. The recipes below use typically Istrian ingredients or combine flavours in a way that Italians normally would not, such as wrapping shellfish in meat. Risotto and polenta are Istrian staples that are becoming widely available either in original or instant versions. Here are some simple recipes that serve four people.

Antipasto

On a large platter arrange eight slices of Istrian prosciutto and eight thinly sliced wedges of *formaggio pecorino* or Istrian sheep cheese around a pile of black olives. Your guests must be strictly limited to two each or they'll lose their appetite for the rest of the meal.

Involtini di Prosciutto Agli Scampi (Shrimp wrapped in prosciutto)

Take 12 prawns and drop them into boiling water. Cook for up to five minutes, depending on the size of the prawn. Remove, peel and cut off the heads and tails. Wrap each prawn in a slice of prosciutto. Heat a third of a cup of good olive oil in a skillet. Brown the prawns quickly over medium-high heat until the prosciutto colours slightly, turning frequently. Add ½ cup of wine and reduce heat to low. Sprinkle with freshly ground pepper and salt to taste. Simmer for eight minutes and serve on top of risotto.

Brodetto all'istriana (Istrian-style fish stew)

Choose about one kilo of mixed shellfish such as shrimp, crab, mussels and clams and one whole white fish such as snapper, sea bass, halibut or groper. Cut 150g (one-third of a pound) of squid into small bite-size rounds. (Unless the squid is young it may need to be beaten with a hammer first to tenderise it.) Clean and wash the fish. Heat ¼ cup of olive oil in a large pot and sauté the fish until brown. Add the shellfish and squid, 250g (½ lb) of sliced onion, four peeled garlic cloves, 300g (two-thirds of a pound) fresh tomatoes cut into quarters, two tablespoons of chopped parsley, two bay leaves and salt and pepper to taste. Add water to cover and bring to a boil. When it reaches a boil add ½ cup wine. Cook for 30 minutes, stirring from time to time. Serve with polenta or large chunks of bread.

Frittelle istriane (Istrian pancakes)

Beat three egg yolks with 120g (¼ cup) sugar until thick. Add ¼ teaspoon each of grated orange and lemon peel and one tablespoon of grappa. Beat egg whites until stiff and fold into the yolk mixture along with 400g (¾ lb) cream cheese or ricotta. Mix until thick and creamy. In another bowl blend three eggs with a pinch of salt. Add 250g (½ lb) flour, one cup milk and one cup mineral water. Ladle onto a hot skillet and fry the pancakes. Add the filling to the fried pancakes on one end only and roll them. Place on a buttered, ovenproof dish and top with a dollop of sour cream. Place under a hot grill until piping hot and serve immediately.

ISTRIA

Although most of the nightlife is out of town in Verudela, in mild weather the cafés along the pedestrian streets, Flanatička and Sergijevaca, are lively people-watching spots. *Rock Club Uljanik*, Dobrilina 2, is great whenever something's on, and you can dance there.

Buffet Pivnica, in the back courtyard at Istarska 34 near the Roman amphitheatre (open daily from 8 am to 4 pm), is one of the least expensive places in Pula to get a draught beer, glass of wine or espresso coffee, and all prices are clearly listed. No food is available but there's a convenient free toilet.

On Verudela, there's **Disco Piramida**, and **Fort Bourguignon** organises techno and rave parties. **Oasis** is within walking distance from the youth hostel.

Getting There & Away

Bus The 20 daily buses to Rijeka (110km, 1½ hours) are sometimes crowded, especially the eight which continue on to Zagreb, so reserve a seat a day in advance if you can. Going from Pula to Rijeka, be sure to sit on the right-hand side of the bus for a stunning view of the Gulf of Kvarner.

Other buses departing from Pula include the following:

destination	distance	frequency
Rovinj	42km	18 daily
Poreč	56km	12 daily
Zagreb	292km	11 daily
Zadar	333km	3 daily
Postojna	161km	2 daily
Trieste	124km	2 daily
Split	514km	2 daily
Portorož	90km	1 daily
Koper	104km	1 daily
Ljubljana	211km	1 daily
Dubrovnik	749km	1 daily

Train Ever since Pula was the main port of the Austro-Hungarian empire, the railway line in Istria has run north towards Italy and Austria instead of east into Croatia but there are two daily trains to Ljubljana (four hours, 92KN) and two to Zagreb (418km, 6½ hours, 145KN).

Boat The fast boat **Marina** connects Pula with Venice (L57,000) and Zadar (75KN) in the summer. See the Sea section in the Getting There & Away chapter. The ferry to Mali Lošinj (28KN) and Zadar (54KN) runs once a week all year. Ask at Jadroagent or Kvarner Express on the harbour.

Getting Around

The only city buses of use to visitors are the No 1 which runs to the camping ground at Stoja and bus Nos 2 and 7 to Verudela which pass the youth hostel and Autocamp Ribarska Koliba. Frequency varies from every 15 minutes to every half-hour, with service from 5 am to 11.30 pm daily. Tickets are sold at newsstands for 8KN and are good for two trips.

AROUND PULA
Brijuni Islands

The Brijuni (Italian: Brioni) island group consists of two main pine-covered islands and 12 islets off the coast of Istria just north-west of Pula. Each year from 1949 until his death in 1980, Maršal Tito spent six months at his summer residences on Brijuni in a style any western capitalist would admire. Tito received 90 heads of state here, and at a meeting on Veli Brijun in 1956 Tito, Jawaharlal Nehru (the first Indian prime minister) and Gamal Nasser (the president of Egypt) laid the foundations of the non-aligned movement.

Tito had three palaces on Veli Brijun: Vila Jadranka, Bijela Vila and Vila Brionka. The famous 1956 Brijuni Declaration was signed in Bijela Vila, Tito's 'White House'. Tourists are driven past these three, but Tito's private retreat on the tiny islet of Vanga cannot be visited. In 1984 Brijuni was proclaimed a national park. Some 680 species of plants grow on the islands, including many exotic subtropical species planted at Tito's request.

As you arrive on **Veli Brijun**, after a half-hour boat ride from Fažana on the mainland, you'll see Tito's two private yachts still tied up in the harbour, and near the landing there are four luxury hotels where his guests once stayed. The four-hour tour of the island begins with a visit to **St German Church**, now a gallery displaying copies of medieval frescoes in Istrian churches. The **Tito on Brijuni** exhibit in another building includes large photos of Tito with film stars such as Gina Lollobrigida, Sophia Loren, Elizabeth Taylor and Richard Burton, all of whom visited Tito here.

ISTRIA

As part of the tour, you're then driven around the island in a small train, past the palaces and through a **safari park**. The fenced area was Tito's private hunting ground, and the exotic animals held there were given to Tito by world leaders. Deer wander wild across the island. You pass the ruins of a 1st century **Roman villa** without stopping, then have a walk around an unexciting zoo. Towards the end of the tour you're herded quickly through the excellent **ethnographic museum** which has Croatian folk costumes.

Getting There & Away

You may only visit Brijuni National Park with a group. Instead of booking an excursion with one of the travel agencies in Pula, Rovinj or Poreč, which costs at least 200KN, you can take a public bus from Pula to Fažana (8km), then sign up for a tour (145KN) at the Brijuni Tourist Service (☎ 525 883) office near the wharf. It's best to book in advance, especially in the summer season.

Also check along the Pula waterfront for excursion boats to Brijuni. The five-hour boat trips from Pula to Brijuni may not actually visit the islands but only sail around them. Still, the trip can still make an enjoyable day out.

ROVINJ
• **pop 12,910**   ☎ **052**

Relaxed Rovinj (Italian: Rovigno) is perhaps the best place to visit in all of Istria. Wooded hills punctuated by low-rise luxury hotels surround the town, while the 13 green offshore islands of the Rovinj archipelago make for pleasant, varied views. Rovinj is still an active fishing port, so you see local people going about their day-to-day business, and the cobbled, inclined streets in the old town are picturesque. There's a large Italian community here. Friendly Rovinj is just the place to rest up before your island-hopping journey further south.

Originally an island, Rovinj was first mentioned in the 7th century as Ruvignio but it's believed that the town emerged at least several centuries earlier – possibly between the 3rd and 5th centuries. It was settled by Slavs in the 7th century and began to develop a strong fishing and maritime industry.

In 1199, Rovinj signed an important pact with Dubrovnik to protect its maritime trade, but in the 13th century the threat of piracy forced it to turn to Venice for protection. The town was fortified under the Venetians but was still subject to attacks from Genoa and the Uskoks.

From the 16th to the 18th centuries, its population expanded dramatically with an influx of immigrants fleeing Turkish invasions of Bosnia and continental Croatia. The town began to develop outside the walls and, in 1763, the islet was connected to the mainland and Rovinj became a peninsula. Perhaps because of its location, Rovinj was spared the epidemics that ravaged the rest of the peninsula and enjoyed greater economic development.

Although its maritime industry thrived in the 17th century, Austria's 1719 decision to make Trieste and Rijeka free ports dealt the town a serious blow. The rise of sailing ships further damaged Rovinj's shipbuilding industry and in the middle of the 19th century it was supplanted by the shipyard in Pula. Like the rest of Istria, Rovinj bounced from Austrian to French to Austrian to Italian rule before finally becoming a part of postwar Yugoslavia.

Orientation

The old town of Rovinj is entirely contained within an egg-shaped peninsula, with the bus station just to the south-east. The left-luggage office is open from 5.15 am to 8.30 pm (ask at the ticket window). There are two harbours – the northern open harbour and small, protected Rovinj Harbour to the south. About 1.5km south of the old town is the Punta Corrente Forest Park and the wooded cape of Zlatni Rt which has several large hotels. A small archipelago of islands lies just offshore, the most popular being Crveni otok (Red island), Sveti Katarina and Sveti Andrija.

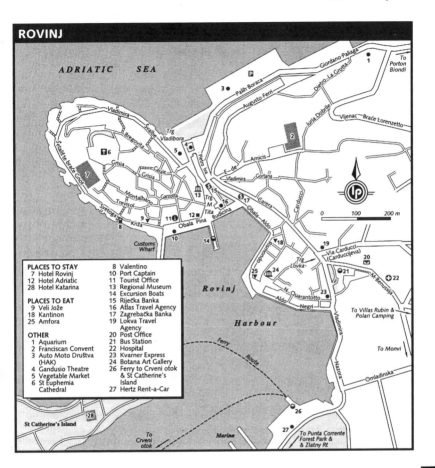

ROVINJ

ADRIATIC   SEA

Rovinj

Harbour

St Catherine's Island

PLACES TO STAY
7 Hotel Rovinj
12 Hotel Adriatic
28 Hotel Katarina

PLACES TO EAT
9 Veli Jože
18 Kantinon
25 Amfora

OTHER
1 Aquarium
2 Franciscan Convent
3 Auto Moto Društva
   (HAK)
4 Gandusio Theatre
5 Vegetable Market
6 St Euphemia
   Cathedral

8 Valentino
10 Port Captain
11 Tourist Office
13 Regional Museum
14 Excursion Boats
15 Riječka Banka
16 Atlas Travel Agency
17 Zagrebačka Banka
19 Lokva Travel
   Agency
20 Post Office
21 Bus Station
22 Hospital
23 Kvarner Express
24 Botana Art Gallery
26 Ferry to Crveni otok
   & St Catherine's
   Island
27 Hertz Rent-a-Car

To Crveni otok
Marina
To Punta Corrente Forest Park & Zlatny Rt

0   100   200 m

Information

Tourist Offices The tourist office (☎ 811 566) is at Obala Pina Budicina 12, just off Trg Maršala Tita, and publishes a useful 'Tourist Information' brochure. It's open daily in the summer from 8 am to 6 pm. During the off-season, the office is open Monday to Friday 8 am to 3 pm, Saturday 8 am to noon.

Eurostar Travel (☎ 813 144), Obala Pina Budicina 1, is a good source of information for boat connections to Italy.

Motorists can turn to the Auto Moto Društva (HAK; ☎ 813 239), next to the large parking lot on Obala Palih Boraca.

Money You can change money at any travel agency, the post office and at any bank. There's an ATM at Zagrebačka Banka, Carera 21, which will give you money on your MasterCard.

American Express cardholders can withdraw cash at the ATM outside the Atlas travel agency on Trg Maršala Tito.

Post & Communications The post office is opposite the bus station on M. Benussija ulica. It's open daily from 7 am to 10 pm in the summer. Off-season hours are Monday to Saturday from 7 am to 9 pm. The post-code for Rovinj is 52210.

Travel Agencies Most travel agencies are conveniently located within the old town. Across the street from the bus station, there's Lokva (☎ 813 365, fax 811 620) at Carducci 4 and Marco Polo (☎ 816 955, fax 816 616, marco-polo@pu.tel.hr) at Trg Lokva 3. The American Express representative is the Atlas travel agency (☎ 811 241) on Trg Maršala Tita, across the square from Kompas (☎ 813 211, fax 813 478) at Trg Maršala Tita 5 and Generalturist (☎ 811 402, fax 813 324). There's also KEI-Kvarner Express (☎ 811 155, fax 815 046, kei-opatija@ri.tel.hr) on Aldo Negri. Agencies are open daily in summer from about 8 am to 1 pm and 6 to 10 pm, but off season they're closed in the afternoon and on Sunday.

Things to See & Do

The massive **Cathedral of St Euphemia** (Katedrala Sveti Eufenija) completely dominates the town from its hill-top location in the middle of the peninsula. Built in 1736, it's the largest baroque building in Istria, reflecting the period during the 18th century when Rovinj was its most populous town, an important fishing centre and the bulwark of the Venetian fleet. Next to the side door of the church is a 14th century marble relief of St Euphemia. Inside the cathedral, don't miss the tomb of St Euphemia behind the right-hand altar. The saint was born around 290, became a Christian and was tortured mercilessly by Emperor Diocletian before being thrown to the lions in 304. Her body was later taken to Constantinople where it remained until 800. According to legend, the body disappeared one dark and stormy night only to appear off the coast of Rovinj in a spectral boat. The townspeople were unable to budge the heavy sarcophagus until a small boy appeared with two cows, also spectral,

and claimed that the saint had appeared to him. The sarcophagus was dragged to the top of the hill and placed in the small Church of St George that preceded the present-day cathedral. On the anniversary of her martyrdom (16 September) devotees congregate here.

The 60m bell tower is the tallest in Istria and was constructed by Italian architects who modelled it after St Mark's bell tower in Venice. The tower is topped by a copper statue of St Euphemia that was created in 1758 and acts as a weather vane.

The **Regional Museum**, on Trg Maršala Tita, contains a collection of 15th to 19th century paintings and works by contemporary artists working in Rovinj as well as several Etruscan pieces. The museum is open Tuesday to Saturday from 9.30 am to 1 pm and 6 to 9.30 pm.

Nearby is the elaborate **Balbi Arch**, built in 1679 on the location of the town gate. The top of the arch is ornamented with a Turkish head on the outside and a Venetian head on the inside. To the right and left over the arch are the coats of arms of the Balbi family and above it there's a relief of the Venetian lion.

The baroque **Franciscan monastery**, ulica de Amicis 36, was built at the beginning of the 18th century and contains a valuable library as well as a small museum of 18th and 19th century paintings and sculptures. It's open daily from 5 to 6 pm.

The best museum is the **Rovinj Aquarium** (established in 1891) at Obala Giordano Paliaga 5. It exhibits a good collection of local marine life, from poisonous scorpion fish to colourful anemones. It's open mid-April to mid-October from 10 am to 5 pm daily, and entrance is 10KN

The winding narrow **backstreets** of the town that lie behind the Balbi Arch are Rovinj's finest attraction. Windows, balconies, portals and squares are a pleasant confusion of styles – Gothic, Renaissance, baroque and neoclassical. Notice the unique exterior chimneys (*fumaioli*), built when the town's population was exploding and entire families were housed in a single room with

Waterfall in Plitvice Lakes National Park

Church of Sveti Donat in Zadar

Parish church of Supetar on the island of Brač

SARA YORKE

SARA YORKE

SARA YORKE

Split, the chief city of Dalmatia

a fireplace. Ulica Grisia is the 'artists street' where local artists sell their work, especially in mid-August for the open-air art show.

When you've seen enough of the town, follow the waterfront south past the Park Hotel to the **Punta Corrente Forest Park**, which was established in 1890 by Baron Hütterodt, an Austrian admiral who kept a villa on Crveni otok. Here you can swim off the rocks, climb a cliff or just sit and admire the offshore islands.

Activities

Diving Center Scuba Rovinj (☎ 830 731, scuba-rovinj@pu.tel.hr, www.istra.com/rovinj/scuba), Trg Matteotti 10, offers boat **dives** for 105KN, wreck dives for 176KN and shore dives for 54KN. The main scuba attraction here is the wreck of the *Baron Gautch*, an Austrian passenger-steamer sunk in 1914 by an Austrian mine that caused 177 fatalities. The wreck lies in up to 40m of water and has plenty of sea life.

There are also 53 **rock climbing** routes in a former Venetian stone quarry in Zlatni Rt.

Organised Tours

Atlas runs all-day 'fish picnics' for 140KN that take you around the surrounding archipelago for swimming and a fish lunch. Delfin Agency (☎ 813 266), near the ferry dock for Crveni otok, runs half-day scenic cruises to the **Lim Fjord** (70KN).

Special Events

The city's annual events include the Rovinj-Pesaro Regata (early May), the 'Rovinj Summer' concert series (July and August), the Rovinj Fair (August) and the ACI Cup Match Yacht Race (September). On the second Sunday in August, Grisia ulica becomes an open-air art-fest where anyone from children to professional painters can display their work. The narrow street is packed with tourists and Istrians as the event is renowned throughout the region.

Places to Stay

Camping The camping ground closest to Rovinj is *Porton Biondi* (☎ 813 557), less than 1km from the town (on the Monsena bus), which charges 15KN per person and 9KN per tent. The camp is relatively small and in a thick pine forest near the beach. It's open from May to September.

A couple of kilometres further on there's *Camping Monsena* (☎ 813 354), a naturist camping ground that can accommodate 2000 campers. At the end of May and beginning of June there's a special gathering of naturists. The site is open from May to October.

Five kilometres south-east of Rovinj is *Polari Camping* (☎ 813 441), part of the Villas Rubin tourist complex. With a capacity of 5800 campers it's not exactly tranquil, but there are sports facilities nearby in Villas Rubin. It's open from May to mid-October and can be reached by the Villas Rubin bus.

Private Rooms Many offices in Rovinj offer private rooms beginning at 72KN per person in the summer season with a 50% surcharge for a stay of less than four nights and a 100% surcharge for a one-night stay. Lovka is the only agency that doesn't impose surcharges. Pula and Poreč are within easy commuting distance from Rovinj, so having to stay four nights may not be such a problem.

Hotels There are a few hotels in town. *Hotel Rovinj* (☎ 811 288) has a splendid location on Svetoga Križa overlooking the sea, and prices at 245/410KN a single/double for a four night stay. *Hotel Adriatic* (☎ 815 088, fax 813 573, P. Budicina bb) is in a 1912 building right in the town centre. The rooms are large and recently renovated. Singles/doubles are 285KN per person per day in high season (mid-July to mid-August), 245KN in the two weeks before and after that period and 212KN off season, but rooms with a view are more expensive.

Most hotels are on Zlatni Rt cape. The cheapest is the 192-room *Hotel Monte Mulin* (☎ 811 512, fax 815 882), on the wooded hillside overlooking the bay just beyond the Hotel Park. It's about a 15 minute walk south of the bus station and is open all year round. Bed and breakfast is 198/310KN a single/double (20% lower in spring and autumn). *Hotel Eden* (☎ *811 088, fax 811 349*) is a luxury hotel with an indoor and outdoor swimming pool and a sauna. Expect to pay about 490/792KN in high season. Nearby is the *Hotel Park* (☎ *811 077, fax 816 977*), a large, luxurious establishment with rooms for 445/648KN.

Places to Eat

Most of the fish and spaghetti places along the harbour cater to well-heeled tourists but *Kantinon* (*18 Obala Alzo Rismondo*) sells fresh grilled fish beginning at 20KN to a local crowd. It's open daily from 10 am to midnight. *Veli Jože* (*Svetoga Križa 1*) is somewhat more expensive but is a good place to try Istrian dishes in an interior crammed with knick-knacks or on tables outside. Try the *bakalar* (codfish) in a white sauce or baked lamb with potatoes. It's open daily from 10 am to 3 am. *Amfora* (*Rismondo 23*) is one of the best restaurants in town. It's expensive unless you order one of the fixed-price full-course meals for 55KN or a small risotto for 30KN. It's open daily from 11 am to 11 pm.

Picnickers can get supplies at the *supermarket* next to the bus station or pick up a *burek* from one of the *kiosks* near the vegetable market.

Entertainment

The best show in town is watching the sunset from *Valentino*, Santa Croce 28. At 20KN for a glass of wine it's not cheap but sitting on the rocks next to the sea with a view of Katarina island is worth the splurge. For a night out, head down to the huge *Zabavni* entertainment complex at Monvi for discos, cabarets and restaurants.

Getting There & Away

The closest train station is Kanfanar, 19km away on the Pula-Divača line.

There's a bus from Rovinj to Pula (34km) every hour or so, seven a day to Poreč (38km), seven a day to Rijeka (84km), eight

a day to Zagreb (278km), two a day to Koper (81km) and Split (509km), and one a day to Dubrovnik (744km) and Ljubljana (190km).

Eurostar Travel (☎ 813 144), Obala Pina Budicina 1, has information about the *Marconi* that shuttles between Rovinj and Trieste and may have tickets (which must be paid for in Italian lire). Otherwise try asking the port captain on the opposite side of the same building.

Getting Around

Local buses run every two hours from the bus station north to Monsena and south to Villas Rubin.

AROUND ROVINJ

One of the most popular day trips from Rovinj is a boat ride to the lovely **Crveni otok** (Red island). Only 1900m long, the island includes two islets – Sveti Andrija and Maškin – which are connected by a causeway. From the 6th century Sveti Andrija housed a Benedictine monastery, later kept by the Franciscans. In the 19th century the island became the property of Baron Hütterodt who transformed it into a luxuriantly wooded park. Maškin is more wooded since Sveti Andrija has been taken over by the Hotel Istra complex. There's an hourly ferry to Crveni otok (15 minutes, 15KN return), and frequent ferries (five minutes, 10KN return) to nearby **Katarina island**, which was forested by a Polish count in 1905 and now houses the Hotel Katarina.

The **Lim Fjord** is the most dramatic sight in Istria. About 9km long and 600m wide, the inlet was formed when the Istrian coastline sunk during the last Ice Age, allowing the sea to rush in and fill the Draga valley. The walls of the valley become steeper the further inland you go, rising to a height of 100m. There are hills on both sides of the inlet and two caves that have revealed traces of prehistoric settlements. Fishing, oyster farming and excursion boats are the only activities in the fjord. Several waterside restaurants serve up the freshest seafood in all Istria. Unless you have your own boat, the only way to see this splendid fjord is to take an organised tour from Rovinj, Pula or Poreč.

POREČ

• pop 17,000   ☎ 052

Poreč (Italian: Parenzo), the Roman Parentium, and the surrounding region is like a country unto itself, one that is completely devoted to tourism. Year after year the town wins a national award for tourism in recognition of its efficiency and imagination in developing the only real industry in the region. Poreč is the centrepiece of a vast system of tourist resorts that stretch north and south along the Istrian coast. The most scenic are south of the city and the largest is Zelena Laguna, with a full range of facilities and accommodation.

These holiday villages and tourist camps offer a somewhat industrialised vacation experience with too much concrete and too many tour buses for some tastes. However, the hotels, restaurants, tourist offices and travel agencies are almost universally staffed by friendly, multilingual people who make a real effort to welcome visitors. Tourism is all they've got – they know it, and they're not ashamed of it. This is not the place for a quiet little getaway (unless you come in January), but there's a World Heritage site basilica, lots going on outside of town and the Istrian interior within easy reach.

The coast of Poreč measures 37km, islands included, but the ancient town is confined to a peninsula 400m long and 200m wide. The Romans conquered the region in the 2nd century BC and made Poreč an important administrative centre from which they were able to control a sweep of land from the Lim Fjord to the Mirna River. Poreč's street plan was laid out by the Romans, who divided the town into rectangular parcels marked by the longitudinal Decumanus and the latitudinal Cardo.

On the collapse of the Western Roman Empire Poreč came under Byzantine rule, which lasted from the 6th to 8th centuries.

It was under the influence of Byzantine culture that the Basilica of St Euphemius was erected, with its magnificent frescoes. The Aquilean patriarchs ruled the city in the early Middle Ages but Poreč was forced to submit to Venetian rule in 1267.

Poreč was particularly hard-hit by the Istrian plague epidemics, with the town's population declining to about 100 in the 17th century. The town was repopulated with refugees fleeing the Turks in the second half of the 17th century.

With the decline of Venice, the town fell under Austrian, French and then Austrian rule before the Italian occupation that lasted from 1918 to 1943. Upon the capitulation of Italy, Poreč was occupied by the Germans and damaged by Allied bombing in 1944 before becoming part of postwar Yugoslavia.

Orientation

The compact old town on the peninsula is bisected by the Roman Dekumanus street which is lined with shops, shops and more shops. Hotels, travel agencies and excursion boats are on the quay, Obala Maršala Tita, which runs from the small-boat harbour to the tip of the peninsula. The interior of the old town is a pedestrian area. Another commercial area lies east of the old town on the mainland, radiating out from Trg J Rakovca. The bus station is directly opposite the small-boat harbour just outside the old town. The left-luggage office is open from 6 am to 8 pm, except Sunday when it closes at 5 pm.

Information

Tourist Offices Poreč's Tourist Information Centre (☎ 451 293, fax 451 665, istra@io.com, www.istra.com/porec) is at Zagrebačka 8, and has a mountain of brochures and leaflets on Poreč and Istria. During summer it's open daily from 8 am to 4 pm and 6 to 9 pm (except in July and August when it's open without a break) and in winter it's open Monday to Saturday from 8 am to 3 pm.

There's no Jadrolinija office but the Sunny Way travel agency (☎/fax 431 295),

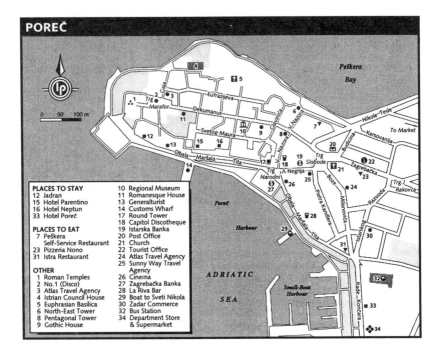

POREČ

PLACES TO STAY	
12	Jadran
15	Hotel Parentino
16	Hotel Neptun
33	Hotel Poreč

PLACES TO EAT	
7	Peškera
	Self-Service Restaurant
23	Pizzeria Nono
31	Istra Restaurant

OTHER	
1	Roman Temples
2	No.1 (Disco)
3	Atlas Travel Agency
4	Istrian Council House
5	Euphrasian Basilica
6	North-East Tower
8	Pentagonal Tower
9	Gothic House
10	Regional Museum
11	Romanesque House
13	Generalturist
14	Customs Wharf
17	Round Tower
18	Capitol Discotheque
19	Istarska Banka
20	Post Office
21	Church
22	Tourist Office
24	Atlas Travel Agency
25	Sunny Way Travel Agency
26	Cinema
27	Zagrebačka Banka
28	La Riva Bar
29	Boat to Sveti Nikola
30	Zadar Commerce
32	Bus Station
34	Department Store & Supermarket

Alda Negrija 1, sells boat tickets and is a good source of information on sailings. It's open daily from 8 am to 10 pm in summer and 9 am to 2 pm in winter.

The Auto-Klub Poreč (☎ 431 665), Partizanska bb, is in the large white building visible across the field north of the market and is open daily from 8 am to 3 pm.

Money Zagrebačka Banka, on Trg Narodni, is open Monday to Friday from 8 am to 12.30 pm and 6 to 8.30 pm, Saturday 8 am to noon. It has an ATM outside where you can get cash on Cirrus or MasterCard as well as an automatic change machine. Istarska Kreditna Banka, Alda Negrija 2, is the place to go if you need to withdraw cash on your Visa card. There's also an ATM outside KEI-Kvarner Express, where you can withdraw cash on Diners Club or American Express cards.

Post & Communications The main post office is at Trg Slobode 14, and is open Monday to Saturday from 7 am to 9 pm, Sunday 9 am to noon. The postcode for Poreč is 52440.

Travel Agencies Atlas (☎ 434 983) has its head office at Eufrazijeva 63 for hotel reservations, but for excursions and changing money head to Boze Milanovića 11 (☎ 432 273), which is open daily in summer from 8 am to 10 pm and in the winter Monday to Saturday from 9 am to 4 pm.

In addition to Atlas and Sunny Way, other travel agencies for booking excursions include KEI Kvarner Express (☎ 451 600), Obala Maršala Tita 17 – the same building as the Hotel Parentino; Generalturist (☎ 451 666), Obala Maršala Tita 19; and Kompas (☎ 451 100), Obala Maršala Tita 16.

Laundry It's about 1km out of town but if you have a pile of dirty clothes, you won't mind trekking out to Laković's laundry (☎ 452 721) on Rovinjska 17. Take Nikole Tesle to Mate Vlašića, which in turn will take you up to Rovinjska. Mrs Laković will wash, dry and fold up to five kilos of clothing for 50KN. She is open Monday to Friday from 9 am to noon and 5 to 7 pm, Saturday 9 am to noon.

Things to See

The main reason to visit Poreč is to see the 6th century **Euphrasian Basilica**, a World Heritage site and one of the finest intact examples of Byzantine art. Built on the site of a 4th century basilica and 5th century church, the complex includes a church, atrium and baptistery. Mosaics from the earlier structures are still visible on the floor of the northern nave but it is the glittering wall mosaics in the apse that packs in the crowds. These 6th century masterpieces feature Biblical scenes, archangels and Istrian martyrs.

Notice the group to the left which shows Bishop Euphrasius, who commissioned the basilica, with a model of the church in his hand. The ciborium over the main altar was erected in 1277, modelled after the one in St Mark's in Venice. The southern wall has three chapels. The western chapel (Chapel of the Holy Cross) is decorated with a large polyptych created in 1440 by Antonio Vivarini and Jacobo Palma Junior's oil painting of The Last Supper. In the central chapel (Chapel of the Crucifixion) there are choir pews carved in 1452. The church is open daily, entry is free, and for 10KN you can climb the belfry. The adjacent **Bishop's Palace** was also built in the 6th century and contains a display of ancient stone monuments.

Trg Marafor is where the Roman forum used to stand; the original pavement has been preserved along the northern row of houses on the square. West of the square are the ruins of the 2nd century **Temple of Neptune** and another large temple from the beginning of the 1st century.

South-east of Trg Marafor on Dekumanus there's an interesting 13th century **Romanesque House** with a wooden balcony, and further east there's a **Gothic House** from the 15th century with a Renaissance portal. The baroque Sinčić Palace at Decumanus 9 houses the **Regional Museum**, which opened in 1884. It contains over 2000 exhibits spanning Poreč's tumultuous history from the Paleolithic era until the 20th century. In addition to furniture, paintings and artefacts, there are mosaic fragments from the 3rd century, crosses, choir stalls and altar paintings. It's open June to September, Tuesday through Sunday from 9 to 11 am and 5 to 10 pm.

The few remaining parts of the ramparts are visible from the northern side of the city and there are three 15th century towers that date from the Venetian rule: the **Pentagonal Tower** (the only preserved part of the former town gates), the **Round tower** on Trg Narodni and the **North-East Tower** on Peškera Bay.

Activities

Nearly every activity you might want to enjoy is outside the town in either Plava Laguna or Zelena Laguna. Most of the sports centres in Plava Laguna are affiliated with hotels and have tennis courts with teachers, basketball and volleyball, windsurfing, rowing, bungee jumping, water-skiing and canoeing. If the weather turns bad, you can always work out in the fitness centre. Call ☎ 410 101 or ☎ 451 955 for further information. In addition there is **parasailing** off the island of Sveti Nikola at a cost of 160KN for 10 minutes. Call ☎ 098 229 571 and they'll twirl you around whatever bay you're on.

The gently rolling hills of the interior and the well-marked bike paths make **cycling** an excellent way to experience the region. The tourist office issues a free map of roads and trails stemming from Poreč, along with suggested routes. You can rent a bike from Generalturist for 16KN an hour or 70KN a day, or in Zelena Laguna at Autotehna (☎ 461 391).

ISTRIA

Hotel Galijot in Plava Laguna has the largest and best equipped **diving** centre in the region. At SUB Centre Plava Laguna (☎ 451 549) you can dive reefs or wrecks for about 235KN a boat dive plus 270KN for full equipment rental. There's another diving centre on Brulo beach, Sub Center Brulo (☎ 451 566, ☎/fax 451 206), which offers boat dives for about the same price. Both centres also offer SSI and PADI certification courses.

From May to mid-October there is a number of passenger boats (12KN return) travelling to **Sveti Nikola**, the small island opposite Poreč harbour. The boats depart every 30 minutes from the new wharf on Obala Maršala Tita.

Organised Tours

Most travel agencies offer tours to the Lim Fjord (120KN), Brijuni Islands (230KN) and boat excursions along the Istrian coast.

Special Events

On 30 April, Porec celebrates two major events – the city's liberation during WWII and the opening of the tourist season. The mayor presents various awards and honours to 'good citizens', which generally means people who have made an effort to further tourism by sweeping the streets or opening a new service. During July and August there's one of the oldest Croatian art exhibitions, which usually centres on a theme. Other annual events include the Folk Festival (June), the Inter Folk Fest (August) and the Musical Summer (May to September). There are summer concerts in Trg Slobode every Thursday at 9 pm. Ask about these at the tourist office.

Places to Stay

Accommodation in Poreč is not cheap and if you come in July or August advance bookings are essential.

Camping There are two camping grounds at Zelena Laguna, 6km south of Poreč. Both *Autocamp Zelena Laguna* (☎ 410 541) and *Autocamp Bijela Uvala* (☎ 410 551) are open from April to mid-October and charge around 24KN per person and 14KN per tent. Take the 'Plava Laguna' bus which runs hourly from the bus station and get off at Zelena Laguna resort. Both camping grounds are a short walk away.

Private Rooms As the rental of private accommodation is not a particularly lucrative occupation, there are fewer and fewer agencies in prosperous Poreč that are willing to make the effort. In the town centre, VITS Turizam (☎ 431 738), Zagrebačka 17, finds private accommodation. Near the vegetable market at Partizanska there is Istra-Line (☎ 451 952, fax 432 116) in a pink building.

If you follow Nikole Tesle until it becomes Kalčića you'll come to Mate Vlašića and at No 6 is Fiore tours (☎/fax 434 075, ☎ 431 397), which also finds private accommodation. Expect to pay 111/198KN for a single/double with a private shower in peak season (the first three weeks in August) and 90/166KN for a single/double with shared facilities. From June to September the agencies are open daily from around 8 am to 10 pm, but outside the main season, make sure to arrive early as most agencies close around noon and all day Sunday.

Hotels Hotels in and around Poreč are expensive but generally in good condition. The prices listed below are for half-pension because it costs only 15KN to 20KN more than a room with breakfast. At this price you will not be eating like a Frankopan duke but the food is decent enough. All prices drop by about 30% during the shoulder seasons of May, June, September and October.

The five-storey *Hotel Poreč* (☎ 451 811), near the bus station, is one of the cheapest hotels in town. The rooms are standard issue and equipped with satellite TV and telephones but they either overlook the bus station or the shopping centre. In July and August rooms here cost 284/460KN for a single/double.

Hotel Neptun (☎ *452 711, fax 431 531, Obala M. Tita 15*) overlooks the harbour and is usually open all year. The hotel and rooms are in excellent condition and freshly renovated. In peak season you'll pay 255/570KN for a single/double. Nearby, the affiliated *Hotel Parentino* (☎ *431 925, Obala Maršala Tita 17*) has somewhat cheaper double rooms in a very elegant 19th century building with high ceilings. Singles/doubles are 270/475KN. The *Jadran* (☎ *431 236, Obala M Tita*) is a solid old building on the waterfront with rooms for 260/454KN.

Farmhouses 'Agritourism' is the newest program in Poreč but it is just getting off the ground. The tourist office has issued a brochure with photos and information about country houses throughout Istria offering visits and stays. Some of the residences are actual farmhouses while others are modern villas with swimming pools and opportunities for hiking and bike riding. You'll need your own car and you can expect to pay about 145KN per person for a double room with half-board.

Places to Eat

Istra (*Milanovića 30*) is where locals go for a special restaurant meal. In addition to the usual offerings of grilled fish, spaghetti and calamari there are delicious local specialties such as a mixed seafood starter and *mučkalica*, stewed chicken and vegetables in a spicy sauce. There's a cosy interior and a covered terrace with wooden booths. It's open daily from noon to 11 pm.

You can tell that *Nono* (*Zagrebačka 4*) serves the best pizza in town because it's always crowded even while other places are nearly empty. With their soft, puffy crust and fresh toppings, these pizzas are actually memorable. Small pizzas are 25KN and large ones are 30KN. It's open daily from noon to 11 pm.

The *Peškera Self-Service Restaurant*, just outside the north-west corner of the old city wall, is one of the best of its kind in Croatia. You can get a main course such as fried chicken, grilled calamari or rump steak for 28KN to 40KN and eat it on a terrace facing the sea. The posted menu is in English and German, and there's a free toilet at the entrance. It's open daily from 9 am to 10 pm.

A large *supermarket* and department store is next to Hotel Poreč, near the bus station.

Entertainment

Most nightlife is out of town at Zelena Laguna but in town you can go to *Capitol Discotheque*, downstairs at V Nazora 9, *No 1* on Marabor or *Easy Rider* underneath the Riva Bar on Obala Maršala Tita.

Getting There & Away

The nearest train station is at Pazin, 30km to the east (five buses daily from Poreč). Buses run twice a day to Portorož (54km), Trieste (89km) and Ljubljana (176km); six times a day to Rovinj (38km, 17KN) and Novigrad (11KN); nine times a day to Zagreb (264km, 81KN); seven times a day to Rijeka (80km, 40KN); eight daily to Umag (16KN); and 12 times a day to Pula (56km, 23KN). Between Poreč and Rovinj the bus runs along the Lim Fjord, a drowned valley. To see it, sit on the right-hand side southbound, or the left-hand side northbound.

For information on the fast motor vessel *Marconi* that shuttles between Trieste and Poreč (2¾ hour, L27,000), inquire at the Sunny Way travel agency and see the Sea section in the Getting There & Away chapter.

Getting Around

From June to mid-September a tourist train operates hourly or half-hourly from Trg Slobode to Zelena Laguna (10KN). There are also hourly buses to Vrsar that stop at Plava Laguna, Zelena Laguna and the other resorts south of the city.

Car The cheapest price for car rental is at Zadar Commerce (☎ 434 103), Istarskog razvoda 11.

ISTRIA

Magic Mushrooms?

The truffle trade is less like a business than a highly profitable cult. It revolves around an expensive, malodorous fungus endowed with semi-magical powers that's collected by shadowy characters who deal in cash and smuggle their booty across borders. Devotees claim that once you've tasted this small, nut-shaped delicacy, all other flavours seem insipid.

Although France, Spain and Italy are the traditional truffle-producing countries, Istrian truffles are rapidly gaining a foothold in the marketplace. Even at 14KN a gram, the price is significantly cheaper than other European truffles and the taste is said to be at least as good as their more expensive counterparts. In fact, there have been unconfirmed reports that certain nefarious parties are collecting Istrian truffles and packaging them as Italian truffles.

The Istrian truffle business is relatively young. In 1932, when Istria was occupied by Italy, an Italian soldier from the truffle capital of Albi allegedly noticed vegetational similarities between his region and Istria. He returned after his military service with specially trained dogs who, after enough sniffing and digging, eventually uncovered the precious commodity.

Dogs are still the key to a successful truffle hunt. Istrian truffle-hunting dogs (called breks) may be mongrels but they are highly educated. Puppies begin their training at two months old but only about 20% of them go on to fully fledged careers as truffle-trackers. Their lives are short. For reasons that remain unclear, breks are peculiarly subject to a variety of cancers.

The truffle-hunting season lasts from October to January, during which time at least 3000 people and 9000 to 12,000 dogs are wandering around Istrian forests. The Motovun region is especially rich in truffles, but they are also found on the slopes of Učka Mountain and in the Labin region. Truffle hunters are so determined to remain underground (for obvious tax reasons) that they will never admit to truffle-hunting, no matter how unmistakable the evidence.

Some people believe truffles are an aphrodisiac, though scientific research has failed to uncover any basis for this claim. Conduct your own experiment: get a truffle and mix a few shavings into scrambled eggs or sprinkle them on top of a risotto. Turn the lights way down low, put on some nice music and see what happens.

AROUND POREČ
Motovun

Poreč is a good base for exploring the interior of Istria, especially the hill towns. Motovun is a captivating little town perched on a hill in the Mirna River valley, about 20km north-east of Poreč. Two sets of walls enclose a typical medieval town of steep, winding streets lined with Romanesque and Gothic residences. The oldest part of town is on top of the hill and contains the Renaissance church of **St Stephen** (Sveti Stjepan) with 17th and 18th century paintings and frescos. Along the inner wall that encloses the old town rises a 16th century bell tower which can be climbed (10KN) for a magnificent view. You can also walk around the outer walls that connect the more recent suburbs on the southern and eastern end of the old town. The view over vineyards, fields and woods is memorable. There are a number of galleries and crafts shops throughout the town, including a free art gallery just after the entrance gate that exhibits contemporary paintings and old weaponry. It's not easy to visit Motovun without your own car but there's at least one daily bus from Poreč to Rijeka that stops there (30 minutes).

Grožnjan

This medieval hill town was revitalised when it was turned into a musicians' colony in 1965. Each year there are music, orchestra and ballet courses and recitals. In summer concerts and musical events are held almost daily, and you can often overhear the musicians practising as you wander through the crooked lanes and leafy squares.

As the seat of Venice's northern Istrian territories, Grožnjan's ramparts and towers were fortified twice in the 14th century but only parts of the walls remain. The baroque parish church on the main square has Renaissance choir stalls, and there are various crafts shops and galleries throughout the town. If you don't have your own wheels, you can take the morning bus that runs from Pula to Poreč and Trieste, and get off at the town of Krasica, before Buje. It's a 3.5km walk to Grožnjan but the road winds along a scenic ridge with great views.

ISTRIA

Zadar Region

In many ways the Zadar region is a microcosm of Croatia. There are two major national parks, the ancient city of Zadar, with its long, tortured history, and an island archipelago that offers some of the Adriatic's most remote, untouched island villages. Whether your interests are poking around in old churches, trekking through unspoiled wilderness or getting away from it all in a sleepy fishing village, you're sure to find it here. Paklenica National Park offers the best hiking and rock climbing opportunities in Croatia, the waterfalls of Plitvice Lakes National Park are a green and watery wonderland, and the islands of Pag and Dugi Otok are good off-the-beaten-track destinations for resort-weary travellers. Zadar has good national and international bus and boat connections, and the national parks are easily accessible. Connections to the islands are slow but worth the extra trouble.

The area around Zadar is heavily urbanised with a sprawl of new construction. The coastal terrain is flat, whether you head north-west to Pag or south-east to Šibenik, but the low-lying coastal region allows the *maestral* to bring refreshing breezes from the west. The Velebit Mountain Range in the north-east containing Paklenica National Park protects the coast from the *bura* in the winter, lending it a mild climate.

ZADAR
- **pop 76,300** ☎ **023**

Zadar (the ancient Zara), the main city of northern Dalmatia, occupies a long peninsula which separates the harbour on the east from the Zadar Channel on the west. The old town, on the north-western part of the peninsula (4km long and only 500m wide), encompasses the port and Jazine Bay. The new suburbs of Voštarnica and Brodarica are along the north-eastern coast outside the peninsula, and the north-western coast is given over to the 'tourist zone' of Borik. The old town has been rebuilt several times

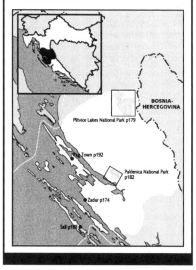

but retains the look and feel of an ancient Mediterranean city. The streets are paved with gleaming white stone, high city walls run along the harbour and as soon as the weather gets warm, people pour into the cafés or wander along the harbourside promenades. A wealth of museums, churches and monuments have recently been repaired and reopened in an attempt to lure tourists from the beaches and camp sites at nearby Borik.

Zadar was inhabited by the Illyrian Liburnian tribe as early as the 9th century BC. At the end of the 3rd century BC, the Romans began their 200-year-long struggle with the Illyrians and by the 1st century BC, Zadar had become a Roman municipality and later a colony. It acquired the characteristics of a typical Roman town, with a rectangular street plan, a forum and baths.

Water came from the nearby Lake Vrana. Zadar does not appear to have been a particularly important town for the Romans but when the Roman Empire was divided, it became the capital of Byzantine Dalmatia. In the 6th and 7th centuries, the city was settled by Slav migrants and Zadar eventually fell under the authority of Croato-Hungarian kings.

All was well until the rise of the Venetian empire in the mid-12th century. For the

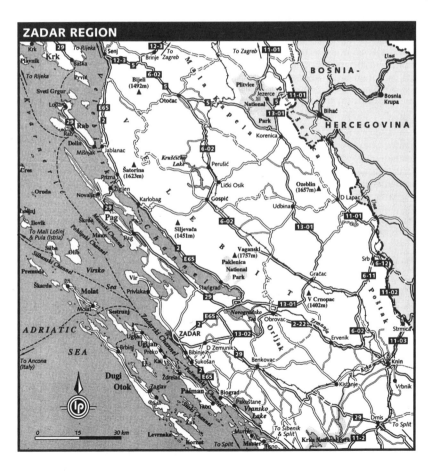

ZADAR REGION

next 200 years Zadar was subjected to relentless assault by Venetians seeking to expand their hold on Adriatic trading interests. There were four unsuccessful citizens' uprisings in the 12th century, but in 1202 the Venetians managed to sack the city and expel its citizens with the help of French Crusaders. The people of Zadar continued to rebel throughout the 13th and 14th centuries, with the help of Croato-Hungarian kings, but finally it was sold to Venice in 1409 along with the rest of Dalmatia.

Zadar's economic growth declined under Venetian rule because of Turkish attacks and frequent Veneto-Turkish wars. The city walls were built in the 16th century but it was not until the end of the 17th century that the Turkish threat finally receded. With the fall of Venice in 1797, the city passed to Austrian, French, then Austrian rule. The Austrians took a city that had an Italianised aristocracy and they imported more Italians from their provinces in Italy to administer the city. Italian influence endured well into the 20th century, Zadar being excluded from the Kingdom of Serbs, Croats and Slovenes and remaining an Italian province. When Italy capitulated to the Allies in 1943, the city was occupied by the Germans and then bombed to smithereens by the Allies; almost 60% of the old town was destroyed.

The city was rebuilt following the original street plan and an effort was made to harmonise the new with what remained of old Zadar. As though the city had some magnetic power to attract trouble, history repeated itself in November 1991 when Yugoslav rockets launched an attack on the city, keeping it under siege for three months. Bombs sailed overhead and the city's residents were virtually imprisoned in their homes with insufficient food or water. Although the Serb gunners were pushed back by the Croatian army during its January 1993 offensive, this experience has embittered many residents and you may encounter some suspicion.

Few war wounds are visible, however. Zadar's narrow, traffic-free stone streets are again full of life and the tree-lined promenade along Obala kralja Petra Krešimira IV is perfect for a lazy stroll or a picnic. Tremendous 16th century fortifications still shield the city on the landward side and high walls run along the harbour. Zadar can be a fascinating place in which to wander and, at the end of the day, you can sample its famous maraschino cherry liqueur.

Orientation

The old town is neatly contained within two roads that run along the quays. Within the old town, you'll find all of the city's museums, churches and monuments. Most travel agencies are along the town's main commercial street, Široka ulica. The Jadrolinija boats are lined up on the north-eastern harbour which is connected by a footbridge across Jazine Bay to Obala Kneza Branimira. Continuing north-west you'll come to the marina and then to Borik, about 3km from the old town. The train and bus stations are a 15 minute walk south-east of the harbour and old town. There is one left-luggage office for both the train and bus stations, open 24 hours a day. From the train and bus stations, Zrinsko-Frankopanska ulica leads north-west past the main post office to the harbour.

Information

Tourist Offices The municipal tourist office is Turistička Zajednica (☎ 212 412), Smiljanića 4, but you're more likely to find the information you need at one of the travel agencies. It's open Monday to Friday from 8 am to 4 pm. Jadroagent (☎ 211 447) on ulica Natka Nodila, just inside the city walls, has tickets for all boats. Jadrolinija (☎ 212 003), Liburnska obala 7 on the harbour, has tickets for all local ferries. It's open Monday to Saturday from 7.30 am to 8 pm and Sunday from 7.30 am to noon and 5 to 8.30 pm.

Money There's a Zagrebačka Banka at Knezova Šubića Bribirskih 4 where you can change money or withdraw cash using MasterCard at the ATM. The bank is open Monday to Friday from 8 am to 1 pm and Saturday 8 to 11.30 am. Travel agencies also change money.

Post & Communications The main post office, at Zrinsko-Frankopanska ulica 8, is open from 7 am to 8 pm daily. You can withdraw cash using MasterCard or Diners Club. The postcode for Zadar is 23000.

Travel Agencies Croatia Express (☎ 211 660) is on Široka ulica. The American Express representative is Atlas travel agency (☎ 314 206), Branimirova Obala 12, across the footbridge over the harbour just north-east of Narodni trg. Kvarner Express (☎ /fax 212 215) is on Kraljice Elizabete Kotromanić 3 and Kompas (☎/fax 433 380) is at Široka 9.

Things to See

City Walls Walking Tour A tour of the City Walls gives an insight into the city's history. If you tour the walls chronologically, you'll begin with the eastern walls near the footbridge. These walls are the only remains of the ancient Roman and early Medieval fortifications, as most of the walls were built under the Venetians. Opposite the footbridge there are four old **city gates**. Heading north-west you'll pass first the **gate of St Rok**, then the **Port Gate** built in 1573 that still sports the Venetian lion, the symbol of Venice. The gate contains part of a Roman triumphal arch and has a memorial inscription of the 1571 Battle of Lepanto in which the Austrians delivered a decisive blow to the Turkish navy.

Heading back in the opposite direction along the quays, you'll come to the **Square of the Five Wells** (Trg 5 Bunara), behind St Šimun's church, built on the site of a former moat in 1574 and containing a cistern with five wells. After the destruction of the Roman water supply system, Zadar did not have a potable running water supply until 1838 under Austrian rule.

Continuing south-west you'll come to the **Town Gate**, the most elaborate of all the gates. Built under the Venetian administration in 1543, the gate's Renaissance-styled decorations include St Krževan on horseback, the Venetian lion, inscriptions and coats of arms.

Churches The main places of interest are near the circular **St Donatus Church** (Sveti Donat), one of the most outstanding monuments in Dalmatia. Dating from the beginning of the 9th century, it was named after Bishop Donat who allegedly had it built following the style of early Byzantine architecture. The unusual circular ground plan is especially visible on the southern side because the southern annexe is missing. The church was built over the Roman forum which was built between the 1st century BC and the 3rd century AD. A few architectural fragments are preserved and two complete pillars are built into the church. The original floors were removed from the church and now slabs from the ancient forum are clearly visible. Notice the Latin inscriptions on the remains of the Roman sacrificial altars.

Outside the church on the north-west side is a pillar from the Roman era that served as a 'shame post' in the Middle Ages, where wrongdoers were chained and publicly humiliated. The western side of the church has more Roman remains, including pillars with reliefs of the Roman gods – Jupiter, Amon and Medusa. Underneath, you can see the remains of the altars used in pagan blood sacrifices. It is believed that this area was a temple dedicated to Jupiter, Juno and Minerva, and dates from the 1st century BC.

The Romanesque **Cathedral of St Anastasia** (Katedrala Svete Stošije) near St Donatus was built in the 12th and 13th centuries on the site of an older church. Behind the richly decorated façade is an impressive three nave interior marked by 13th century wall paintings in the side apses. Notice particularly the fresco of a gateway in the southern apse which was used as a model for the door frame of the main portal. On the altar in the left apse is a marble sarcophagus containing the relics of St Anastasia, commissioned by Bishop Donat in the 9th century. The presbytery contains choir stalls lavishly carved by the Venetian artist Matej Morozon in the 15th century. The cathedral was badly bombed during WWII and has since been reconstructed.

ZADAR

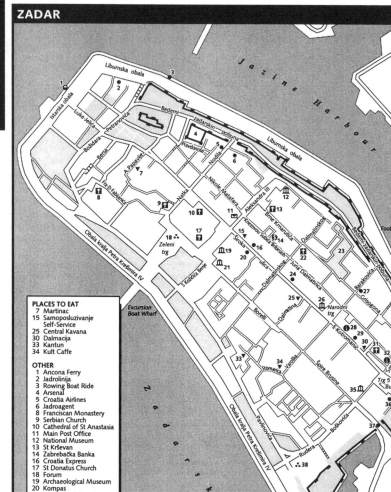

PLACES TO EAT
7 Martinac
15 Samoposluzivanje
 Self-Service
25 Central Kavana
30 Dalmacija
33 Kantun
34 Kult Caffe

OTHER
1 Ancona Ferry
2 Jadrolinija
3 Rowing Boat Ride
4 Arsenal
5 Croatia Airlines
6 Jadroagent
8 Franciscan Monastery
9 Serbian Church
10 Cathedral of St Anastasia
11 Main Post Office
12 National Museum
13 St Krševan
14 Zabrebačka Banka
16 Croatia Express
17 St Donatus Church
18 Forum
19 Archaeological Museum
20 Kompas
21 Museum of Church Art
22 St Petar Stari
23 Vegetable Market
24 National Theatre
26 Town Watchtower
 & Ethnological Museum
27 Grocery Store
28 Liburnija Tourist Office
29 Kvarner Express
31 St Šimun
32 Turistička Zajednica
35 Art Gallery
36 Medieval Tower
37 Town Gate
38 Ruins

0   50   100 m

To Bus &
Train Stations
& Hotel Kolovare

The **Franciscan monastery and church** (Samostan Svetog Frane) a few blocks away is in better shape. Although it's the oldest Gothic church in Dalmatia – it was consecrated in 1280 – the interior has a number of Renaissance features such as a lovely chapel of St Anthony which contains a 15th century wooden crucifix. In the sacristy a memorial tablet commemorates the seminal event in Zadar's history – the 1358 treaty under which Venice relinquished its rights to Dalmatia in favour of the Croato-Hungarian king, Ludovic. The large Romanesque painted crucifix in the treasury behind the sacristy is worth seeing. St Donatus, the Franciscan monastery and the cathedral are open daily from 6.30 am to noon and 5 to 6.30 pm May to September; the rest of the year it's the same in the morning but 4 to 5.30 pm in the afternoon. Other churches are only open for daily Mass but the schedule varies – check at one of the travel agencies.

St Krševan's Church (Crkva Sveti Krševan) was part of a 12th century Benedictine monastery that was destroyed by Allied bombs in 1944. The church has a baroque altar constructed in 1701 and Byzantine frescoes on the north wall and in the north apse. Frescoes on the southern apse are poorly preserved.

Notable churches include **St Šimun** (Sveti Šime), reconstructed in the 16th and 17th centuries on the site of an earlier church. The sarcophagus of St Šimun is a masterpiece of medieval goldsmith work. Commissioned in 1377, the coffin is made of cedar and covered inside and out with finely executed gold-plated silver reliefs. The middle relief showing Christ's presentation in the Temple is a copy of Giotto's fresco from *Capella dell'Arena* in Padua. Other reliefs depict scenes from the lives of the saints and King Ludovic's visit to Zadar. The lid shows a reclining St Šimun.

Museums The outstanding **Museum of Church Art**, in the Benedictine monastery opposite St Donatus, offers a substantial display of reliquaries and religious paintings. Along with the goldsmith's works in the first hall, notice the 14th century painting of the Madonna. In the second hall, the most notable works are the marble sculpture of the Madonna and Paolo Veneziani's painting of the Madonna. On the second floor you'll find 15th and 16th century sculptures and embroidery, and six pictures by the 15th century Venetian painter Vittor Carpaccio. The obscure lighting deliberately re-creates the environment in which the objects were originally kept. The museum is open daily from 10 am to 12.30 pm and 6 to 7.30 pm except Sunday evening.

Nearby is the modern **Archaeological Museum** (closed Sunday) with pottery fragments dating back to the Neolithic era. From the Liburnian era, there are bronze swords, jewellery and pottery. Also interesting is a model of Zadar as it existed in Roman times and statues of emperors Tiberius and Augustus. It's open Monday to Friday May to September, from 9 am to 1 pm and 6 to 9 pm; the rest of the year the morning hours are the same but afternoons it's 5 to 7 pm. Saturday hours are 9 am to 2 pm.

The **National Museum**, Polojana Pape Aleksandra III, in the Benedictine monastery of St Krševan's Church, is an excellent historical museum featuring scale models of Zadar from different periods and old paintings and engravings of many coastal cities. It's open Monday to Friday from 9 am to 2 pm. The same 5KN admission ticket will get you into the local **art gallery** on Šmiljanića. The captions in all Zadar's museums are in Croatian only.

Other Attractions Apart from the museums and churches, a number of other sights scattered around town add distinction to the city. **Narodni trg** was traditionally the centre of public life. The west side of the square is dominated by the late-Renaissance **Town Watchtower** dating from 1562. The clock tower was built under the Austrian administration in 1798. Public proclamations and judgments were announced from the **Town Loggia** across the square, which is now an exhibition space.

Organised Tours

Any of the many travel agencies around town can supply information on the tourist cruises to the beautiful Kornati Islands, which include lunch and a swim in the sea or a salt lake for 250KN. As this is about the only way to see these 101 barren, uninhabited islands, islets and cliffs, it's worthwhile if you can spare the cash. Check with Kvarner Express, Kompas or Croatia Express.

Also ask about excursions to Krka National Park which is difficult to access individually from Zadar (Šibenik is better). There are too few tourists in the region to run the excursion regularly, but if there's a group going you can tag along.

Special Events

Major annual events include the town fair (July and August), the Dalmatian Song Festival (July and August), the Musical Evenings in St Donatus Church (August) and the Choral Festival (October).

Places to Stay

Staying in town is nearly impossible. Most visitors head out to the 'tourist settlement' at Borik on the Puntamika bus (every 20 minutes from the bus station, 6KN), where there are hotels, a hostel, a camp site and numerous *sobe* (room) signs. If you arrive off season, try to arrange accommodation in advance, since hotels, hostels and camp sites will probably be closed.

Camping *Zaton* (☎ 264 303) is 16km northwest of Zadar on a sandy beach and should be open May to September, but call first to check. It's a huge development with a 5000 person capacity. It's not attractively landscaped – the terrain is flat and uninteresting but there is a long stretch of beach and enough sports facilities to keep you busy. There are eight buses daily marked 'Zaton' from the bus station (fewer on weekends) which drop you off in Zaton village, about 1km from the camp. Expect to pay 22KN for your tent and 18KN per person.

Nearer to Zadar is *Autocamp Borik* (☎ 332 074), a smaller site, only steps away

from Borik beach and much closer to town. It'll cost you 20KN per tent plus 13KN per person. It should also be open from May to September, but check ahead.

Hostels Also near the beach at Borik, the *Borik Youth Hostel* (☎ 331 145, fax 331 190, Obala Kneza Trpimira 76) is in a small, tidy building. It's open from May to September. Bed and breakfast costs 70KN and full board is 100KN.

Private Rooms Agencies finding private accommodation include Kompas, Kvarner Express or Marlin Tours (☎/fax 313 194), around the corner from Atlas at Jeretova 3. Liburnija tourist office (☎ 211 039) next to Kvarner Express might also have rooms. Prices vary so check around. Expect to pay around 120KN per person with a 30% surcharge for stays less than three nights. Breakfast is an extra 6KN.

Hotels There are no budget hotels within the town and only one regularly operating hotel, the *Hotel Kolovare* (☎ 203 200, fax 203 300, Bože Peričića 14). It has recently been transformed into a first-rate luxury hotel with a modern phone system, a new swimming pool, air-con, modern bathrooms and a small beach. Clearly going for an international clientele, the hotel has adopted international prices – 430/660KN for a single/double. Prices stay the same all year.

The only other choice is to head out to nearby Borik. The portion of this residential suburb that is closest to the beach has been carved out as a tourist ghetto. In addition to the hostel and autocamp, there are several hotels that were none too attractive to begin with but now could use renovation. On Majstora Radovana 7, the mid-range *Novi Park* (☎ 206 443, fax 332 065), *Zadar* (☎ 211 096) and *Donat* (☎ 332 184) all offer rooms but you must take half-board for 224/369KN. *Hotel Barbara* (☎ 332 194, fax 332 065) is the best of the bunch since it has a swimming pool and costs only slightly more.

Places to Eat

Dalmacija, at the end of Kraljice Elizabete Kotromanić, is a good place for pizza, spaghetti, fish and local specialties at prices that won't break your budget. It's open daily from 11 am to midnight. *Kantun (Stomarica 6)* is a casual, simple place that nevertheless serves excellent plates of fried fresh fish for 25KN. It's open daily from noon to 11 pm.

The newly renovated *Samoposluzivanje* is a self-service restaurant in the passage at Nikole Matafara 9, with hot dishes starting at 25KN. There's not much ambience but it has the advantage of letting you point to the dishes you want rather than try to pronounce them. It's open Monday to Saturday from noon to 9 pm. *Martinac (Papavije 7)* has a secluded terrace behind the restaurant that provides a relaxed atmosphere to sample delicious dishes such as risotto (35KN), fish (40KN to 45KN) and excellent clams. It's open daily from 11 am to 11 pm.

Central Kavana on Široka is a spacious café and hang-out with live music on weekends, while *Kult Caffe (Stomarica)* draws a young crowd to listen to rap music indoors or relax on the large shady terrace outside. In summer the many **cafés** along Varoška and Klaića place their tables on the street – great for people-watching. There's a *grocery store* at Grisogona that sells bread and cold meats for sandwiches, and you'll find a number of *burek stands* around the vegetable market.

Local people usually head out to Borik to eat. One of the most popular establishments is *Restaurant Albin (put Dikla 47)* on the road to Borik. Although somewhat more expensive than the places in town, the fish is extremely well prepared and the surroundings are spacious. It's open daily from 8 am to midnight. *Roko (put Dikla 74)* is more touristy but also offers a good assortment of pizza, pasta and fish. It's open daily from 11 am to midnight.

Entertainment

The **National Theatre** box office on Široka ulica sells tickets to the cultural programs advertised on posters outside. Zadar's most popular disco is *Saturnus*, in Zaton near Zadar. It's the largest disco in Croatia, resembling a space-ship dropped in the flatlands. Built for the tourist encampment in Zaton, you'll find many more Germans and Italians here than Croatians during the summer season. Saturnus is on the main road to Zaton and is open daily in July and August; the rest of the year it's open weekends only.

Getting There & Away

Train There are two daily trains to Zagreb (11 hours, 80KN) that change at Knin. The bus to Zagreb (320km, 70KN) is quicker. There are also buses from Zadar to Rijeka (228km), Split (158km), Mostar (four daily, 301km), Dubrovnik (393km, seven daily, 114KN) and Sarajevo (twice daily, 93KN).

Bus Croatia Express sells bus tickets to many German cities, including Munich (366KN), Frankfurt (576KN), Cologne (666KN) and Berlin (720KN).

Boat From late June to September the fast boat *Marina* runs from Venice to Zadar twice a week and from Pula to Zadar four times a week, stopping at Mali Lošinj. There are weekly local ferries all year (four weekly in summer) from Mali Lošinj (six hours, 30KN) and Pula (eight hours, 58KN). The Jadrolinija coastal ferry from Rijeka to Dubrovnik calls at Zadar four times a week (116KN). In summer, other Jadrolinija lines from Ancona in Italy stop at Zadar (four weekly, 224KN). From May to September, Atlas runs a fast boat between Zadar and Ancona (three hours, 340KN).

On Tuesday and Thursday, there's a late morning ferry to Zaglav on Dugi Otok (1½ hours, 21KN) which connects by bus to Sali. Even better is an early boat on Sunday that connects to Sali, with a late afternoon boat back. There are boats on other days but the schedules do not allow a day trip to Dugi Otok.

Getting Around

Buses run frequently from the bus station to the harbour and to Borik. Buses marked 'Poluotok' run to the harbour and buses marked 'Puntamika' run to Borik. Tickets are 6KN which you can buy in *tsioks* (kiosks) or from the driver.

AROUND ZADAR
Ugljan

The island of Ugljan is easily accessible by boat from Zadar, making it a popular getaway for the locals and a kind of residential suburb for people who work in Zadar. The 50 sq km island is densely populated, housing about 7500 people, and it can get crowded on summer weekends. There are few forests but much macchia (shrubs), some pines and a good deal of farmland with vegetable gardens, olive groves and vineyards. The eastern coast is the most indented and the most developed part of the island, while the west is relatively deserted.

The port of entry is **Preko**, directly across from Zadar, with two small harbours and a ferry port. Although there's a town beach, the best beach is on the little island of **Galovac**, only 80m from the town centre. Small, pretty and wooded, Galovac has a Franciscan monastery dating from the 15th century. If you have your own wheels, you could visit Ugljan village positioned on an indented bay with a sandy beach, the fishermen's village of Kali and the nearby islet of Ošljak, which is covered with pine and cypress trees.

Getting There & Away

There are hourly ferries that make the 30 minute run between Zadar and Preko year-round.

PLITVICE LAKES NATIONAL PARK
☎ 053

Plitvice Lakes National Park lies midway between Zagreb and Zadar. The 19.5 hectares of wooded hills enclose 16 turquoise lakes which are linked by a series of waterfalls and cascades. Wooden footbridges follow the lakes and streams over, under and across the rumbling water for an exhilaratingly damp 18km. In 1979, the Plitvice Lakes were proclaimed a World Heritage site by UNESCO, and the lakes and forests are carefully regulated to ensure their continuing preservation.

The extraordinary natural beauty of the site merits at least a three day visit but you can experience a lot simply on a day trip from Zadar or Zagreb. There's no worst time to visit – in the spring the falls are flush with water, but in summer the surrounding hills are greener; there are fewer visitors in autumn and you'll be treated to the changing colours of leaves.

The lake system is divided into the upper and lower lakes. The upper lakes lying in a dolomite valley are the most impressive, surrounded by dense forests and interlinked by several gushing waterfalls. The lower lakes are smaller and shallower, surrounded only by sparse underbrush. Most of the water comes from the Bijela and Crna Rijeka (White and Black Rivers) which join south of Prošćansko Lake but the lakes are also fed by underground springs. In turn, water disappears into the porous limestone at some points only to re-emerge in another place. All the water empties into the Korana River near Sastavci.

The upper lakes are separated by dolomite barriers which expand with the mosses and algae that absorb calcium carbonate as river water rushes through the karst. The encrusted plants grow on top of each other, forming travertine (porous rock) barriers and creating waterfalls. The lower lakes undergo a similar process but they were formed by cavities created by the water of the upper lakes. Travertine is constantly forming and reforming itself into new combinations so that the landscape is ever changing. This unique interaction of water, rock and plant life has continued more or less undisturbed since the last Ice Age.

The colours of the lakes also change constantly. From azure to bright green, deep blue or grey, the colours depend upon the quantity of minerals or organisms in the

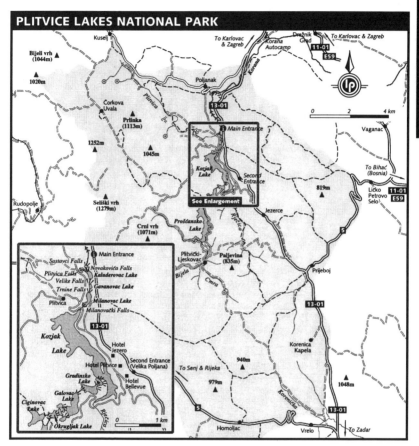

PLITVICE LAKES NATIONAL PARK

water, whether rain has deposited mud, and the angle of sunlight.

The luxuriant vegetation of the national park is another delight. The north-eastern part of the park is covered by beech forests while the rest is covered with beech, fir spruce and white pine dotted with patches of whitebeam, hornbeam and flowering ash that change colour in autumn.

Animal life flourishes in the unspoiled conditions. The stars of the park are bears and wolves but there are also deer, boar,

rabbits, foxes and badgers. There are over 120 different species of birds such as hawks, owls, cuckoos, thrushes, starlings, kingfishers, wild ducks and herons. You might occasionally see black storks and ospreys – and flocks of butterflies flutter throughout the park.

After prehistoric settlements, the first recorded inhabitants in the region were the Thracians who arrived in the first millennium BC, followed by the Illyrians and then the ubiquitous Romans who visited in 59

ZADAR

BC and stayed for 600 years. Slavs migrated to the area in the 7th century and were eventually organised into the feudal system that dominated the early middle ages. The Turks seized power in 1528 and when they were driven out 150 years later, the Austrians tried to attract new settlers by making it a feudal-free zone. The area became part of the Krajina military frontier and was settled by Vlachs and Morlachs who followed the Serbian Orthodox faith.

Even as early as 1896 when the first hotel was built, the tourism potential of the lakes was apparent. A preservation society founded in 1893 ensured the protection of the lake environment well into the 20th century. The boundaries of the national park were set in 1951 with a view toward minimising degradation and maximising tourism. Before the recent war, the lakes were a major tourist attraction but their presence within the Serb-dominated Krajina region made trouble inevitable when the former Yugoslavia began to crack up.

The civil war in ex-Yugoslavia actually began in Plitvice on 31 March 1991, when rebel Serbs from the Krajina region took control of the park headquarters. The murder of a Croatian police officer, Josip Jović, that Easter Sunday was the first casualty of this ruthless war. Rebel Serbs held the area for the duration of the war, turning the hotels into barracks and plundering park property. When the Croatian army finally retook the park in August 1995, they found the natural beauty intact but the hotels and facilities completely gutted. Reconstruction has been proceeding at a furious pace and most hotels, camping grounds and facilities should be in good working order by the time you visit.

Orientation & Information

You can pick up maps and brochures at the tourist office (☎ 751 015, fax 741 013), 53231 Plitvička jezera, at the main entrance, open daily from 8 am to 6.30 pm. The secondary entrance is at Velika Poljana, near the hotels. Park admission is 60/40KN for adults/students and includes a

3½ hour orientation tour by bus and a boat ride across the main lake, and is valid for the entire stay. Admission is 10KN cheaper in the shoulder season and 20KN cheaper off season. The post office is near the hotels. There are well-marked trails throughout the park and a system of wooden walkways that allows you to appreciate the beauty of the landscape without disturbing the environment.

Things to See

The lower lakes string out from the main entrance and are rich in forests, grottoes and steep cliffs. **Novakovića Brod** is nearest the entrance and is followed by **Kaluderovac Lake** near two caves – the Blue Cave and Šupljara. Next is **Gavanovac Lake** with towering waterfalls and last is **Milanovac Lake**, notable for colours that are variously sky-blue, azure or emerald green.

Kozjak is the largest lake and forms a boundary between the upper and lower lakes. Three kilometres long, the lake is surrounded by steep, forested slopes and contains a small oval island, composed of travertine. Past the hotels, you'll see **Gradinsko Lake** bordered by reeds that often harbour nesting wild ducks. A series of cascades links Gradinsko to **Galovac Lake**, considered the most beautiful lake of all. An abundance of water has formed a series of ponds and falls. A set of concrete stairs over the falls, constructed long ago, have eventually been covered by travertine forming even more falls in a spectacular panorama. Several smaller lakes are topped by the larger **Okrugljak Lake**, supplied by two powerful waterfalls. Continuing upward you'll come to **Ciginovac Lake** and finally **Prošćansko Lake** surrounded by thick forests.

Places to Stay & Eat

Camping *Korana* (☎ 053-751 015) is a large, well-equipped autocamp about 1km north of the main entrance along the main road to Zagreb. The charge is 25KN per person and 18KN per tent and the site is open from May to October.

Hotels The hotels are clustered on Velika Poljana overlooking Lake Kozjak. *Hotel Bellevue (☎ 053-751 700, fax 053-751 965)* offers rustic accommodation within the park for 260/400KN a single/double, but at the hotels *Jezero (☎ 053-751 400),* which should re-open soon, and *Plitvice (☎ 053-751 100)* you'll pay about 50% more. Prices are not substantially lower in the shoulder season but drop about 30% January through April and from November to December.

Check at the Plitvice Lakes National Park office in Zagreb (☎ 46 13 586), Trg Kralja Tomislava 19, Zagreb 10000, for information on private accommodation, but it will obviously be outside the park and therefore inconvenient unless you have your own car.

There are two restaurants on Velika Poljana, one of which is self-service. There's also a small restaurant on Lake Koznjak and a minimarket near the second entrance to pick up picnic supplies.

Getting There & Away
All the Zagreb-Zadar buses stop at Plitvice (140km, 40KN). It's possible to visit Plitvice for the day on the way to or from the coast, but be aware that buses will not pick up passengers at Plitvice if they are full. On summer weekends you could spend a good part of the day stuck in traffic since the road to Plitvice is the main artery to the coast for holidaying city folk. Luggage can be left at the tourist information centre at the main entrance to the park or at one of the hotels.

PAKLENICA NATIONAL PARK
Rising high above the Adriatic, the stark peaks of the Velebit Massif stretch for 145km in a dramatic landscape of rock and sea. Paklenica National Park covers 3657 hectares of the Velebit Range, extending in a rough circle from the park entrance in the village of Marasovići. From Sunday strollers to rock climbers and serious hikers, the park offers a wealth of opportunities to trek across steep gorges, crawl up slabs of stone, or meander along shady paths next to a rushing stream. The panorama inside the

Park Rules in Paklenica

- Do not damage trees and bushes, or pick flowers or plants.
- Do not frighten, disturb, hunt, catch or kill any kind of animal.
- Do not bring weapons into the park.
- Do not damage nests and animal burrows.
- Do not touch or break cave stalactites and stalagmites.
- Do not touch light fixtures in Manita peć cave, which may only be visited with a guide.
- Do not camp or light fires.
- Carry all litter back to the park entrance or throw it away in specified places.
- Do not pollute the water.
- No dogs are allowed loose in the park.
- Keep to the tracks and paths.
- Visitors must purchase a ticket and show it to park attendants on request.

park is ever changing and much greener than you would think when looking at the chalky mountains from the sea.

The national park circles around two deep gorges, Velika Paklenica (Great Paklenica) and Mala Paklenica (Small Paklenica), which scar the mountain range like hatchet marks, with cliffs over 400m high. The dry limestone karst that forms the Velebit Range is highly absorbent, but several springs in the park's upper reaches provide a continuous source of water which explains the unusually lush vegetation. About half the park is covered with forests, mostly beech and pine followed by white oak and varieties of hornbeam. The vegetation changes as you ascend, as does the climate, which progresses from Mediterranean to continental to subalpine. The lower regions, especially those with a southern exposure, can be fiercely hot in the summer and the cold bura (gale force winds) that whips through the range in winter brings rain and sudden storms.

Animal life is scarce but interesting. The park's most celebrated inhabitants are griffon vultures, whose 2.5m wing spans make them hard to miss, at least while they're in flight. Although they have traditionally nested in the cliffs just beyond the car park, their numbers have been dwindling in recent years, and at last report they are down to only four nesting pairs. You'll have better luck seeing other birds – Egyptian vultures, golden eagles, striped eagles and peregrine falcons also nest on the cliffs of the two gorges and, if you've forgotten what they look like, there's an illustrated signboard at the park's entrance. Rumour has it that bears and wolves live in the park's upper regions, but your chances of actually seeing one are minuscule.

The best time to visit the park is in May, June or September. In late spring the park is

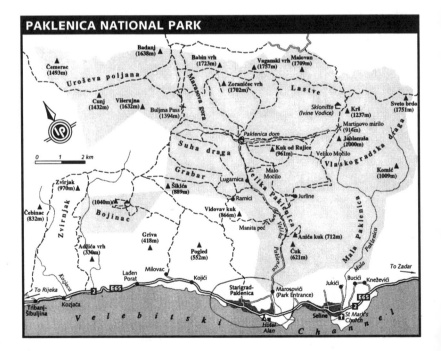

PAKLENICA NATIONAL PARK

greenest, the streams become torrents and there are few other visitors. In July and August you'll still find the trails uncrowded, since most people come to the region for the sun and sea, but it might be too hot to hike comfortably. In September the weather is mild during the day and cool at night, making it perfect hiking weather, plus you can still finish off a day on the trails with a refreshing swim.

Orientation

The best base for exploring the park is Stari Grad (sometimes also referred to as Stari Grad-Paklenica, to differentiate it from another Stari Grad near Senj which has nothing to do with Paklenica National Park).

Stari Grad is the site of the national park office and has the most possibilities for restaurants and accommodation. It's also near the entrance to Velika Paklenica which offers the most varied walks and climbs. The entrance to the national park is near the village of Marasovići, which is about 2km north of the town of Stari Grad. The road to the entrance is not particularly interesting, so a lot of people drive to the car park past the reception area. The entrance to Mala Paklenica is on the far side of Seline village about 2.5km south-east of Stari Grad on the road to Zadar. Follow the road opposite St Mark's (Sveti Marko) church toward the canyon. Trails throughout the park are marked by small white and red posts.

Information

The Paklenica National Park Office (☎/fax 369 202, np-paklenica@zd.tel.hr, www .tel.hr/paklenica) is on the main road in Stari Grad and is open April through October from 8 am to 3 pm. It sells booklets and maps, and is in charge of maintaining the park. The *Paklenica National Park* guide gives an excellent overview of the park and suggests various walks. Rock climbers should talk to one of the guides employed by the park administration who can provide detailed advice on climbing routes and their difficulty levels. The Croatian Climbing Federation (☎/fax 448 774), Kozaričeva 22, Zagreb 10000, also has up-to-date information and publishes a useful map to the park with clearly marked routes. It's on sale in the national park office or at larger bookstores in Zagreb. Admission to Paklenica is 20KN and it's open from 6 am to 8.30 pm

Walking

Most walks are one-day affairs either from 'base camp' at Stari Grad or Seline or from one of the mountain huts. The most convenient is the Planinarski Dom Paklenica (which translates as 'Mountain Lodge, Paklenica'), which costs 50KN a night plus 5KN for use of the kitchen. There's no hot water or electricity but you can reach the highest peaks of Velebit from here. Planinarski Dom has 40 beds in four rooms but a sleeping bag is advisable since the lodge provides blankets but no sheets. You can also throw a sleeping bag on the floor and negotiate a price with the groundskeeper.

East of Planinarski Dom, there's the Ivine Vodice hut at Sklonište. Ivine Vodice has no beds but can host 10 people with sleeping bags. It's free, and it's not necessary to reserve in advance. Both huts are open daily from June to September, and weekends only for the rest of the year.

Mala Paklenica to Velika Paklenica Mala Paklenica is smaller and less visited than Velika Paklenica, which is why you stand a better chance of glimpsing a griffon vulture. The karst formations are outstanding in Mala Paklenica but the trail can get slippery in spring and autumn and you may have to cross Mala Paklenica stream a few times. You'll be following the stream through rocks and boulders for the first four hours or so and then zigzagging uphill to about 680m. Take the left-hand path marked Stari Grad and Jivile. You'll pass through fields and pastures before descending to a rocky gully that leads to the valley floor. You'll arrive at Velika Paklenica, enjoy a marvellous view and then follow the path through the gorge with Anića Kuk on your left down to the valley floor.

ZADAR

The Threatened Griffon Vulture

Of all Croatia's birds, the griffon vulture is the most majestic. With a wing span of almost 3m, measuring about 1m from end to end, and weighing seven to nine kilos, the bird looks big enough to take on passengers. They're speedy as well, cruising comfortably at 40 to 50km/h and reaching speeds of up to 120km/h. The vulture's powerful beak and long neck is ideally suited for rummaging around the entrails of its prey which is most likely to be a dead sheep.

Finding precious sheep carcasses is a team effort for griffon vultures. Usually a colony of birds will set out and fly in a comb formation of up to a kilometre apart. When one of the vultures spots a carcass, it circles as a signal for its neighbours to join in the feast. Shepherds don't mind griffons, reasoning that the birds prevent whatever disease or infection killed the sheep from spreading to other livestock.

The total known number of griffon vultures in Croatia is 150, with 142 of them living on the coastal cliffs of Cres and eight living in the gorges of Paklenica National Park. The bird's dietary preferences mean that griffons tend to follow the sheep. Shepherding is still active on Cres but in Paklenica the sheep population has thinned out over the years. Krk island used to host griffon colonies but the lack of sheep plus over-development has eliminated the population. On Cres, the best area to spot a griffon vulture is on the sea crags from Orlec south to Belej, Plat and Verin.

Their breeding habits discourage a large population, as a griffon couple produces only one fledgling a year and it takes five years for the young bird to reach maturity. During that time, the growing griffons travel widely: one griffon tagged in Paklenica National Park was found in Chad, 4000km away.

The griffon population does not enjoy protection as an endangered species in Croatia, which leaves them subject to potentially lethal harassment. Because the young birds cannot fly more than 500m on a windless day, tourists who provoke them into flight often end up killing them, as the exhausted birds drop into the water and drown. The Eco Centre in Beli on Cres island serves as a kind of hospital and rest home for injured or exhausted vultures and is urging that stronger measures be taken to protect the griffon.

Stari Grad to Planinarski Dom Immediately after the entrance to the park you'll find yourself at the floor of the Velika Paklenica Gorge, with grey stone massifs looming on either side. In July and August, you're sure to find rock climbers making their way up the cliffs. About 200m up from the car park on the left is the entrance to tunnels that were carved out of the rock by the federal Yugoslav army before the recent war. Entrance is free to the well-lit, neat halls and rooms but they are only open in August on Thursday and Sunday from 9 am to noon.

When you pass a rock fall with a stream on your right you'll be at Anića luka, a green, semicircular plateau. In another kilometre or so there's a turn-off to Manita Peć (cave). Take the steps down from the ante-hall to the centre of the cave, with a wealth of stalagmites and stalactites enhanced by strategically placed lighting. The area is 40m long and reaches a height of 32m. The cave is open from 10 am to 1 pm and must be visited with a guide. It's about a two hour walk from the car park.

From the cave you can follow the trail to Vidakov Kuk (1½ hours). The ascent up the 866m peak is fairly rugged, but on a clear day you'll be rewarded with an unforgettable view over the sea to Pag. You can continue on an easy trail to Ramići and then head east to the main trail up to Planinarski Dom.

You can also bypass the Manita Peć detour and continue up to the Game Warden's Hut in the Lugarnica area (about an hour's walk from the car park), open in July and August only. You can buy snacks and drinks in the hut before continuing on up to Planinarski Dom. You'll pass beech and pine forests before coming to the shelter.

In another route to the hut, take the right path after Anića Luka past the little farm-house at Jurline. The left fork leads to the black pine forests of Mala Močilo but you can also continue straight ahead to Veliko Močilo and rest beside a spring of drinkable water (three hours from the car park). From here you can take the right fork to the Ivine Vodice hut, or at Martinovo Marilo you can take the left path along the southern slope of the upper Velika Paklenica valley, following the Velika Paklenica River to Planinarski Dom (about 1½ hours from Velika Močilo).

Upper Velebit From the mountain lodge, you can easily reach each of the Velebit peaks in a day but you'd need about a week to explore all the peaks. The highest point in the Velebit Range is Vaganski vrh (1757m). From the flat, grassy top you have a view of up to 150km inland over the Velebit peaks on a clear day. It may be a long, hard day – depending on your level of fitness – but it can be reached in a day with enough time to return to the shelter by nightfall.

Another popular destination is Babin vrh (Grandmother's Peak, 1741m). Follow the trail with the Brezimenjača stream on the left to the pass of Buljma (1394m) and then continue to Marasova gora through decidu-ous forest. There's a 7m lake at the foot of Babin vrh which never dries up (but the water has been polluted by sheep).

It's also possible to reach all the peaks along the Velebit ridge from Mala Pakleni-ca, but make sure you have survival equipment, a map and the assurance that both huts are open. Past Sveti Jakov in Mala Paklenica take the right path to the Ivine Vodice hut. Marked trails lead past Sveto Brdo (1751m), Malovan (1709m), Vagan-ski vrh and Babin vrh before descending to the Planinarski Dom hut.

Rock Climbing

The national park offers a tremendous variety of rock climbing routes from begin-ners' level to borderline suicidal. The firm, occasionally sharp limestone offers graded climbs, including 72 short sports routes and 250 longer routes. You'll see the beginners' routes at the beginning of the park with cliffs reaching about 40m, but the best and most advanced climbing is on Anića Kuk which offers over 100 routes up to a maximum of 350m. Nearly all routes are well equipped with spits and pitons, except for the appro-priately named *Psycho Killer* route. The most popular climbs are Mosoraški (350m, graded 5+, or 5.7 in the US grading system), Velebitaški (350m, graded 7-/5.10b), and Klin (300m, graded 8-/5.11b). Spring is the best climbing season as summers can be quite warm and winters too windy. The na-tional park offers a week-long beginners' course for 720KN, and guides for 720KN a day. A rescue service is also available. For more information and a few pictures, check out the 'Free Climbing in Croatia' site at http://public.srce.hr/hpd–zeljeznicar/AO/climbing.htm on the Net.

STARI GRAD

• pop 1160   ☎ 023

Stari Grad is on either side of the main coastal road from Rijeka to Zadar. All buses from Rijeka or Zadar stop in front of the Hotel Alan and 2km north in the centre of town.

The tourist office (☎ 369 245, fax 369 255) is in the centre of town on the main road across from the small harbour. In the summer it's open daily from 9 am to 9 pm but off-season it's open Monday to Saturday from 8 am to 3 pm. Splitskabanka is between the tourist office and the Hotel Alan and is open Monday to Friday from 8 am to noon and 6 to 8 pm and Saturday 8 am to noon. There are no ATMs but you can change money in the post office, which is between the tourist office and the Hotel Alan on the main road. It's open Monday to Saturday from 7 am to 9 pm, Sunday 7 am to noon.

Places to Stay & Eat

Although camping is not permitted in the national park, there are numerous camping grounds in and around Stari Grad. The largest sites are at the *Hotel Alan (☎ 369 236)* and the adjoining *National Park Camping (☎ 369 202)*, both of which overlook a pebble beach and are only 50m from the road leading to the entrance of the national park. National Park Camping is open from April to November while the one at the Hotel Alan is only open in July and August. *Camping Plantaža (☎ 369 188)* is about 2km north-west of the town centre on the road to Rijeka and *Camping Pisak (☎ 369 662)* is about 3km south-east of the town centre on the road to Zadar. Both sites are unreliably open from June to September. Small, private camping grounds are stationed along the main road leading into and out of town.

Private accommodation is also abundant in and around Stari Grad. Although no agency 'officially' finds accommodation, the tourist office makes it its business to connect people looking for rooms or apartments with the many residents offering them. Prices are from 29KN to 72KN per person for a room, depending on the season, and 144KN to 162KN (per unit) for a studio not including residence tax or breakfast (17KN) and based upon a three night stay. Full board and larger apartments are also available. You can find accommodation for yourself by walking along the main road and checking out the many sobe signs.

The two hotels in town are not in great shape but they don't cost very much either. Rooms at the *Hotel Alan (☎ 369 236, fax 369 203)* are 176/317KN a single/double in high season including breakfast. The hotel could use renovation and there is no TV or telephone in the rooms but nearly all of them have balconies with great views. Rooms in the *Hotel Vicko (☎ 369 304)* are slightly more expensive and better equipped but you don't get the views. Prices drop by about a third outside of the July and August season. Both hotels are closed from October to April.

The best place to eat is *Rajna (☎ 369 130)*. Not only is the food good and inexpensive but the restaurant is a popular meeting place for climbers. The owner also has a few rooms to rent.

Getting There & Away

Stari Grad is 45km from Zadar and 200km from Rijeka. All buses between those cities stop at Stari Grad.

DUGI OTOK

• pop 1800   ☎ 023

Dugi Otok may not be the place to find artfully designed villages or historic old towns but the natural, unspoiled beauty of the island makes it a perfect getaway for those seeking a peaceful, relaxing vacation. The island has a brief season around the first three weeks of August when Italian vacationers boat over on the ferry from Ancona or on private vessels, and then all is quiet for another year. Among the highlights of the island are the Telašćica Bay nature park with its cluster of small islands, the nearby saltwater Mir Lake, sandy Sakarun Bay and a panoramic drive along the rocky, indented coast. There isn't much to do here besides swim, scuba dive and enjoy the spectacular scenery, but you'll certainly be free of package tourists, cruise lines and souvenir sellers.

The name Dugi Otok means long island. Stretching north-east to south-west, the island is 43km long and only 4km wide. The south-west coast is marked by steep hills and cliffs, while the northern half is cultivated with vineyards, orchards and sheep pastures. In between is a series of karstic hills rising to 338m at Vela Straža, its highest point.

Ruins on the island reveal early settlement by Illyrians, Romans and then early Christians but the island was first documented in the mid-10th century. It later became the property of the monasteries of Zadar. Settlement expanded with the 16th century Turkish invasions, which prompted residents of Zadar and neighbouring towns to flee to the island.

Dugi Otok's fortunes have largely been linked with Zadar as it changed hands between Venetians, Austrians and French, but when northern Dalmatia was handed over to Mussolini, the island stayed within Croatia. Old-timers still recall the hardships they endured when the nearest medical and administrative centre was in Šibenik, a long, hard boat ride up the coast.

Economic development of the island has always been hampered by the lack of any freshwater supply – drinking water must be collected from rainwater or, in the dry summers, brought over by boat from Zadar. The capital town of Sali is the site of a fish processing factory that is being revived after years of neglect.

Like many Dalmatian islands, the population has drifted away over the last few decades, leaving a few hardy souls to brave the dry summers and bura-chilled winters.

The best base for a stay on the island is Sali, on the south-eastern coast, which has the best hotel, the most private accommodation and the most opportunities for excursions. Božava, across the island on the north-eastern coast, is a sleepy little village near Veli Rat Bay, but accommodation is scarcer and more expensive. Roughly in the middle is Brbinj, which is the main ferry stop.

Getting There & Away

Transportation to and within the island is limited, which is why the island attracts relatively few visitors. In summer, the large Jadrolinija coastal ferries stop at Brbinj once a week and the Ancona (Italy) to Zadar line stops at Brbinj twice a week (5½ hours from Ancona). There are also daily ferries all year from Zadar to Brbinj, Zaglav and Sali which take about 1½ hours and cost 21KN.

Getting Around

There is little public bus transportation throughout the island, only a weekly bus taking Božavo villagers to Sali and back. On days when the ferry stops at Zaglav and not Sali, there is a bus that connects Sali with the ferry stop.

If you're entering the island at Brbinj without your own transport, you may have little choice but to head to Božava. There are no buses between Brbinj and Sali but buses to Boz from Brbinj (14km) meet all ferries except the one from Ancona that lands at 6 am on Sunday.

Sali
• **pop 1190**

As the island's largest town and port, Sali is a metropolis compared to the other small towns and villages scattered along Dugi Otok's coast. Named after the saltworks that had occupied villagers during the medieval period, the town has a rumpled, lived-in look that is comfortable and unpretentious.

Sali's low-key appeal is undisturbed by the yachts and small passenger boats that dock there during the summer on the way to and from Telašćica Bay and the Kornati Islands. Although the town is tantalisingly close to these natural wonders, you'll need to either come with a boat, rent a boat or take a boat tour to visit them.

Orientation & Information The town centres around the port on Porat Bay, where you'll find restaurants, small cafés and offices. West of the town centre is sparkling Šašćica Bay, tucked between two hills with swimming coves. From the foot of the port, a path and stairs lead to the upper town, surrounded by small vineyards and fields.

The Turistički Ured (☎ 377 094) is on Obala Kralja Tomislava and is the source of all information about Sali. From June to September it's open daily from 8 am to 8 pm but off season it's only open Monday to Friday from 8 am to noon. It finds private accommodation, books excursions and distributes the few available brochures and maps.

There is no bank but you can change money or get cash on your MasterCard or Diners Club card at the post office on Obala Petra Lorinija, which is open Monday to Saturday from 8 am to noon and 6 to 9 pm. The postal code for Sali is 23281.

Things to See & Do Sightseeing within the town is limited but there is the interesting **St Mary's Church** (Crkva Sveti Marije), built in the 15th century on the site of an earlier church. It is especially notable for the wooden altar and several Renaissance paintings but is only open for Mass.

The town's proximity to the underwater marine park at the Kornati Islands makes it an excellent base for **scuba diving**. Dive Centre Sali (☎/fax 377 194) at the foot of Selašćica Bay organises a two-dive day trip around Dugi Otok and/or the Kornati Islands for 288KN, not including equipment rental of 144KN. Diving in the Kornati Islands is marked by steep drop offs and numerous caves because of its position facing the open sea. There are also possibilities for cave diving on the north side of Dugi Otok where the caves are relatively shallow and large, making them suitable for beginners.

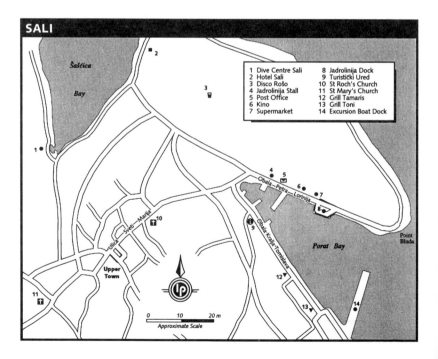

SALI

1 Dive Centre Sali	8 Jadrolinija Dock
2 Hotel Sali	9 Turistički Ured
3 Disco Rošo	10 St Roch's Church
4 Jadrolinija Stall	11 St Mary's Church
5 Post Office	12 Grill Tamaris
6 Kino	13 Grill Toni
7 Supermarket	14 Excursion Boat Dock

The tourist office will book you on **boat trips** that include a leisurely tour of Telašćica Bay and a stop on one of the Kornati Islands. There are three boats that do the excursion – two small boats for 100KN and 110KN and a large boat for 130KN.

The tourist office will also arrange for you to rent a small motorboat for 150KN a day which is the only available option for self-transport since there are, as yet, no scooter or bike rentals.

Special Events The weekend before the Assumption (15 August) the island hosts the Saljske Užance Festival, which draws visitors from the entire region. Highlights are the donkey races and the candlelight procession of boats around the harbour. Men and women don traditional costumes, play instruments devised from cow horns and perform traditional village dances.

Places to Stay – Camping There are no functioning camping grounds on Dugi Otok, which is an unfortunate omission since there are some splendid sites. There used to be a Slovenian-run site on the edge of Mir Bay, but since the war no-one seems to know what to do with it and camping is officially forbidden. Despite the illegality and the lack of plumbing, at the time of writing, people were camping there anyway.

Places to Stay – Private Rooms Private accommodation is reasonable in Sali especially out of the main season, and the tourist office can connect you with some wonderful, out-of-the-way places including a house on its own little island. Even in high season you can find a room for 54KN to 72KN per person, usually with a shared bath. The price is based on double occupancy so, if you're travelling solo in peak season, you may have to pay the price of a double. Off season you have a lot more bargaining power to push the price down 20% to 30%.

A fully equipped studio runs from 180KN to 200KN and a two room apartment is priced at 288KN. All prices are based upon a three night minimum stay with a 30% surcharge for fewer nights. The surcharge is usually waived off season.

If you come in the summer, it would be a good idea to ask the proprietor if there are any restrictions on water use. Even if nothing is spelled out, chances are that long, luxurious showers will not be appreciated.

Places to Stay – Hotels If you prefer the comforts of a hotel, you're in luck because the *Hotel Sali* (☎ *377 049, fax 377 078*) offers just about the best deal on the coast. In 1997, Zagreb entrepreneurs bought the dreary old state-run structure and managed to whip it into shape in less than a year. On a hill overlooking Sašćica Bay, with access to swimming coves, the hotel is freshly painted in white and marine blue. All rooms have modern baths, air-con, satellite TV and balconies, many with views over the sea. Considering its location and excellent condition, the price is a steal at 177/316KN in high season plus residence tax. The price falls 25% in early July and late August, and 50% in June and September.

Places to Eat Although there are a few restaurants along Obala Kralja Tomislava, the best is the *Grill Tamaris* which offers spaghetti with mixed seafood for 25KN and freshly grilled shrimp and fish for 180KN a kilogram. *Grill Toni* is not bad either, offering a similar menu. Both restaurants are open daily in summer from 10 am to midnight but close for several months in winter. There's also a *supermarket* near the Jadrolinija dock open Monday to Saturday from 7 am to 10 pm and 7 am to noon on Sunday.

Telašćica Bay

The south-eastern tip of Dugi Otok is split in two by the deeply indented Telašćica Bay, dotted with five small islands and five more even tinier islets. In fact, the 8200m bay contains five smaller bays which form an indented coastline of 28km and one of the largest and most beautiful natural harbours in the Adriatic.

The Kornati Islands extend nearly to the edge of Telašćica Bay and the topography of the two island groups is identical – stark white limestone with patches of brush. The tip of the western side of the island faces the sea where the wind and waves have carved out sheer cliffs dropping 166m. There are no towns, settlements or roads on this part of the island, only a couple of restaurants on Mir Bay catering to the boaters who spend days or even weeks cruising the islands.

Next to Mir Bay is the saltwater Mir Lake, fed by underground channels through the limestone to the sea. The lake is surrounded by pine forests and the water is much warmer than the sea. The lake is clear but has a muddy bottom. Like most mud in unusual places, it's supposed to be very good for you – cure ailments, keep you young etc.

Boz

• pop 115

For visitors who think even Sali is too urban, there's always Božava which is smaller still and more remote. You'll pay for your isolation however, since accommodation, excursions and boat rental is at least 10% more expensive than in Sali.

If you arrive by bus, walk downhill from the bus stop to the tiny town centre where you'll find the tourist office (☎/fax 377 607), open daily June to September from 9 am to noon and 6 to 9 pm. It can find you private accommodation or pack you off to the only hotel in town, *Hotel Božava* (☎ /fax 377 618/19), which has mediocre rooms overlooking a cove for 200/344KN a single/double in high season.

The town is on a harbour with many opportunities for swimming and strolling on pine-shaded paths. **Veli Rat** is a village on the furthest north-western point of the island on the scenic Čuna Bay, about 6km north-west of Božava. Although the area is lovely, there's no transport. Unless you come with your own wheels, you'll be relegated to hitching, walking or paying a resident to drive you out there.

PAG

A barren, rocky island with no trees, little vegetation, no rivers or streams, Pag nonetheless has a stark, ethereal beauty enhanced by a highly original culture. The sharp-flavoured cheese and intricate lace from Pag is renowned throughout Croatia, while the 15th century Pag town reflects Croatia's great builder, Juraj Dalmatinac, who designed the neat, orderly streets.

The 63km karstic island is a strange moonscape defined by two mountain ridges, patches of shrubs and a dozen or so villages and hamlets. There are peaceful coves and bays for swimming around the main towns of Pag and Novalja as well as the smaller settlements of Šimuni, Mandre and Straško on the south-western coast, but the island is never overrun by tourists. Pag town is roughly in the centre of the island on the south-eastern coast of the large Pag Bay (Paški zaljev), while Novalja is 20km north-west on a small cove. The island is linked to the mainland by Pag Bridge in the south-east.

The island was inhabited by the Illyrians before falling to the Romans in the 1st century BC. The Romans constructed forts and aqueducts. The Slavs settled around Novalja in the 7th century AD and began building churches and basilicas. In the 11th century a new settlement emerged in the south of the island, called Stari Grad, 2km south of today's Pag, near the saltworks that became the foundation of the island's economy. The next centuries were turbulent for the island as it competed fiercely with Zadar and Rab over the salt trade. Zadar launched brutal attacks on the island in the 13th and 14th centuries but in 1409 it was sold to Venice along with Zadar and the rest of Dalmatia. Pag eventually fell under Austrian rule in 1797, then French and finally Austrian rule until 1918.

Today the primary occupations are agricultural as islanders attempt to wring a living from their unforgiving land. The sandy soil yields a decent domestic white wine, *žutica*, and the hardy sheep graze on herbs and salty grass, lending their meat

Delicate & Durable: Pag Lace

The exact origins of the lace-making tradition in Pag are unknown but it probably began in the Renaissance as ornamentation for the traditional white linen shirts and neckerchiefs worn on Pag island. As traditional dress began to die out in the 20th century, lace edging decorated tablecloths, altar cloths, bedspreads and handkerchiefs. In 1906 a School for Lace Making was established in Pag and the lace began to assume the geometrical shapes you see today. In 1911, Pag's lace received wider attention as a result of the efforts of an Austrian writer, Natalie Bruck-Auffenberg, who presented a lace blouse to the Archduchess Maria Josephine. The archduchess travelled to Pag to place an order and more noble ladies followed suit. The lace-making school was closed for a time but re-opened three years ago to keep the craft alive.

Lace-making requires a needle, thread, clean hands, good eyesight and a lot of time. The needle is an ordinary mending needle and the work is done on a backing which is usually a hard stuffed pillow. Lace-makers work without drawings, based on designs handed down from generation to generation to which each lace-maker adds their own personal touch. Within the many variations, there is a solid geometric structure called the *reticela* that is the skeleton of each design. At the centre is a circle that is traversed by eight thread sticks that radiate outward through an intricate web of circles and triangles. The result is a piece of handiwork that is as delicate as a snowflake but stiff and durable enough to withstand laundering.

and milk a distinctive flavour. Pag sheep cheese (*Paški Sir*) soaked in olive oil and aged in stone is a prized specialty of Croatian cuisine. The marvellous lace from the island is a slim underpinning for economic viability but it does help bring in tourists. In a curious administrative decision, the half of the island that includes Pag town is part of Zadar County while the rest is part of Kvarner County.

Getting There & Away

There are two buses a day from Pag town to Zadar (one hour, 25KN), two buses a day to Rijeka from Monday to Saturday and one on Sunday (4½ hours, 85KN) and five buses a day to Zagreb (six hours, 110KN). Five buses a day make the 30 minute trip between Pag town and Novalja (15KN). If you're travelling up the coast by car, note that there are regular car ferries from Žigljen on the north-east coast to Prizna on the mainland that run roughly hourly in winter and nonstop from June to September.

Pag Town

• pop 2420   ☎ 023

The appeal of Pag town is the straight, narrow streets and low stone houses with living rooms that are practically on the street. There's a sense of intimacy and involvement with the residents who socialise, repair appliances and make lace on stools outside their houses. The small town ambience is captivating and there are pebble beaches to relax upon after a morning of lace-shopping.

In the early 15th century, the increasingly prosperous salt business prompted the construction of Pag town when nearby Stari Grad could no longer meet the demands of its burgeoning population. The Venetians engaged the finest builder of the time, Juraj Dalmatinac, to design a new city and the first cornerstone was laid in 1443. In accordance with what were then the latest ideas in town planning, the main streets and the cross streets intersect at right angles and lead to four city gates. In the centre, there's a square with a cathedral, St Mary's Church

(Sveti Marija), a ducal palace, and a bishop's palace that remained unfinished because Pag never succeeded in having its own bishop. In 1499, Dalmatinac began working on the city walls but only the north corner, with parts of a castle, remains.

Orientation The old town, bordered by Vangrada and Podmir streets, is a pedestrian zone that retains the original simplicity of its architecture. Everyone congregates around the cafés and benches on the main square, Trg Kralja Krešimira IV. Outside the old town there's a newer section with a couple of hotels, narrow beaches on the bay, travel agencies and restaurants. The bus station (no left-luggage facility) is next to the Hotel Jadran, just outside the old town. A bridge across the bay to the southwest leads to a residential quarter that contains the large hotels, bigger beaches and most private accommodation.

Information The unhelpful Turistički Ured (☎ 611 286) on Katine is open May to September from 7 am to 11 pm, but you'll generally have better luck getting information from one of the travel agencies.

There are no ATMs in town but you can change money at any travel agency or at Riječka Banka, Vela ulica 18, which is open Monday to Friday from 8 am to 8 pm and Saturday 8 am to 12.30 pm.

The post office on Antuna Šimića (down a side street of the 'main' side street) is open Monday to Saturday from 7 am to 9 pm and Sunday 9 am to noon. You can change money and access cash using MasterCard or Diners Club. The postcode for Pag town is 23250.

Since there are few excursions, travel agencies are mostly occupied with changing money and finding private accommodation. Try Sunturist (☎/fax 612 060), Šetalište Gradac Carbonere 1; Mediteran (☎ 611 238),

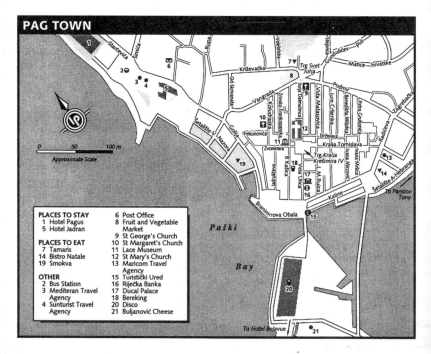

PAG TOWN

PLACES TO STAY	6 Post Office
1 Hotel Pagus	8 Fruit and Vegetable
5 Hotel Jadran	Market
	9 St George's Church
PLACES TO EAT	10 St Margaret's Church
7 Tamaris	11 Lace Museum
14 Bistro Natale	12 St Mary's Church
19 Smokva	13 Maricom Travel
	Agency
OTHER	15 Turistički Ured
2 Bus Station	16 Riječka Banka
3 Mediteran Travel	17 Ducal Palace
Agency	18 Bereking
4 Sunturist Travel	20 Disco
Agency	21 Buljanović Cheese

Trg Sveti Stjepana with the Cathedral Sveti Stjepana in Hvar town

Idyllic, laid-back Lumbarda

Boats at Cavtat

Korčula town

Cavtat harbour

Nazora 12; Meridijan (☎ 612 162, fax 612 161), Starčevića 1 in the Hotel Pagus; or Maricom (☎/fax 611 331), Radićeva 8. Travel agencies are open daily from May to September and Monday to Saturday only for the rest of the year.

Things to See The simple, Gothic **St Mary's Church** (Crkva Sveti Marija) built by Dalmatinac on Trg Kralja Krešimira IV is in perfect harmony with the simple, modest structures surrounding it. The lunette over the portal shows the Virgin with women of Pag in medieval blouses and headdresses and there are two rows of unfinished sculptures of saints. Completed in the 16th century, the interior was renovated with baroque ceiling decorations in the 18th century. The Gothic wooden crucifix on the altar dates from the 12th century and there are a variety of gold and silver liturgical objects in the church's treasury. The church is open daily May to September from 9 am to noon and for Mass only for the rest of the year. Other notable churches include **St Margaret's** (Sveti Margarita) with a Renaissance-baroque façade and a treasury with paintings and reliquaries and **St George's** (Sveti Juraj) which houses changing art exhibits (open 8 pm to 10 pm). Notice also the elaborate portal over the **Ducal Palace** (Kneževa Palaća) attributed to a disciple of Dalmatinac.

No visit to Pag would be complete without a look at the **Lace Museum** on Kralja Zvonimira off the main square. Entrance is free and the small museum gives a good overview of the island's most famous craft. It's open daily in the summer from 6 pm to 9 pm but is closed for the rest of the year.

Special Events The last day of July is the Pag Carnival, which is a good opportunity to see the traditional *kolo* dance and appreciate the elaborate traditional dresses of Pag. The main square is filled with dancers and musicians and a theatre troupe presents the traditional folk play *Paška Robinja* (*The Slave Girl of Pag*).

Places to Stay - Camping *Camping Šimuni* (☎/fax 698 208) is on the southwestern coast, about halfway between Pag town and Novalja, near the port of Šimuni. It's on a rocky beach and is open from April to November. All buses from Pag to Novalja stop at Šimuni. Two kilometres south-west of Novalja, near the village of Straško, you'll find *Camping Straško* (☎ 661 226), also on a beach. It's open from May to October.

Places to Stay – Private Rooms Prices vary a bit so it pays to shop around. Any of the travel agencies listed above will find you private accommodation, but at the time of writing Sunturist was the cheapest, offering top range singles/doubles for 72/130KN. If there are no ladies offering sobe at the bus station, you'll find a lot of sobe signs on ulica Prosika across the bridge.

Places to Stay – Hotels *Hotel Jadran* (☎ 611 145, Šetalište Grade Carbonere) is an older hotel on the harbour that is awaiting renovation. Rooms are basic and communal showers and toilets are in the hall, but you can get a double room for only 180KN. *Hotel Pagus* (☎ 053-611 310) is in good condition and has relatively spacious rooms furnished in a light Mediterranean style. Rooms have telephone but no TV and cost 200/350KN a single/double. The hotel is on a narrow beach in the bay, and is open all year.

Pansion Tony (☎ 611 989, Dubrovačka 39) is a casual place along the shore, about 1km east of Hotel Pagus. It's quiet and relaxing but somewhat isolated in the bushes and reeds. Rooms are 118KN per person with no single supplement but you may wish to take half-board at 162KN per person with a 30% surcharge for one-night stays. *Hotel Bellevue* (☎ 611 091, Gajeva bb) is across the Paški Zaljev Bay, which means you get a striking view of the town and the surrounding hills. The hotel is nothing special but you're close to a gravelly beach for swimming. There are only double rooms for 314KN.

Places to Eat Most restaurants offer a little bit of everything – pizza, pasta, fish, meat and salads. Curiously, the price of a starter of Pag cheese isn't much cheaper than anywhere else on the coast, but the quality is apt to be better. *Smokva* on Golija is a good place to sample Pag specialties such as cheese, lamb and the *gegić* and *žutica* wines. Main courses of fish or meat run from 35KN to 50KN and the tables are snuggled under fig trees. *Tamaris* (*Križevačka bb*) offers pizza from 22KN to 32KN, green pasta for 25KN to 30KN and a plate of fried calamari for 35KN. *Bistro Natale* (*Radićeva 2*) serves up pizza and pasta in a narrow courtyard and is popular with kuna-counting locals.

Entertainment The only disco in town is in a former salt warehouse just over the bridge. The cavernous interior was restored by a prize-winning local architect who carefully updated the original rustic features. The disco is sometimes called the *Fifth Magazine* after the old name for a salt warehouse. It's open daily from 10 pm in summer but weekends only off season.

Shopping Pag offers the most distinctive products in all Croatia. It would be a shame to leave the island without buying lace, since the prices are relatively cheap and buying a piece helps keep the tradition alive. A small circle or star about 10cm in diameter costs about 80KN, but it takes a good 24 hours to make. Larger pieces cost from 150KN to 300KN. The Lace Museum is being reorganised to allow shopping, but it's more fun to walk down ulica Tomislava or Zvonimira in the morning while the women are lace-making and buy from them directly. Prices are marked on a card and bargaining is usually futile.

Unlike lace, Pag cheese is not sold in town and requires some effort to find. Usually there's just a home-made sign, *Pakši Sir*, posted outside a house on a remote road somewhere. Close to town, try the pungent cheese made by Tonći Buljanović at Prosika 6. Asking price for a kilo is usually 100KN but you can often bargain down to 70KN or 80KN a kilo. It can get you through a lot of dreary hotel breakfasts.

Šibenik Region

Šibenik is the capital of Šibenik-Knin county which contains two of Croatia's most beautiful national parks: the Krka waterfalls and the Kornati Islands.

The city spreads over several hills on the north-east coast of a 10km bay that spreads from Zaton in the north-west to Mandalina in the south-east. The Krka River which discharges into this bay extends deep into the karstic interior as far as Knin. The bay is connected to the Šibenik Channel, separating Zlarin island from the mainland. The relatively flat coast that runs north-west and south-east of Šibenik contains a string of resorts and tourist settlements and the waters between the city and Kornati Islands National Park contain several small islands.

The interior of the region includes part of the Vojna Krajina military frontier established by the Austrians in the 16th century as protection from the Turks. It was settled by Vlachs and Morlachs belonging to the Orthodox church and thus developed a large Serbian population. Upon the Croatian declaration of independence in 1990, the Krajina Serbs, with the help of arms from Belgrade, established their own state and made Knin its capital. When Croatia retook the territory in 1995, virtually the entire Serbian population fled, leaving a landscape of smashed buildings and ruined villages. Most of the damage has now been repaired, but the interior villages have remained depopulated.

Knin is still a vital transit point between the coast and the Croatian heartland but its remoteness has made it hard for the government to attract residents or visitors. Since there are no hotels or tourist facilities of any kind in Knin, Šibenik is the only viable base for exploring the region.

ŠIBENIK
- pop 41,012   ☎ 022

Although Šibenik is not often promoted as a tourist destination, the town centre has a remarkable cathedral and a network of streets

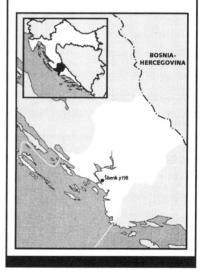

ŠIBENIK

BOSNIA-HERCEGOVINA

Šibenik p198

and squares laid out in the 15th and 16th centuries. Restaurants, hotels and entertainment are scattered among the tourist complexes along the coast but if you find a place to stay in town, you can take some interesting strolls along the harbour and through the steep back streets and alleys. The city also makes an excellent base for exploring the two parks, especially the Krka waterfalls which can be visited independently.

Unlike many other Dalmatian coastal towns, Šibenik was settled first by Croat

195

Vlachs, Nomads of the Balkans

The first settlers of the Krajina region north of Šibenik were a pastoral, nomadic people known as Vlachs or Morlachs. Darker skinned than their Slavic neighbours (Morlach is derived from Maurus, Latin for black), their origins are uncertain. They may have come from Serbia or Bosnia or they may have been Roman legionaries who were pushed into the Dalmatian interior by the 7th century Slavs. By the time Austria invited them to settle the Vojna Krajina (Military Frontier) in the 16th century, most, although not all, belonged to the Orthodox Church.

Vlachs had little to do with their Austrian and Italian neighbours, preferring to live within their own unusual culture. The Catholic and Orthodox Vlachs detested each other and both viewed Venetians and Italianised coastal Dalmatia with contempt. As nomadic people, they were more comfortable with their livestock than with other people, whom they tended to avoid. The Venetians were horrified by their habit of sleeping with their animals and baffled by their refusal to eat frogs, which were considered a great delicacy. They were said to be violent people who slept with a gun under their head and devoted more time to drunken festivals than working. Vlachs firmly believed in the existence of witches and fairies and were inclined to tear apart the dead body of anyone suspected of being a vampire.

Vlach marriages were especially peculiar. On her wedding day, the bride's parents would enumerate all her bad qualities to the groom who frequently responded by beating her. Upon marriage, the husband got the bed and the wife curled up on the ground. When she went to confession, the priest would deliver absolution by whacking her with a club.

The brutality inflicted upon Vlach women was probably not unusual in peasant cultures and, at least, the Vlachs allowed women to opt out of the system by entering into a same-sex marriage. Two women could swear oaths to each other in a church ceremony after which they were pronounced *posestre* (half-sisters). The 18th century Italian writer Alberto Fortis witnessed a posestre ceremony between two women and commented upon the "satisfaction that sparkled in their eyes when the ceremony was performed".

The status of the Vlachs was a constant bone of contention between Austria and the Croatian Sabor. For Austria, the Vlach soldiers were an essential bulwark against the Turks and well worth the exemption from serfdom they received in exchange for their military service. The Croatian Sabor was made up of noblemen who were profoundly threatened by the existence of free peasants, fearing that such a dangerous notion could radicalise their own serfs. It was not until the mid-nineteenth century when feudalism was in its death throes that the issue faded away. At the same time, the Orthodox Vlach majority in the region began to identify themselves as Serbs and the terms Vlachs and Morlachs gradually disappeared.

tribes, not Illyrians or Romans. First mentioned in the 11th century by the Croatian King Krešimir IV, the city was conquered by Venice in 1116 but was tossed back and forth among Venice, Hungary, Byzantium and the kingdom of Bosnia until Venice seized control in 1412 after a three year fight. At the end of the 15th century Ottoman Turks burst into the region as part of their struggle against Venice. Over the course of the succeeding two centuries, Turks periodically attacked the town, disrupting trade and agriculture. The fortresses built by the Venetians in defence of the town are still visible, most notably the fortress of St Nikola at the entrance to the Šibenik channel. The Turkish threat receded with the 1699 treaty of Karlowitz but the city continued to suffer from Venetian rule until it passed into the hands of Austria in 1797, where it remained until 1918.

Šibenik fell under attack in 1991 from the federal Yugoslav army and was subject to shelling until its liberation as part of 'Operation Storm' by the Croatian army in 1995. Little physical damage is visible, but the city's aluminium industry, which was an important part of the regional economy, was shattered by the war. The city is trying to make a comeback but the struggle to survive leaves people with little money for cafés, restaurants or other luxuries.

Orientation

The city spreads like an amphitheatre from the harbour uphill to the surrounding hills. The main road is Kralje Zvonimira and the old town lies between it and the harbour, which is in a large bay. The entire old town is a pedestrian area and contains the cathedral and several other notable churches. The oldest part of the town is on Zagrebačka ulica and the streets running north. The bus station is in a modern jumble of concrete blocks in the city's southern corner. The left-luggage office at the bus station is open from 6.30 am to 9 pm. The main commercial street is Ante Starčevića and Ante Šupuka south-east of the old town with the railway station lying south-west. The left-luggage is open 24 hours.

Information

Tourist Offices The Turistički Ured (☎ 212 075, fax 219 073), Fausto Vrančića 18, is open in the summer Monday to Saturday from 8 am to 9 pm, Sunday 6 to 9 pm and off season Monday to Friday 8 am to 3 pm.

Jadrolinija (☎ 213 468) at Obala Oslobođenja 8 is a good source of information for ferry sailings. Hours vary according to the ferry schedule but it is usually open at least an hour before each departure or Monday to Saturday from 5 am to 3.30 pm and 5 to 7 pm, and Sunday from 5 to 9 am and 6 to 8 pm.

Croatia Express at the train station is open Monday to Friday from 8 am to 1 pm and 5 to 10 pm, Saturday from 7 am to 2 pm. They change money and sell train tickets.

Money Zagrebačka Banka, Šupuka 10, is open Monday to Friday from 8.30 am to 1.30 pm, Saturday 8.30 am to noon and has an ATM machine where you can withdraw cash using Eurocard, MasterCard or Cirrus. You can change money at the bank, at any travel agency listed below or the post office.

Post & Communications The main post office is at Vladimira Nazora 51 and is open Monday through Saturday from 7 am to 9 pm. You can make calls and change money there. The postcode for Šibenik is 22000

Travel Agencies Atlas travel agency (☎ 330 224), Krešimirov dom, changes money, and books excursions. In summer it is open Monday to Saturday from 8 am to 3 pm and 6 to 9 pm, Sunday 6 to 9 pm, but off season it is open weekdays only from 8 am to 3 pm.

There are other travel agencies that find private accommodations and arrange excursions to Krka waterfalls. NIK travel agency (☎/fax 338 540), Šupuka 5, is the largest travel agency in town and sells international bus and air tickets as well as excursions. It is open from 7.30 am to 8 pm in the summer but weekday mornings only off season. Mihovil Tours (☎ 216 666, fax 214 841), Trg Pavla Šubića 1, is another place to try.

Things to See

Juraj Dalmatinac was the sculptor and the **Cathedral of St Jacob** (Katedrala Sveti Jakova) is his masterpiece. Unquestionably the crowning glory of the Dalmatian coast, the cathedral is worth a considerable detour to see. Its most unusual feature is the frieze of 71 heads on the exterior walls of the apses. These portraits in stone are vivid character studies of ordinary 15th century citizens. Placid, annoyed, proud or fearful, their expressions convey the timelessness of human emotion across the centuries.

Juraj Dalmatinac was not the first or the last builder to work on the cathedral.

Construction began in 1431 but after 10 years of toying around with various Venetian builders, the city appointed the Zadar native, Dalmatinac, who increased the size and transformed the conception of the church into a transitional Gothic-Renaissance style.

In addition to the exterior frieze, other examples of Dalmatinac's style include the two aisle staircases descending into the sacristy on one side and baptistery on the other, and the exquisite baptistery in which three angels support the baptismal font. The latter was carved by Andrija Aleši after Dalmatinac's designs. Other interior art worth noting are the crypt of bishop Šižigorić (by Dalmatinac) who supported the building of the cathedral, the altar painting of St Fabijan and Sebastijan (by Zaniberti), the painting *The Gift of the Wise Men* (by Ricciardi) and, next to it, two marble reliefs of

angels (by Firentinac). Notice also the *Lion's Portal* on the north side, created by Dalmatinac and Bonino da Milano, on which two lions support columns containing the figures of Adam and Eve, who appear to be excruciatingly embarrassed by their nakedness.

The cathedral was constructed entirely of stone, quarried from the islands of Brač, Korčula, Rab and Krk, and is considered to be the largest church built completely of stone without brick or wood supports. The unusual domed roof complex was completed after Dalmatinac's death by Nikola Firentinac, who continued the facade in a pure Renaissance style.

The church was finally completed in 1536. The Cathedral is open for visits May to October from 8 am to noon during the day and from 6 to 8 pm in the evening The rest of the year it's only open for mass.

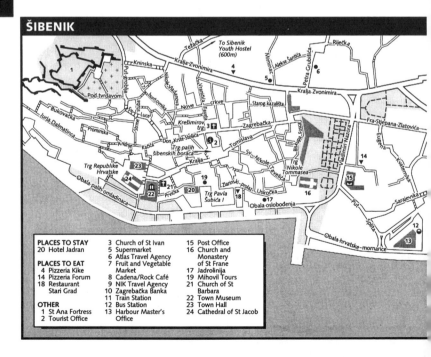

ŠIBENIK

PLACES TO STAY	3 Church of St Ivan	15 Post Office
20 Hotel Jadran	5 Supermarket	16 Church and
	6 Atlas Travel Agency	Monastery
PLACES TO EAT	7 Fruit and Vegetable	of St Frane
4 Pizzeria Kike	Market	17 Jadrolinija
14 Pizzeria Forum	8 Cadena/Rock Café	19 Mihovil Tours
18 Restaurant	9 NIK Travel Agency	21 Church of St
Stari Grad	10 Zagrebačka Banka	Barbara
	11 Train Station	22 Town Museum
OTHER	12 Bus Station	23 Town Hall
1 St Ana Fortress	13 Harbour Master's	24 Cathedral of St Jacob
2 Tourist Office	Office	

Across the square from the Cathedral is the **Town Hall**, a harmonious Renaissance arrangement of columns and a balustrade that was constructed between 1533 and 1546. Destroyed during an Allied air attack in 1943, the building was completely rebuilt to its original form which explains its shiny, new appearance.

On the south side of the Cathedral is the **Town Museum**, which recounts the story of Šibenik and the surrounding region from the end of the Paleolithic era to the end of WWII. Archaeological finds from the nearby village of Danilo are the most interesting part of the collections. Theoretically, the museum is open July to December from 10 am to 1 pm and 7 to 10 pm, but don't count on it.

The city has a wealth of beautiful churches but they are only open for mass and non-worshiping visitors are not appreciated. The **Church of St Ivan** on the square of John Paul II is a fine example of Gothic-Renaissance architecture from the end of the 15th century; the Church and Monastery of St Francis (St Frane) from the end of the 14th century has 14th and 15th century frescoes and an array of Venetian Baroque paintings; the **Church of St Barbara** on the east side of the Cathedral contains a museum of church art exhibiting paintings, engravings and sculptures from the 14th to the 18th centuries.

You can climb to the top of **St Ana fortress** in the north-east for a magnificent view over Šibenik and the surrounding region.

Special Events
Šibenik hosts a renowned International Children's Festival the last week of June and first week of July. There are workshops in crafts, music and dance, children's film and theatre, puppets and parades.

Places to Stay
Camping Camping grounds *Zablaće* (☎ 354 015) and *Solaris* (☎ 364 000) are part of the Solaris resort complex (see below for further details). The *Solaris* camping ground (open from May to October) is more attractive. Besides, *Zablać* (open May to September) is next to the *Midnight Club* disco, which is something to consider if you're in the habit of sleeping at night.

Hostels The *Šibenik Youth Hostel* (☎ 216 410, Put Luguša 1) is open July, August and September and charges 60KN a bed for a two, four or six-bed room. There are 40 beds and breakfast is 15KN extra. The hostel is about 600m north of Kralja Zvonimira.

Private Rooms Most private accommodation is in neighbouring villages along the coast such as Primošten, Tribunj and Vodice easily reachable by bus from Šibenik. NIK agency has first category rooms for 118/168KN a single/double, studio apartments

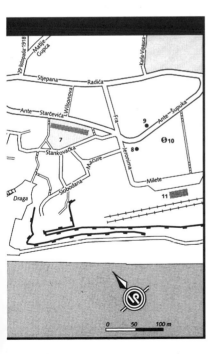

for 237KN and larger apartments for 284KN. Mihovil has rooms for 80KN per person. The 30% surcharge for stays less than three nights may be waived if business is slow. Prices drop about 30% outside the peak July/August season. In July and August, you may be met by women at the bus or train station offering *sobe* at much lower prices.

Hotels The only hotel in town is the *Hotel Jadran* (☎ *212 644, Obala Oslobođenja 52)*, a modern hotel conveniently located along the harbour, which has singles/doubles for 240/400KN in July and August but up to 25% less in other months. The hotel and rooms are somewhat impersonal but in excellent condition and equipped with satellite TV. The hotel can be warm in the summer; try to get a room overlooking the harbour to get some breezes.

The resort complex *Solaris* (☎ *363 999, fax 361 081, Solaris bb)* is about 6km out of town on the road to Split. The complex includes two camping grounds, four hotels and a stony beach. If you wish to be isolated in a concrete development where you'll meet no one but other tourists, this is for you. In July and August, you'll pay 320/561KN a single/double but prices drop about 15% in the shoulder season and 25% off season. There are also two-person apartments available for about 750KN. Buses run between the bus station and Solaris about 15 times a day.

Places to Eat
Like the rest of the Dalmatian coast, the menus in Šibenik restaurants lean heavily toward fish with a nod to the pastas and risottos of Italy. Fish can be expensive but there are plenty of pizzerias. Try *Pizzeria Forum (Vladimira Nazora 7),* near the post office, which is an unpretentious local place serving up good pizza that costs from 25KN to 35KN. It's open daily from 7 am to midnight. *Pizzeria Kike (Zadarska 1)* is another simple, inexpensive pizzeria with pizzas that range from 23KN to 30KN but don't expect elaborate décor. It is open Monday

to Saturday from 7 am to 11 pm and Sunday from 5 pm to 11 pm.

Besides pizzerias, there are very few places to eat in Šibenik. Most residents head out of town for dining and entertainment, but near the port you'll find the excellent *Restaurant Stari Grad (Obala Oslobođenja 12)* where the fish is always fresh and priced at a reasonable 200KN a kilogram. The spaghetti with seafood makes a tasty meal for only 35KN.

Out of town, locals like *Steak House (Trg Dinka Zavorovića 4)* in Brodarica just past the Solaris complex. Not only the steaks but the salads are reported to be superb. The restaurant is open daily from 11 am to midnight.

Entertainment
The terrace of the Hotel Jadran is the site of live music nightly in the summer but the only disco is out of town at the *Midnight Club (Zablać e)* near the Solaris complex. *Cadena/Rock Café (Šupuka 2)* is an outdoor café in the summer and a basement bar in the winter, but a pleasant, relaxed place to hang out in all seasons and there's a live band once a week, usually Thursday.

Organised Tours
Atlas travel agency organises full day trips to the Kornati Islands with a lunch stop at Piškera and a few swim stops for 210KN, a half-day trip to the Krka waterfalls for 115KN, and a full-day trip that includes Skradinski buk and Visovać for 210KN. All admission fees are included in the prices. NIK agencies offers an excursion to the Krka waterfalls for 144KN, but it only includes Skradinski buk.

Getting There & Away
There are two overnight trains daily between Zagreb and Šibenik (nine hours, 81KN) and from Monday to Saturday there are six trains a day between Šibenik and Split (1½ hours, 23KN) which drops to four trains on Sunday.

Šibenik is well connected by bus to local and international destinations.

destination	frequency	duration	cost
Murter	9 daily	45 minutes	11KN
Primošten	6 daily	25 minutes	11KN
Dubrovnik	8 daily	6 hours	104KN
Split	every ½ hour	1¾ hours	31KN
Zadar	every ½ hour	1½ hours	28KN
Zagreb	15 daily	6½ hours	96KN
Rijeka	13 daily	6 hours	104KN
Pula	4 daily	8 hours	145KN
Osijek	1 daily	8½ hours	205KN

International lines worth knowing about include a weekly bus to Vienna (14½ hours, 325KN and daily buses to about 20 German cities including Berlin (24 hours, 666KN), Munich (15 hours, 288KN) and Cologne (22 hours, 612KN).

AROUND ŠIBENIK

The city is surrounded by small villages on the sea that become major tourist resorts in the summer. The largest resort is **Vodice**, 11km north-west of Šibenik on the Adriatic Highway. The small fishing village on the harbour has been amplified by the construction of several large hotels and apartment complexes. There's a baroque church and a 16th century tower but most people head to one of the beaches and coves around the town centre. From Monday to Saturday there are three ferries a day between Šibenik and Vodice and two on Sunday.

Tribunj is on a small peninsula 4km west of Vodice and claims to have the largest fishing fleet in Central Dalmatia making it a good place to sample fresh fish, mussels and crabs. The local specialty is fish ragout with polenta.

By far the most attractive town within reach of Šibenik is **Primošten**, 30km south-east of the city centre. The small village of medieval streets dominated by a large belfry is neatly contained within a peninsula, making it resemble the Istrian town of Rovinj. Across the bay is another peninsula thickly wooded with pines and bordered by pebbly beaches. The hotels are discrete enough not to spoil the landscape.

Šibenik is easily connected by ferry to several small islands which can be explored in a day trip. **Zlarin** is only a half hour by boat and is known for the coral that used to be abundant before it was torn from the sea and sold for jewellery. Because there are no cars allowed on the island, it makes a tranquil retreat from Šibenik and boasts a sand beach, pine woods and a spacious port. **Prvić** island is only 15 minutes further than Zlarin and contains two villages, Prvić Luka and Šepurine (10 minutes further on the ferry), that retain the flavour of simple fishing settlements, probably because there are no large hotels on the island, only private accommodation.

The island of **Murter** is 29km north-west of Šibenik, separated from the mainland by a narrow channel. The steep south-western coast is indented by small coves, most notably the cove of Slanica which is the best for swimming. The village of Murter is in the north-west and has a good harbour and not-so-good beach. The tourist office (☎ 434 995) is at Rudina 2 and is open from 7.30 am to 9.30 pm in summer but closes at noon off season.

Although the village is unremarkable, it is an excellent base from which to explore the Kornati Islands. Booking an excursion to the Kornati Islands from Murter will allow you to see more of the archipelago than booking from Šibenik or Zadar, since it is much closer. Atlas travel agency (☎ 434 999), Hrvatskih Kraljeva 8, and Žut-Tours (☎ 434 401), Hrvatskih Vladara 23, are two of the many agencies that offer day trips to the Kornati Islands for about 180KN including a lunch stop and swim on one of the islands.

If you'd like to splurge and stay on an island, Žut Tours and Koserinatours (☎ 438 508), Komirića 6, in the nearby town of Tislo arrange private accommodation on one of the islands. It will cost about 280KN a night for a two-person apartment plus the boat transfer of about 366KN return.

Keep in mind that the Murter inhabitants are the owners of the Kornati Islands and visit it occasionally by private boat to tend

ŠIBENIK

ŠIBENIK-KNIN REGION

their land. Asking around town may put you in touch with someone who will run you out there and arrange for you to stay overnight in their cottage on one of the islands for less money.

KRKA NATIONAL PARK

From the western foot of the Dinara Mountains into the sea near Šibenik, the 72.5km Krka River and its waterfalls defines the landscape of Šibenik-Knin county. Like Plitvice Lakes the Krka waterfalls are a karstic phenomenon. The river water formed a deep canyon (up to 200m) through the limestone and brought with it calcium carbonate. Mosses and algae retain the calcium carbonate and encrust it in their roots. The material is called travertine, or tufa, and is formed by billions of plants that grow on top of one another. The growths create barriers in the river which produce waterfalls. Unlike Plitvice Lakes, the

volume of water rushing through the canyon is much greater, averaging 55 cubic metres of water per second at the last cascade Skradinski Buk, making the spectacle even more dramatic.

The landscape of rocks, cliffs, caves and chasms is a remarkable sight, but the National Park also contains several important cultural landmarks. Near its northernmost point there's an Orthodox monastery, sometimes called Arandjelovac, or Holy Archangel, or often simply referred to as the Krka monastery.

First mentioned in 1402 as the endowment of Jelena Šubić, the sister of Emperor Dušan of Serbia, it was built and rebuilt until the end of the 18th century. The monastery has a unique combination of Byzantine and Mediterranean architecture and had a valuable inventory dating back to the 14th century, at least some of which may have been destroyed during the recent war.

Below the monastery the river becomes a lake created by the Roški Slap barrier downstream and the valley narrows into a 150m gorge. At the end of the gorge is the Roški Slap, a 650m long stretch that begins with shallow steps and continues in a series of branches and islets to become 27m high cascades. On the eastern side of the falls you can see water mills that used to mill wheat.

Between Roški Slap and the Skradinski Buk falls, the river becomes a peaceful lake. The first kilometre is bordered by reeds and bulrushes sheltering marsh birds. Next downstream is the Medu Gredama gorge with cliffs 150m high cut into a variety of dramatic shapes. Then the gorge opens out into Lake Visovac with Samostan Visovac, its lovely island monastery. In the 14th century hermits built a small monastery and church which they abandoned under threat from the Turks in 1440. They were succeeded by Bosnian Franciscans in 1445, who remained throughout Turkish rule until 1699. The church on the island dates from the end of the 17th century and the bell tower was built in 1728. On the western bank of the river is a forest of holm oak and on the eastern bank is a forest of white oaks.

Six kilometres downstream you come to the largest waterfall, Skradinski Buk, with an 800m long cascade covering 17 steps and rising to almost 46m. As at Roški Slap, watermills used to grind wheat, mortars pounded felt and huge baskets held rugs and fabrics. The mills are deserted now but Venetians used to collect a small fortune in taxes upon the Krka mills. Downstream from Skradinski Buk the river is less interesting due to the construction of the Jaruga power plant in 1904.

Getting There & Away

Although countless agencies sell excursions to the falls from Šibenik, Zadar and other cities, it is possible and certainly more interesting to visit the falls independently if you base yourself in Šibenik. You can begin your exploration from either Skradin or

Lozovac entrances which lie on the west and east banks respectively.

There are nine daily buses from Šibenik that make the 15 minute run to Skradin. At Skradin you pay a park entrance fee of 40KN which allows you to board a boat to Skradinski Buk. If you take a bus to Lozovac which are also very frequent, you can take a bus to Skradinski Buk (also included in the park admission) but you miss out on the boat ride through the canyon that you can enjoy from Skradin.

The advantage of Lozovac is that you can catch a different boat going to Visovac and the Roški falls. You need to take the bus to Skradinski Buk (or walk along the road) and about halfway to Skradinski Buk you'll see a sign pointing you toward the boats to Visovać. During the summer there are four boats a day to Visovać and one to Roški falls but off season you should call the Krka National Park Office first (☎ 217 740) or ask at the tourist office in Šibenik to find out the boat schedule. You'll pay 60KN for a boat to Visovać and 100KN for the four hour trip to Roški falls in addition to the park admission.

KORNATI ISLANDS

'On the last day of the Creation God desired to crown His work, and thus created the Kornati Islands out of tears, stars and breath,' wrote George Bernard Shaw. Composed of 147 mostly uninhabited islands, islets and reefs covering 69 sq km, the Kornati Islands are the largest and densest archipelago in the Adriatic. Typically karst terrain, the islands are riddled with cracks, caves, grottoes and rugged cliffs. Since there are no sources of fresh water on the islands, they are mostly barren, sometimes with a light covering of grass. The evergreens and holm oak that used to be found on some islands were long ago burned down in order to clear the land. Far from stripping the islands of their beauty, the deforestation has highlighted startling rock formations, whose stark whiteness against the deep blue Adriatic is an eerie and wonderful sight.

The Kornati Islands form themselves into four series running north-west to south-east. The first two series of islands lie closer to the mainland and are known locally as Gornji Kornat. The largest and most indented of these islands is Žut. The other two series of islands, facing the open sea, comprise the Kornati National Park and are the most dramatically indented. The island of Kornat is by far the largest island, extending 25km in length but only 2.5km in width.

Not only the land but the sea is within the protection of the National Park. Fishing is strictly limited now in order to allow the regeneration of fish shoals that had been severely overfished. Groper, bass, conger eel, sea bream, pickerel, sea scorpion, cuttlefish, squid, octopus and smelt are some of the fish trying to make a come-back in the region.

Human presence on the Kornati Islands appears to extend back to the Neolithic era and remains of Illyrian settlements were found on the largest island, Kornat. Romans and early Christians inhabited Kornat island, which has a small tower that was probably built in the sixth century AD. The island of Piškera was also inhabited during the Middle Ages and served as a collection and storage point for fish. Until the 19th century the islands were owned by the Zadar aristocracy but about one hundred years ago peasant ancestors of the residents of Murter and Dugi Otok bought the islands, built many kilometres of rock walls to divide their property and used the islands to raise sheep.

The islands remain privately owned, 90% belonging to Murter residents and the remainder to residents of Dugi Otok. Although there are no longer any permanent inhabitants on the islands, many owners have cottages and fields which they visit from time to time to tend the land. Olive trees account for about 80% of the land under cultivation followed by vineyards, orchards and vegetable gardens. All told, there are about 300 buildings on the Kornati Islands, mostly clustered on the south-western coast of Kornat, the main island.

Getting There & Away

The best way to visit the islands is by boat, especially if you have your own. The largest marina is on the island of Piškera, on the southern part of the strait between Piškera and Lavsa. There's another large marina on the island of Žut and a number of small coves throughout the islands where boaters can dock.

Otherwise, you can book an excursion from Zadar, Šibenik, Split and other coastal cities or arrange for private accommodation from the island of Murter (see above). There is no ferry transport between the Kornati Islands and the mainland.

Central Dalmatia

Roman ruins, spectacular beaches, old fishing ports, medieval and Renaissance architecture and unspoiled islands make Central Dalmatia the ideal region to combine hedonism with historical discovery.

The early Roman ruins in Solin and the late Roman Diocletian's Palace in Split (a World Heritage site) recall the region's Latin heritage. Trogir, also a World Heritage site, provides many outstanding examples of medieval sculpture and Hvar town is richly ornamented with Renaissance architecture.

Beach buffs can choose the unusual Zlatni Rat beach on Brač, the long coastline of the Makarska Riviera or one of the countless secluded coves on Brač, Šolta, Vis and Hvar islands. Boat transportation efficiently links all the islands, especially in the summer, which makes it easy to see a lot in a short stay.

Central Dalmatia runs from Trogir in the north-west to Ploče in the south-east and includes the large islands of Brač and Hvar as well as the smaller islands of Vis, Biševo and Šolta. The dramatic coastal scenery is due to the rugged Dinaric Alps which form a 1500m barrier separating Dalmatia from Bosnia.

A warm current flowing north up the coast keeps the climate mild – dry in summer, damp in winter. Dalmatia is noticeably warmer than Istria or the Gulf of Kvarner, and it's possible to swim in the sea from the beginning of May right up until the end of September.

Split is the largest city in the region and a hub for bus and boat connections along the coast. Hvar, which receives more hours of sunshine than anywhere else in Croatia, is Central Dalmatia's most popular destination, followed by Brač and the Makarska Riviera. Lovely Vis and Šolta islands attract relatively few visitors, preserving a lazy Mediterranean ambience even at the height of the summer season.

HIGHLIGHTS

- Rambling through the Roman ruins of Solin
- Swimming in the Blue Grotto of Biševo
- Taking a moonlight stroll through Diocletian's Palace in Split
- Sunbathing on Zlatni Rat beach in Bol
- Visiting the Renaissance architecture and lively nightlife of Hvar town
- Admiring the sculpture in the Cathedral of St Lovro in Trogir

SPLIT

- **pop 189,390   ☎ 021**

Split (Italian: Spalato), the second largest city in Croatia, is the heart of Dalmatia. The old town is built around the harbour, on the south side of a high peninsula sheltered from the open sea by many islands. Ferries

CENTRAL DALMATIA

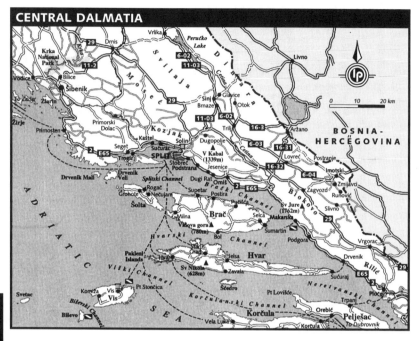

to these islands are constantly coming and going. The entire west end of the peninsula is a vast wooded mountain park, while industry, shipyards, limestone quarries and the ugly commercial/military port are mercifully far enough away on the north side of the peninsula. High coastal mountains set against the blue Adriatic provide a striking frame to the scene.

Split achieved fame when the Roman emperor Diocletian (245-313 AD), noted for his persecution of early Christians, had his retirement palace built here from 295 to 305. After his death the great stone palace continued to be used as a retreat by Roman rulers. When the nearby colony of Salona was abandoned in the 7th century, many of the Romanised inhabitants fled to Split and barricaded themselves behind the high palace walls, where their descendants live to this day.

First Byzantium and then Croatia controlled the area, but from the 12th to the 14th centuries medieval Split enjoyed a large measure of autonomy which favoured its development. The western part of the old town around Narodni trg, which dates from this time, became the focus of municipal life, while the area within the palace walls proper continued as the ecclesiastical centre.

In 1420 the Venetians conquered Split, which led to a slow decline. During the 17th century, strong walls were built around the city as a defence against the Turks. In 1797 the Austrians arrived; they remained until 1918, with only a brief interruption during the Napoleonic wars.

Since 1945, Split has grown into a major industrial city with large areas of apartment block housing. Much of old Split remains, however, and this combined with its exuberant nature makes it one of the most fascinating cities in Europe. It's also the perfect base for excursions to many nearby attractions, so settle in for a few days.

Orientation

The bus, train and ferry terminals are adjacent on the east side of the harbour, a short walk from the old town. The *garderoba* (left-luggage) kiosk at the bus station is open from 4 am to 10 pm. The left-luggage office at the train station is about 50m north of the station at Domagoja 6 and is open from 5 am to 10.30 pm. Obala hrvatskog

narodnog preporoda, the waterfront promenade, is your best central reference point in Split. Most large hotels and the best restaurants, nightlife and beaches lie east of the harbour along Bačvice, Firule, Zenta and Trstenik bays. The wooded Marjan hill dominates the western tip of the city and has many beaches at its foothills.

Information

Tourist Offices The Turistički biro (☎/fax 342 142) at Obala hrvatskog narodnog preporoda 12 will sell you a guidebook to Split for 116KN, book private accommodation

---

Uskoks: The Pirates of Senj

As a tale of adventure on the high seas, derring-do and murderous rebellion, the history of the Uskoks surpasses anything that could be dreamt up by a novelist. This remarkable tribe appeared in Dalmatia in the middle of the 16th century when the Ottoman Turks were laying waste to Serbia, Bulgaria and Bosnia. Many Catholic residents of the afflicted region fled westward in the face of the Turkish advance, eventually arriving at the fortress of Klis, near Split. They called themselves Uskoci, or Fugitives, and battled the Turks for five years before Venice signed a pact with the invaders and directed the Uskoks to abandon the position in 1537.

They settled in Senj, north of Zadar, and were confronted with the perennial refugee problem – how to make a living in their new home. Unfazed by their total lack of naval experience, the Uskoks learned how to make light, fast boats that were uniquely adapted to the Dalmatian coast. Reasoning that they had every right to punish the Turks who had driven them from their homes, the Uskoks pursued Turkish ships up and down the coast, stripping and sinking every one they could get their hands on.

For nearly 30 years they attacked only Turkish ships, receiving blessings and subsidies from the Catholic Church. Then Venice changed its policy and decided to make peace with the Turks. Suddenly the Uskoks were outcasts. Since the two Adriatic powers, Venice and Austria, refused their requests to resettle them in the interior where they could farm, nothing was left for them but piracy.

In 1566, the Uskoks began to attack Venetian ships and brought new ferocity to their exploits. The Austrians were unmoved by the problems of their naval rival but the Venetians were greatly perturbed. Captured Uskoks were treated with merciless cruelty and the Venetians eventually launched a blockade of Senj to starve out the inhabitants. The Uskoks continued to harass the Venetians, their numbers enhanced by adventure-seekers, bored noblemen and thugs from all over Europe.

In 1615, Venice and Austria used the Uskoks as a pretext for a short war. As part of the peace treaty Austria agreed to liquidate the pirates' nest. A number of the pirates were hanged or beheaded while the rest were transported to the interior as they had wanted all along. Although they were allegedly deported to villages in the Krajina, no certain trace of them has ever been found.

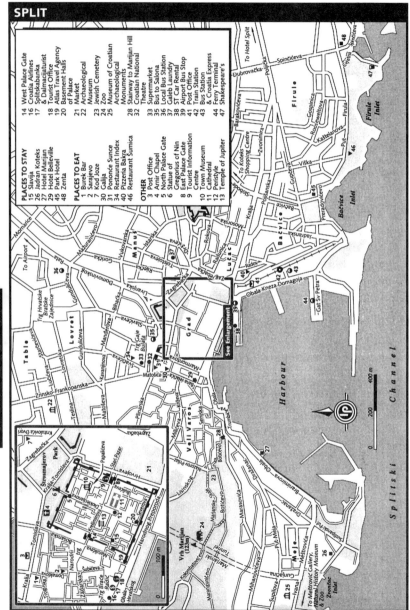

SPLIT

PLACES TO STAY
15 Slavija
26 Jadran Koteks
27 Hotel Marjan
29 Hotel Belleville
45 Park Hotel
48 Zenta

PLACES TO EAT
1 Burek Bar
2 Sarajevo
7 Kavkaz
30 Galija
31 Ponor'ce Sunce
34 Restaurant Index
40 Pizzeria Bakra
46 Restaurant Šumica

OTHER
3 Post Office
4 Arnir Chapel
5 North Palace Gate
6 Statue of
 Gregorius of Nin
8 East Palace Gate
9 Tourist Information
 Centre
10 Town Museum
11 Cathedral
12 Peristyle
13 Temple of Jupiter
14 West Palace Gate
16 Croatia Airlines
17 Splitskabanka
 & Dalmacijaturist
18 Tourist Office
19 Atlas Travel Agency
20 Basement Halls
 of Palace
21 Market
22 Archaeological
 Museum
23 Jewish Cemetery
24 Zoo
25 Museum of Croatian
 Archaeological
 Monuments
28 Stairway to Marjan Hill
32 Croatian National
 Theatre
33 Supermarket
35 Bus to Salona
36 Local Bus Station
37 Galeb Laundry
38 ST Car Rental
39 Airport Bus Stop
41 Post Office
42 Train Station
43 Bus Station
 & Croatia Express
44 Ferry Terminal
47 Shakespeare's

and provide transportation information. In the summer it's open Monday to Saturday from 8 am to 6 pm, Sunday 9 am to noon (closed Sunday off season). The Jadrolinija office (☎ 355 399) is in the ferry terminal (open daily from 8 am to 1.30 pm and 5 to 8 pm off season and without interruption in the summer). Motorists can turn to HAK (☎ 356 333), Komulovića 2.

Money Splitskabanka, obala preporoda 10, has the only ATM in town where you can withdraw cash using MasterCard. You can change money at Splitskabanka or at any travel agency, most of which are located around the bus and train stations.

Post & Communications Poste restante mail can be collected at window No 7 at the main post office, Kralja Tomislava 9. The post office is open weekdays from 7 am to 8 pm, and Saturday 7 am to noon. The telephone centre here is open daily from 7 am to 9 pm. On Sunday and in the early evening there's always a line of people waiting to place calls, so it's better to go in the morning. There is also a window where you can get cash using your MasterCard. You can send international packages from the post office near the train station at Obala Kneza Domagoja 3. The postcode for Split is 21000.

Travel Agencies The American Express representative, Atlas travel agency (☎ 343 055), is at Trg Braće Radića, and is open Monday to Saturday from 8 am to 1.30 pm and 2 to 8.30 pm, Sunday 8.30 am to noon and 6.30 to 8.30 pm. The agency holds mail for American Express clients. Dalmacijaturist (☎ 345 166 or ☎ 345 078), Trg Braće Radić, sells tickets for the fast boats they run to the islands in the summer. Croatia Express (☎ 342 645), Obala kneza Domagoja 8, sells international bus tickets and is a good source of bus information. It's open daily from 8 am to 8 pm.

Laundry Although it's not cheap, necessity may dictate a stop at Galeb (☎ 589 297), Višeslava 3, weekdays from 9 am to 5 pm.

It will cost 20KN to wash trousers and dresses and 3KN for socks and underwear.

Things to See

Diocletian's Palace Walking Tour Facing onto the harbour, **Diocletian's Palace** is one of the most imposing Roman ruins in existence. Although the original structure was modified in the Middle Ages, the alterations have only served to increase the allure of this fascinating site. Far from being a museum, the 220 buildings within the palace boundaries are still home to about 3000 people as well as shops, cafés and restaurants.

The palace was built from lustrous white stone from the island of Brač and construction lasted 10 years. Diocletian spared no expense, importing marble from Italy and Greece, and columns and sphinxes from Egypt. A military fortress, imperial residence and fortified town, the palace measures 215m from east to west (including the square corner towers) and 181m wide at the southernmost point. The walls at their highest point measure 26m and the entire structure covers 31,000 sq m.

There are fortified gates in the centre of the eastern, northern and western walls, as well as a smaller gate in the southern wall which led from the living quarters to the sea. From the eastern to the western gate there's a straight street (Krešimirova or Decumanus) which separates the imperial residence on the southern side, with its state rooms and temples, from the northern side which was intended for soldiers and servants. From the northern gate, another straight road (Dioklecijanova ulica or Cardo) leads to the Peristyle. To the east is the imperial mausoleum and to the south is the imperial residence.

Begin the walk at the imposing statue of **Gregorius of Nin** (Grgur Ninski) the 10th century Croatian bishop who fought for the right to use old Croatian in liturgical services. Sculpted by Ivan Meštrović, this powerful work is one of the defining images of Split. Notice that his left big toe has been polished to a shine. It's said that touching it brings good luck. To the right of the statue is the well-preserved corner tower of the palace. Between the statue and the tower is the remains of the pre-Romanesque church of St Benedict with the 15th century **Chapel of Arnir.** Peer through the protective glass and you'll see the altar slab and altar sarcophagus carved by the early Renaissance master Juraj Dalmatinac.

The statue is right outside the **Northern Gate** which was once the starting point for the road to Solin. From the fragments that remain, it's possible to visualise the statues, columns and arches that once decorated the gate. Turn left at Papalićeva ulica and at number 5 is **Papalić Palace** with a courtyard, loggia and external staircase. Built by Juraj Dalmatinac for one of the many noblemen who lived within the palace in the Middle Ages, it is considered a fine example of late Gothic style with an elaborately carved entrance gate that proclaimed the importance of its original inhabitants. The exterior of the palace is closer to its original state than the interior, which has been thoroughly restored to house the **Town Museum**. Captions are in Croatian but wall panels in a variety of languages provide a historical framework for the exhibits. The museum has three floors, with drawings, heraldic coats of arms, 17th century weaponry, fine furniture, coins and documents from as far back as the 14th century. Admission is 10KN (5KN for students) and the museum is open Tuesday to Friday from 9 am to noon and 5 to 8 pm, weekends 10 am to noon.

Return to Dioklecijanova, turn left and you'll see the **Peristyle**, the ceremonial entrance court to the imperial quarters, measuring 35m by 13m and three steps below the level of the surrounding streets. The longer side is lined by six granite columns, linked by arches and decorated with a stone frieze. The southern side of the Peristyle is enclosed by the Protiron, which is the entrance into the Imperial quarters. The square has an outdoor café and the ancient stones provide handy seats to relax and people-watch in this popular meeting place.

Turn right onto the narrow street of Kraj Sveti Ivana which leads to what used to be the ceremonial and devotional section of the palace. Although the two temples that once flanked the streets have long since disappeared, you can still see parts of columns and a few fragments. At the end of the street is the **Temple of Jupiter**, later converted into a baptistery. The temple once had a porch supported by columns but the one column you see dates from the 5th century. The headless sphinx in black granite guarding the entrance was imported from Egypt at the time of the temple's construction. The walls of the temple support a barrel-vaulted ceiling and there's a decorative frieze around the other three walls. Below the temple is a crypt which was once used as a church.

Returning to the Peristyle, go up the eastern stairs to the **Cathedral of St Domnius** (Sveti Dujam), originally built as Diocletian's mausoleum. The mausoleum has almost completely preserved its original octagonal form, encircled by 24 columns. The domed interior is round with two rows of Corinthian columns and a frieze showing Emperor Diocletian and his wife, Prisca.

The oldest monuments in the cathedral are the remarkable scenes on the wooden entrance doors from the life of Christ. Carved by Andrija Buvina in the 13th century, the scenes are presented in 28 squares, 14 on each side, and recall the fashion of Romanesque miniatures of the time.

Notice the right altar carved by Bonino da Milano in 1427 and the vault above the altar decorated with mural paintings by Dujam Vušković. To the left is the altar of St Anastasius (Sveti Staš) by Juraj Dalmatinac in 1448, with a relief of *The Flagellation of Christ* that is one of the finest sculptural works of its time in Dalmatia. The main altar dates from the 13th century and the vault is ornamented with paintings by M. Pončun.

The choir is furnished with 13th century Romanesque seats which are the oldest in Dalmatia. Cross the altar and follow signs to the **Treasury**, rich in reliquaries, icons, church robes, illuminated manuscripts and documents in glagolitic script. Admission to the Treasury is 5KN and it's open in June and September from 10 am to noon and in July and August from 8 am to noon and 4 to 7 pm.

The Romanesque **belfry** was constructed between the 12th and 16th centuries and was reconstructed in 1908 after it collapsed. You can climb the tower for 5KN. Notice the two lion figures at the foot of the belfry and the Egyptian black granite sphinx dating from the 15th century BC on the right wall. South of the mausoleum, there are remains of the Roman baths, a Roman building with a mosaic and the remains of the Imperial dining hall in various stages of preservation.

Immediately to the left of the cathedral are the massive steps leading down through the Protiron into the **Vestibule** which is the best-preserved part of the Imperial residence. The circular ground floor is topped by a cupola once covered in mosaics and marble, although the centre of the dome has disappeared. Today the cellars are filled with stands selling souvenirs and handicrafts. To the left is the entrance to the **basement halls** of the Palace. Although mostly empty, the rooms and corridors emit a haunting sense of timelessness that is well worth the 6KN (3KN for students) ticket. You can visit daily from 9 am to 9 pm. The cellars open onto the southern gate.

Other Attractions Although it's north of the town centre, the **archaeological museum** (Archeološki muzej) at Zrinjsko-Frankopanska 25 is worth the walk. The emphasis is on the Roman and early Christian period, with exhibits devoted to burial sculpture and excavations at Salona. The quality of the sculpture is high and there are interesting reliefs based on Illyrian mythical figures. There's also jewellery, ceramics and coins. The museum is open Monday to Friday from 9 am to 1 pm.

The **Museum of Croatian Archaeological Monuments** (Muzej hrvatskih arheoloških), Spomenika Šetalište Ivana Mestrovica bb, concentrates on medieval Croatian rulers, with inscribed stone fragments, parts of altars and furniture, late medieval tombstones, swords and jewellery. Captions are in Croatian, however, which makes it difficult to identify the exhibits. The museum is open Tuesday through Saturday from 9 am to 3 pm and Sunday 10 am to noon.

Split's finest art museum is the **Meštrović Gallery**, Šetalište Ivana Meštrovića 46. You'll see a comprehensive, well-arranged collection of works by Ivan Meštrović, Croatia's premier modern sculptor, who built the gallery as a personal residence in 1931-39. Although Meštrović intended to retire here, he emigrated to the USA soon after WWII. It's open Tuesday to Saturday from 10 am to 6 pm and Sunday 10 am to 2 pm. Also within the park is the **Natural History Museum** (Pirondoslovni muzej) and **zoo**. From October to March the zoo is open from 8 am to 4 pm; from April to September it's 8 am to 8 pm.

From the Meštrović Gallery it's possible to hike straight up **Marjan Hill**. Go up ulica Tonća Petrasova Marovića on the west side of the gallery and continue straight up the stairway to Put Meja ulica. Turn left and walk west to Put Meja 76. The trail begins on the west side of this building. Marjan Hill offers trails through the forest, lookouts, old chapels and the local zoo.

Organised Tours

Atlas runs excursions to Krka waterfalls once a week (215KN). They also offer a canoe picnic on the Cetina River for 275KN including lunch and a fast boat to Bol on Brač, every Sunday (120KN return).

Special Events

The Split Summer Festival from mid-July to mid-August features opera, drama, ballet and concerts on open-air stages. There's also the Feast of St Dujo (7 May), a Flower Show in May and the four-day Festival of Popular Music around the end of June. The traditional February Carnival has recently been revived and from June to September a variety of evening entertainment is presented in the old town, usually around the Peristyle.

Ivan Meštrović

Croatia's greatest 20th century sculptor was born in 1883 in the Sava valley and grew up in Otavice, a small village in the mountains north-west of Split. He received no formal education but his obvious artistic talent drew the attention of a stone-cutter in Split and, at the age of 15, he was invited to live in the stone-cutter's workshop as an apprentice. After only nine months, an Austrian mine-owner consented to pay for Meštrović to study at the Vienna Academy of Art.

In 1904 he married Ruza Klein, the daughter of a Jewish merchant, and in 1905 received his first major commission: *The Well of Life* that stands outside the Croatian National Theatre in Zagreb. Its impressionism reflects the influence of the French sculptor August Rodin, whom Meštrović had befriended in Vienna. In 1910 he participated in the Viennese Secession exhibition where he attracted attention with his sculptures of south-Slavic heroes who had battled the Turks. His sculpture of the Serbian hero Kraljević Marko now stands in the Meštrović studio in Zagreb.

The choice of a Serbian hero reflected Meštrović's commitment to a union of the southern Slavs. His political activism against the Austro-Hungarian empire forced him to flee Split in 1914 and move to Rome where he and two other Dalmatian activists organised the Yugoslav Committee on National Independence.

Fearful of the consequences of the Treaty of London, in which Dalmatia would be given to Italy as a reward for entering WWI, the group moved to London to agitate for independence. A Meštrović one-man show in the Victoria & Albert Museum in London helped publicise their cause and secure popular support in Britain for the postwar Kingdom of Serbs, Croats and Slovenes.

After WWI, Meštrović returned to Zagreb and built a studio. His work turned away from political themes and from 1919 to 1922 he executed the Racic Memorial Chapel in Cavtat for the dying daughter of a shipowner. In 1926 he produced the monument of Gregorius of Nin and gave it to Split.

His first marriage ended in divorce and in nearby Dubrovnik he met his second wife, Olga Kestercanek. In the 1930s, Meštrović built a summer home for his wife and new family in Split which, in accordance with his wishes, has now become a museum of his work. In his

Places to Stay

The hotel situation in Split is slowly improving after years of housing refugees and international peacekeepers, but budget places are still in short supply. Prices quoted here are for the high season – July and August – but they don't descend much (if at all) in the off season.

Camping The nearest camp site used to be *Autocamp Trstenik* (☎ *521 971*), 5km east of the centre near the beach, but it has been closed for several years. Call to find out if it has reopened. See the camp sites listed in Trogir for more reliable alternatives.

Private Rooms In the summer, you may be met at the bus station by women offering *zimmer*. Otherwise, you'll need to head for the Turistički biro, (☎/*fax 342 142, Obala hrvatskog narodnog preporoda 12*). Prices begin at 130/158KN for a single/ double. There will also be a 30% surcharge added to your bill for stays less than four nights.

Ivan Meštrović

home town of Otavice, he built the Church of the Holy Redeemer which was to serve as the family mausoleum.

When the quisling government of Ante Pavelić was installed in Zagreb in 1941, Meštrović was pressured to cooperate with the regime but he refused and was imprisoned for almost five months. Although highly unpopular because of his ties with the Yugoslav Committee, Meštrović's international reputation eventually forced Pavelić to release him. He sought safety in Rome but was soon forced to flee again to Switzerland for the duration of the war.

Although Tito implored Meštrović to return to postwar Yugoslavia, in 1946 the sculptor accepted a professorship at Syracuse University and sailed for the United States.

It was not his first visit. After a successful exhibi-

tion in 1924, he received a commission for the Chicago Indians series which is his best known work in the United States. Soon after his arrival, the Metropolitan Museum of New York staged an exhibition of his work, the first time in its history that a living artist was honoured with a one-person show. He became a US citizen in 1954 and in 1955 became Professor of Sculpture at the University of Notre Dame in Indiana. In addition to bestowing a number of his works on both Syracuse and Indiana campuses, Meštrović sent 59 statues from the United States to Yugoslavia.

Meštrović died in 1962 and was buried in the Church of the Holy Redeemer in Otavice. The town was occupied by Serbian rebels from 1991 to 1995. The Croatian forces that retook the area in 1995 discovered that the church had been savagely attacked and the tombs desecrated. Reconstruction is in progress.

Hotels – Budget The 32-room *Slavija* (☎ *47 053, Buvinova 3)* in the old town has the cheapest rooms at 170/220KN a single/double without bath and 211/260KN a single/double with bath.

Hotels – Mid-Range The *Park Hotel* (☎ *515 411, fax 591 247, Šetalište Bačvice 15)* is a bland sprawling complex that provides a kind of resort experience near a beach. Rooms have air-con and you pay 390/500KN for a single/double. Mid-level is the *Zenta* (☎ *357 229, Ivana Zajca 2)*,

farther east than the Park Hotel but still within walking distance from town. You can also take bus No 3 to the hospital. When you get off, take Spinčića about 30m heading toward the sea. Rooms cost 250/ 360KN a single/double.

Hotels – Top End In town the *Hotel Bellevue* (☎ *585 655, fax 363 383, Bana Jelačića 2)* has the best location, located right on the edge of Trg Republike.Singles/doubles cost 375/500KN. The rooms vary in size but have recently been upgraded and the hotel retains an old-fashioned appeal that is a rarity in Dalmatia.

The most luxurious and most expensive hotel in town is the **Hotel Marjan** (☎ *342 866, fax 342 930, obala Kneza Branimira 8)*, near the marina about 1km west of the town centre. Rooms cost 414/547KN a single/double.

Just west and past the marina is the **Jadran Koteks** (☎ *361 599, Sustipanski put 23)*, which has single rooms that will cost you 390/580KN.

East of town is the **Hotel Split** (*☎/fax 303 111, Put Trstenika 5)*, another luxury establishment with an outdoor pool, sauna and beach. Top price rooms with a sea view run 540/ 842KN a single/double and 281/425KN without view, but you need to have a car since the hotel is far from the town centre.

Places to Eat

Town Centre *Sarajevo (Domaldova 6)* is a spacious restaurant in the heart of town that specialises in traditional Dalmatian meat dishes such as *pastičada*. There are also several fish dishes on offer. Main courses run from 35KN to 55KN and the restaurant is open daily from 10 am to 11 pm. *Kod Joze (Sredmanuška 4)* is a popular local restaurant/tavern, slightly off the beaten track. The home-made green tagliatelle with seafood is a standout and good value at 50KN. It's open daily from 11 am to midnight. The best pizza in town is served at *Galija* on Tončićeva (daily until 11 pm); pizzas start at 22KN. *Pizzeria Bakra (Radovanova 2)*, off ulica Sv Petra Starog just down from the market, is not bad either. The vegetarian salad bar at *Ponoćno Sunce (Teutina 15)* is excellent

Best Restaurants & Pizzerias on the Coast

Pizzeria Nono, Poreč. Oh my, what a pie. You could make a meal out of the light, fluffy crust even without the savoury toppings.

Valsabbion Pula. You'll have to dig deeply into your wallet for this one, but you couldn't find a better splurge. The dishes are imaginatively concocted but portions are less than copious.

Korkyra, Rijeka. The quality-price ratio is always good here but the pre-lunch specials for 20KN are outstanding value. This is a good place to try *brodetto* and *bakalar*.

Ponoćno Sunce, Split. Vegetarians can feast at the salad bar where you might find grilled eggplant, bean salads, rice salads and leafy greens. There's also a full menu of other Dalmatian specialties.

Restaurant Šumica, Split. The usual array of fresh seafood is expertly prepared, the pastas and sausage are home made and food is served under pine trees on a terrace overlooking the sea.

Paradise Garden, Hvar. The spaghetti with shellfish is celestial. Elsewhere on the coast the sauce is tomato based but here the lightly herbed butter and wine sauce perfectly complements the fresh seafood.

Pizzeria Busola, Jelsa. Even if the chef here is not in the mood to create one of his authentically Italian pizzas (which happens), the pasta dishes are equally scrumptious.

Villa Kaliopa, Vis. Dine on Dalmatian dishes in a beautifully landscaped garden replete with soft lighting and classical sculpture.

Adio Mare, Korčula. It may be getting a wee bit too popular for its own good but the excellent fish served in a spacious, attractively decorated interior will keep the crowds coming.

Club Nautika, Dubrovnik. Dubrovnik's most elegant dining spot offers pricey but first-rate Adriatic cuisine in an unforgettable setting overlooking the sea.

value at 30KN. It also serves reasonably priced pastas and grilled meat. It's open Monday to Saturday from 11 am to 11 pm. The cheapest place in town is **Restaurant Index** *(Svačićeva 8)*, a self-service student eatery. Vegetarians should avoid this place, but you can get a plate of meat and cabbage for 19KN. It's open Monday to Friday from noon to 8 pm.

The spiffy **Burek Bar** *(Domaldova 13)*, just down from the main post office, serves a good breakfast or lunch of burek and yoghurt for about 12KN. The vast *super-market/delicatessen (Svačića 1)* has a wide selection of meat and cheese for sandwiches and nearly everything else you might want for a picnic. Sit around the square and eat your goodies.

East of Centre *Bekan (Ivana Zajca 1)*, next to the Hotel Zenta, serves an array of fish prepared Dalmatian style. It's not cheap (unless you order the spaghetti with seafood for 48KN) but you can sample a savoury shrimp *buzara* on an airy terrace overlooking the sea. It's open daily from 10 am to midnight.

For a splurge, you couldn't do better than **Restaurant Šumica** *(put Firula 6)*. The pasta is home-made and combined with salmon or other fish in imaginative sauces. The grilled scampi is perfection but you pay a steep 280KN a kilogram. Before your meal you'll be served a dish of home-made fish pâté with bread to whet your appetite and the meal is served on an open air terrace under pine trees with a view of the sea. The restaurant is open daily from 10 am to midnight.

Entertainment
In summer everyone starts the evening at one of the cafés along Obala hrvatskog narodnog preporoda, Ujevićeva Poljana or around the cathedral before heading to a disco.

During winter, opera and ballet are presented at the **Croatian National Theatre** *(Trg Gaje Bulata)*. The best seats are about 60KN and tickets for the same night are usually available. Erected in 1891, the theatre was fully restored in 1979 in the original style; it's worth attending a performance for the architecture alone.

Currently, **Night Café** is a popular dance spot. You'll find it in the Koteks shopping centre, a huge white complex 10 minutes walk east of the old town. There are live concerts every Monday, Tuesday, Wednesday, Thursday and Sunday with a Tombola on Thursday. In the summer, **Shakespeare** *(Uvala Zenta 3)* takes over. This open air disco near the Hotel Zenta is open nightly from June to September.

Shopping
Diocletian's Cellars have been turned into a market for crafted jewellery, reproductions of Roman busts, silver cigarette cases, candlestick holders, wooden sailing ships, leather goods and other odds and ends. Prices aren't too steep and you might find the perfect lightweight item to fulfil back-from-a trip gift-giving obligations.

There's a daily market above Obala Lazerata where you can buy fruit, vegetables, shoes, confectionery, clothing, can openers, string, flowers, souvenirs and other products. If you can't find what you're looking for in this market, chances are it doesn't exist in Split.

Getting There & Away
Air Croatia Airlines operates one-hour flights to/from Zagreb up to four times a day (568KN in peak season, 50% cheaper off season).

Bus Advance bus tickets with seat reservations are recommended. There are buses from the main bus station beside the harbour to the following destinations:

destination	distance	frequency
Zadar	158km	26 daily
Zagreb	478km	26 daily
Rijeka	404km	14 daily
Ljubljana	532km	1 daily
Pula	514km	4 daily
Dubrovnik	235km	12 daily

CENTRAL DALMATIA

To Bosnia-Hercegovina there are seven daily buses from Split to Međugorje (156km), 11 to Mostar (179km) and six to Sarajevo (271km).

Bus No 37 to Solin, Split airport and Trogir leaves from a local bus station on Domo-vinskog, 1km north-east of the city centre (see the map).

Croatia Express (☎ 342 645), Obala Kneza Domagoja 9 near the bus station, has buses to many German cities, including Munich (912km, daily, 378KN) and Berlin (Saturday and Sunday, 738KN). It's open daily from 7 am to 10 pm.

Agencija Touring (☎ 361 797) at the bus station also has many buses to Germany and a weekly bus to Amsterdam (810KN). Next door, the agency Split Tours (☎ 342 522) is the representative for Eurolines, with buses to most major European destinations.

Train There are three or four trains a day between Split and Zagreb (nine hours, 91KN), and two trains a day between Split and Šibenik (74km, 25KN).

Boat Jadrolinija (☎ 355 399), in the large ferry terminal opposite the bus station, handles services to Hvar island and operates three or four times a week all year round. The local ferry is cheaper though (23KN), and calls at Vela Luka on Korčula island (25KN) daily.

There are five or six Jadrolinija ferries a week all year round between Ancona and Split (10 hours, 249KN); in July and August, these stop twice a week at Stari Grad on Hvar island.

Adriatica Navigazione connects Ancona and Split three times a week in the summer for about the same price, and twice a week in the winter. The schedule and tickets are available from Jadroagent, located in the ferry terminal.

From May to September, Atlas travel agency runs a fast boat between Zadar and Ancona (three hours, 340KN) and a new Croatian company, SEM (☎ 021 589 433), runs a daily boat between Split, Trieste and Ancona for 234KN, Split-Ancona.

Car Rental Try ST (☎ 355 797) at Obala Lazareta 8, Budget (☎ 345 700) in the Hotel Marijan or Mack (☎ 342 994) in Obala Branimira 1.

Getting Around

To/From the Airport The bus to Split airport (20KN) leaves from Obala Lazareta 3, a five minute walk from the train station. This bus departs 90 minutes before flight times. You can also get there on bus No 37, as described in Getting There & Away (two-zone ticket).

Bus Local buses run about every 20 minutes and connect the town centre and the harbour with outlying districts. To stay within Split you'll buy a one-zone ticket which costs 5KN for one trip but 7KN for two trips if you buy tickets from the kiosk outside the Prima Department store on Trg Gaja Bulata or at a *Tisak*. A two-zone ticket is 7.50KN, three-zone 10.50KN and four-zone 13.50KN.

AROUND SPLIT
Šolta

This lovely, wooded island is a popular getaway for Split inhabitants looking to escape the sultry summer heat. Only 59 sq km, the island's most accessible entry points from Split are Rogač and Nečujam on the northern coast. In **Rogač** the ferry ties up in front of the tourist office (☎ 654 491) and on the edge of a large bay. A shady path leads around the bay to smaller coves with rocky beaches and a small road leads uphill to a market. There are year-round car ferries from Split (45 minutes, 16KN), making it an easy day trip.

Nečujam is 7km from Rogač; set on a curving beach, it has a hotel, snack bar and outdoor shower. Transportation to Nečujam is patchier, however. There are only a few buses from Rogač (9km) and no car ferries; there is however a private operator that runs a daily boat from Split at 8.30 am to Nečujam and returns at 6.15 pm. Look for the Manon boat at the harbour or ask at Dalmacijaturist.

Solin

The ruins of the ancient city of Solin (Roman Salona), among the vineyards at the foot of mountains just north-east of Split, are the most important archaeological site in Croatia.

Today surrounded by noisy highways and industry, Solin was first mentioned in 119 BC as the centre of the Illyrian tribe. The Romans seized the site in 78 BC and under the rule of Augustus it became the administrative headquarters of the Roman Dalmatian province.

When Emperor Diocletian built his palace in Split at the end of the 3rd century AD, it was the proximity to Salona that attracted him. Salona was incorporated into the Eastern Roman Empire in the 6th century but was levelled by the Slavs and Avars in 614. The inhabitants fled to Split and neighbouring islands, leaving Salona to decay.

Things to See A good place to begin your visit is at the large car park near the Snack Bar Salona. **Manastirine**, the fenced area behind the car park, was a burial place for early Christian martyrs prior to the legalisation of Christianity. Excavated remains of the cemetery and the 5th century basilica are highlights, although this area was outside the ancient city itself. Overlooking Manastirine is **Tusculum**, an archaeological museum with interesting sculpture embedded in the walls and in the garden.

The Manastirine/Tusculum complex is part of an **archaeological reserve** open from 8 am to 3 pm. Pick up a brochure in the information office at the entrance to the reserve.

A path bordered by cypresses runs south to the northern **city wall** of Salona. Notice the covered aqueduct along the inside base of the wall. It was probably built around the

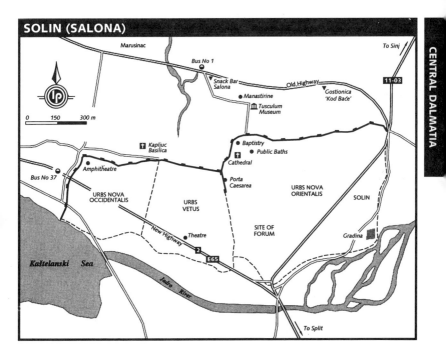

SOLIN (SALONA)

CENTRAL DALMATIA

11-03

1st century and supplied Salona and Diocletian's Palace with water from the Jadro River. The ruins you see in front of you as you stand on the wall were an early Christian site; they include a three-aisled 5th century **cathedral** with an octagonal baptistery, and the remains of Bishop Honorius' Basilica with a ground plan in the form of a Greek cross. **Public baths** adjoin the cathedral on the east.

South-west of the cathedral is the 1st century east city gate, **Porta Caesarea**, later engulfed by the growth of Salona in all directions. Grooves in the stone road left by ancient wheels can still be seen at this gate.

Walk west along the city wall 500m to **Kapljuc Basilica** on the right, another martyrs' burial place. At the west end of Salona is the huge 2nd century **amphitheatre**, destroyed in the 17th century by the Venetians to prevent it from being used as a refuge by Turkish raiders. At one time it could accommodate 18,000 spectators, which gives an idea of the size and importance of this ancient city.

Getting There & Away The ruins are easily accessible on Split city bus No 1 direct to Snack Bar Salona (look for the yellow bus shelter on the left) every half-hour from Trg Gaje Bulata.

From the amphitheatre at Solin it's easy to continue on to Trogir by catching a west-bound bus No 37 from the nearby stop on the adjacent new highway (buy a four-zone ticket in Split if you plan to do this). If, on the other hand, you want to return to Split, use the underpass to cross the highway and catch an eastbound bus No 37.

TROGIR
- **pop 1600**   ☎ **021**

Trogir (formerly Trau) is a jewel of a walled town with a wide waterfront promenade that encloses a maze of medieval streets. No other town in Dalmatia better encapsulates the cultural life that flourished along the coast in spite of a series of foreign rulers. The profusion of Romanesque and Renaissance style within 15th century city

walls, as well as the magnificent cathedral at the town centre, inspired UNESCO to name the town a World Heritage site in 1997. Trogir is an easy day trip from Split and a relaxed place to spend a few days, taking a trip or two to nearby islands.

Backed by high hills in the north, the sea to the south and snug in its walls, Trogir (Tragurion to the Romans) proved an attractive place to settlers. The early Croats settled the old Illyrian town by the 7th century. Its defensive position allowed Trogir to maintain its autonomy throughout Croatian and Byzantine rule while trade and exploiting nearby mines insured its economic viability. In the 13th century sculpture and architecture flourished, reflecting a vibrant, dynamic culture. When Venice bought Dalmatia in 1409, Trogir refused to accept the new ruler and the Venetians were forced to bombard the town into submission. While the rest of Dalmatia stagnated under Venetian rule, Trogir continued to produce great artists who enhanced the beauty of the town.

Orientation
The old town of Trogir occupies a tiny island in the narrow channel between Čiovo island and the mainland, just off the coastal highway. Many sights are seen on a 15 minute walk around this island. The nearest beach is 4km west at the Medena Hotel.

The heart of the old town is divided from the mainland by a small channel and a few minutes walk from the bus station. After crossing the small bridge near the station, go through the North Gate. Turn left at the end of the square and you'll come to Trogir's main street, ulica Kohl-Genscher (named jointly after the German chancellor and foreign minister who initially campaigned to recognise Croatia's independence in 1991). Trogir's finest sights are around trg Ivana Pavla, straight ahead. The old town is connected to Čiovo island to the south by a drawbridge.

There's no left-luggage office in Trogir bus station, so you'll end up toting your bags around town if you only visit on a stopover.

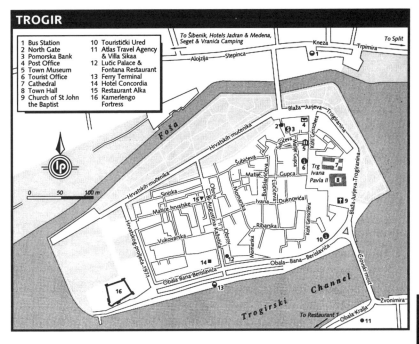

TROGIR

1	Bus Station	10	Touristički Ured
2	North Gate	11	Atlas Travel Agency
3	Pomorska Bank		& Villa Sikaa
4	Post Office	12	Lučic Palace &
5	Town Museum		Fontana Restaurant
6	Tourist Office	13	Ferry Terminal
7	Cathedral	14	Hotel Concordia
8	Town Hall	15	Restaurant Alka
9	Church of St John	16	Kamerlengo
	the Baptist		Fortress

Information

Tourist Offices A private tourist office (☎ 881 554) opposite the cathedral on Kohl-Genscher 21 sells maps, guidebooks and arranges private accommodation. The Turistički Ured town tourist office (☎ 881 412) is further down the street at obala Bana Berislavića 12 and is another good source of information, although it doesn't arrange private accommodation. In summer the offices are open from 8 am to 7 pm but off-season hours are shorter. Atlas travel agency (☎ 881 374, fax 884 744) is at obala kralja Zvonimira 10 and is open Monday to Saturday from 8 am to 9 pm, Sunday 8 am to noon and 6 to 9 pm. In winter the office closes at 7 pm weekdays, noon Saturdays and is closed all day Sunday.

Money Pomorska Banka is on Gracška vrata, just inside the North gate. It's open Monday to Friday from 7.30 am to noon and 2.30 to 7 pm. Saturdays hours are 8 to 11.30 am. During opening hours, you can get cash using MasterCard or Cirrus.

Post & Communications The main post office and telephone centre is at the beginning of ulica Kohl-Grenscher. It's open Monday to Saturday from 7 am to 9 pm, Sunday 9 am to noon. As usual, you can make phone calls and send faxes from here. The postcode for Trogir 21220.

Things to See

There's a lot to see in Trogir, as the town has retained many intact buildings from its age of glory – between the 13th and 15th century. As you enter, notice the Renaissance **North Gate** with the statue of the town protector, St Ivan Orsini, hovering overhead. As you proceed down ulica

Kohl-Grenscher you may wish to stop in the **town museum** housed in the former Garanjin-Fanfogna palace. The five rooms exhibit books, documents, drawings, documents and period costumes from Trogir's long history. The museum is open from June through September, Monday to Saturday from 9 am to noon and 6 to 9 pm. In winter, it's open by appointment only (ask at one of the tourist offices).

The glory of the town is the three-naved Venetian **Cathedral of St Lovro** built from the 13th to 15th century on trg Ivana Pavla and one of the finest architectural works in Croatia. Note first the Romanesque portal (1240) by Master Radovan. The sides of the portal depict lion figures (the symbol of Venice) with Adam and Eve above them, the earliest example of the nude in Dalmatian sculpture. The outer pilasters show saints, the centre scenes representing the calendar months and the small posts feature hunting scenes. Overhead is the Nativity of Christ. At the end of the portico is another fine piece of sculpture – the baptistry sculpted in 1464 by Andrija Aleši. Enter the building through an obscure back door to see the richly decorated Renaissance Chapel of St Ivan, created by the masters Firentinac and Duknović from 1461 to 1497. Within the sacristy there are paintings of St Jerome and John the Baptist. Take a look at the treasury which contains an ivory triptych and several medieval illuminated manuscripts.

A sign informs you that you must be 'decently dressed' to enter the cathedral, which means that men must wear tops (women too, of course) and shorts are a no-no. For a small fee, you can even climb the 47m cathedral tower (if it's open) for a delightful view. To be sure of visiting the cathedral, it's best to come in the morning between 9 am and noon, although in the summer it's also open between 5 and 9 pm. Before leaving the square, look at the 15th century **town hall** opposite the cathedral with a Gothic yard decorated with coats of arms and a stone head. Next to the cathedral, the tourist office occupies the **Cipiko**

palace with its stunning carved triforium, the work of Firentinac and Aleši.

South-east of the cathedral, look at the magnificent carved portal on the **church of St John the Baptist** representing the mourning of Christ. Inside, the church has become a kind of art museum (*Pinakoteka*) exhibiting 14th to 17th century paintings and statues. Admission is 10KN. Walk along the waterfront and notice the portal and courtyard of the Renaissance **Lučić Palace** next to the Fontana restaurant. If you keep walking you'll come to the **Kamerlengo Fortress** which looks exactly as a medieval fortress should look. Once connected with the city walls, the fortress was built around the 15th century. At the farthest end, you'll see an elegant gazebo (now graffiticovered) built by the French Marshal Marmont during the Napoleonic occupation of Dalmatia, from which he used to sit and play cards amidst the waves. At the time, the western end of the island was a lagoon; the malarial marshes were not drained until the 20th century.

Special Events

Every year from mid-June to mid- August, Trogir hosts a summer music festival with classical and folk concerts presented in churches and open squares. Posters advertising the concerts are all around town and you can reserve tickets through the private tourist office.

Places to Stay

Camping *Vranića Camping* (☎ 894 141) is just off the highway to Zadar about 5km west of Trogir by bus 24. The *Seget* (☎ 880 394), 2km west of Trogir is reliably open from June to September. The *Seget* is smaller but both camping grounds offer tennis, biking, windsurfing, waterskiing, sailing and horseback riding.

Private Rooms The Turist Office (☎/fax 881 554) opposite the cathedral has private rooms for 150/288KN a single/double plus a 30% surcharge for stays less than three nights. Prices are lower off season.

Hotels The best deal in town is the new *Villa Sikaa* (☎ 881 223, fax 885 149, styepan.runtic@st.tel.hr) over the Atlas office. The seven large rooms are air-conditioned, equipped with double-glazed windows and satellites and some have stunning views over the town. In an unusual touch, the owner offers a free Internet connection in each room for the price of a local phone call. Singles/doubles are 200/300KN in the summer and 150/200KN off season including breakfast. Also in town is the *Concordia* (☎ 885 400, obala Bana Berislavić 22) right on the waterfront. The 15 rooms are slightly smaller but still pleasant, air-conditioned and some have sea views. Singles/doubles are 250/400KN in high season and about 25% less off season. Three kilometres west of Trogir there is the budget *Hotel Jadran* (☎ 880 008, fax 880 401) that offers basic rooms for 180/364KN and, a little further on, the mid-range *Hotel Medena* (☎ 880 588, fax 880 019), which has better rooms for 252/366KN. Both hotels have small private beaches (rocks) but the Medena also offers a sauna and gym as well as rooms with telephone and TV. To get there, take any Medena bus from Trogir bus station which run every hour or so on weekdays but infrequently on Sunday.

Places to Eat

When locals want to have a night out they usually head to the *Fontana Restaurant* with its large terrace on the waterfront. You can get almost anything there – from inexpensive pizza and omelettes to pricier grilled fish and meat, but the specialty is fish. *Alka* is another popular choice at the same price and it also has an outdoor terrace. For a splendid view of the town, head to *Restaurant No 1* in the ACI marina about 200m west of Atlas. There's a full menu of grilled seafood and meat, no more and no less expensive than anywhere else.

Getting There & Away

Southbound buses from Zadar (130km) will drop you off in Trogir. Getting buses north can be more difficult, as they often arrive full from Split.

City bus No 37 runs between Trogir and Split (28km) every 20 minutes throughout the day, with a stop at Split airport en route. In Split bus No 37 leaves from the local bus station. You can buy the four-zone 13.50KN ticket from the driver in either direction. There's also a ferry once a week from Split that docks in front of the Hotel Concordia.

AROUND TROGIR

Although there are beaches to the west of Trogir, it's a much better idea to head to the beaches on Drvenik Mali and Drvenik Veli islands, an easy boat trip from town. Boats leave from in front of the Hotel Concordia. Both islands are sparsely inhabited and idyllic getaways.

The smaller island is **Drvenik Mali** with olive trees, a population of 56 and (finally) a sand beach that curves around the cove of Vela Rina.

Drvenik Veli also has secluded coves and olive trees plus a few cultural highlights to get you off the beach. The church of St George dates from the 16th century and houses Baroque furniture and a Venetian altarpiece. Outside Drvenik Veliki village is the unfinished 18th century church of St Nicholas, whose builder never quite got past the monumental front.

Unfortunately, the boat schedules are geared to islanders working in Trogir and not day trippers, but on Thursday and Saturday you can catch a 10 am boat to the islands and spend a few hours before catching the 3 pm boat back from Drvenik Veli. If you're interested in spending more time on the islands, the tourist office in Trogir can find you private accommodation.

MAKARSKA

- pop 11,743   ☎ 021

This attractive town and port is the centrepiece of the 'Makarska Riviera', a 50km stretch of coast at the foot of Biokovo Mountain. The steep, barren mountain descends to the coast in a series of cliffs and ridges, forming an impressive backdrop to a string of beautiful pebble beaches. The foothills are protected from harsh winds and covered in lush Mediterranean greenery – pine forests, olive groves, figs and fruit trees.

With an abundance of hiking and swimming possibilities in such a spectacular natural setting, it's unsurprising that tourism has a long history in this region. The recent war in the former Yugoslavia severely disrupted the flow of visitors however, and, outside of a short summer season that runs from about six weeks in July and August, you should find the area relatively uncrowded the rest of the year.

Makarska is the largest town in the region and makes a good base for exploring both the coast and Biokovo Mountain. Located on a large cove bordered by Cape Osejava in the south-east and the Sveti Petar Peninsula in the north-west, the landscape is dominated by the Biokovo Mountain looming over the town. The roads and trails that crisscross the limestone massif may be irresistible to hikers but the less energetic can simply lie on the beach and watch the day-long play of light and shadow on the mountain's cracks and crevices.

Makarska owes its name to the Roman settlement of Muccurum which probably existed in the village of Makar about 2km north of Makarska. Excavations on Sveti Petar peninsula, however, reveal that there was another linked settlement along the coast, Inaronia, that served as a way station between Salona and the important trading town of Narona down the coast. Both settlements were allegedly destroyed in 548 by Totila, king of the Eastern Goths.

The region was populated by migrating Slavs in the 7th century who eventually set up a booming piracy business that disrupted Venetian shipping. The Venetian warships that sailed into Makarska in 887 were severely trounced in battle and the Venetians were thereafter forced to pay for the right to sail past the settlement. In the 11th century, Makarska came under the rule of the Croato-Hungarian kings which lasted until 1324 when it fell to the Bosnian ruler Kotro-manić. In 1499, the town was taken by the Ottoman Turks who were pushing against the Venetians for control of the Adriatic coast. During the 150 years that Makarska was under Turkish rule, it became an important port for the salt trade from Bosnia and Hercegovina. The Venetians took over the town in 1646 and held it until the end of their empire in 1797. Trade prospered and a new aristocracy built baroque mansions to the east and west of the town. After the fall of Venice, Makarska was then subject to Austrian, French and again Austrian rule before becoming part of the Kingdom of Yugoslavia.

Orientation

The bus station on Ante Starčevica is about 300m uphill from the centre of the old town that opens like an amphitheatre onto the sea. Take Kralja Zvonimira from the bus station downhill to Obala Tomislava and you'll be on the main promenade of the old town with travel agencies, shops and restaurants.

There's a long pebble beach that stretches from the Sveti Petar park at the beginning of Obala Tomislava north-west along the bay, which is where you'll find most of the large hotels. The south-east side of town is rockier but you can still find plenty of places to stretch out on the rocks and take a swim. The bus station has a left-luggage facility that's open from 6 am to 10 pm daily.

Information

Tourist Offices The Turistički Ured (☎/fax 612 002) at Tomislava 16 is open Monday to Friday from 8 am to 3 pm. They publish a useful guide to the city with a map which you can pick up there or at any travel agency.

Money Splitska Banka, Tomislava 15, is open Monday to Friday from 8 am to 4 pm, Saturday 8 am to noon. You can change money or withdraw cash on your Visa card. Zagrebačka Banka, Trg Tina Ujevića 1, has an ATM where you can withdraw cash on MasterCard.

Post & Communications The post office at Trg 4 Svibnja 533 is open Monday to Saturday from 7 am to 9 pm, Sunday 9 am to noon. You can change money, make telephone calls or withdraw cash on MasterCard. The postal code for Makarska is 21300.

Travel Agencies SB Tours (☎ 611 005, fax 611 202) at Tomislava 14 is open daily from 8 am to 1 pm and 6 to 9 pm, and changes money and finds private accommodation. The Turist biro (☎ 611 688, fax 615 352) at Tomislava 2 sells tickets for Jadrolinija international and coastal routes as well as international bus tickets. It's open daily from 8 am to 9 pm in summer and 8 am to 7 pm off season.

Atlas travel agency (☎ 617 038), Franjevački 16, is at the far end of town. In addition to money exchange and private accommodation services, Mornar Tours (☎ 616 834, fax 616 836), Prvosvibanjska bb, handles airline tickets for Croatia Airlines in case you need to change your ticket.

Things to See

Makarska is more renowned for its natural beauty than its cultural highlights but on a rainy day you could check out the **Town Museum** on Tomislava 17 which traces the town's history in a less than gripping collection of photos and old stones. The museum is open Monday to Saturday from 9 am to 2 pm. More interesting is the **Franciscan monastery** at Franjevački put 1, built in 1400 and restored in 1540 and 1614. The single-nave church is worth visiting for the shell collection in the cloister and a painting of the Assumption by the Flemish artist Pieter de Coster (1760). The monastery and museum are open daily from 9 am to noon and 5 to 8 pm. The 18th century **St Mark's Church** (Sveti Marka) on Kačićev trg features a baroque silver altar from 1818 and a marble altar from 18th century Venice, but the church is only open for Mass.

Activities

Biokovo Mountain, rising behind the city, offers wonderful **hiking** opportunities. The Vošac peak (142m) is the nearest target for hikers, only 2.5km from the city centre. From St Mark's church in Kačićev trg, you can walk or drive up put Makra following signs to the village of Makar where a trail leads to Vošac (one to two hours). From Vošac a good marked trail leads to Sveti Jure, the highest peak at 1762m (two hours). Take plenty of water.

Another popular destination is the Botanical Garden near the village of Kotišina which can be reached by a marked trail from Makar that passes under a series of towering peaks.

Biokovo Active Holidays (☎ 616 974, fax 616 455), Dalmatinska 5, is an excellent source of hiking and other information about Biokovo Mountain.

For **scuba diving** try More Sub (☎ 611 727, ☎ 098 265 241) which has a booth in the Hotel Dalmacija. They offer one dive for 137KN and two dives for 245KN as well as a two day discover scuba course for 350KN plus equipment rental of 175KN.

Organised Tours

Biokovo Active Holidays offers guided walks and drives on Biokovo for all levels of physical exertion from very easy to medium hard. You can go part way up the mountain by minibus and then take a short hike to Sveti Jure peak for 125KN or take a 5½ hour hike through black pine forests and fields of chamois and sheep for 140KN including lunch. There's also an early drive to watch the sun rise over Makarska for 90KN.

Places to Stay

Camping The closest autocamp is *Baško Polje* (☎ 612 329) between Makarska and Baška Voda. It's on the beach and is open from June to October.

Private Rooms Any of the travel agencies listed above (except Atlas) can find singles/doubles for 86/130KN in the high season for top end rooms and 58/86KN for bottom end rooms plus the usual 30% surcharge for stays less than three nights or you can rent a studio for 180KN a day.

Hotels The most luxurious hotel in town is the four star *Meteor* (☎ *606 600, fax 611 419, Šatalište Donja Luka 1*), 400m west of the town centre on a pebble beach. Each of the 280 rooms is air-conditioned and has a balcony with a sea view. There are indoor and outdoor swimming pools, shops and tennis courts. Rooms are 486/756KN a single/double in high season and not much cheaper the rest of the year. *Hotel Dalmacija* (☎ *615 777, fax 612 211, Kralja Krešimira bb*) is a towering structure of 190 air-con rooms with a swimming pool and enclosed private beach. Singles/doubles are 352/486KN in high season. *Hotel Biokovo* (☎ *615 244, fax 615 081*) on Tomislava is an attractive 50-room hotel right on the promenade, with double-glazed windows to keep out noise. A single/double room with breakfast is 308/440KN in high season. Half-board is an extra 52KN per person. *Hotel Makarska* (☎/*fax 616 622, Potok 17*) is a small, family-owned hotel in town about 200m from the beach. Rooms have telephone and TV and cost 180/366KN a single/double in high season.

Places to Eat

On one of their rare nights dining out, local people usually head to *Riva (Tomislava 6)* for good quality at low prices. The menu is the usual range of dishes such as scampi, beef cutlet or squid and you can sit under the trees on an outdoor terrace. It's open daily from 11 am to midnight. *Pizzeria Lungomare* next to the Hotel Biokovo serves hearty, fresh-baked pies for 30KN and there's a comfortable outdoor terrace. It's open daily from 9 am to midnight. Picnickers can pick up supplies at the *fruit and vegetable market* next to Sveti Marka church or the *supermarket (Tomislava 14)* that's open Monday to Saturday from 6.30 am to 9 pm, and Sunday 6.30 to 11.30 am.

Entertainment

Pjer (Prvosvibanjska bb) along the harbour is a popular bar, open daily from 8 pm to 4 am. The two most popular discos in town are *Opera (Šetalište Fra Jure Radića)* and *Gaudeamus (Don M. Pavlinovića 1)*. During the summer they are open nightly but off-season hours are limited to Friday and Saturday nights.

Getting There & Away

In summer there are three to five ferries a day between Makarska and Sumartin on Brač, reduced to two a day in winter. The Jadrolinija stall selling ferry tickets is in front of SB Tours, on Tomislava 14.

There are ten buses a day to Dubrovnik (three hours, 61KN), 11 buses daily to Split (1¼ hours, 20KN), two buses a day to Rijeka (nine hours, 174KN) and two buses a day to Zagreb (six hours, 110KN).

There's a daily bus to Sarajevo (5½ hours, 109KN) and a weekly bus to Stuttgart and Frankfurt (440KN).

AROUND MAKARSKA
Brela

The town of Brela, 14km north-west of Makarska, is surrounded by the longest and loveliest coastline in Dalmatia. Six kilometres of pebble beaches curve around coves thickly forested with pine trees, largely unmarred by ugly tourist developments. A shady promenade winds around the coves, the sea is crystal clear and there are convenient outdoor showers on some beaches.

Orientation & Information The bus stop (no left-luggage facility) is behind the Hotel Soline, a short walk downhill to Obala Kneza Domagoja, the harbour street and town centre. The Turistički Ured (☎/fax 618 337) is on Obala Kneza Domagoja along with most travel agencies, shops and restaurants. The tourist office is open daily from 8 am to 9 pm in summer, but only Monday to Friday from 8 am to 2 pm off season. Beaches and coves are on both sides of the town but the longest stretch is the 4km coast west of the town centre.

Places to Stay Camping is at *Baško Polje* (see Camping in the Makarska section) and the tourist office can arrange private accommodation at about the same rates as in

Shelling in 1991 and 1992 did considerable damage to Dubrovnik's much admired roof tiles; they are now being painstakingly repaired

Dubrovnik, the crowning glory of Croatia's Dalmatian Coast

Makarska. There are no cheap hotels but the least expensive is the *Hotel Marina (☎ 603 666, fax 603 688)* which offers singles/doubles for 270/410KN in high season. The most luxurious is the *Hotel Soline (☎ 603 222, fax 618 501)* with air-con, a sauna and an indoor swimming pool. Singles/doubles with half-board are 488/712KN.

Getting There & Away All buses between Makarska and Split stop at Brela, making it an easy day trip from either town.

VIS
• pop 4338   ☎ 021
Ask a Croatian to name their top three islands and one of them is likely to be Vis. In addition to its unspoiled beauty, Vis has the allure of the forbidden. Used as a military base for the former Yugoslav army, it was off-limits to the public until 1989 and is only now struggling to attract tourists. Rather than sprawling tourist resorts, the island has two small towns – Vis and Komiža – at the foot of two large bays and a rugged coast dotted with coves, caves and a couple of sand beaches.

The interior of the island is planted with vineyards producing Vis's well-known Vugava (white) and Plavac (red) wines. Fishing is the other cornerstone of the island's economy. The surrounding waters are rich in marine life and there's a sardine canning plant near Komiža. Like many islands, Vis has become dramatically depopulated in the years since WWII and sees tourism as its only chance for survival. In addition to the charms of sun and sea, the island's long history has produced an archaeological treasure trove of amphorae, sculpture, jewellery and other remnants of antiquity that you can see in the Issa museum and around the town of Vis.

Inhabited first in Neolithic times, the island was settled by the ancient Illyrians who brought the Iron Age to Vis in the first millennium BC. In 390 BC a Greek colony was formed on the island, known then as Issa, from which the Greek ruler Dionysius the Elder controlled other Adriatic posses-

sions. The island eventually became a powerful city-state and established its own colonies on Korčula island, Trogir and Stobreč. Allying itself with Rome during the Illyrian wars, the island nonetheless lost its autonomy and became part of the Roman Empire in 47 BC. By the 10th century Vis had been settled by Slavic tribes and was sold to Venice along with other Dalmatian towns in 1420. Fleeing Dalmatian pirates, the population moved from the coast inland. With the fall of the Venetian Republic in 1797 the island fell under control of Austria, France, England, Austria again and then Italy during World War II as the Great Powers fought for control of this strategic Adriatic outpost. The island was an important military base for Tito's Partisans. He established his Supreme Headquarters in a cave in Hum Mountain from which he coordinated military and diplomatic actions with Allied forces and allegedly made his famous statement, 'We will not have what is theirs but we will not give what is ours'.

Getting There & Away
Vis town is best reached by car ferry from Split but, like many small islands, the boat schedules are set to accommodate islanders working in town, not visitors popping out to the island. In July and August, however, there's a daily boat at 9 am from Split, and on weekends you can take a 6 pm boat back from Vis which makes a pleasant day trip. In the spring and fall, there's a morning boat only on Monday, Wednesday and Friday and in winter only on Monday and Friday – but no afternoon boat back so you'll have to spend the night. The trip takes 2½ hours and costs 30KN. There's an afternoon boat on Tuesday all year that stops in Hvar town.

Vis is also on the main Jadrolinija coastal line which leaves Hvar on Tuesdays at 9.20 am and arrives in Vis at 11.05 am before going on to Korčula. The return boat leaves Korčula on Sunday at 12.20 pm and arrives at Vis at 3.25 pm before going on to Split. In July and August, the fast passenger boat *Adriana* connects Vis with Split, Korčula and Hvar on Wednesday. There's a boat from Vela Luka on Korčula at 6.45 am on Wednesday, arriving in Vis 30 minutes later (50KN), and a boat from Split at 6 pm on Wednesday that stops in Hvar before arriving in Vis 30 minutes later (60KN).

Vis town is also connected to Italy by a Jadrolinija ferry three times a week that stops in Split before heading to Ancona; there's also the Collegamenti boat to Pescara which leaves on Monday evenings for the three-hour trip to Vis and Monday mornings from Vis town for the trip to Pescara. The price is 600KN one way and tickets can be bought from Atlas travel agency.

Komiža is connected by the Collegamenti boat to Italy (three hours, 600KN in high season) which leaves Pescara on Friday evening at 7 pm and Komiža on Friday morning at 7.15 am.

The only island bus transport connects Vis with Komiža. The bus meets the morning and afternoon Jadrolinija ferries and there's a bus at 3 pm.

Vis Town

On the north-east coast of the island, at the foot of a wide, horseshoe-shaped bay, lies the ancient town of Vis, the first settlement on the island. In only a short walk you can see the remains of a Greek cemetery, Roman baths and an English fortress. Regular ferry arrivals give spurts of activity to an otherwise peaceful town of coastal promenades and crumbling 17th century buildings.

Orientation The town is on the southern slope of Gradina hill and is a merger of two settlements: Luka on the north-west part of the bay and Kut in the south-east. The ferry ties up at Luka and a harbourside promenade runs from Luka to Kut. Most beaches are along this promenade while the ancient ruins and another beach in front of the Hotel Issa are a short walk north along the coast.

Information The Turistički Ured (☎ 711 114) at Šetalište Stare Isse 5 is right next to the Jadrolinija ferry dock. It's open daily

from 8 am to 1 pm and 6 to 8 pm in the summer but mornings only the rest of the year.

Jadrolinija (☎ 711 032) adjoins the tourist office and is open Monday to Saturday from 4.45 to 6 am, 10 am to 1 pm and 5 to 7 pm and Sunday 2 to 4 pm, as well as one hour before ferry departures.

Splitska Banka, obala Sveti Jurja 34, is open Monday to Friday from 8 to 11 am and 6 to 8 pm, Saturday 8 to 11 am, and you can withdraw cash on your Visa card. You can change money at the bank, the post office or any travel agency but there are no ATMs on the island.

The post office, obala Sveti Jurja 25, is open Monday to Saturday from 7 am to 9 pm, Sunday 9 am to noon. The postcode for Vis is 21480.

Mare Issae (☎/fax 711 877), Korzo 9 behind the Tamaris hotel, finds private accommodation, arranges excursions, rents wheels, changes money and sells local wine and souvenirs. Across the square from the tourist office is Darlić & Darlić (☎/fax 711 663), which offers the same services (minus the wine and souvenirs) and has an outlet in Komiža. Atlas travel agency (☎/fax 711 532), obala Sveti Jurja 36, arranges excursions. All agencies are open daily from 8 am to 1 pm and 6 to 9 pm in the summer, but keep shorter hours the rest of the year.

Things to See & Do The Archaeological Collection Issa at the Baterija Fortress, ŠetalisViški boj 12, is a good introduction to the town's historical sights. Exhibits include Greek and Roman pottery, jewellery and sculpture, including an exquisite 4th century bronze head of a Greek goddess that could be either Aphrodite or Artemis. The museum is open Tuesday to Sunday from 9 am to 1 pm and 5 to 7 pm in summer, but mornings only in winter. Admission is 10KN and you'll receive a leaflet giving an overview of the exhibits, the history of Vis and a useful map showing the locations of the ruins around town. Walk north from the dock about 100m and, behind the tennis court, you can see remains of a **Greek cemetery** next to remains of **Greek walls**. A few metres further along the coastal road, you'll see remains of **Roman Baths** behind a fence. During their four-year rule over the island during the Napoleonic Wars (1811-1815), the English built several **fortresses** on hills around the bay; the one on the northern corner is the most prominent.

Scenic coastal roads with dramatic cliffs and hairpin turns make it worthwhile to rent your own wheels for a day. You can rent scooters for 170KN a day at Mare Issae or Darlić & Darlić travel agencies, mountain bikes for 60KN a day and Go-Peds for 120KN a day.

Diving is excellent in the waters around Vis. Fish are plentiful and there's a wreck of an Italian boat dating from the 1866 naval battle between Austria and Italy. Poseidon Diving in the Hotel Issa (☎ 711 124) arranges boat dives for about 160KN per dive not including equipment. You could also try Manta Diving Center (☎/fax 711 663) in Komiža.

Organised Tours The island is best appreciated by boat and a trip that includes the Blue Grotto at Biševo (see below) is a must. You can book an all-day 'fish picnic' at Darlić & Darlić for 150KN which includes a visit to the Blue Grotto, stops at various secluded beaches and a fish lunch with wine aboard the boat in the 'Green Cave'. If the agency is closed look for the boat with the 'Fish Picnic' sign on the dock.

Places to Stay There are no camping grounds in Vis and only two hotels but you should have no trouble finding private accommodation, whether rooms or apartments. You'll have to rent through an agency however, since women offering *sobe* at the ferry landing are rare.

Private Rooms Mare Issae and Darlić & Darlić travel agencies have private rooms and apartments at reasonable rates. You'll pay about 70KN per person for a room and 210KN for a small studio with a kitchenette

and bathroom plus a 30% surcharge for stays under three nights. Darlić & Darlić has cheaper budget and mid-range rooms for as low as 50KN per person in high season.

Hotels The two hotels in town are located on opposite ends of Luka town and have exactly the same prices. *Hotel Tamaris* is on Sveti Jurja about 100m south-east of the ferry dock, while *Hotel Issa* is larger and on a pebbly beach about 200m north of the town centre. A single/double costs 252/414KN in high season, about 30% less in the shoulder season and 40% less off season.

Places to Eat There are a few pizzerias, a market in the square next to *Tamaris* hotel, and *AS* seafood restaurant on the ferry dock, but none can match the extraordinary experience of eating in the *Villa Kaliopa* (*V. Nazora 32*) between Luka and Kut. The restaurant is located in the exotic gardens of the 16th century Gariboldi mansion. Palm trees, bamboo and classical statuary provide a romantic setting for a menu of Dalmatian specialties that are pricey but manageable if you choose carefully.

Komiža

On the western coast at the foot of Hum hill, Komiža is a captivating small town on a bay, with sand and pebble beaches on the eastern end. Narrow back streets lined with tawny 17th and 18th century houses twist uphill from the port which has been used by fishermen at least since the 12th century. To the east of the town is a 17th century church on the site of a Benedictine monastery and at the end of the main wharf is a Renaissance citadel dating from 1585.

The bus from Vis stops at the edge of town next to the post office and a few blocks away from the Citadel. Walking all the way around the harbour you'll come to the municipal tourist office (☎ 713 455) at Riva 1. Next door is the Darlić & Darlić travel agency (☎ 713 137), which can arrange private accommodation (same prices as Vis town). If you're in the mood to spend more money, head in the opposite direction around the harbour and you'll come to **Hotel Biševo** (*☎ 713 144, Ribarska 72*), which has rooms for 290/440 a single/double in high season. Nearby is the restaurant **Bako** (*Gundulićeva 1*), with a cool stone interior that contains a fish pond and a collection of Greek and Roman amphorae.

Around Komiža

Biševo The tiny islet of Biševo has little but vineyards, pine trees and a spectacular **Blue Grotto** (Modra Špilja). Between 11 am and noon the sun's rays pass through an underwater opening in this coastal cave to bathe the interior in an unearthly blue light. Beneath the crystal-blue water, rocks glimmer in silver and pink to a depth of 16m. Wear a bathing suit and bring a face mask and snorkel since the boats stop for a 10 minute swim. The experience is unforgettable. Unless you have your own boat you'll

need to book an excursion from a travel agency in Vis or Komiža. At a price of 65KN, it's one of the world's great bargains.

BRAČ

• pop 13,824   ☎ 021

As the largest island in Central Dalmatia, Brač offers two major resorts, several sleepy villages and a dramatic Mediterranean landscape of pines, maquis and steep cliffs sloping onto a rocky coast. The climate is sunny, hot and dry in the long summer and mild and rainy in winter. The island boasts over 2700 hours of sunshine a year, which is great for tourism but makes farming a challenge. In the interior you'll see piles of rocks, gathered by women throughout the ages to prepare the stony land for cultivation. With such backbreaking labour, the islanders have produced wine, olive oil, figs, almonds and sour cherries,

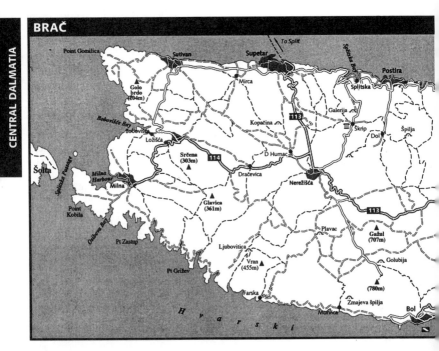

but Brač's main export is stone. Diocletian's palace in Split and the White House in Washington DC were built from Brač's lustrous white stone which is still quarried and exported.

Breaking rocks for a living has its drawbacks, of course. Many islanders have emigrated, leaving villages in the dry interior nearly empty. The coastal villages of Supetar and Bol are now a magnet for sun-and-sea-holiday tourists but the stone streets still evoke the intimacy of small-town life.

Remnants of a Neolithic settlement were found in Kopačina cave near Supetar but the first recorded inhabitants were the Illyrians, who built a fort in Škrip to protect against Greek invasion. The Romans arrived in 167 BC and promptly set to work exploiting the stone quarries near Škrip and building summer mansions around the island. Slavs settled the island in the 9th century, gather-ing in the interior to escape the notorious Dalmatian pirates. During the four centuries of Venetian rule (1420-1797), the interior villages were devastated by plague and the inhabitants moved to the 'healthier' settlements along the coast, revitalising the towns of Supetar, Bol, Sumartin and Milna. After a brief period of Napoleonic rule, the island passed into Austrian hands. Wine cultivation expanded until the phylloxera epidemic at the turn of the 20th century ravaged the island's vines and people began leaving for North and South America, especially Chile. The island endured a reign of terror during the WWII when German and Italian troops looted and burned villages, imprisoning and murdering inhabitants. Tourism on the island developed under the former Yugoslavia but has been much reduced since the recent war, even though Brac was untouched by the fighting.

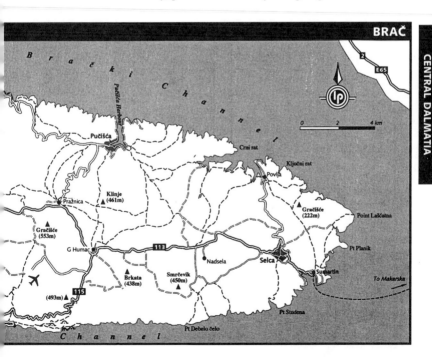

Getting There & Away There are 13 car ferries a day between Split and Supetar in summer (one hour, 16KN) and seven a day at other times of the year. The ferry drops you off in the centre of town only steps from the bus station. Buses leave five times a day for the 40 minute ride to Bol, five times a day to Milna and three times a day to Škrip.

Public transport to island highlights is sparse so you may wish to have your own wheels if you want to see a few sites in a short time.

Jadrolinija runs a passenger hydrofoil between Bol and Split (70KN return) daily but the scheduling is largely for the convenience of islanders who work in Split and you can only get an evening boat back from Bol to Split from Thursday through Sunday in the summer. The boat has air-con and the trip only takes 1¼ hours, with a stop at Milna. Boats leave from the small boat harbour in Bol and you can buy your ticket aboard the boat, but if you're coming from Split it's cheaper to buy a return ticket there.

Getting Around Supetar is the hub for bus transport around the island. There are five buses a day that connect Supetar with Bol (40 minutes) but not all of them connect with the ferries from Split. There are also five buses a day to Milna and three daily buses to Škrip. With such infrequent service you may wish to have your own wheels if you want to see a number of sites in a short time.

Supetar

With regular year-round ferry connections to Split and buses to villages around the island, Supetar makes an excellent day trip from Split or jumping-off point for an island visit. The beaches are an easy stroll from the town centre and the cluster of Austrian-style buildings around the port lend the town an easy-going charm.

Orientation Supetar is easy to navigate since most offices, stores and agencies are on the main road that radiates roughly east-west from the harbour. Called Porat at the harbour, the road becomes Hrvatskih Velikana in the east and Vlačica on to Put Vele Luke as it travels west. There are five rocky beaches on the coast. Vrilo beach is about 100m east of the town centre. Walking west, you'll come first to Vlačica then Banj beach lined with pine trees, then Bili Rat, site of the water sports centre, and then cut across St Nikolaus Cape on to Vela Luka beach. The bus station is next to the Jadrolinija office and has no left-luggage office.

Information The Turistički Ured (☎/fax 630 551), Porat 1, is only a few steps east of the harbour and has a full array of brochures and leaflets on activities and sights in Supetar. It's open daily from 8 am to 10 pm in the summer. Jadrolinija (☎ 631 357), Hrvatskih Vekikana bb, is about 50m east of the harbour.

In addition to travel agencies you can change money at Privredna Banka Zagreb at the dock, open Monday to Friday from 8 am to 2 pm and 3 to 8.30 pm.

Splitska Banka, Vlačića 13, is open Monday to Friday from 8 to 11 am and 6 to 8 pm, Saturday 8 to 11 am. There's an ATM outside the Jadrolinija office.

The main post office on Vlačica 9 is open Monday to Saturday from 7 am to 9 pm and Sunday 9 am to noon. You can change money or withdraw cash on your Master-Card. The postal code for Supetar is 21400.

Supetar Tours (☎ 631 066, fax 630 022) at Hrvatskih Velikana bb is about 50m east of the ferry dock and is open daily from 7 am to 3 pm and 5 to 10 pm in the summer; it keeps shorter hours off season. Atlas travel agency (☎/fax 631 088) at Porat 10 is also near the harbour and holds mail for American Express clients.

MB Rent-a-Car (☎ 630 709) is a few doors up from the Jadrolinija office and rents cars for 320KN a day (unlimited kilometres, tax and insurance are included in this price), scooters for 150KN a day (85KN for three hours) and bicycles for 15KN an hour, or 60KN a day.

CENTRAL DALMATIA

Things to See & Do The baroque **Church of the Annunciation** west of the harbour was built in 1733. Although the exterior is plain except for the semicircular entrance staircase, the interior is painted in cool, minty pastels and contains an interesting set of altar paintings, particularly the altar painting of the Annunciation from the school of Giambattista Pittoni.

The cemetery is at the tip of St Nikolaus Cape and you can't miss the monumental **Mausoleum of the Petrinović family**. The sculptor Toma Rosandić from Split incorporated elements of Byzantine style into this impressive structure that dominates the tip of the cape.

The best **diving** on the island is found off the south-western coast between Bol and Milna, making Bol a better base for divers, but you can book dives, take a diving course and rent equipment at the Hotel Pliva or Hotel Kaktus. Two boat dives in a day cost 285KN, but this doesn't include equipment, which can run up to 200KN a day.

Although the island is too big to circle around in a day, **renting a boat** to explore the various coves and inlets makes a great outing. You can rent a motorboat from Lucija (☎ 631 131) who has a stall at Banj beach and at the dock. The price is 80KN an hour and 300KN a day.

Speedboats are available at Bili Rat beach at a cost of 100KN for 15 minutes or you can **water ski** (70KN for 15 minutes), or hire a fast boat to tug you in a 'banana' (30KN for 15 minutes) or in small rubber rafts (150KN for 15 minutes).

Special Events Supetar Summer Cultural Festival lasts from June through September. Folk music, dances and classical concerts are presented several times a week in public spaces and churches. Tickets to festival events are usually free or cost very little, and there are also frequent art exhibits around town.

Places to Stay For such a small place, Supetar has a good range of accommodation options.

Camping Camping Supetar (☎ 631 066) is a mid-sized autocamp about 300m east of town behind *Babura* (☎ 631 634), a smaller and more recent operation. Both camps have access to a small rocky beach.

Private Rooms During the summer women often meet the ferries offering sobe at a good price but without the quality control of an agency. The most reliable agency is Supetar Tours, which offers singles in good quality rooms, often with private facilities, for 138/202KN in the high season (plus a 30% supplement if you stay less than three nights). The price drops 20% in the shoulder season and 30% off season. They will also find you private apartments for 724KN a night for a four-person apartment.

Pensions Pansion Palute (☎ 631 541, Put Pašika 16) is a small, family run pension that is open all year. Rooms cost 140/240KN a single/double with breakfast plus residence tax. Half board costs 190KN per person in a single and 175KN per person in a double. The food is good so it may be worthwhile to take half board and enjoy the occasional outdoor cook-outs for the guests.

Pansion Zelić (☎ 630 018, Šibnja 15) is a little cheaper at 126KN per person but also offers a pleasant, familial environment.

Hotels Hotel Kaktus and its annexes Olea and Savia, together with Kaktus Apartments and Hotel Palma, are part of a huge tourist complex on the western edge of town that includes a sports centre, tennis school, two outdoor pools and a panoply of outdoor activities, including diving and windsurfing. For a sprawling development of this kind, the landscaping is surprisingly pleasant with pine trees, shrubbery and a nearby beach.

Hotel Kaktus (☎ 631 133, fax 631 344) and its annexes are the most luxurious and expensive of these establishments with prices that begin at 186/278KN a single/double in the off season and jump to

CENTRAL DALMATIA

470/614KN in July and August. The large rooms have balconies, satellite TV and minibars. *Hotel Palma (☎ 631 363)* offers simpler rooms (no telephone or TV) that begin at 162/240KN off season and go up to 357/464KN in high season. *Kaktus Apartments (☎ 631 133)* offers fully equipped apartments that cost around 700KN a night for a four-person apartment with TV, telephone, balcony (sometimes with barbecue facilities), two double rooms plus a pull-out bed for two other people.

Reservations for all the above establishments are made by Supetrus Agency (☎ 630 200, fax 631 344) at Put Vele Luke 4.

Hotel-Restaurant Bretanide (☎/fax 631 038, Hrvatskih velikana 26) is a small hotel and restaurant on the eastern end of town across the street from the autocamp Babura and a narrow, rocky beach. All rooms are pleasantly furnished in a Mediterranean style with telephone and satellite TV but try to get one of the rooms facing the sea for the view and the cool breeze. Prices in high season are 210/330KN with breakfast. Half and full board are also available.

Pliva Complex (☎ 631 247, fax 630 011, put Vele Luke) is another tourist development farther west out of town that offers basic but clean rooms for 100KN per person. The hotel was built as a 'workers resort' by the ex-Yugoslavian government but the simple rooms are clean and well maintained. There are three buildings in the complex; Vrilo and Vlačica are closest to the beach.

Places to Eat *Vinotoka (put Gustirne Luke)* is a rustic tavern-style restaurant that pays special attention to serving shellfish in a variety of sauces. Fish is served by the portion rather than by weight, which makes ordering easier; there are also a few vegetarian plates including a crispy Greek salad. You'll see signs on the western edge of the harbour. It's open daily from noon to midnight.

Jastog (ulica Ive Lole Ribara 7) near the Hotel Palma offers somewhat more elegant dining and an excellent selection of seafood

and local dishes. It's open Monday to Saturday from noon to midnight.

Bistro Palute next to Atlas travel agency on the harbour specialises in grilled meat but fish dishes are also good. Dining is casual and you can get local dishes for only 32KN to 55KN. It's open daily from 10 am to 1 am.

Entertainment *Fenix (put Vele Luke 2)* is the local disco on the western edge of town, and there's a nightclub and small disco in *Hotel Kaktus*.

Bol

• pop 1478　　☎ 021

Bol is an example of how to maximise tourism without wrecking the landscape. Virtually all hotels are in a pine forest west of town within easy reach of Zlatni Rat beach. A coastal promenade shaded by pine trees connects the town centre with the hotels, preserving the rustic tranquillity of the beaches and coves. The old town is attractive but the real highlight is Zlatni Rat, the protruding sliver of beach that appears in almost all Croatian tourist brochures.

Orientation The town centre is a pedestrian area that stretches east from the bus station. Zlatni Rat beach is 2km west of town and in between are Borak and Potočine beaches. Behind them are several hotel complexes including the Borak, Elaphusa and Bretanide.

Information The Turistički Ured (☎ 635 122, fax 635 638) at Porat Boskih Pomoraca is a good source of information on town events. It's open daily from 8 am to 11 pm in the summer.

You can change money at Splitska Banka, Frana Radica, open Monday to Friday from 8 am to noon and 6 to 8 pm, or at Zagrebačka Banka, Uz Pyacu 4, open Monday to Friday from 8 am to 1 pm and Saturday 8 to 11.30 am. There are also a number of change places in the port area. There's an ATM outside Zagrebačka Banka where you can get a cash advance on MasterCard.

The post office, Uz Pjacu 1, is open Monday to Saturday from 7 am to 9 pm and Sunday 9 am to noon. You can change money, get cash on MasterCard, or make phone calls from here. The postcode for Bol is 21420.

Boltours (☎ 635 693), Vladimira Nazora 18, books excursions and finds private accommodation. It's open daily during the summer from 8.30 am to 10 pm but keeps shorter hours off season. Atlas travel agency (☎ 635 233, fax 635 695) at Rudina 12 is open from 8 am to 1 pm and 6 to 9 pm in summer but mornings only off season.

Things to See Most people come to Bol for the unusual **Zlatni Rat** beach which extends like a tongue into the sea for about 500m from the western end of town. Made up of smooth white pebbles, the tip of the beach changes shape according to the wind and waves. Pine trees provide shade and rocky cliffs rise sharply behind the beach, making the setting one of the loveliest in Dalmatia.

East of the town centre on the Glavica peninsula is the **Dominican monastery** (Samostan Dominikanaca) and the **Church of Our Lady of Mercy** (crkva Gospe od Milosti). The monastery and church were built in 1475 on the site of a 12th century episcopal palace. The late Gothic church is notable for a late 16th century altar screen as well as ceiling paintings by the Croatian baroque painter Tripo Kikolija. The church is partly paved with tombstones, some of which have initials of various monastic orders or inscriptions in glagolitic script. Nearby is the monastery **museum** presenting prehistoric items excavated from the nearby Kopačina cave, a collection of ancient coins, amphorae and church vestments. The highlight of the collection is the altar painting *Madonna with Child and Saints* attributed to Tintoretto, for which the museum retains the original invoice of 270 Venetian ducats. The museum is open daily April to October from 10 am to noon and 5 to 7 pm. Admission is 5KN. The church can be visited free of charge.

Galerija Dešković on Porat Bolskih Pomoraca has interesting exhibitions of contemporary Croatian art.

Activities Bol is the **windsurfing capital** of Croatia and the action takes place at Potočine beach, west of town. Although the westerly *maestral* blows from April to October, the best windsurfing is at the end of May and beginning of June, and at the end of July and beginning of August. The wind generally reaches its peak in the early afternoon and then dies down at the end of the day.

There are three outfitters along the beach: Orca, Big Blue and Bic Centar. Prices are roughly the same, so pick your spot according to where the wind is whipping up. A half-day 'funboard' rental costs from 165KN to 180KN; five hours on a school board runs from 200KN to 235KN, and an eight hour beginners' course will cost you about 800KN.

There are professional-quality clay tennis courts at the **Tennis Centre** (Zlatni Rat) along the road to Murvica; call ☎ 306 253 for bookings. Prices run from 35KN to 55KN an hour, depending on the time of day, and a tennis pro will help you work on your serve (or whatever) for 85/125KN an hour (one/two people). Rackets and balls can be rented.

You can **scuba dive** with Big Blue (☎/fax 635 614) at Potočine beach, which offers a certification course for 1765KN, a beginners' introduction to diving for 255KN and boat dives for 165KN. There are no wrecks to dive but there are some coral reefs at 40m and a large cave. Their office adjoins the Borak hotel and boats go out regularly during the season.

You can rent **motorboats** from a stall at Potočine Beach opposite the Bretanide hotel for 300KN a day or 70KN an hour. In the evening the same stall is in the harbour. Call the Bretanide (☎ 635 367) for information.

Delta Rent-a-Bike has a stall in front of the Bretanide and will rent mountain **bikes** for 15KN an hour and 70KN a day.

CENTRAL DALMATIA

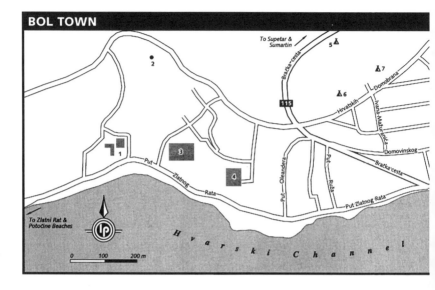

BOL TOWN

To Supetar &
Sumartin

5

To Zlatni Rat &
Potočine Beaches

0   100   200 m

H   v   a   r   s   k   i   C   h   a   n   n   e   l

Organised Tours Most of the excursions are run by Atlas travel agency. You can go to Mljet for 315KN, Krka waterfalls for 270KN, the 16th century monastery at Blaca for 60KN and rafting on the Cetina River for 350KN. You can also go by foot to Dragon's Cave, an extremely unusual set of reliefs probably carved by an imaginative 15th century friar. Carved angels, animals and a gaping dragon decorate the walls of this strange cave in a blend of Christianity and Croat pagan symbols. The cave is closed to the public but the manager of Galerija Dešković on Porat Bolskih Pomoraca has the key to the cave and can be persuaded to walk you out there for about 100KN. First you walk 5km to Murvica and then it's a one hour walk to the cave. The gallery is open daily from 5 to 10 pm.

Special Events There's a 'Summer Cultural Festival' in Bol in which dancers and musicians from around the country perform in churches and open spaces. The patron saint of Bol is Our Lady of Carmel; on her feast day (5 August) there's a procession

with residents dressed up in traditional costumes as well as music and feasting on the streets.

Places to Stay As elsewhere along the coast, there are few small hotels but several large tourist complexes. The hill between the town and the coast has been almost entirely given over to the Borak, Elaphusa and Bretanide resorts; the area remains appealing though as the development blends in well with the landscape.

Camping The campsites are near town and relatively small-sized. West of town, near the big hotels, try *Camping Barhanović* (☎ 635 630) or *Camp Ranč* (☎ 635 132). Both are on Hrvatskih Domobrana. *Camp Kito* (☎ 635 551) is nearby on Bračka Cesta. East of town near the Dominican monastery there's *Dominikanski Samostan* (☎ 635 132) on Šetalište Andeleka Rabadana.

Private Rooms Bol Tours finds private accommodation for 80/110KN a single/double in high season with private bath-

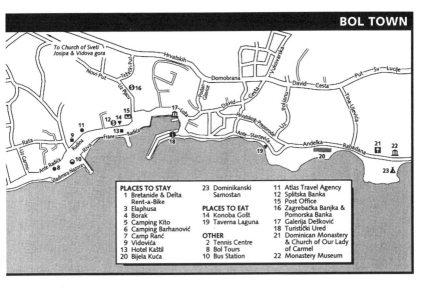

BOL TOWN

PLACES TO STAY
1 Bretanide & Delta
   Rent-a-Bike
3 Elaphusa
4 Borak
5 Camping Kito
6 Camping Barhanović
7 Camp Ranć
9 Vidovića
13 Hotel Kaštil
20 Bijela Kuća

23 Dominikanski
   Samostan

PLACES TO EAT
14 Konoba Gošt
19 Taverna Laguna

OTHER
2 Tennis Centre
8 Bol Tours
10 Bus Station

11 Atlas Travel Agency
12 Splitska Banka
15 Post Office
16 Zagrebačka Banjka &
   Pomorska Banka
17 Galerija Dešković
18 Turistički Ured
21 Dominican Monastery
   & Church of Our Lady
   of Carmel
22 Monastery Museum

---

room and 64/84KN for a room with a shared bathroom. Prices drop about 10% in the shoulder season and about 25% April through June and September through October. A four-person equipped apartment costs 390KN in high season. Add residence tax and a 20% surcharge for stays less than three nights.

Hotels The best deal for active vacationers is a stay at the hotel **Borak** which is ground zero for nearly all sporting activities. The hotel offers an all-inclusive rate of 630/ 1050KN a single/double in high season that includes all food and drinks as well as unlimited hours diving, windsurfing or playing tennis. The rate drops to 560/910KN at the beginning and end of July and August, 385/630KN in June and September and 297/490 other times. Prices are based on a minimum three night stay. Children under 12 get reductions and there are scheduled activities for kids. As might be expected, the clientele includes families, sporty types and boozers.

Also on the hill are the hotels Bretanide and Elaphusa. The **Bretanide** charges 468/648KN a single in high season and the Elaphusa slightly less since the hotel is awaiting renovation. Of all three hotels, the Bretanide is closest to Zlatni Rat beach.

On the eastern end of town is the hotel **Bijela Kuća** (*Šetalište Andelka Rabadana*), a 201 room concrete structure that charges 270/414KN a single/double in high season. *Hotel Kaštil (Frane Radić a 1)*, in the town centre, is slightly less expensive but noisy on summer nights.

Reservations at all the above hotels are handled by Zlatni Rat Marketing (☎ 635 222, fax 306 215, www.bol.hr).

Vidovića (*☎/fax 635 450 or ☎/fax 635 158, Rubina 36*) is a small hotel-restaurant offering only nine rooms that are air-conditioned and equipped with satellite TV and telephone. For a bed and breakfast you pay 270/400KN a single/double but half-board is only 90KN per person extra and the food is excellent.

Places to Eat It would be hard to find a definitively bad meal in Bol since the restaurant scene is competitive. Fish is

CENTRAL DALMATIA

always fresh; the only difference is in the subtlety of the sauces and the chef's ability to cook it at exactly the right temperature.

Vidovića (Rubina 36) is one of the best seafood places in a town, filled with fresh, tasty fish and shellfish. It's pricier than other establishments but the chef has a way with sauces and the dining is slightly more elegant than usual. Locals come here for a special night out. *Konobo Gušt*, behind the Hotel Kaštil, offers good, informal tavern-style dining in a setting of burnished wood, old photos and knick knacks. The fish and meat dishes are prepared simply but correctly and you can get a plate of fried calamari with vegetables and potatoes for 60KN. *Taverna Laguna* is in a romantic spot next to a quiet lagoon east of the town centre that would make the restaurant a stand-out even if the food was mediocre. The pasta and seafood dishes are far better than average and you can have a decent meal with a drink for 70KN.

Entertainment After strolling the harbourside promenade or the marble road to Zlatni Rat, night-owls usually head to *Faces Club*, the 2000-person disco on the road to Gorni Humac, about 1km out of town. There are also small nightclubs at the Elaphusa and Bretanide hotels, and live entertainment on the patio of the hotel Borak.

Sumartin

Sumartin is a quiet, pretty port with a few rocky beaches and little to do, but it makes a nice retreat from the busier tourist centres of Bol and Supetar. The bus station is in the centre of town next to the ferry, and Tourism Sumartin (☎ 648 028) right on the dock will help you find private accommodation if you decide to stay.

Getting There & Away Sumartin is the entry point on Brač if you're coming from Makarska. There are from two to five daily car ferries from Makarska to Sumartin, depending on the season. Buses go from Sumartin to Supetar but only very early in the morning and late afternoon.

AROUND BRAČ

Illyrians, Romans and early Christians came, stayed and built on Brač, mostly in the interior. One of the more interesting sites is the village of **Škrip**, the oldest settlement on the island, about 8km south of Supetar. Formerly a refuge of the ancient Illyrians, the Romans took over the fort in the 2nd century BC, followed by inhabitants of Solin fleeing 7th century barbarians and eventually early Slavs. Remains of the Illyrian wall are visible around the citadel in the south-east corner. The most intact Roman monument on the island is the mausoleum at the base of Radojković's tower, a fortification built during the Venetian-Turkish wars. The tower is now a museum. Sarcophagi from the early Christian period are near Cerinić's citadel with a nearby quarry containing a relief of Hercules from the 3rd or 4th century. You can catch an early morning bus from Supetar and an early afternoon bus back.

The port of **Milna**, 20km south-west of Supetar, is the kind of lovely, intact fishing village that, in any other part of the world, would have been long ago commandeered by package tourists. The 17th century town is set at the foot of a deep natural harbour that was used by Emperor Diocletian on the way to Split. Paths and walks take you around the harbour which is studded with coves and rocky beaches that are usually deserted. Besides the picture-perfect setting, there's the 18th century Church of Our Lady of the Annunciation with a baroque front and early 18th century altar paintings. Milna is an easy day trip from Supetar, with a morning bus to the town and an afternoon bus back to Supetar. During the summer, the early evening hydrofoil from Bol stops at Milna before going on to Split.

HVAR
- pop 11,459   ☎ 021

Called the 'Croatian Madeira', Hvar receives a total of 2724 hours of sunshine each year, more than anywhere else in the country. Yet the island is luxuriantly green, with brilliant patches of lavender, rosemary and heather. The fine weather is so reliable that hotels give a discount on cloudy days and a free stay if you should ever see snow. There have been eight snowy days in the last ten years.

The island's allure has not gone unnoticed by cruise ship operators who regularly call on Hvar town. The town centre can become frenzied in July and August but there's so much to explore around the island that you won't mind escaping the town for a breather.

Part of Hvar's scenic splendour is Sveti Nikola, the crest that stretches across the middle of the island, 628m at the highest peak. The northern part of the island is defined by the fertile Velo Polje plain and a highly indented coastline dotted with coves and inlets. Most of the interior villages developed around Velo Polje, which produces grapes, olives, figs and fruit. Lavender is cultivated on the slopes of the nearby hills. Most of the original forests were cleared, leaving small groves of fir and holm oak interspersed by low shrubs and macchia.

The island was first settled by the Illyrians, who fought numerous battles with Greek colonisers in the 4th century BC. The Greeks won and established the colony of Faros on the site of present-day Stari Grad. The Romans conquered the island in 219 BC but it was not an important outpost for the Romans and there are few remains from that period. With the collapse of the Roman Empire, Hvar came under Byzantine rule.

In the 7th and 8th centuries Slavic tribes settled the island and in the 11th century it became part of Croatia under King Petar Krešimir. After several centuries in which Venice, Byzantium and Croatian-Hungarian kings ruled the island, in 1331 it opted for the most powerful of the lot – Venice – as protection against the notorious pirates of Omiš. With a few interruptions, Venetian rule lasted until 1797.

The island staged several serious rebellions that were ruthlessly crushed by Venice's superior forces. After the fall of Venice in 1797, the island's history followed that of Dalmatia, passing to Austrian, French then Austrian rule before finally becoming part of the kingdom of Serbs, Croats and Slovenes after WWI.

Getting There & Away

The Jadrolinija ferries between Rijeka and Dubrovnik call at Hvar three or four times a week all year, stopping in Hvar town in winter and Stari Grad in summer before continuing on to Korčula. The Jadrolinija agency beside the landing sells tickets.

The local ferry from Split calls at Stari Grad (two hours, 23KN) three times a day and connects Hvar town with Vela Luka on Korčula island in the afternoon. Besides the local ferries that run from Split to Stari Grad there's a weekly Jadrolinija car ferry from Stari Grad to Ancona, Italy (244KN), stopping at Split.

The passenger boat *Adriana* sails July, August and the beginning of September connecting Hvar town with Split daily (one hour, 56KN) and travelling once a week to Vela Luka and three times a week to Korčula town.

It's possible to visit Hvar on a (hectic) day trip from Split by catching the morning Jadrolinija ferry to Stari Grad, a bus to Hvar town, then the last ferry from Stari Grad directly back to Split.

Getting Around

Buses meet all ferries that dock at Stari Grad and go to Hvar town and Jelsa. There are six buses a day between Stari Grad and Hvar town in the summer season (13KN) but services are reduced on Sunday and off season.

Hvar Town

Medieval Hvar lies between protective pine-covered slopes and the azure Adriatic, its Gothic palaces hidden among narrow backstreets below the 13th century city walls. A long seaside promenade winds along an indented coast dotted with small, rocky beaches. The traffic-free marble streets of Hvar have an air of Venice, and it was under Venetian rule that

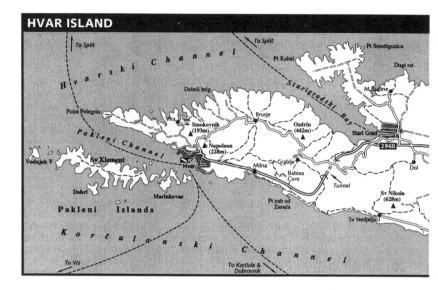

HVAR ISLAND

Hvar's citizens developed the fine stone carving skills that resulted in a profusion of beautifully ornamented buildings.

Orientation The main commercial street is the wide promenade that runs along the harbour which is where you'll find most sights. Trg Sveti Stjepana is the town square. On the northern slope above the square and within the old ramparts are the remains of some palaces which belonged to the Hvar aristocracy. Some hotels are along this stretch while others are north-west of the town centre. From the bus station to the harbour, the town is closed to traffic which preserves the medieval tranquillity of the town.

Information Hvar is a small, easily manageable town, and you'll have little trouble finding the information you need.

Tourist Offices The tourist office (☎ 741 059) is in the arsenal building on the corner of Trg Sveti Stjepana and is open Monday to Saturday from 8 am to 1.30 pm and 3.30 to 10 pm, Sunday 10 am to noon and 6 to 10 pm. Off season it's closed afternoons and all day Sunday.

The Jadrolinija office (☎ 741 132) on the harbour is open Monday to Saturday from 6.30 am to 1 pm and 2 to 9 pm, Sunday from 7 to 11.30 am, 2 to 5 pm and 7 to 8 pm.

Money There is an ATM outside the Jadrolinija office where you can withdraw cash using MasterCard, Eurocard or Cirrus. There is a Splitskabanka next to the Hotel Slavija that is open Monday to Friday from 8 am to 11.30 am and 6 to 8 pm and Saturday 8 to 11.30 am. Privedna Banka is open Monday to Friday from 9 am to noon and from 6 to 9 pm. Stedionica, the currency exchange place next to the Pelegrini travel agency, has good rates, and it's open daily between 7 am to 11 pm.

Post & Communications The post office is on the harbour and is open Monday to Friday from 7 am to 8 pm, Saturday 7 am to 5 pm. The postal code for Hvar is 21450.

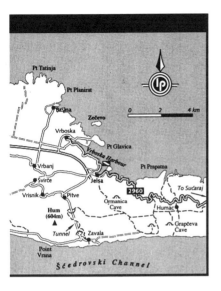

Travel Agencies Atlas travel agency (☎ 741 670) facing the harbour is open Monday to Saturday from 8 am to noon and 5.30 to 9.30 pm, Sunday 6 to 9 pm. Mengola travel agency (☎/fax 742 099) on the harbour is open Monday to Saturday from 8.30 am to 1 pm and 4 to 10 pm, Sunday 9 am to noon and 6 to 10 pm. Pelegrini (☎ 742 250) is also on the harbour and is open Monday to Saturday from 8 am to 12.30 pm and 4 to 10 pm, Sunday 9 am to noon and 6 to 10 pm.

Left Luggage There's no left-luggage facility at the bus station but the attendant at the public toilets beside the market adjoining the bus station holds luggage for 6KN a piece. The toilets are only open during market hours, so check the closing time carefully.

Things to See Begin your tour around town at the main square, **Trg Sveti Stjepana**, which was formed by filling in an inlet that once stretched out from the bay. At 4500 sq m, it's one of the largest old squares in Dalmatia. The town first developed in the 13th century to the north of the square and later spread south of the square in the 15th century. Notice the well in the middle of the square which was built in 1520, and has a wrought iron grill dating from 1780.

On the south side of the square is the **Arsenal** built in 1611 to replace a previous building destroyed by the Turks. Mentioned in Venetian documents as 'the most beautiful and the most useful building in the whole of Dalmatia', the Arsenal once served as a repair and re-fitting station for war galleons. Although the 10m span of the arches now curves over souvenir shops, you can try to visualise the immense interior of this structure.

The north side of the building was used to store food, and in 1612 a **theatre** was built that is reported to be the first theatre in Europe open to plebeians and aristocrats alike. The theatre remained a regional cultural centre throughout the centuries, and plays are still staged there for small audiences only – the old building is too unstable to support crowds. The theatre can be entered from the adjoining **Gallery of Contemporary Croatian Art** which is open daily from 9 am to noon and 8.30 to 10.30 pm summers only as well as Christmas week and Holy Week.

Another landmark building in Hvar town is the **Cathedral of St Stjepan** which forms a stunning backdrop to the square. The bell tower rises four levels, each more elaborate than the last in a biforium, triforium and quatriforium design. The cathedral was built in the 16th and 17th centuries at the height of the Dalmatian Renaissance on the site of a previous cathedral destroyed by the Turks. Parts of the older cathedral are visible in the nave and in the carved 15th century choir stalls but most of the interior dates from the 16th and 17th centuries. The cathedral can be visited twice a day, half an hour before Mass.

Behind the tower and adjoining the cathedral is the **Bishop's Palace** which houses the cathedral treasury of silver vessels, embroidered Mass robes, numerous Madonnas, a couple of 13th century icons and an elaborately carved sarcophagus. It's open in summer only from 9 am to noon and 5 to 7 pm as well as Christmas week and Holy Week.

West of the square, you'll come first to the unfinished Gothic **Hektorović Mansion**. Go up a few stairs to the **Benedictine monastery**, which has a collection of paintings and icons from the convent treasury and an interesting collection of lace painstakingly woven by the nuns from dried agave leaves. It's open in summer from 9 am to noon and 5 to 7 pm as well as Christmas week and Holy Week.

Next you'll see the 16th century **Loggia** in front of the Palace hotel. In front of it is an 18th century column *Štandarac* from which governmental decisions used to be announced. The same road will take you to the remains of the Dominican **Church of St Marko**, which was destroyed by the Turks in the 16th century. In the apse there's a small **archaeological museum** which is usually closed.

Return to the **Town Gate** and you'll find yourself in a network of tiny streets with small palaces, churches and old houses.

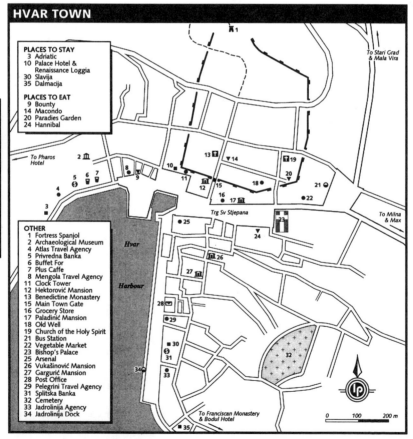

HVAR TOWN

PLACES TO STAY
3 Adriatic
10 Palace Hotel & Renaissance Loggia
30 Slavija
35 Dalmacija

PLACES TO EAT
9 Bounty
14 Macondo
20 Paradies Garden
24 Hannibal

OTHER
1 Fortress Spanjol
2 Archaeological Museum
4 Atlas Travel Agency
5 Privredna Banka
6 Buffet For
7 Plus Caffe
8 Mengola Travel Agency
11 Clock Tower
12 Hektorović Mansion
13 Benedictine Monastery
15 Main Town Gate
16 Grocery Store
17 Paladinić Mansion
18 Old Well
19 Church of the Holy Spirit
21 Bus Station
22 Vegetable Market
23 Bishop's Palace
25 Arsenal
26 Vukašinović Mansion
27 Gargurić Mansion
28 Post Office
29 Pelegrini Travel Agency
31 Splitska Banka
32 Cemetery
33 Jadrolinija Agency
34 Jadrolinija Dock

To Stari Grad & Mala Vira

To Pharos Hotel

Trg Sv Stjepana

To Milna & Max

Hvar

Harbour

To Franciscan Monastery & Bodul Hotel

0   100   200 m

Climb up through a park to the **Fortress Španjol** citadel, built on the site of a medieval castle to defend the town from the Turks. It was strengthened in 1557 and then again in the 19th century by the Austrians who added barracks. Inside is a tiny collection of ancient amphorae recovered from the seabed, and the view over the harbour is magnificent.

Returning to town, proceed south along the harbour to the 15th century **Franciscan monastery** that overlooks a shady cove. The elegant bell tower was built in the 16th century by a well-known family of stone masons from Korčula. The Renaissance cloister leads to a refectory containing lace, coins, nautical charts and valuable documents such as an edition of Ptolemy's *Atlas* printed in 1524. Your eye will immediately be struck by *The Last Supper*, an 8m x 2.5m work by the Venetian Matteo Ingoli dating from the end of the 16th century. The cypress in the cloister garden is said to be more than 300 years old. The adjoining church, named Our Lady of Charity, contains more fine paintings such as the three polyptichs created by Francesco da Santacroce in 1583, which represent the summit of this painter's work, and the *Cruxifixion* by Leandro Bassano on the altar. Below the altar is the tomb of Hannibal Lucić, 16th century author of *Female Slave*, the first non-religious drama in Croatia. The Renaissance relief over the portal, *Madonna with Child*, is a small gem created by Nikola Firentinac in 1470. The monastery is open daily in the summer from 9 am to noon and 5 to 7 pm as well as Christmas week and Holy Week.

As you return north, stroll through the old streets and notice the **Vukašinović palace** with its seven balconies, monumental entrance and the 15th century **Gargurović palace**.

Activities The Diving Center (☎ 742 490) at the Hotel Amphora offers **scuba diving** for 122/245KN for one or two boat dives respectively plus full equipment rental of 175KN. They also offer mountain bike rentals for 53KN a day and 245KN a week, motorboat rental for 182KN a day, snorkelling equipment for 31KN a day and waterskiing at 70KN for 15 minutes.

There are coves around the hotel Amphora and the Hotel Dalmacija for **swimming** but most people head to the Pakleni Islands (Pakleni Otoci) which got their name from Paklina, the resin that once coated boats and ships. Taxi boats leave regularly during the season from in front of the Arsenal to the islands of Jerolim and Stipanska which are popular naturist islands (although nudity is not mandatory) and then continue on to Zdrilca and Palmižana. The cost is 10KN to 25KN depending on the destination.

If you can tear yourself away from the sea, Hvar town makes a good starting point for several gentle **hikes**. You can walk to Vira cove (about 4km) by taking the path toward the Venetian fortress and then heading north-west. You'll come to the Austrian watchtower on Smokovnik hill (193m) and then descend to the tranquil cove where there are ten stone mounds, part of an Illyrian burial site.

There are two paths to the village of Milna on a cove, 2km south-east of town. You can walk along the coast or take a path that cuts through vineyards, olive groves and orchards. From Milna you can continue on what used to be the main road from Hvar to Stari Grad which partly follows an old Roman road.

After Milna head north-east to Malo Grablje past the church of St Vitus. You'll come to the Maslinica cove which you follow east to Stari Grad.

Street Names

A curious feature of Hvar is its lack of street names. You may stumble across a faded name on a plaque every so often but, in a small town where everyone knows everyone (except in the summer), street names seem superfluous to the residents.

CENTRAL DALMATIA

Organised Tours Atlas organises an island tour for 125KN, Biševo-Vis island hydrofoils for 220KN and a slower boat to Biševo for 170KN. They also run an 8km walking tour each Sunday that involves a bus to Veliko Grablje, a walk to Malo Grablje and then on to Milna for lunch.

Places to Stay – Camping A recent fire on the northern part of the island destroyed the only camp site convenient to Hvar town but there are frequent buses to Jelsa (see later in this chapter) where you can pitch a tent outside town.

Places to Stay – Private Rooms Mengola Travel and Pelegrini (☎/fax 742 250) are the only two agencies that find private accommodation. Expect to pay 100/158KN for a single/double with a 30% surcharge for stays less than three nights. Outside the peak season (which lasts from the final week in July through August), you can negotiate a much better price.

Places to Stay – Hotels As one of the Adriatic's most popular resorts, don't expect any bargains in the summer. The cheapest hotels are the *Dalmacija* (☎/fax 741 120) and the *Delfin* (☎/fax 741 168) on either side of the harbour, both charging 270/460KN a single/double with a 20% surcharge for a stay less than four nights. Both hotels open mid-June. The *Slavija* (☎ 741 820, fax 741 147) is open all year and offers better value for about 10KN more per person.

Then there is the *Pharos* (☎/fax 741 028) overlooking the town, with singles/doubles for 310/460KN a single/double. It's very near the disco Veneranda. The unattractive *Bodul* (☎/fax 741 744) is another package tour favourite and has singles/doubles for 334/504KN.

The *Hotel Palace* (☎ 741 966, fax 742 420) has more character than any of the modern hotels. Built at the turn of the century on the site of the Ducal palace, the hotel is behind an elegant 16th century loggia. Its luxuries include air-con and an

indoor swimming pool. Prices are from 378KN to 432KN for a single and 583KN to 684KN a double depending on the size and location of the room.

The two other luxury establishments are the *Adriatic* (☎/fax 741 024), on the western side of the harbour, and the *Amphora* (☎ 741 202, fax 741 711) around the cove. The Amphora costs 560/662KN a single/double, and the Adriatic is about 25KN less.

Places to Eat The pizzerias along the harbour offer the most predictable inexpensive eating, but for a step up try *Bounty*, next to the Mengola travel agency, which has good quality fish, pasta and grilled meat at prices that won't dent your budget.

Hannibal on the south side of Trg Sveti Stjepana has a good selection of pasta cooked with shrimp, lobster, fish or mushrooms and also grilled meat and fish dishes. Prices start at 35KN and you can either eat at a table on the square or in the spacious interior.

Paradise Garden up some stairs on the north side of the cathedral serves up a memorable spaghetti with seafood as well as the usual excellent assortment of grilled or fried fish. Dining is outdoors on an enclosed patio. Expect to pay about 45KN to 65KN for a main course.

Macondo, in a narrow alley over the main square, is slightly more expensive than the other restaurants and slightly better. The cold mixed plate offers two fish patés, octopus salad and salted anchovies which make a tasty opening to the main meal (fish specialties) or good light meal. The restaurants serve daily from noon until 2 pm and 6.30 pm to midnight.

The *grocery store* (Trg Sv Stjepana) is your best alternative to a restaurant, and there's a nice park in front of the harbour just made for picnics.

Entertainment Hvar has a very lively nightlife when the tourist season is in full swing. *Buffet For* is where local men drink but *Plus Caffe* next door is a 'meet market' for the suave set that cluster around the high tables and chairs sporting their tans. On summer evenings there's live music on the terrace of the Slavija hotel, just as you would expect to see in Venice. *Veneranda* above the Hotel Delfin is a former fortress that becomes an open-air cinema around 9.30 pm and then a disco later on. Raves are sometimes organised. *Max*, a new disco-club outside of town on the road to Milna, is another option. During the summer there are shuttle buses operating between the town and the club.

Shopping Lavender, lavender and more lavender is sold in small bottles, large bottles, flasks or made into sachets. Depending on the time of year, there will be anywhere from one to 50 stalls along the harbour selling the substance, odour saturating the air. Various herbal oils, potions, skin creams and salves are also hawked. Prices run anywhere from 10KN to 50KN depending on the size of the bottle.

Stari Grad

Stari Grad (Old Town), on the island's north coast, is older than Hvar town and is certainly attractive, though it can't compete with the stylish architecture and stunning setting of its more fashionable sister.

Although most ferries connecting the island to the mainland list Stari Grad as their port of call, in fact the town is a couple of kilometres north-east of the ferry dock and, since buses connect the ferries to Hvar town and Jelsa, Stari Grad can easily be bypassed. There are some worthwhile sights in the town however, and when Hvar town is wall to wall with vacationers, Stari Grad provides a little more breathing room.

Road signs around Stari Grad note a secondary name, 'Faros', a reference to the Greek colony that was founded here in 385 BC. The local population resisted Greek rule but the Greek navy from Issa (now Vis) defeated the islanders in one of the oldest historically confirmed naval battles.

The Romans ousted the Greeks in 219 BC, and razed the town. Later, Slavs settled the town and it became the political and cultural capital of the island until 1278, when the bishopric moved to Hvar town.

The town occupied itself with navigation and shipbuilding and in the 16th century the poet Petar Hektorović built a mansion here which has become the highlight of a visit to Stari Grad.

Orientation & Information Stari Grad lies along a horseshoe-shaped bay with the old quarter on the south side of the horseshoe. The bus station (no left-luggage facility) is at the foot of the bay and the north side is taken up by residences, a small pine wood and the sprawling Hotel Helios complex.

The Turistički Ured (☎ 761 763), Riva 2, has a good map and is open daily from 8 am to 2 pm and 6 to 9 pm in the summer but weekday mornings only off season. The post office is on the main square, Trg Tvrdalj, and is open from Monday to Saturday from 7 am to 9 pm, Sunday 9 am to noon. The postal code for Stari Grad is 21460.

Splitska Banka at Riva 12 is open Monday to Friday from 8 am to noon and 6 to 8 pm, Saturday 8 am to noon.

Things to See Tvrdalj on the square of the same name is Petar Hektorović's 16th century fortified castle. The leafy fish pond reflects the poet's love for fish and fishermen. His poem *Fishing and Fishermen's Chat* (1555) paints an enticing portrait of his favourite pastime. The castle also contains quotes from the poet's work inscribed on the walls in Latin and Croatian. From June to September the castle is open from 8 am to noon and 6 to 8 pm.

Another highlight of Stari Grad is the **Dominican monastery** which was founded in 1482, damaged by the Turks in 1571 and later fortified with a tower. In addition to the library and archaeological findings in the monastery museum, there is a 19th century church with *The Interment of Christ* attributed to Tintoretto, and two paintings by Gianbattista Crespi. The museum and monastery is open June to September from 9 am to noon and 6 to 8 pm.

CENTRAL DALMATIA

Places to Stay Off the harbour just east of the old town is *Kamp Jurjevac* (☎ 765 555), near swimming coves and open from June to early September. There are also fully equipped four-person bungalows for 237KN.

The only agency finding private accommodation is Mistral Agency (☎/fax 765 281, Grofa Vranjicanija 2) near the bus station. Singles/doubles with private facilities cost 100/162KN in July and August but 20% to 30% less the rest of the year.

The hotel complex *Helios* (☎ 765 555) has commandeered the north wing of the town with a string of modern hotels: the *Arkada*, the *Adriatic* and the *Helios*, with prices that run from 180KN to 200KN for a single and 300KN to 380KN for a double.

Jelsa

Jelsa is a small town, port and resort 27km north-east of Hvar town surrounded by thick pine forests and high poplars. Although it lacks the Renaissance buildings of Hvar, the intimate streets and squares are still pleasant and the town is within easy reach of swimming coves and sand beaches. Hotel accommodation is cheaper than Hvar town and there are two camping grounds outside of town.

Jelsa first emerged in the 14th century as a port for the inland village of Pitve and spread around the churches of Saints Fabian and Sebastian and St John in the Field. In the 16th century a fort was erected over the town to protect it from the Turks and by the 19th century it had grown into a prosperous fishing village.

In the middle of the 19th century the marshes around the coast were drained and the town gradually spread out. In 1881 it became the centre of Matica Hrvatska, a celebrated Croatian literary circle, and in 1868 the public library became the first public reading room in the Dalmatian islands.

Like most coastal villages, fishing has now given way to tourism and the town has become a popular alternative to Hvar.

Orientation & Information Jelsa is wrapped around a bay with several large hotels on each side and the old town at the foot of the harbour. A promenade stretches from the west end of the bay and rises up the hill on the eastern side leading to a sandy cove. The bus station is on the edge of the main road leading into town (no one bothers with street names) but has no left-luggage facility. As you proceed into town you'll come to the post office which is open Monday to Saturday from 7 am to 9 pm, Sunday 9 am to noon. The postal code for Jelsa is 21465.

Turning left at the harbour you'll find Atlas travel agency (☎ 761 038) at Obala bb. Across the street and along the quay is the Turistički Ured (☎/fax 761 017), Obala bb. It's open Monday to Saturday from 8.30 am to 12.30 pm and 6 to 8 pm, Sunday 9 am to noon.

Splitska Banka is on Trg Tome Gamulina on the east side of the harbour and is open Monday to Friday from 8 to 11.30 am and 6 to 8 pm, Saturday 8 to 11 am. You can change money at any travel agency but there is no ATM in Jelsa.

Things to See & Do Unfortunately, the Church of Saints Fabian & Sebastian is only open for Mass, but if you get there within 30 minutes before the service you can see a 17th century baroque altar by wood carver Antonio Porri and a wooden statue of the Virgin Mary brought by refugees from the village of Čitluk, near Sinj, who were fleeing the Turks in the 16th century.

In addition to the sand beach near the Hotel Mina, there is a daily taxi boat to the naturist beaches of Zečevo and Glavice (20KN return) or you can rent wheels and head across the hill to the coves surrounding the village of Zavala.

The hair-raising road is superbly scenic and takes you through the tiny village of Pitve, before descending to a number of isolated coves. The Island Tours agency (☎ 761 404) on the road to Mina rents scooters for 240KN a day and motorcycles for 300KN a day.

Dive Centre Jelsa (☎/fax 761 822) on the coastal road to the Hotel Fontana is the place to go for **scuba diving**, charging 122/245KN (not including equipment) for one or two boat dives.

Organised Tours Atlas offers more or less the same program as in Hvar town but the prices are sometimes a few kuna more or less. For example, it also offers rafting on the Cetina River for 350KN from Jelsa and 380KN from Hvar town.

Places to Stay & Eat Around the hotel Mina are the camping grounds *Grebišće* (☎ 761 191) and *Mina* (☎ 761 227), both of which have access to a beach. Island Tours finds private rooms for 8OKN per person in high season with a 30% surcharge for stays less than three nights. There is also the *Hotel Fontana* (☎ 761 028) that has singles/doubles for 270/396KN and *Mina* (☎ 761 122) with singles for 300/415KN. *Pizzeria Busola* on the road to Mina is Italian owned and makes extraordinarily good pizza and pasta.

Southern Dalmatia

Steeped in sunshine and bathed in mild Mediterranean breezes, the south-eastern tip of Croatia is a lush region of coves, forested islands and, its crowning jewel, the walled city of Dubrovnik. The coastal belt stretches from the disputed town of Ploče in the north to the Montenegrin border, and is separated from Hercegovina by the Dinaric mountains. Off the rocky shores lies the large island of Korčula and a flurry of smaller islands, including the idyllic national park of Mljet island. Together with the mountainous Pelješac Peninsula, the entire area comprises Dubrovnik-Neretva county. With the exception of Korčula island, the county largely follows the borders of the former independent Republic of Ragusa (Dubrovnik).

The lack of heavy industry or a large port has encouraged the inhabitants to rely on agriculture and tourism. The region is famous for its wines, especially the Postup and Dingač red wines of Pelješac, and the Posip and Grk white wines of Korčula. The production of wine and olive oil, fishing, and the cultivation of mussels and livestock has gradually given way to tourism as the main focus of economic activity, spearheaded by the international appeal of Dubrovnik.

Outside this magical city, large parts of the region attract relatively few tourists, surprising given the spectacular scenery and pristine sea. Unlike other parts of the Adriatic coast, however, there are no megaresorts here and no sprawling tourist settlements – which has discouraged mass tourism but makes individual travel especially rewarding.

HIGHLIGHTS

- Taking a walk on top of Dubrovnik's walls

- Watching the street action from a café on Placa

- Seeing a production of *Hamlet* in Croatian during Dubrovnik's summer festival

- Biking through the forests of Mljet Island

- Kayaking or canoeing on Mljet's lakes

- Sampling the white wines of Lumbarda

- Visiting the beaches of Orebić

- Approaching Korčula town by boat

BOSNIA-HERCEGOVINA

Korčula Island & Pelješac pp264-5

Korčula Town p267

Mljet pp262-3

Dubrovnik pp252-3
Dubrovnik-Old Town p254

Dubrovnik

• pop 49,700   ☎ 020

Only a handful of the world's cities can claim to represent an ideal larger than themselves and Dubrovnik is one of them. The thick stone walls that have protected the city for seven centuries against assault proclaim invincibility in the face of aggression. The wide marble street, Placa, lined with businesses, cafés, churches and palaces, encourage the fusion of commerce, pleasure and faith into a vibrant community life. The profusion of fine sculpture and architectural detail on public buildings and monuments underscores a common artistic heritage available to anyone who cares to look. The way in which the towering walls both define and blend into the landscape of sea, sky and hills is an argument for a human presence that enhances rather than spoils the environment.

For those who watched the shelling of Dubrovnik on TV in late 1991, here's a bit of good news: the city is still there, as beautiful as ever, with few visible reminders of recent trauma. Some buildings on back streets are still damaged but you don't see it as the shutters will be down and the windows closed. However, the eight-month siege by the federal army from October 1991 to May 1992 tore through the town's distinctive honey-coloured clay roofs. Replacing them with matching tiles was extremely problematic and you'll notice a patchwork of colours as you walk around the city walls (see the boxed aside overleaf, *Dubrovnik: Destruction and Reconstruction*). The most severe blow to Dubrovnik was in the catastrophic decline of tourism which left its residents feeling abandoned and apprehensive as well as much poorer. The city has recently begun to climb back and in July and August the streets are again crowded with visitors.

HISTORY

The story of Dubrovnik begins with the 7th century onslaught of barbarians that wiped out the Roman city of Epidaurum (site of present day Cavtat). The residents fled to the safest place they could find which was a rocky islet separated from the mainland by a narrow channel.

Recent excavations reveal that the islet was probably inhabited at the time but the new settlers increased the population and named their new sanctuary Laus, Greek for 'rock'. Eventually it became known as Rausa, Ragusa and Ragusium. This inaccessible settlement was located around the southern walls of present-day Dubrovnik.

Building walls was a matter of pressing urgency at the time, when barbarian invasions were a constant threat; it appears that the city was well fortified by the 9th century when it resisted a Saracen siege for 15 months.

The town had help in the form of the powerful Byzantine empire, however, under whose protection Ragusa remained from the 7th to the 12th century. Meanwhile another settlement emerged on the mainland, stretching from Zaton in the north to Cavtat in the south. This settlement became known as Dubrovnik after the holm-oak (*dubrava* in Croatian) that carpeted the region. The two settlements merged in the 12th century, and the channel that separated them was paved over to become Placa.

By the end of the 12th century Dubrovnik had become an important trading centre on the coast, providing an important link between the Mediterranean and Balkan states. From the hinterlands, cattle and dairy products, wax, honey, timber, coal, silver, lead, copper and slaves were exported along with Dubrovnik products such as salt, cloth, wine, oil and fish.

As the city grew increasingly prosperous it posed a threat to the other major commercial interest in the Adriatic – Venice. Dubrovnik came under Venetian authority in 1205 and remained under its control for 150 years. Despite accepting governance from Venice the city continued to establish its own independent commercial relations and finally broke away from Venetian control in 1358. Although the city thereafter acknowledged the authority of the Croatian-Hungarian kings and paid them tribute, it was largely left alone to do what it did best – make money.

By the 15th century 'Respublica Ragusina' – the Republic of Ragusa – had extended its borders to include the entire coastal belt from Ston to Cavtat, having previously acquired Lastovo island, the Pelješac Peninsula and Mljet island. It was now a force to be reckoned with. The city turned toward sea trade and established a fleet of its own ships which were dispatched

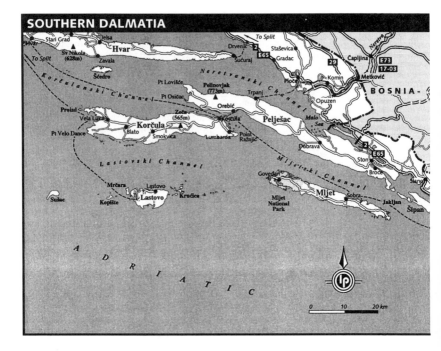

SOUTHERN DALMATIA

to Egypt, Syria, Sicily, Spain, France and later Turkey. Through canny diplomacy the city maintained good relations with everyone – even the Ottoman Empire, to whom Dubrovnik began paying tribute in the 16th century.

Centuries of peace and prosperity allowed art, science and literature to flourish. Marin Držić (1508-1567) was a towering figure in Renaissance literature, best known for his comic play *Dundo Maroje*. Ivan Gundulić (1589-1639) was another Dubrovnik poet/ dramatist whose greatest work was the epic *Osman*. To the world of science, Dubrovnik gave Ruder Bošković (1711-1787) who produced a seminal work in the field of theoretical physics as well as numerous tomes on optics, geography, trigonometry and astronomy. Composers, poets, philosophers and painters turned Dubrovnik into a major cultural centre on the Adriatic.

Tragically, most of Dubrovnik's Renaissance art and architecture were destroyed in the earthquake of 1667 which killed 5000 people and left the city in ruins. Only the Sponza palace and the Rector's Palace survived to give an idea of what Renaissance Dubrovnik must have looked like. The city was rebuilt in a uniform baroque style with modest dwellings in rows and shops on the ground floor. The earthquake also marked the beginning of the economic decline of the town accentuated by the opening of new trade routes to the east and the emergence of rival naval powers in Western Europe.

The final *coup de grace* was dealt by Napoleon whose troops entered Dubrovnik in 1806 and announced the end of the republic. The Vienna Congress of 1815 ceded Dubrovnik to Austria where the city maintained its shipping but succumbed to social

hostel and most of the town's hotels. The old walled town lies south-east of Lapad at the foot of Srd Hill halfway between the port of Gruž and the cape of Sveti Jakov. The entire old town is closed to cars and is divided nearly in half by the wide street Placa, also referred to as Stradun. There are no hotels in the old town but plenty of restaurants.

Pile Gate is the western entrance to the town and the last stop for local buses from Lapad and Gruž. The eastern gate is Ploce, which leads to several luxury hotels along ulica Frana Supila. The Jadrolinija ferry terminal and the bus station are a few hundred metres apart at Gruž which is about 2km west of the old town. Left-luggage at the bus station is open from 4.30 am to 10 pm. To get to the old town from the bus station, go around the corner, cross the street and take any bus except No 7.

The city boundaries also include the Elafiti Islands (Šipan, Lopud, Koločep, Olipe, Tajan and Jakljan).

INFORMATION
Tourist Offices
The Tourist Information Centar (☎ 426 354) is on Placa, opposite the Franciscan monastery in the old town and is open daily from 8 am to 8 pm in the summer and Monday to Saturday 8 am to 6 pm in winter. They find private accommodation, change money and sell brochures. The Dubrovnik City Guide is a good source of practical information on the city's sights and services as well as monthly events. The Jadrolinija office (☎ 418 000) at Obala S. Radića 40 is open daily from 8 am to 8 pm. The Croatia Airlines office (☎ 413 777), Brsalje 9, outside the Pile Gate is open Monday to Friday from 8 am to 4 pm, Saturday 9 am to noon. Motorists can turn to Autoklub Dubrovnik (☎ 413 604) at Vladimira Nazora 39 for help.

disintegration. It remained a part of the Austro-Hungarian empire until 1918 and then slowly began to develop its tourist industry.

Like Venice, Dubrovnik's fortunes now depend upon tourism. Stari Grad, the perfectly preserved old town, is unique for its marble-paved squares, steep cobbled streets, tall houses, convents, churches, palaces, fountains and museums, all cut from the same light-coloured stone. The intact city walls keep motorists at bay and the city's renowned Summer Festival has re-established its position as a coastal cultural centre.

ORIENTATION
The town extends about 6km from the mouth of the Rijeka River in the west to the cape of Sveti Jakov in the east and includes the promontory of Lapad. This leafy residential suburb with rocky beaches contains the

Money
Travel agencies change money but if you arrive by bus, the nearest change place is the post office in the department store near the bus station, open Monday to Friday from 8 am to 8 pm, Saturday 8 am to 2 pm.

SOUTHERN DALMATIA

Dubrovnik: Destruction & Reconstruction

Caught in the cross hairs of the civil war that ravaged former Yugoslavia, Dubrovnik was pummelled with some 2000 shells in 1991 and 1992. When the smoke finally cleared in June 1992, the extent of the damage revealed was severe.

Shells struck 68% of the 824 buildings in the old town, leaving holes in two out of three tiled roofs. Building façades and the paving stones of streets and squares suffered 314 direct hits and there were 111 direct hits on the great wall. Nine historic palaces were completely gutted by fire while the Sponza Palace, Rector's Palace, St Blaise's Church, Franciscan monastery and the carved fountains, Amerling and Onofrio, sustained serious damage. The total damage was estimated at US$10 million.

In order to handle the complex process of restoring the ancient city, an Expert Advisory Commission for the Rehabilitation of Dubrovnik was formed. The Commission was composed of technical experts from UNESCO, Austria, France, Germany and Italy, as well as representatives from the Croatian Ministry of Culture & Education and the local Committee for the Rehabilitation of Dubrovnik. The committee developed a master plan for the restoration work which would guarantee that all the repairs and reconstruction would be done with traditional techniques, using traditional materials whenever feasible.

One of the first and most urgent problems confronted by the committee's experts was repairing the city's tiled roofs in order to prevent water damage from rainfall. The rosy terracotta tiles that had topped all of Dubrovnik's buildings were originally produced in a tile factory in Kupari, south of Dubrovnik, that had long since closed.

The traditional method was to knead the clay like dough and then shape it to a curve on a man's thigh before baking it. Such a procedure was far too lengthy under the circumstances, and the committee launched a desperate search for an existing supply of tiles to plug up the most critical holes. Replacements of the same colour proved impossible to find.

The closest match came from the town of Agen in south-west France, which provided the first 200,000 tiles, followed by another 400,000 from a factory in Slovenia. The tiles are now produced in a factory near Zagreb, though the brick-red colour of the new tiles blends badly with the more subdued shade of the old Kupari tiles.

The restorers faced a similar problem in finding a source of the fine white limestone used to build the city. The original stone came from nearby Vrnik, off the island of Korčula, but the quarries have since fallen into disuse and are only capable of producing small amounts of stone.

The island of Brač has a long tradition of stonemasonry and a ready supply of high-quality stone; even with this stone, though, restorers worried that the obvious differences in colour and texture would only magnify over time. The solution was to use the Brač stone in places that had already used the stone or where it would not be readily visible, such as in drainage

In the old town, Dubrovačka Banka on Placa is open Monday to Friday from 7.30 am to 1.30 pm and 2 to 8 pm.

You can withdraw cash on your Visa card. There's also an ATM on Placa 4 where you can withdraw cash on Master-Card.

Post & Communications

The main post office is at Ante Starčevića 2, a block from Pile Gate. It's open Monday to Saturday from 7 am to 8 pm, Sunday 8 am to 2 pm. There's another post office/telephone centre at Lapad near Hotel Kompas and one in town on the corner of Široka and

Dubrovnik: Destruction & Reconstruction

gutters. A supply of stone for the long-term needs of the city has yet to be found.

To the casual observer, Dubrovnik has regained most of its original grandeur. The great town walls are once again intact, the streets are smoothly paved and famous monuments like the 15th century Onofrio Fountain and the Clock Tower have been lovingly restored. Visible damage to the Sponza Palace, the Rector's Palace, St Blaise's Church and the Cathedral has been repaired with the help of an international brigade of specially trained stoneworkers.

Still, much work remains to be done. Behind the imposing façades, the interiors of many buildings are in tatters. Some residences along the side streets leading to the Placa are little more than shells enclosing piles of rubble. Repairs are just beginning on nine 17th century palaces. Smaller churches such as the Church of St Saviour and the Church of St Roche await rehabilitation, as do the interiors of the Rector's Palace and the Franciscan monastery.

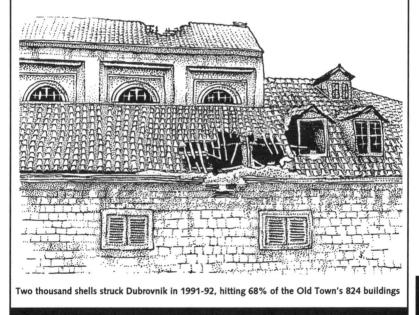

Two thousand shells struck Dubrovnik in 1991-92, hitting 68% of the Old Town's 824 buildings

Od Puča. You can change or withdraw money on Diners Club or MasterCard. The postal code for Dubrovnik is 20000.

Travel Agencies

The American Express representative is Atlas travel agency (☎ 442 222, 411 100), on Brsalje 17 outside Pile Gate next to the old town, but mail is held at another office (☎ 432 093) across from the Revelin Fort at Frana Supila 2. There's also an office in the harbour at Gruz (☎ 418 001) and another in Lapad at Lisinskog 5 (☎ 442 555). The offices are open Monday to Saturday from 8 am to 7 pm.

Generalturist (☎ 432 974) has an office at Frana Supila 9 for handling air tickets and arranging excursions. Melmar Tours (☎ 416 860, fax 432 570) arranges private accommodation and rents cars and scooters.

Globtour (☎ 428 144, fax 426 322) on Placa is in a convenient location to arrange private accommodation. Next to the Hotel Petka is Gruž OK (☎ 418 940, fax 418 950), Obala Stjepana Radića 32, which finds private accommodation, changes money and rents cars and scooters.

THINGS TO SEE

You'll probably begin your visit at the city bus stop outside **Pile Gate** which dates from 1537. Notice the statue of Saint Blaise, the city's patron saint, set in a niche over the Renaissance arch. Originally the drawbridge at the gate's entrance was lifted every evening, the gate was closed and the key handed to the prince.

As you pass through the outer gate you come to an inner gate dating from 1460 and then Placa, Dubrovnik's wonderful pedestrian promenade. In front of you is the

Onofrio Fountain, one of Dubrovnik's most famous landmarks. It was built in 1438 as part of a water supply system that involved bringing water from a well 12km away. Originally the fountain was adorned with sculpture but it was heavily damaged in the 1667 earthquake and only 16 carved masks remain with water jets gushing from their mouths into a drainage pool.

On the left is lovely **St Saviour Church** (Crkva Sveti Spasa) which was built from 1520 to 1528 and was one of the few buildings to have survived the earthquake of 1667.

Next to St Saviour Church is the **Franciscan monastery** at Placa 2. Over the door of the monastery church is a remarkable *Pietá* sculpted by the local masters, Petar and Leonard Andrijić in 1498. Unfortunately, the portal is all that remains of the richly decorated church that was destroyed in the 1667 earthquake.

Inside the monastery complex is the mid-14th century **cloister**, one of the most beautiful late-Romanesque structures in Dalmatia. Notice how each capital over the dual columns is topped by a different

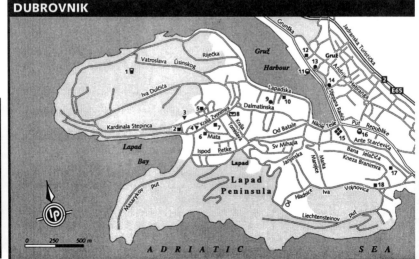

figure, portraying human heads, animals and floral arrangements.

Further inside you'll find the third-oldest functioning pharmacy in Europe, in business since 1391. The pharmacy may have been the first pharmacy in Europe open to the general public. Before leaving, visit the monastery museum with its collection of relics, liturgical objects, paintings, gold work and pharmacy items such as lab gear and medical books. The monastery is open daily from 9 am to 5 pm.

As you proceed down Placa you may wish to make a detour up Božidarevića St to Od Puća, site of a **Serbian Orthodox Church** dating from 1877, and then onto Žudioska ulica to see the 15th century **synagogue**, the oldest Sephardic and the second-oldest synagogue in Europe.

At its eastern end Placa widens into Luža Square, formerly used as a market place. The **Orlando Column** (Roland's Column) is a popular meeting place and used to be the place where edicts, festivities and public verdicts were announced. Carved in 1417, the forearm of this medieval knight was the

official linear measure of the Republic – the ell of Dubrovnik which measures 51.1 cm.

The **Clock Tower** dominates the square and makes an elegant punctuation point at the end of Placa. First built in 1444, it was restored many times, most recently in 1929, and is notable for the two bronze figures in the bell tower that ring out the hours.

Across the square is the 16th century **Sponza Palace** which was originally a Customs House, then a minting house, a State treasury and a bank. Now it houses the State Archives with a priceless collection of manuscripts dating back nearly a thousand years. This superb structure is a mixture of Gothic and Renaissance styles beginning with an exquisite Renaissance portico resting on six columns. The first floor has late-Gothic windows and the second floor windows are in a Renaissance style with an alcove containing a statue of St Vlaho. The interior follows a complex, harmonious plan but cannot be visited.

Crossing the square you'll pass **Little Onofrio's Fountain**, part of the same water project as its larger cousin to the west but built to supply water to the market place on Luša Square. In front of you is the imposing **St Blaise's Church** (Crkva Sveti Vlaha), built in 1715 to replace an earlier church destroyed in the earthquake. Built in a baroque style following the church of St Mauritius in Venice, the ornate exterior contrasts strongly with the sober residences surrounding it. The interior is notable for its marble altars and a 15th century silver gilt statue of St Blaise who is holding a scale model of pre-earthquake Dubrovnik in his hand.

Continuing along the broad street beside St Blaise is the Gothic-Renaissance **Rector's Palace**, Pred Dvorom 3, built in the late 15th century with outstanding sculptural ornamentation. Although rebuilt several times, it retains a striking compositional unity. Notice the finely carved capitals and the ornate staircase in the atrium which is often used for concerts during the Summer Festival. Also in the atrium is a statue of Miho Pracat, who bequeathed his wealth to the Republic and

PLACES TO STAY
2 Hotel Kompas
5 Begovic
  Boarding House
6 Hotel Sumratin
7 Hotel Zagreb
10 Hotel Lapad
12 Hotel Petka
17 Youth Hostel
18 Hotel Lero

PLACES TO EAT
3 Restauracija Eden
  & Konobo Atlantic
4 Restauracija Konavoka

OTHER
1 Divine Folie
8 Lapad Post Office
9 Open-air Cinema
11 Jadrolinija
  Ferry Wharf
13 Jadroagent
14 Market
15 Department Store
16 Bus Station
19 Post Office
20 Fort Lovrjenac
21 Lazareti
22 Ploče Beach

SOUTHERN DALMATIA

was the only commoner in the one thousand years of the Republic's existence to be honoured with a statue (1638). We may assume that the bequest was considerable.

The palace was built for the rector who governed Dubrovnik and contains the Rector's Office, his private chambers, public halls and administrative offices. Interestingly, the elected rector was not permitted to leave the building during his one-month term without the permission of the senate. Today the palace has been turned into a museum with artfully restored rooms,

figures in ceremonial dress, portraits, coats of arms, and coins that evoke the glorious history of Dubrovnik. The museum is open Monday to Saturday from 9 am to 1 pm.

Across the square from the Rector's Palace is the **Cathedral of the Assumption of the Virgin** (Stolna crkva Velike Gospe) on Poljana M. Držića. The church was built on the site of a 7th century basilica that was enlarged in the 12th century, supposedly as the result of a gift from England's King Richard I, the Lionheart, who was saved from a shipwreck in the nearby island of Lokrum.

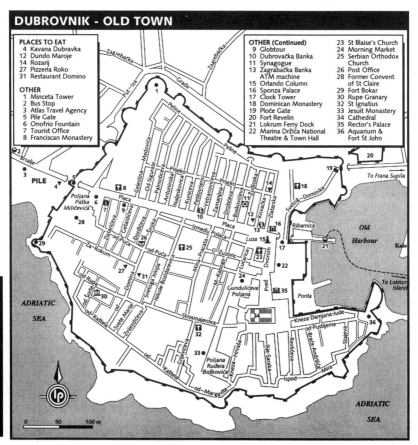

DUBROVNIK - OLD TOWN

PLACES TO EAT
4 Kavana Dubravka
12 Dundo Maroje
14 Rozarij
27 Pizzeria Roko
31 Restaurant Domino

OTHER
1 Minceta Tower
2 Bus Stop
3 Atlas Travel Agency
5 Pile Gate
6 Onofrio Fountain
7 Tourist Office
8 Franciscan Monastery

OTHER (Continued)
9 Globtour
10 Dubrovačka Banka
11 Synagogue
13 Zagrabačka Banka ATM machine
15 Orlando Column
16 Sponza Palace
17 Clock Tower
18 Dominican Monastery
19 Ploče Gate
20 Fort Revelin
21 Lokrum Ferry Dock
22 Marina Držića National Theatre & Town Hall

23 St Blaise's Church
24 Morning Market
25 Serbian Orthodox Church
26 Post Office
28 Former Convent of St Claire
29 Fort Bokar
30 Rupe Granary
32 St Ignatius
33 Jesuit Monastery
34 Cathedral
35 Rector's Palace
36 Aquarium & Fort St John

Soon after the earlier cathedral was destroyed in the 1667 earthquake, work began on this new cathedral which was finished in 1713 in a purely baroque style. The cathedral is notable for its fine altars, especially the altar of St John Nepomuk made of violet marble. The cathedral **treasury** contains relics of St Blaise as well as 138 gold and silver reliquaries largely made in the workshops of Dubrovnik's goldsmiths between the 11th and 17th centuries. Among a number of religious paintings, the most striking is the polyptych of the Assumption of the Virgin, made in Titian's workshop. The treasury is open daily from 9 am to noon and 3 to 6 pm.

From the cathedral walk down Androvića to the **St Ignatius Church** (Crkva Sveti Ignacija) on Uz Jezuite, built in the same style as the cathedral and completed in 1725. Inside are frescoes displaying scenes from the life of St Ignatius, founder of the Jesuit society. Abutting the church is the **Jesuit College** at the top of a broad flight of stairs leading down to Gundulićeva Poljana, a bustling morning market. The monument in the centre is of Dubrovnik's famous poet, Ivan Gundulić. The reliefs on the pedestal depict scenes from his epic poem *Osman*.

Return to the cathedral and take Od Pustijerne to the **aquarium** in St John Fort at Kneza Damjana Jude 2. Fed by fresh sea water, there are tanks with electric rays, sting rays, conger eels, scorpion fish and spotted dogfish, sea breams, grouper, poisonous snakelike morays and seahorses. Smaller glass tanks display colourful sponges, sea-anemones, sea stars, shells, snails, urchins and an eight-footed octopus which varies its shape and colour as it swims. The aquarium is open Monday to Saturday from 10 am to 6 pm and is a great favourite with kids.

Return to the Sponza Palace and follow the road to the Ploce Gate. On your left, you'll see the **Dominican monastery and church**, Sveti Dominika 4, another architectural highlight in a transitional Gothic-Renaissance style with a rich trove of paintings. Built at the same time as the city walls in the 14th century, the stark exterior re-

sembles a fortress more than a religious complex.

The interior contains a graceful 15th century cloister constructed by local artisans after the designs of the Florentine architect Massa di Bartolomeo, and a large, single-naved church with an altarpiece by Vlaho Bukovac. The eastern wing contains the monastery's impressive art collection that includes paintings from Dubrovnik's finest 15th and 16th century artists. Notice the works of Božidarević, Dobričević and Hamzić. The monastery is open daily from 9 am to 5 pm.

By this time you'll be ready for a leisurely walk around the **city walls** themselves. Built between the 13th and 16th centuries and still intact today, these powerful walls are the finest in the world and Dubrovnik's main claim to fame.

The first set of walls to enclose the city were built in the 13th century. In the middle of the 14th century the 1.5m thick walls were fortified with 15 square forts. The threat of attacks from the Turks in the 15th century prompted the city to strengthen existing forts and add new ones so that the entire old city is now contained within a curtain of stone over 2km long and up to 25m high. The walls are thicker on the land side – up to 6m – but run 1.5 to 3m on the sea side. The round Minčeta Tower protects the northern edge of the city from land invasion while the western end is protected from land and sea invasion by the detached Lovrjenac Fort. The Pile Gate is protected by the Bokar Tower and the Revelin Fort protects the eastern entrance.

The views over the town and sea are great, so make this walk the high point of your visit. The entrance to the walls is immediately to the left of Pile Gate when you enter the city. They are open daily from 7 am to 7 pm and cost 10KN. You can also visit the Lovrjenac Fort Monday to Saturday from 9 am to 6 pm. Admission is 5KN. Shakespeare's plays are staged on the fortress terrace during the Summer Festival.

In addition to a profusion of old churches that can be visited before or after mass,

Dubrovnik has other attractions. There's an **Ethnographic Museum** in the 16th century Rupe Granary that contains exhibits relating to agriculture. It is open Sunday to Friday from 9 am to 1 pm. There's also a **Maritime Museum** in the St John Fort that traces the history of navigation in Dubrovnik with ship models, navigational objects and paintings. It's open Tuesday to Sunday from 9 am to 1 pm. Art lovers may wish to head up to the **Fine Arts Museum** at Frana Supila 23 for a look at modern and contemporary Croatian artists, particularly the local painter Vlaho Bukovac. It's open Monday to Saturday from 10 am to 1 pm and 5 to 8 pm.

ACTIVITIES

The waters around Dubrovnik offer excellent **scuba diving** opportunities. There are wrecks, caves, and walls to explore, especially around Koločep island. Nimar Dive Centre (☎ 417 123, fax 428 857) at Lazarina 3 offers single dives for 175KN and a six-dive package for 775KN. Full equipment rental is 125KN.

The closest beach to the old city is just beyond the 17th century **Lazareti** (former quarantine station) outside Ploče Gate. There are also 'managed' hotel beaches on the **Lapad Peninsula**, but you could be charged admission unless they think you're a guest.

A far better option is to take the ferry which shuttles hourly in the summer to **Lokrum island**, a luxuriantly wooded island with a rocky nudist beach, a botanical garden and the ruins of a medieval Benedictine monastery.

ORGANISED TOURS

Atlas travel agency offers a day trip rafting the Neretva River (370KN), a trip to Mljet (250KN) and a canoe trip down the Trebižat River in Hercegovina (300KN) as well as various other sightseeing tours of the region.

SPECIAL EVENTS

The Dubrovnik Summer Festival from mid-July to mid-August is the most prestigious summer festival in Croatia and has taken place every year since 1950. For five weeks

in July and August, a program of theatre, concerts and dance are presented on open-air stages throughout the city. The opening ceremony takes place on Luža Square and usually includes fireworks and a band.

In addition to attracting the best national artists and regional folklore ensembles, the program usually includes one or two big-name international artists. Theatre productions feature the plays of Marin Držić, Shakespeare, Moliére and the Greek tragedians. Tickets run from 30 to 200KN and are available from the Dubrovnik Summer Festival box office, Poljana Paska Milićevića 1, or on site one hour before the beginning of each performance.

The Feast of St Blaise (3 February) is another citywide bash marked by pageants and processions. Carnival festivities heralding the arrival of Lent in February are also popular.

PLACES TO STAY
Camping

Porto (☎ 487 078) is a small camping ground 8km south of Dubrovnik near a quiet cove. Right next door is *Camping Matkovića (☎ 486 096)*. Both sites should be open from June through September, but it's best to call first. The No 10 bus to Srebeno leaves you nearly at its gate. Otherwise, there's the much larger *Zaton (☎ 280 280)* about 15km west of the city, reliably open May to October. A few kilometres further west at Trsteno is a small, private camping ground, *Trojanović (☎ 751 060)*.

Hostels

The *YHA hostel (☎ 423 241, fax 412 592)*, up Vinka Sagrestana from Bana Josipa Jelačića 17, was refurbished in 1996. A bed in a room for four with breakfast is 75KN. Lunch and dinner can also be arranged but the hostel is on one of the liveliest streets in Lapad, full of bars, cafés and pizzerias.

Private Rooms

The easiest way to find a place to stay is to accept the offer of a *sobe* from one of the women who approach you at the bus or

Cathedral of the Assumption of the Virgin in Dubrovnik

JEANNE OLIVER

SARA YORKE

JON DAVISON

The walls, squares and roofs of beautiful Dubrovnik

ferry terminal. Their prices are lower than those charged by the room-finding agencies and, unless you arrive in July or August, they're open to bargaining.

Officially, there are no single rooms but off season you may be able to knock 20% off the price of a double room; prices begin at 108KN in May, June and September for a room with shared bath, but rise to 198KN in July and August for a room with private facilities. Prices do not include breakfast or residence tax and are subject to a 30% surcharge for stays less than three nights. If it's a busy season, expect to pay even more. Apartments are also available beginning at about 250KN for a studio in July and August. Agencies that handle private accommodation include Atlas, Gulliver (☎ 411 088) next to Jadroagent, Melmar and Globtour (☎ 428 144, fax 426 322) on Placa. The tourist office on Placa opposite the Franciscan monastery is another place to try.

Hotels

Lapad Most of the less expensive hotels are in Lapad as well as a few more luxurious establishments. On the whole, the suburb is not a bad place to stay. Since it's a mixed residential and 'tourist' neighbourhood, you don't get the feeling that you've been banished to some faraway tourist ghetto. The main road is Kralja Tomislava while the pedestrian tree-lined Zvonimira makes a pleasant stroll past stalls and outdoor cafés. A walk along the coast past the Hotel Kompas leads to lots of spots for stretching out along the rocks and taking a swim. After about 1km you'll come to the Hotel Neptune and a series of package tour hotels. Buses 1A, 1B and 6 run between Pile Gate and the bus stop in Lapad near the post office.

The **Begović Boarding House** (☎ 428 563, Primorska 17), a couple of blocks up from Lapad post office (bus No 6), has three rooms with shared bath at 70KN per person and three small apartments for 90KN per person. There's a nice terrace out the back with a good view.

Hotel Sumratin (☎ 431 031, fax 423 581, Šetalište kralja Zvonimira 31) and **Hotel**

Zagreb (☎ 431 011, Šetalište kralja Zvonimira 27) are near each other and under the same ownership but Hotel Zagreb is in a restored 19th century building with more character than you usually find along the coast. Prices are the same at 190/320KN a single/double including bath and breakfast in July and August, cheaper the rest of the year.

Along a busy road through Lapad, **Hotel Lero** (☎ 411 455) is a modern structure that has rooms from 263/374KN a single/double in July and August. It has 162 rooms and is located along Miramare Bay a little over 1km from the old town. There are telephones in the rooms and you have access to a small beach near the Hotel Bellevue.

Hotel Lapad (☎ 413 576, fax 424 782, Lapadska Obala 37) is a better bet with 200 rooms, many equipped with air-conditioning and satellite TV. The hotel is a solid old limestone structure with simple but cheerful rooms and an outdoor swimming pool. There's no beach access but the hotel runs a daily boat to a remote beach near Zaton at no extra charge. Rooms are 338/436KN for a single/double in July and August but drop to 247/389KN in the shoulder season.

The **Hotel Kompas** (☎ 416 797, fax 416 877) is a sprawling complex along the coast with an indoor and outdoor swimming pool, air-conditioning and a sauna. Rooms are 317/504KN in high season but rooms with a view are somewhat more expensive.

Gruž The renovated **Hotel Petka** (☎/fax 418 058, Obala Stjepana Radića 38), opposite the Jadrolinija ferry landing, has 104 rooms at 198/342KN a single/double with bath and breakfast.

Ploče East of the old town along Frana Supila is where you'll find the best luxury establishments within easy walking distance of the town centre. **Hotel Argentina** (☎ 440 555, fax 432 524, Frana Supila 14) is a favourite with journalists who were there to record the bombardment of the city in 1991. There's an indoor and outdoor swimming pool but the swimming is excellent from the rocks next to the hotel. Rooms have (unreliable) air-conditioning and you have access to a sauna and fitness room. Rooms start at 465/760KN a single/double in high season but rooms overlooking the sea are at least 25% more expensive.

Next door is Dubrovnik's most expensive hotel, the *Villa Orsula* (☎ *440 555, fax 432 524)*, with suitably plush surroundings that share some facilities with the Hotel Argentina. Rooms are 828/1152KN a single/double in high season.

PLACES TO EAT
Old Town

For a quick snack of pastries, small pizzas or sandwiches in the 10KN range try *Kavana Dubravka* right outside Pile Gate. It's open daily from 7 am to 2 am and there's an outdoor terrace behind the comfortable, air conditioned interior.

You can get a decent meal at one of the touristy seafood or pasta places along ulica Prijeko, a narrow street parallel to Placa, but you may prefer the quieter atmosphere at *Pizzeria Roko* on Za Rokum which serves good pies starting at 28KN.

The spaghetti with shrimp and squid risotto at *Dundo Maroje* on Kovačka is excellent and there are a full range of other seafood or pasta dishes in the 40KN range. It's open daily from 11 am to 3 pm and 7 pm to midnight. Nearby is *Rosarij (Zlatarska 4)*, a romantic spot tucked away in a quiet corner of town. Grilled fish or scampi runs about 70KN. It's open daily from 11 am to midnight.

Then there's *Restaurant Jadran* in the atrium of the Convent of St Claire. It may be touristy but the ambience is great and prices are reasonable. You can get fried calamari for 40KN, octopus salad for 40KN, the Serbian dish Mućkalica for 40KN and a vegie platter for 30KN. It's open daily from 9 am to midnight.

The elegant *Nautika (Brsalje 3)* next to Atlas travel agency offers the best dining in town and a spectacular view over the sea. The food is pricey but good. Main courses run from 80KN to 95KN with vegetable side dishes and salads for 20KN and a

scampi risotto at 80KN. If the prices make you wince, at least enjoy a drink in the downstairs coffee shop with an outdoor terrace. The restaurant is open daily from noon to midnight and the coffee house is open from 10 am to midnight.

For a meat fix head to *Restaurant Domino (Od Domina 6)*, which offers a selection of cow cuttings as well as other meat dishes and an assortment of grilled fish at about the same prices as Nautika.

In Gruž there's *Restauracija Primorka (Nikole Tesle 7)*, just west of the department store, with a good selection of seafood and national dishes at medium prices. In summer you dine below the trees on a lamp-lit terrace. It's open daily from 7 am to 11 pm.

Lapad

The *Restauracija Konavoka (38 Šetalište kralja Zvonimira)*, near the Hotel Sumartin, has an upstairs roofed terrace attractively decorated with potted plants making it a pleasant place to hang out or enjoy a cheap pizza. Seafood runs from 45KN to 75KN and vegetarian platters are available. It's open daily from noon to midnight.

Konobo Atlantic (Kardinala Stepinca 42) is not terribly atmospheric since the outdoor tables are next to a bus stop. Install yourself indoors, however, and you can sample superb home-made pasta such as a vegetarian lasagna for 25KN and tagliatelle with assorted seafood sauces that run from 23KN to 35KN. It's open daily from noon to midnight.

The best dining in Lapad is at *Restauracija Eden (Kardinala Stepinca 54)*. The leafy terrace upstairs is an agreeable spot to enjoy meat, pasta or fish dishes that run from 50KN to 80KN. It's open daily from noon to midnight.

ENTERTAINMENT

In May, June and September there are open-air folklore shows on Sunday at 11 am in front of St Blaise's Church. The Dubrovnik orchestra regularly gives concerts in the atrium of the Rector's Palace and the Dubrovnik String Quartet gives concerts throughout the autumn on Thursday night in St Blaise's Church.

The newest addition to Dubrovnik nightlife is the *Divine Folie* disco in Babin kuk which booms out techno to 6000 people under tents. *Sun City Disco (put Republike 28)* is an old standby next to the bus station. Both places are open nightly from 10 pm to 5 am.

Watch movies by starlight at the open-air cinema on Kumičića in Lapad. Club *Nautika (Brsalje 3)* outside the Pile Gate is an expensive restaurant but you can enjoy the two open-air terraces overlooking the sea for the price of a coffee or a drink.

GETTING THERE & AWAY
Air
Daily flights to/from Zagreb are operated by Croatia Airlines. The fare is about 620KN one way in the summer but much less off season.

Bus
Daily buses from Dubrovnik include:

destination	distance	frequency	cost
Rijeka	639km	3 daily	230KN
Zadar	393km	6 daily	113KN
Split	235km	13 daily	77KN
Zagreb	713km	8 daily	135KN
Orebić Korčula	113km	1 daily	35KN
Mostar	143km	3 daily	70KN
Sarajevo	278km	2 daily	155KN

International buses go to Rome (twice weekly, 25 hours), Paris (once a week, 26 hours), London (twice weekly, 26 hours), Tel Aviv (once a week, 28 hours), Brussels (once a week in summer, 26 hours), Frankfurt (once a week, 26 hours), Hamburg (once a week, 27 hours) and Cologne (once a week, 26 hours). In a busy summer season and on weekends, buses out of Dubrovnik can be crowded, so book a ticket well before the scheduled departure time.

Boat
All ferries from Dubrovnik leave from the Jadrolinija ferry landing in Gruž, except ex-cursion boats to Lokrum and Cavtat which leave from the Old Town port.

In addition to the Jadrolinija coastal ferry north to Korčula, Hvar, Split, Zadar, and Rijeka, which runs four times a week in summer and twice a week in winter, there's a local ferry that leaves Dubrovnik for Sobra on Mljet island (2½ hours, 21KN) at 2 pm daily except Sunday throughout the year.

There's a local boat to the Elafiti Islands (Kolačep, Lopud, Šipan) two or three times a day all year round.

Adriatica Navigazione runs a ferry between Bari and Dubrovnik once a week all year and Jadrolinija connects the two cities four times a week in the summer and once a week in the winter. The eight hour trip costs about 249KN.

During the summer, Jadrolinija runs a ferry twice a week between Dubrovnik and Igoumenitsa, stopping in Bari (17½ hours, 265KN). Unless the ferry service to Albania resumes, there is no choice but to connect via Ancona or Bari. Both the Jadrolinija line to Bari and the Adriatica Navigazione line to Ancona connect well to other Adriatica Navigazione ferries to Durrës. From Ancona and Bari it is also possible to catch the Anek Lines boats to Igoumenitsa, Patrasso and Corfu.

GETTING AROUND
To/From the Airport
Čilipi international airport is 24km southeast of Dubrovnik. The Croatia Airlines airport buses (20KN) leave from the main bus terminal 1½ hours before flight times.

Local Buses
Pay your 6KN fare in exact change on city buses as you board – have small coins ready.

Car Rental
Try Gulliver (☎ 411 088), S. Radića 31; Mack (☎ 412 732), Fr. Supila 3; Melmar (☎ 416 860), Fr. Supila 5; or Madra (☎ 412 290), Vojnovic 69. There's also Budget at Dulčića 18 (☎ 432 685) and Avis (☎ 22043) at V. Nazora 9.

AROUND DUBROVNIK
Elafiti Islands

A day trip to one of the islands in this archipelago north-west of Dubrovnik makes a perfect escape from the summer crowds. The most popular islands are Koločep, Lopud, and Šipan which are easily reachable during the summer by a morning boat from Dubrovnik (off season there are only afternoon boats).

Koločep is the nearest island (25 minutes) and has several sand and pebble beaches as well as centuries-old pine forests, olive groves and orange and lemon orchards. **Lopud** is 25 minutes further and has a number of interesting churches and monasteries dating from the 16th century, when the inhabitants' seafaring exploits were legendary. The village is composed of stone houses surrounded by exotic gardens and there's a beach nearby. No cars are allowed on the island.

Šipan is the largest of the islands (1¼ hours from Dubrovnik) and was a favourite with the Dubrovnik aristocracy, who built houses there in the 15th century. The boat lands in Šipanska Luka in the north-west of the island which has remains of a Roman villa and a 15th century Gothic duke's palace.

Cavtat

- **pop 1930**   ☎ **021**

Cavtat is a small town that curves around an attractive harbour bordered by beaches. Although not as interesting as Dubrovnik, it makes a good alternative place to stay if Dubrovnik is fully booked or the summer crowds become overwhelming. The town's proximity to Dubrovnik means that you can do a little sightseeing in the morning, relax on a beach and still get back to Dubrovnik for dinner.

Originally a Greek settlement called Epidauros, it became a Roman colony around 228 BC and was later destroyed during the 7th century Slavic invasions. Throughout most of the Middle Ages it was part of the Dubrovnik republic and shared the cultural and economic life of the capital city. It's

most famous personage was the painter Vlaho Bukovac (1855-1922), one of the foremost exponents of Croatian modernism.

Orientation & Information

The old town is on the harbour and several gargantuan tourist complexes lie on the eastern edge, along the town's best beach. The Turistički Ured (☎/fax 478 025) is near the bus station at Tiha 3 and is open all year, Monday to Saturday from 8 am to 2pm, Sunday 9 am to noon. However, you'll get more reliable information from the travel agencies. The post office, Kneza Domagoja 4, is near the bus station and is open Monday to Saturday from 7 am to 9 pm. The postal code for Cavtat is 20210.

Things to See

Several sights make the city well worth a stop. Near the bus station is the Renaissance **Rector's Palace** that houses a rich library (which belonged to 19th century lawyer and historian Balthazar Bogišić) as well as lithographs and a small archaeological collection. It's open daily from 10 am to 1 pm. Next door is the baroque **St Nicholas Church** (Crkva Sveti Nikole) with wooden altars (open 10 am to noon daily).

From the church follow the coast to the **Franciscan monastery**, which houses a valuable art collection (open 10 am to noon daily in summer). A path leads uphill from the monastery to the cemetery which contains the **Mausoleum** of the Račić Family, built by Ivan Meštrović; the elaborately sculpted monument reflects the sculptor's preoccupation with religious and spiritual concerns. It's open daily April to November from 10 am to noon and 3 to 7 pm; it's open mornings only the rest of the year.

Places to Stay & Eat

For private accommodation try Atlas travel agency (☎ 478 464), Astarea (☎ 471 165) next to the bus stop, or the helpful Filomena Agency (☎ 478 212) a short walk away at Put Tiha 4a. Top-end hotel rooms in the high season will cost you 148/178KN a single/double.

The cheapest hotel in town is the *Hotel Supetar* (☎ 478 278) which has very basic singles/doubles for 250/400KN in high season, including an obligatory half-pension. The *Hotel Cavtat* (☎ 478 246) has 94 rooms in the town centre overlooking the beach. The warmly decorated rooms are in excellent condition and equipped with satellite TV. A single/double with breakfast runs 390/520KN in high season.

Restaurant Kolona on a verdant terrace overlooking the bus stop has the freshest fish in town which is evident when you order the starter of sliced raw fish in olive oil (30KN). Grilled fish, squid and an assortment of risottos are excellently prepared and run from 40KN to 50KN. The restaurant is open daily from 10 am to midnight.

Getting There & Away

Bus No 10 runs hourly to Cavtat from Dubrovnik's bus station (20km) or you can take a boat from the Lokrum boat dock (three times daily, 35KN return), near Ploce gate.

Mljet

• pop 1237   ☎ 020

Of all the Adriatic islands, Mljet may be the most seductive. Over 72% of the island is covered by forests and the rest is dotted by fields, vineyards and small villages. The western half of the island has been named a national park where the lush vegetation and gentle coves are unmarred by development schemes, large resorts or nearly any other trappings of tourism. You may pay more or have to go to more trouble to stay here, but you'll be rewarded by an unspoiled oasis of tranquillity that, according to legend, captivated Odysseus for seven years. I'm sure he didn't regret a moment.

Ancient Greeks called the island 'Melita' or 'honey' for the many bees humming in the forests. It appears that Greek sailors came to the island for refuge against storms, to gather fresh water from the springs and probably to unwind a little. At that time the island was populated by Illyrians who erected hill forts and traded with the mainland. They were conquered by the Romans in 35 BC who expanded the settlement around Polače by building a palace, baths and servants quarters.

The island fell under the control of the Byzantine empire in the 6th century and was later subject to the 7th century invasions of Slavs and Avars which pushed inhabitants of neighbouring regions to flee to the island. After several centuries of regional rule from the mainland it was given to the Benedictine order in the 13th century, who constructed a monastery in the middle of Veliki Jezero, one of two lakes on the island's western end. Dubrovnik was extending its influence in the region at the time and formally annexed the island in 1410.

Although Mljet's fortunes were thereafter tied to those of Dubrovnik, the inhabitants maintained their traditional activities of farming, viticulture, livestock rearing and seafaring. Except for seafaring, the traditional activities are still the foundation of the economy. The island's inhabitants produce wine and olive oil, cultivate medicinal herbs and fish. Establishing the national park in 1960 helped bring tourism to Mljet, but the islanders are deeply ambivalent about the many depredations that tourism often entails and seem content to keep visitors down to manageable levels. Priorities here are peace and quiet, even if it means foregoing needed cash.

Orientation

The island is 37km long, and has an average width of about 3km. Fifty-four sq km on the island's north-western end are set aside as a national park. Tour boats from Korčula arrive at Pomena wharf just outside the park's west end and site of the island's only hotel, the Odisej. There's a good island map posted at the wharf.

The other harbour in the park is at Polače, a small village with a couple of restaurants and a tourist office (☎ 744 086) which is open only in July and August from 8 am to noon and 6 to 9 pm.

The administrative centre of the island is at Babino Polje, 18km south-east of Polače, where there is another tourist office (☎ 745 125) and a post office.

The postcode for Polače and Pomena is 20226; the postcode for Babino Polje is 20225.

Things to See & Do

The highlights of the island are **Malo Jezero** and **Veliko Jezero**, the two lakes on the island's western end connected by a channel. Veliko Jezero is connected with the sea by the Soline Canal, which makes the lakes subject to tidal flows.

In the middle of Veliko Jezero is an islet with a **Benedictine monastery**; it was originally built in the 12th century but has been rebuilt several times, adding Renaissance and baroque features to the Romanesque structure. The monastery contains the **Church of St Mary** (Crkva Svete Marije), built around the same time. In addition to building the monastery, the Benedictine monks deepened and widened the passage between the two lakes, taking advantage of

the rush of sea water into the valley to build a mill at the entrance to Veliko Jezero. The monastery was abandoned in 1869 and the structure housed the government's forest management offices for the island until 1941. It was then converted into a hotel that was trashed during the recent war. Now it contains a restaurant and there are plans to convert it into a cultural-scientific centre.

There's a boat from Mali Most (about 1.5km from Pomena) on Malo Jezero that leaves for the island monastery four times a day (12KN return). It's not possible to walk right around the larger lake as there's no bridge over the channel connecting the lakes to the sea. If you decide to swim it, keep in mind that the current can be strong.

Polače features a number of remains dating from the 1st to 6th centuries. The most impressive is the **Roman Palace** probably dating from the 5th century. The floor plan was rectangular and on the corners of the front are two polygonal towers separated by a pier. On a hill over the town you can see the remains of a late antique fortification and north-west of the village are the

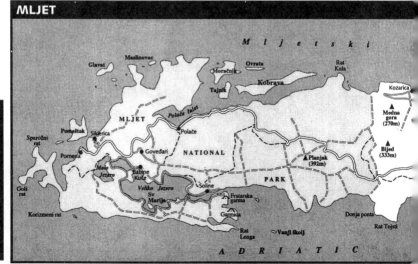

SOUTHERN DALMATIA

remains of an early Christian basilica as well as a 5th century church.

Renting a kayak or a canoe is an excellent way to enjoy the lakes. You can rent kayaks for 15KN an hour or 60KN a half-day and canoes for 30KN an hour or 90KN a half-day from the Hotel Odisej or a private operator on Mali Most. The hotel also rents bicycles for 15KN an hour or 60KN a half-day.

The island offers some unusual opportunities for **scuba diving**. There's a Roman wreck dating from the 3rd century in relatively shallow water. The remains of the boat, including amphorae, have calcified over the centuries which has protected them from pillaging. There's also a German torpedo boat from WWII and several walls to dive. Contact Nimar in Dubrovnik (see above) or in the Hotel Odisej (☎ 744 022).

Organised Tours

Atlas travel agency (☎ 711 060) in Korčula offers day trips to Mljet twice a week from May to mid-October. The tour lasts from 8.30 am to 6 pm, and is 122KN per person,

including the 48KN park entry fee. The boat trip from Korčula to Pomena takes at least two hours, less by hydrofoil. From Pomena it's a 15-minute walk to a jetty on **Veliko Jezero**, the larger of the two lakes. Here the groups board a boat to the monastery island where lunch is served. Those who don't want to spend the rest of the afternoon swimming and sunbathing on the monastery island can catch an early boat back to the main island, and spend a couple of hours walking along the lake shore before catching the late-afternoon excursion boat back to Korčula.

Atlas in Dubrovnik also offers a day trip to Mljet by hydrofoil for 250KN. Lunch isn't included in the tour price and meals are expensive, so it's best to bring a picnic lunch.

Places to Stay

There's no camping in the national park but there's a small *camping ground* (☎ 745 071) in Ropa, about 1km from the park, open from June to September. The tourist office in Polače (☎ 744 086) arranges private accommodation at 148KN for a

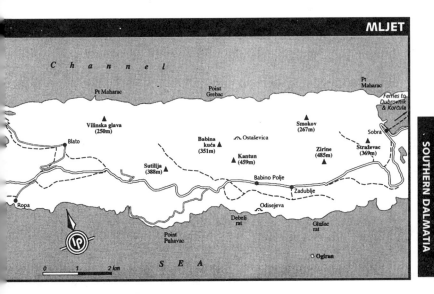

double room in peak season but it's essential to make arrangements before arrival as the supply of rooms is not large. You could also try the tourist office in Babino Polje. Don't count on *sobe* signs. The only hotel is the luxury *Odisej* in Pomena with rooms at 361KN *per person* in July and August with half-board, 50% less off season.

Places to Eat

The restaurants in Mljet all serve good quality food at prices that are somewhat higher than in Dubrovnik. The emphasis is on seafood and prices of fresh fish run about 220KN a kilogram. Meals run from 60KN to 80KN per person but as elsewhere, pasta and risotto is usually available for a light meal.

In Polače try *Stella Maris* on the main road overlooking the sea or the nearby *Ogigija Market*. Opposite the Hotel Odisej in Pomena, *Galija* and *Nine* are on the sea and serve good food. The Hotel Odisej offers a fixed price lunch for 45KN. If you're on the monastery island, there's *Taverna Melita* with an open-air terrace on the sea.

Getting There & Away

Most people take a day trip to Mljet from Korčula but there's a regular ferry (daily except Sunday, 21KN) that leaves from Dubrovnik at 2 pm and docks in Sobra. The return ferry leaves from Sobra at 5.30 am which means a very early morning departure by local bus from the national park. There are additional ferries in both directions in July and August.

The big Jadrolinija coastal ferries also stop at Sobra twice, on the northern coast 7km east of Babino Polje, a week in summer and once a week the rest of the year. Local buses meet the ferry in Sobra and stop in Babino Polje, Ropa, Goveđari, Polače and Pomena.

Korčula Island

- pop 17,038 ☎ 020

Separated from the Pelješac Peninsula by a narrow channel, Korčula (Italian: Curzola) is the sixth largest Adriatic island, reaching nearly 47km in length and 5km to 8km in width. Besides the dense woods that led the

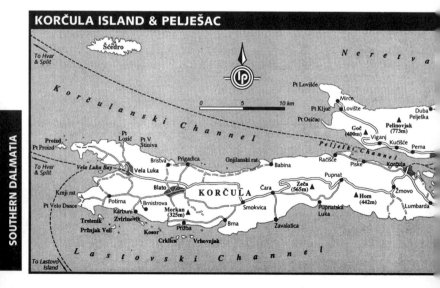

KORČULA ISLAND & PELJEŠAC

original Greek settlers to call the island Korkyra Melaina (Black Korčula), the island is graced with indented coves, rolling hills and a walled old town that resembles a miniature Dubrovnik.

The interior is rich in vineyards, olive groves, small villages and hamlets. The steep southern coast is dotted with quiet coves and small beaches while the northern shore is flatter and has several natural harbours. Traditional culture flourishes on the island. The devout population keeps alive age-old religious ceremonies and an influx of tourism insures that folk dances and music have an eager audience.

A neolithic cave (Vela Špilja) near Vela Luka on the island's western end points to the existence of a prehistoric settlement on the island but it was Greeks who first began spreading over the island in the 6th century BC. Their most important settlement was in the area of today's Lumbarda around the 3rd century BC. Romans conquered the island in the 1st century, giving way to the Slavs in the 7th century. The island was first conquered by Venice in 1000 and then passed under Hungarian rule. It was briefly part of the Republic of Dubrovnik before again falling under Venetian rule in 1420, where it remained until 1797. Under Venetian rule, the island became known for its stone which was quarried and cut for export by skilled local artisans. Shipbuilding also flourished despite Venetian attempts to restrict competition with its own shipyards. After the Napoleonic conquest of Dalmatia in 1797, Korčula's fortunes followed those of Dalmatia which changed hands among the French, Austro-Hungarians and English before finally becoming a part of Yugoslavia in 1921.

Besides tourism, the most important economic activity on the island is agriculture. Although islanders produce cereals, vegetables and citrus fruit, the most important product is olive oil from the many olive groves. Unfortunately a ferocious fire in the summer of 1998 decimated a huge portion of the olive trees and the future of that industry remains uncertain. Korčula is also known for its wine, especially the dessert wine made from the *grk* grape cultivated around Lumbarda. The shipbuilding tradition continues on a lesser scale in a shipyard near Vela Luka.

Getting There & Away

Boat The island has two major entry ports – Korčula town and Vela Luka. All the Jadrolinija ferries between Split and Dubrovnik stop in Korčula town. From the second week in July to the first week in September, Jadrolinija runs the passenger boat *Adriana* four times a week from Split to Korčula town (two hours, 70KN) stopping at Hvar and once a week from Split to Vela Luka stopping at Hvar.

There's at least one car ferry a day from Vela Luka to Split (three hours, 25KN), calling at Hvar five times a week throughout the year. It leaves Vela Luka very early in the morning, so you might want to spend the night if you'll be catching it, although a bus from Korčula does connect. The ferry from Split is met by a bus at Vela Luka to go to Korčula town (15KN).

Once a week from June to September Jadrolinija runs a car-ferry between Korčula and Ancona, Italy (16 hours, 249KN) stopping at Split and Vis.

To go to Orebić look for the passenger launch (four times a day year-round except weekends, 15 minutes, 8KN one way) that leaves from the Hotel Korčula right below the old town's towers. If you're coming from Orebić and want to camp or stay at the hotel take the car-ferry to Bon Repos in Dominče (6.80KN, 15 minutes). The car-ferry is the only alternative on weekends. On Saturdays, it connects with the bus from Lumbarda but on Sunday there's only one bus in the morning from Korčula to Orebić and one late afternoon bus coming back.

Bus There's a daily bus to Dubrovnik (113km, 35KN) stopping at Orebić as well as a daily bus to Zagreb (150KN) and two buses a week to Sarajevo (145KN).

Six daily buses link Korčula town to Vela Luka at the west end of the island (48km, 1½ hours, 15KN). But service is sharply reduced on weekends.

KORČULA
- pop 3000   ☎ 020

The town of Korčula at the north-east tip of the island hugs a small, hilly peninsula jutting into the Adriatic. With its round defensive towers and compact cluster of red-roofed houses, Korčula is a typical medieval Dalmatian town. It's a peaceful little place with grey stone houses nestling between the deep green hills and gunmetal-blue sea. There are rustling palms all around and lots to see and do, so it's worth planning a relaxed four-night stay to avoid the 30% surcharge on private rooms. Day trips are possible to Lumbarda and Vela Luka, to Orebić on the Pelješac Peninsula, and to the islands of Badija and Mljet.

Although documents indicate that a walled city existed on this site in the 13th century, it wasn't until the 15th century that the current city was built. Construction of the city coincided with the apogee of stone carving skills on the island, lending the

buildings and streets a distinctive style. The town's layout was cleverly designed to insure the comfort and safety of its inhabitants. Streets running west are straight in order to open the city to the refreshing *maestral* wind from the west while streets running east are slightly curved to minimise the force of the *jura* from the north-east. Streets fan out toward the north, allowing the city's defenders to easily reach the towers and walls, especially the critical northern portion facing the Pelješac channel.

In the 16th century, carvers added decorative flourishes such as ornate columns and coats-of-arms on building facades which gave a Renaissance look to the original Gothic core. People began building houses south of the old town in the 17th and 18th centuries as the threat of invasion diminished and they no longer needed to protect themselves behind walls. The narrow streets and stone houses in the 'new' suburb attracted merchants and artisans and, even today, this is where you'll find most commercial activity.

Orientation
The big Jadrolinija car-ferry usually drops you off below the walls of the old town of Korčula in the east harbour unless there's too much wind, in which case the ferry ties up in the west harbour in front of the Hotel Korčula and the tourist office. The passenger launches to Orebić also tie up in the west harbour. The bus station (no left-luggage office) is south of town past the marina on the way to the large hotels.

Most people head to the beaches of Orebić but the waters around town are clean enough to swim from any point. There's a small cove next to the large Governor's Gate, and rocky beaches around the hotels and around the Sveti Nikole promenade south-west of the old town.

Information
Tourist Offices The Turistički Ured (☎ 715 701) is in the loggia next to the Hotel Korčula. It's a good source of information for events in town and around the island and

is open daily from 8 am to 8 pm. The Jadrolinija office (☎ 711 101) about 25m up from the harbour is open Monday, Wednesday, Friday and Saturday from 5 am to 5 pm, Tuesday 7.30 am to 7.30 pm, Thursday 8 am to 3 pm and Sunday 6 am to 1 pm.

Money There's no ATM machine on the island but you can change money at the post office or any of the travel agencies listed above. There's also Splitskabanka where you can change money or get a cash advance

on your Visa card. It's open Monday to Friday from 7.30 am to 7.30 pm, Saturday 7.30 am to 1 pm.

Post & Communications The post office (with public telephones) is rather hidden next to the stairs up to the old town and is open Monday to Friday from 7 am to 8 pm and Saturday 7 am to 5 pm. The postcode for Korčula is 20260. You can check your email and surf the net at Tino Computers (☎ 715 048, tino.computers@ibm.net) on

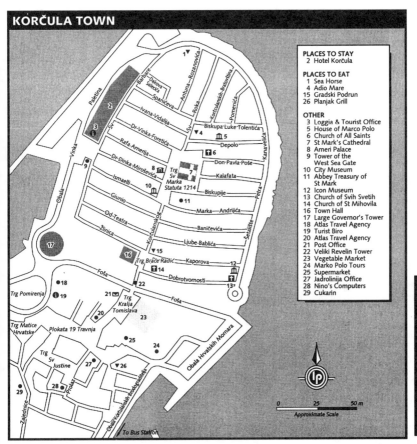

KORČULA TOWN

PLACES TO STAY
2 Hotel Korčula

PLACES TO EAT
1 Sea Horse
4 Adio Mare
15 Gradski Podrun
26 Planjak Grill

OTHER
3 Loggia & Tourist Office
5 House of Marco Polo
6 Church of All Saints
7 St Mark's Cathedral
8 Arneri Palace
9 Tower of the West Sea Gate
10 City Museum
11 Abbey Treasury of St Mark
12 Icon Museum
13 Church of Svih Svetih
14 Church of St Mihovila
16 Town Hall
17 Large Governor's Tower
18 Atlas Travel Agency
19 Turist Biro
20 Atlas Travel Agency
21 Post Office
22 Veliki Revelin Tower
23 Vegetable Market
24 Marko Polo Tours
25 Supermarket
27 Jadrolinija Office
28 Nino's Computers
29 Cukarin

SOUTHERN DALMATIA

Sveti Justina and it costs only 4.80KN for ten minutes. It's open Monday to Saturday from 10 am to 2 pm and 6 to 10 pm, and Sunday 6 to 10 pm.

Travel Agencies The Turist Biro (☎ 711 067) is near the old town and is open Monday to Saturday from 8 am to 9 pm and Sunday 8 am to 1 pm during the summer. Atlas travel agency (☎ 711 231) is the local American Express representative, open Monday to Saturday from 7 am to 1 pm and 6.30 to 9 pm, Sunday 8 am to 1 pm. Both offices close afternoons and Sunday during the winter. Marko Polo Tours (☎ 715 400, fax 715 800, marko-polo-tours@du.tel.hr) is right on the harbour and is open daily from 8 am to 8 pm.

Things to See

Take a closer look at the remaining **walls and towers** that make a sea approach to the town particularly striking. On the west harbour the **Tower of the West Sea Gate** has an inscription in Latin from 1592 stating that Korčula was founded after the fall of Troy. Nearby is the conical **Large Governor's Tower** (1483) and **Small Governor's Tower** (1449) which protected the harbour and the Governor's Palace which used to stand next to the town hall.

The entrance to the old city is through the **Veliki Revelin** southern land gate. Built in the 13th century and later extended, the tower is adorned with coats-of-arms of the Venetian Doge and Korčulan governors. There was originally a wooden drawbridge here but it was replaced in the 18th century by the wide stone steps that give a sense of grandeur to the entrance. The only remaining part of the town walls stretch west of this tower.

Other sightseeing is centred on Cathedral Square dominated by the magnificent **St Mark's Cathedral** (Katedrala Sveti Marka). This 15th century cathedral was built from Korčula limestone in a Gothic-Renaissance style by Italian and local artisans. Over the solemn portal, the triangular gable cornice is decorated with a two-tailed mermaid, an

elephant and other sculptures. The bell tower that rises from the cathedral over the town is topped by a balustrade and ornate cupola, beautifully carved by the Korčulan Marko Andrijić.

The interior of the cathedral features modern sculptures in the baptistery including a *Pietá* by Ivan Meštrović. The ciborium was also carved by Andrijić and behind it is the altarpiece painting *Three Saints* by Tintoretto. Another painting attributed to Tintoretto or his workshop, *The Annunciation*, is on the baroque altar of St Antony. Other noteworthy works include a bronze statue of St Blaise by Meštrović near the altar on the north aisle and a painting by the Venetian artist Jacopo Bassano in the apse of the south aisle. In the summer the cathedral is open from 10 am to 1 pm and 5 to 7 pm but off season it's open for mass only.

The **treasury** in the 14th century Abbey Palace next to the cathedral is also worth a look. Past the ante-room with it's collection of icons you'll enter the hall of Dalmatian art with an excellent selection of 15th and 16th century Dalmatian paintings. The most outstanding work is the polyptych of *The Virgin* by Blaž Trogiranin. There are also liturgical items, jewellery, furniture and ancient documents relating to the history of Korčula. The treasury is open Monday to Saturday from 10 am to 1 pm and 5 to 7 pm.

The **town museum** is in the 15th century Gabriellis Palace opposite the treasury and traces the history and culture of Korčula throughout the ages beginning with a tablet recording the Greek presence on the island in the 3rd century BC. The stone-carving collection follows the development of that craft with sculptures and stone-mason tools, and the shipbuilding hall displays tools and models of local ships. There's also an archaeology collection with prehistoric objects, and an art collection with furniture, textiles and portraits. Explanations are in English and the museum is open all year Monday to Saturday from 9 am to 1 pm and 6 to 7 pm.

Before leaving the square, notice the elegantly ornamented **Arneri Palace** next door

Marco Polo, First Son of Korčula

Adventurer, merchant and author of the world's first travel book, Marco Polo had a controversial, action-packed life. He spent 17 years in China as a close personal friend of Kublai Khan and then dictated a fantastical account of his experience to a fellow inmate in a Genoese prison who happened to be a popular romance writer. Although rich in detail about 13th century China, mainland Asia and even Japan and Zanzibar, his tales were widely discounted at the time. Yet, it got Western Europeans thinking about the Far East and, for 700 years, his book remained an essential source on Mongol China. Modern researchers are now questioning whether he ever visited China or only rehashed accounts from Arab and Persian sources. How did he miss Chinese women's bound feet, the popularity of tea or the Great Wall of China?

Korčulans are untroubled by such piddling details. They claim that he was born in Korčula in 1254, went to Venice with his family in 1269, wandered the world, returned to Venice and was captured in the great Venice-Genoa naval battle of 1296 which landed him in the Genoese prison. The house in which he was allegedly born is being turned into a small museum in honour of his voyages. Korčulans celebrated the 700th anniversary of his birth in 1954, the 700th anniversary of his return from China in 1995 and recently celebrated the 700th anniversary of the Venice-Genoa naval battle that took place near Korčula. Plans are afoot for a Marco Polo Information Centre.

Evidence for the claim that Marco Polo was born in Korčula is sketchy. Korčulans point to the Depolo family that has evidently been based in Korčula for many centuries, at least as far back as Marco Polo's birth. Records indicate that the house on Depolo ulica, considered as his birthplace was given to the Depolo family in 1400, 76 years after Marco Polo's death. Perhaps they reclaimed it?

The claim that Marco Polo came from a Dalmatian family is somewhat more strongly supported. A number of early Italian chroniclers theorise that his family was Dalmatian and a more recent writer, HH Hart in his book *Venetian Adventurer: Marco Polo*, propounded the view that Marco Polo's family came from Šibenik. Under this theory, his name was originally *Pile*, which means chicken in Croatian, and over time became *Polo* – chicken in Italian.

Wherever Marco Polo was born, it is the Korčulans who are now the most devoted to him. He deserves to be remembered even if it turns out that his travel book was written about a place he never visited (which could never happen today, rest assured). Over the centuries he has come to symbolise the unquenchable human need to explore faraway lands, to boldly go where no one has gone before, and then produce an 'as-told-to' bestseller about it all.

to the museum and extending west down the narrow street of the same name.

It's said that Marco Polo was born in Korčula in 1254; for a small fee, you can climb the tower of the house on ulica Depolo that is supposed to have been his. It's open from 10 am to noon and from 5 to 7 pm. There's also an **icon museum** in the old town which is open Monday to Saturday from 10 am to noon and 5 to 7 pm. It isn't much of a museum, but there are some interesting Byzantine icons painted on wood on a gold background as well as 17th and 18th century ritual objects. Visitors are let into the beautiful old **Church of All Saints** next door as a bonus. This 18th century baroque church features a carved and painted 15th century rood screen and a wooden late-18th century *Pietá* besides a wealth of local religious paintings.

In the high summer season, water taxis at the Jadrolinija port collect passengers to visit various points on the island as well as **Badija island**, which features a 15th century Franciscan monastery (now a budget hotel) and a naturist beach.

Activities

You can rent a bike in Hotel Park (☎ 726 473) for 15KN an hour or 60KN a day or rent a motorcycle from Đir (☎/fax 715 872, ☎ 098 243 209 or ☎ 715 120) on Ante Starčevića which has a variety of motorcycles starting at 100KN for two hours and 220KN for 24 hours, 550KN for three days and 1150KN for a week. It's open daily from 9 am to noon.

Organised Tours

Marko Polo tours and Atlas travel agency offer tours to Mljet (122KN) and guided tours of Korčula island (105KN), as well as a half-day boat trip around the surrounding islands (74KN).

Special Events

Every visitor who happens to be in Korčula on Thursday in July or August inevitably winds up at the Moreška Sword Dance. Tickets cost 35KN and can be purchased from the Turist Biro or Marko Polo tours. If you can work out the transportation, the Kumpanija dances in Pupnat, Smokvica, Blato and Čara make a fun night out but, as yet, there's no bus that makes the run.

Holy Week celebrations in town are particularly elaborate. Beginning on Palm Sunday, the entire week before Easter is devoted to ceremonies and processions organised by the local religious brotherhoods dressed in traditional costumes. The townspeople sing medieval songs and hymns, Biblical events are re-enacted and the city gates are blessed. The most solemn processions are on Good Friday when members of all the brotherhoods parade through the streets. A schedule of events is available at the tourist office but keep in mind that these are religious events and spectators are expected to be discreet about photos.

Sword Dances

One of the island's most colourful traditions is the Moreška Sword Dance, performed in Korčula since the 15th century. Although probably of Spanish origin, Korčula is now the only place in which it is performed. The dance tells the story of two kings – the White King (dressed in red) and the Black King – who fight for a princess abducted by the Black King. In the spoken introduction the princess declares her love for the White King and the Black King refuses to relinquish her. The two armies draw swords and 'fight' in an intricate dance accompanied by a band. Enthusiastic townspeople perform the dance which takes place outside the southern gate. Although traditionally performed only on Korčula's town day, 29 July, the dance now takes place every Thursday evening in July and August. There are also Kumpanija dances around the island regularly in Pupnat, Smokvica, Blato and Čara. The dance also involves a 'fight' between rival armies and culminates in the unfurling of a huge flag. The dance is accompanied by the local instrument *mišnice* – a sort of bagpipe – and drums.

Places to Stay

Camping The campsite closest to town is *Autocamp Kalac* (☎ 711 182) in a pretty spot near the Hotel Bon Repos. It's open from June to September and charges 21KN a person and 14KN a tent. There are other camping grounds near Vela Luka and in Orebić.

Private Rooms The Turist Biro (☎ 711 067), Atlas travel agency and Marko Polo Tours arrange private rooms, charging 72/108KN for a single/double, except in peak season, when prices increase by 20 to 50%, depending on the period. There are few mid-range rooms and there is usually a 30% surcharge for stays less than four nights. You may get a better deal from the private operators who meet the boats but check with the agencies first, since they're only a few steps from the harbour.

Hotels The cheapest place to stay is the budget *Badija* (☎ *711 115, fax 711 746*) on Badija island which has a pool, beach, handball courts and other sports facilities. The hotel is in a restored monastery and the rooms are as basic as you would expect from monk's quarters. Singles/doubles are 162/281KN with full board; bathrooms are shared.

Hotel Bon Repos (☎ *711 102*) outside of town on the road to Lumbarda has manicured grounds and a large pool overlooking a small beach. Rates are 316/489KN a single/double with bath and breakfast. There are also four-person apartments available for 482KN. In town, the *Hotel Park* (☎ *726 004*) charges 316/489KN a single/double with bath and breakfast.

The most luxurious hotel in town is the *Hotel Liburna* (☎ *726 006, fax 711 746*) on the south-eastern tip of Obala Hrvatskih Mornara with a pool, tennis courts and other facilities. Singles/doubles in high season cost 288/576KN.

The *Hotel Korčula* (☎ *711 078, fax 711 746*) on the west harbour has the most character and a wide terrace to linger over coffee. Rooms vary in size but are in very good condition and the location is ideal for exploring the town. Singles/doubles in high season cost 288/576KN.

Places to Eat

Just around the corner from Marco Polo's house on ulica Sveti Roka, *Adio Mare* has a charming maritime decor and a variety of fresh fish, but on summer evenings you may have a long wait to get in. The fresh fish and mussels are worth it though. Expect to pay from 55KN to 100KN for a meal. The restaurant is open daily from 10 am to midnight. *Sea Horse* on Šetalište Petra Kanavelica is another good seafood place for about the same price, also open daily from 10 am to midnight.

Gradski Podrum just inside the southern gate is less expensive and serves fish

Korčula style – boiled with potatoes and topped with tomato sauce for 60KN. Pasta and seafood dishes are also reasonable. The restaurant is open daily from 8 am to 10 pm. Restaurant-grill *Planjak*, between the supermarket and the Jadrolinija office in town on Plokata 19 Travnja is popular with a local crowd who appreciate the fresh, Dalmatian dishes as much as the low prices. It's open daily from 9 am to 11 pm.

A 20 minute walk outside town on the road to Lumbarda takes you to another local favourite, *Gastrionica Hajuk*, which serves up delicious home-cooked food in a laidback ambience. It's open daily from noon to midnight.

Pick up picnic supplies at the supermarket (open Monday to Saturday from 6 am to 9 pm and Sunday 7 to 11 am). For dessert head to *Cukarin* which serves up scrumptious local pastries such as *Cukarini*, which is a sweet biscuit, *Klajun*, a pastry stuffed with walnuts, and *Amareta*, a round, rich cake with almonds. It's open daily from 8 am to 8 pm.

LUMBARDA

Surrounded by vineyards and coves, Lumbarda is a laid-back village around a harbour on the south-east end of the island. The sandy soil is perfect for the cultivation of grapes, and wine from the Grk grape is Lumbarda's most famous product. Greeks were the first to settle the island followed by Romans. In the 16th century aristocrats from Korčula built summer houses around Lumbarda and it remains a bucolic retreat from more urbanised Korčula town. The town beaches are small but sandy. A good ocean beach (Plaza Pržina) is on the other side of the vineyards beyond the supermarket.

Information

The bus stops in the town centre. The tourist office (☎ 712 005) is up the street from the bus stop and is open daily from 8 am to 2 pm and 7 to 10 pm in the summer but is closed evenings and Sunday in winter. The post office is next door and is open Monday to Saturday from 7 am to 9 pm.

Places to Stay & Eat

The Turist Biro (☎/fax 712 023) in town arranges private accommodation and there are several small, inexpensive camp sites up the hill from the bus stop.

The **Bebić** pension *(☎ 712 183)* and restaurant has a breathtaking view over the coast and serves good food. Located on a cove across from town, the pension has a small beach for swimming. A double room or apartment is 200KN with bath and breakfast or 234KN per person with half-board which is highly advisable since the food is delicious. Even if you're staying elsewhere try to grab a meal at Bebić's place. You'll only pay 30KN for a risotto and 45KN for grilled scampi.

Hotel Borik *(☎ 712 188, fax 712 433)* is set back from the road up a small hill in the centre of town and open from June to September. Rooms are 128KN per person in high season (no single supplement) with a 20% surcharge for a sea view. Half-board can also be arranged and it's definitely quiet.

Getting There & Away

In Korčula town, water taxis wait around the Jadrolinija port for passengers to Lumbarda and you'll only pay 5KN to 10KN depending on the number of passengers. Buses to Lumbarda run about hourly in the morning (7km, 5KN) but there's no service on Sunday.

VELA LUKA

Vela Luka, at the west end of Korčula, is the centre of the island's fishing industry because of its large sheltered harbour. There isn't a lot to see at Vela Luka but if you have some time to kill, take a look at the neolithic **Vela Špilje Cave**, which is spacious enough to make cave-dwelling seem like a viable accommodation option. Signs from town direct you to the cave which overlooks the town and harbour.

There are no real beaches, so if you're arriving by ferry from Split or Hvar you might jump right on the waiting bus to Korčula town and look for a room there.

Places to Stay & Eat

Camping Mindel *(☎ 812 494)* is 6km northwest of Vela Luka but there's no bus service there. The Turist Biro (☎ 812 042), open in summer only from 8 am to 6 pm, arranges private rooms.

If the Turist Biro is closed your next best bet is the **Pansion u Domaćinstva Barćot** *(☎ 812 014)*, directly behind the Jadran Hotel which is about 50m from the ferry stop. This attractive 24-room guesthouse is open all year and prices are just a little above what you'd pay for private rooms. Some rooms on the 3rd floor have balconies. It's beside the Jadran Hotel *(☎ 812 036)*, on the waterfront 100m from the ferry landing. **Hotel Posejdon** *(☎ 812 227)* is a large, bland hotel but its location on a cove with a narrow beach is one saving grace. Singles/doubles with half-board are 280/460KN.

The restaurant **Pod Bore** on the harbour is good and inexpensive, serving spaghetti starting at 18KN, a mixed meat platter for 44KN and seafood for 180KN a kilogram.

Orebić

• **pop 1489**　　☎ 020

Orebić, on the south coast of the Pelješac Peninsula between Korčula and Ploče, has the best beaches in southern Dalmatia – wide sandy coves bordered by groves of tamarisk and pine. Only 2.5km across the water from Korčula, Orebić is a perfect day trip from Korčula or an alternative place to stay.

After enough lazing on the beach, you can take advantage of some excellent hiking up and around Mt Ilija or poke around in a couple of churches and museums. Mt Ilija protects the town from harsh northern winds, allowing Mediterranean vegetation to flourish. The temperature is usually a few degrees warmer than Korčula; spring arrives earlier and summer leaves later.

Orebić and the Pelješac Peninsula became part of Dubrovnik in 1333 when it was purchased from Serbia and remained in the Republic until 1806. Until the 16th century, the town was known as Trstenica (the name of its eastern bay) and was an important maritime centre. In fact, the town is named after a family of sea captains who, in 1658, built a citadel as a defence against the Turks. Many of the houses and exotic gardens built by prosperous sea captains still grace Orebić and its surroundings. The height of Orebić seafaring occurred in the 18th and 19th century when it was the seat of one of the largest companies of the day – the Associazione Marittima di Sabioncello. With the decline of shipping, Orebić has reverted to the classic fallback position of all struggling local economies – tourism.

Orientation & Information
The ferry from Korčula ties up in the town centre, just steps from the tourist office (☎ 713 718), open from 8 am to 8 pm in summer, 8 am to 1 pm off season (closed from October to March). The bus station (no left-luggage) is at the end of the ferry dock.

There's a beach west of the dock but the best beach is the long stretch at Trstenica cove about 500m east of the dock along Šetalište Kneza Domagoja.

The post office is next to the tourist office and is open Monday to Saturday from 7 am to 9 pm, Sunday 7 am to noon. The postcode for Orebić is 20250.

Things to See & Do
The Maritime Museum on Obala Pomoraca, next to the tourist office is interesting, although not a must. There are paintings of boats, boating memorabilia, navigational aids and prehistoric finds from archaeological excavations in nearby Majsan. It's open Tuesday to Sunday from 9 am to 1 pm and explanations are in English.

Orebić is great for hiking so pick up a map of the hiking trails from the tourist office. A trail through pine woods leads from Hotel Bellevue to a 15th century Franciscan monastery on a ridge 152m above the sea. From their vantage point, Dubrovnik patrols could keep an eye on the Venetian

ships moored on Korčula and notify the authorities of any suspicious movements. The village of Karmen near the monastery is the starting point for walks to picturesque upper villages and the more daring climb to the top of Mt Ilija (961m), the bare grey massif that hangs above Orebić. Your reward is a sweeping view of the entire coast. On a hill east of the monastery is the Lady of Karmen Church (Gospa od Karmena) next to several huge cypresses as well as a baroque loggia and the ruins of a duke's castle.

Places to Stay
The camping grounds *Hauptstrand (☎ 713 399)* and *Trstenica (☎ 713 348)* overlook the long, sandy Trstenica beach. The latter also rents rooms for 72KN per person, not including breakfast, and with a shared bathroom.

The helpful tourist office rents private rooms (50/137KN a single/double) and can provide a town map. If the office is closed, try Orebić Tours (☎ 713 367), Jelačića 84a, or just walk along the main road or the coastal road looking for *sobe* signs – you'll soon find something.

All the modern resort complexes are west of town. The closest is the *Hotel Bellevue (☎ 713 148, fax 713 193)* on a rocky beach. Facilities include tennis courts and watersports and rooms run 338/525KN a single/double in high season.

Getting There & Away
If you're coming from the coast, there are four daily ferries (six in summer) from Ploče to Trpanj that connect with a bus to Orebić. Korčula buses to Dubrovnik, Zagreb and Sarajevo stop at Orebić. See Korčula for additional bus and ferry information.

Language

Croatian is a southern variant within the Slavonic language family. Other languages in this group include Serbian, Bosnian and Slovene. Croatian and Serbian are still often referred to as one language (with various titles such as Serbo-Croat or Croato-Serbian); until recent events in the former Yugoslavia, Bosnian was also classified within the general 'Serbo-Croatian' moniker. Politics aside the three languages are, in linguistic terms, structurally and lexically so similar that they are effectively dialectal variants of the one language.

Pronunciation

The Croatian writing system is phonetically consistent: every letter is pronounced and its sound will not vary from word to word. With regard to the position of stress, only one rule can be given: the last syllable of a word is never stressed. In most cases the accent falls on the first vowel in the word.

Croatian uses a Roman alphabet (unlike Serbian, which uses the Cyrillic alphabet); many letters are pronounced as in English – the following are some specific pronunciations.

c	as the 'ts' in 'cats'
ć	as the 'cu' in 'cure'
č	as the 'ch' in 'chop'
đ	as the 'gu' in 'legume'
dž	as the 'j' in 'just'
j	as the 'y' in 'young'
lj	as the 'lli' in 'million'
nj	as the 'ny' in 'canyon'
š	as the 'sh' in 'hush'
ž	as the 's' in 'pleasure'

Basics

Hello.	*Zdravo.*
Goodbye.	*Doviđenja.*
Yes.	*Da.*
No.	*Ne.*
Please.	*Molim.*
Thank you.	*Hvala.*

That's fine/	*U redu je/*
You're welcome.	*Nema na čemu.*
Excuse me.	*Oprostite.*
Sorry. (excuse me, forgive me)	*Pardon. (izvinite)*
Do you speak English?	*Govorite li engleski?*
How much is it ...?	*Koliko košta ...?*
What's your name?	*Kako se zovete?*
My name is ...	*Zovem se ...*

Getting Around

What time does the ... leave/arrive?	*Kada ... polazi/dolazi?*
boat	*brod*
bus (city/ intercity)	*autobus (gradski/ međugradski)*
train	*vlak*
tram	*tramvaj*
one-way ticket	*kartu u jednom pravcu*
return ticket	*povratnu kartu*
1st/2nd class	*prvu/drugu klasu*
Where is the bus/ tram stop?	*Gdje je autobuska/ tramvajska postaja?*
Can you show me (on the map)?	*Možete li mi pokazati (na karti)?*
Go straight ahead.	*Idite pravo naprijed.*
Turn left.	*Skrenite lijevo.*

Signs	
ENTRANCE	*ULAZ*
EXIT	*IZLAZ*
NO VACANCIES	*NEMA SLOBODNE*
INFORMATION	*SOBE*
	INFORMACIJE
OPEN	*OTVORENO*
CLOSED	*ZATVORENO*
POLICE	*POLICIJA*
POLICE STATION	*POLICIJA*
PROHIBITED	*ZABRANJENO*
ROOMS AVAILABLE	*SLOBODNE SOBE*
TOILETS	*ZAHODI*

Turn right.	*Skrenite desno.*
near/far	*blizu/daleko*

Around Town

bank	*banka*
... embassy	*... ambasada*
my hotel	*moj hotel*
market	*tržnica*
post office	*pošta*
telephone centre	*telefonska centrala*
tourist office	*turistički informativni biro*

Accommodation

hotel	*hotel*
guesthouse	*privatno prenoćište*
youth hostel	*omladinsko prenoćište*
camping ground	*kamping*

Do you have any rooms available?	*Imate li slobodne sobe?*

How much is it ...?	*Koliko košta za ...?*
per night	*jednu noć*
per person	*po osobi*

Does it include breakfast?	*Dali je u cijenu uključen i doručak?*

I'd like a ... room.	*Želim sobu ... krevetom.*
single	*sa jednim*
double	*sa duplim*

Time, Days & Numbers

What time is it?	*Koliko je sati?*
today	*danas*

Emergencies

Help!	*Upomoć!*
Call a doctor!	*Pozovite liječnika!*
Call the police!	*Pozovite policiju!*
Go away!	*Idite!*
I'm lost.	*Izgubio sam se.* (m)
	Izgubila sam se. (f)

tomorrow	*sutra*
yesterday	*jučer*
in the morning	*ujutro*
in the afternoon	*popodne*
Monday	*ponedeljak*
Tuesday	*utorak*
Wednesday	*srijeda*
Thursday	*četvrtak*
Friday	*petak*
Saturday	*subota*
Sunday	*nedjelja*

1	*jedan*
2	*dva*
3	*tri*
4	*četiri*
5	*pet*
6	*šest*
7	*sedam*
8	*osam*
9	*devet*
10	*deset*
100	*sto*
1000	*tisuća*

one million	*jedan milijun*

Glossary

ACI Club – Adriatic Croatia International Club, an association of Croatian marinas

amphora – large, two-handled vase in which wine or water was kept

apse – the altar area of a church

autobusni kolodvor – bus station

Avars – Eastern European people that waged war against Byzantium from the 6th to 9th centuries

ban – viceroy or governor

basilica – early Christian church

benzil – petrol

bife – snack bar

brijeg – hill

britva – razor

brod – boat

bura – cold north-easterly wind

cesta – road

ciborium – permanent arched canopy over an altar

cijena – price

crkva – church

dolazak – arrivals

dom – dormitory, mountain cottage or lodge

doručak – breakfast

frizer – hairdresser

galerija – gallery

gardaroba – left-luggage office

glagolitic – ancient Slavonic language put into writing by Greek missionaries Cyril and Methodius

gora – mountain

gostionica – family-run restaurant sometimes with a few rooms to rent

grad – city

HAK – Croatian Automobile Association

HDZ – Hrvatska Demokratska Zajednica, the ruling political party

HPT – Croatian post and telecommunications system

hrid – rock

Illyrians – ancient inhabitants of the Adriatic coast, defeated by the Romans in the 2nd century BC

izlaz – exit

jezero – lake

kasa – cash register

karst – porous limestone marked by underground rivers, gorges and caves

karta – ticket

kavana – cafe

kazalište – theatre

kino – cinema

knjižara – bookshop

kolo – a Slavic circle dance often accompanied by a *tamburitza*

kolodvor – train station

konoba – The traditional term for a small, intimate dining spot, often located in a cellar, now applies to a wide variety of restaurants

krajina – frontier

ljekarna – pharmacy

luka – harbour, port

maestral – strong, steady westerly wind

malo – little

maquis – a dense growth of mostly evergreen shrubs and small trees

mjenjačnica – exchange office

moški – men (toilet)

most – bridge

muzej – museum

nave – central part of a church flanked by two aisles

obala – waterfront

odlazak – departures, also *polazak*

otok – island

otvoreno – open

partisans – WWII anti-fascist liberation organisation lead by Maršal Tito

peć – cave

pivnica – pub, beer hall

pleter – plaited ornamentation often found in churches
plaža – beach
plovidba – navigation
polje – collapsed limestone area often under cultivation
poltrone – reclining seats
potok – stream
put – path, trail

restauracija – restaurant
rijeka – river
rt (sic) – cape, promontory
ručak – lunch

Sabor – Parliament
samoposluzivanje – self-service restaurant
sobe – rooms available
stanica – stop (bus or tram)
sveti – saint
tamburitza – a three or five-string mandolin
tisak – newsstand

toplice – spa
trajekt – ferry
trg – square
turistički ured – tourist office
turistički zajednica – tourist association

ulica – street
uvala – bay
ulaz – entrance
uskoks – a community of pirates that lived in 16th century Senj

večera – dinner
velik – large
vlak – train large

vozni red – timetable
vrh – summit, peak

zatvoreno – closed
ženske – women (toilet)
ZET – Zagreb tram system

Food Glossary

bakalar – cod
bijelo vino – white wine
blitva – green, leafy vegetable indigenous to Croatia
brodet – fish soup
burek – a heavy pastry stuffed with meat or cheese

češnjak – garlic
čevapčići – spicy beef or pork meatballs
crno vino – red wine

govedina – beef

jelovnik – menu
juha – soup

kava – coffee
kruh – bread
krumpir – potatoes

lignje – squid
luk – onion

maslac – butter
meso – meat
miješano meso – mixed grill
milijeko – milk
mlince – baked noodles

na roštilju – grilled

oštriga – oyster

palačinke – pancakes
papar – pepper
pastrva – trout
pečeno – roasted
pile – chicken
piletina – chicken
piti – drink
pivo – beer
pršut – prosciutto
prženo – fried

račun – bill
rajčica – tomatoes
rakovi – crabs
ražnjiči – shish kebab
riba – fish
risotto – cooked rice dish made from Arborio rice, often served with seafood

sendviče – sandwich
senf – mustard
sipe – cuttlefish
sir – cheese
sladoled – ice cream
slastičarna – pastry shop
sok – juice
sol – salt
svinjetina – pork
škampi – shrimp
šunka – ham

voda – water

LONELY PLANET

Phrasebooks

Lonely Planet phrasebooks are packed with essential words and phrases to help travellers communicate with the locals. With colour tabs for quick reference, an extensive vocabulary and use of script, these handy pocket-sized language guides cover day-to-day travel situations.

- handy pocket-sized books
- easy to understand Pronunciation chapter
- clear & comprehensive Grammar chapter
- romanisation alongside script to allow ease of pronunciation
- script throughout so users can point to phrases for every situation
- full of cultural information and tips for the traveller

'...vital for a real DIY spirit and attitude in language learning'
– Backpacker

'the phrasebooks have good cultural backgrounders and offer solid advice for challenging situations in remote locations'
– San Francisco Examiner

Arabic (Egyptian) • Arabic (Moroccan) • Australian *(Australian English, Aboriginal and Torres Strait languages)* • Baltic States *(Estonian, Latvian, Lithuanian)* • Bengali • Brazilian • Burmese • Cantonese • Central Asia • Central Europe *(Czech, French, German, Hungarian, Italian, Slovak)* • Eastern Europe *(Bulgarian, Czech, Hungarian, Polish, Romanian, Slovak)* • Ethiopian (Amharic) • Fijian • French • German • Greek • Hill Tribes • Hindi/Urdu • Indonesian • Italian • Japanese • Korean • Lao • Latin American Spanish • Malay • Mandarin • Mediterranean Europe *(Albanian, Croatian, Greek, Italian, Macedonian, Maltese, Serbian, Slovene)* • Mongolian • Nepali • Papua New Guinea • Pilipino (Tagalog) • Quechua • Russian • Scandinavian Europe *(Danish, Finnish, Icelandic, Norwegian, Swedish)* • South-East Asia *(Burmese, Indonesian, Khmer, Lao, Malay, Tagalog Pilipino, Thai, Vietnamese)* • Spanish (Castilian) *(also includes Catalan, Galician and Basque)* • Sri Lanka • Swahili • Thai • Tibetan • Turkish • Ukrainian • USA *(US English, Vernacular, Native American languages, Hawaiian)* • Vietnamese • Western Europe *(Basque, Catalan, Dutch, French, German, Greek, Irish)*

LONELY PLANET

Guides by Region

L onely Planet is known worldwide for publishing practical, reliable and no-nonsense travel information in our guides and on our Web site. The Lonely Planet list covers just about every accessible part of the world. Currently there are nine series: travel guides, shoe-string guides, walking guides, city guides, phrasebooks, audio packs, travel atlases, diving and snorkeling guides and travel literature.

AFRICA Africa – the South • Africa on a shoestring • Arabic (Egyptian) phrasebook • Arabic (Moroc-can) phrasebook • Cairo • Cape Town • Central Africa • East Africa • Egypt • Egypt travel atlas • Ethiopian (Amharic) phrasebook • The Gambia & Senegal • Kenya • Kenya travel atlas • Malawi, Mozambique & Zambia • Morocco • North Africa • South Africa, Lesotho & Swaziland • South Africa, Lesotho & Swaziland travel atlas • Swahili phrasebook • Trekking in East Africa • Tunisia • West Africa • Zimbabwe, Botswana & Namibia • Zimbabwe, Botswana & Namibia travel atlas
Travel Literature: The Rainbird: A Central African Journey • Songs to an African Sunset: A Zimbabwean Story • Mali Blues: Traveling to an African Beat

AUSTRALIA & THE PACIFIC Australia • Australian phrasebook • Bushwalking in Australia • Bush-walking in Papua New Guinea • Fiji • Fijian phrasebook • Islands of Australia's Great Barrier Reef • Melbourne • Micronesia • New Caledonia • New South Wales & the ACT • New Zealand • Northern Ter-ritory • Outback Australia • Papua New Guinea • Papua New Guinea (Pidgin) phrasebook • Queensland • Rarotonga & the Cook Islands • Samoa • Solomon Islands • South Australia • Sydney • Tahiti & French Polynesia • Tasmania • Tonga • Tramping in New Zealand • Vanuatu • Victoria • Western Australia
Travel Literature: Islands in the Clouds • Sean & David's Long Drive

CENTRAL AMERICA & THE CARIBBEAN Bahamas and Turks & Caicos • Bermuda • Central America on a shoestring • Costa Rica • Cuba • Eastern Caribbean • Guatemala, Belize & Yucatán: La Ruta Maya • Jamaica • Mexico • Mexico City • Panama
Travel Literature: Green Dreams: Travels in Central America

EUROPE Amsterdam • Andalucía • Austria • Baltic States phrasebook • Berlin • Britain • Central Europe • Central Europe phrasebook • Czech & Slovak Republics • Denmark • Dublin • Eastern Europe • Eastern Europe phrasebook • Edinburgh • Estonia, Latvia & Lithuania • Europe • Finland • France • French phrasebook • Germany • German phrasebook • Greece • Greek phrasebook • Hungary • Iceland, Greenland & the Faroe Islands • Ireland • Italian phrasebook • Italy • Lisbon • London • Mediterranean Europe • Mediterranean Europe phrasebook • Paris • Poland • Portugal • Portugal travel atlas • Prague • Romania & Moldova • Russia, Ukraine & Belarus • Russian phrasebook • Scan-dinavian & Baltic Europe • Scandinavian Europe phrasebook • Scotland • Slovenia • Spain • Spanish phrasebook • St Petersburg • Switzerland • Trekking in Spain • Ukrainian phrasebook • Vienna • Walking in Britain • Walking in Italy • Walking in Switzerland • Western Europe • Western Europe phrasebook
Travel Literature: The Olive Grove: Travels in Greece

INDIAN SUBCONTINENT Bangladesh • Bengali phrasebook • Bhutan • Delhi • Goa • Hindi/Urdu phrasebook • India • India & Bangladesh travel atlas • Indian Himalaya • Karakoram Highway • Nepal • Nepali phrasebook • Pakistan • Rajasthan • South India • Sri Lanka • Sri Lanka phrasebook • Trekking in the Indian Himalaya • Trekking in the Karakoram & Hindukush • Trekking in the Nepal Himalaya
Travel Literature: In Rajasthan • Shopping for Buddhas

LONELY PLANET

Mail Order

Lonely Planet products are distributed worldwide. They are also available by mail order from Lonely Planet, so if you have difficulty finding a title please write to us. North and South American residents should write to 150 Linden St, Oakland, CA 94607, USA; European and African residents should write to 10a Spring Place, London NW5 3BH, UK; and residents of other countries to PO Box 617, Hawthorn, Victoria 3122, Australia.

ISLANDS OF THE INDIAN OCEAN Madagascar & Comoros ● Maldives ● Mauritius, Réunion & Seychelles

MIDDLE EAST & CENTRAL ASIA Arab Gulf States ● Central Asia ● Central Asia phrasebook ● Iran ● Israel & the Palestinian Territories ● Israel & the Palestinian Territories travel atlas ● Istanbul ● Jerusalem ● Jordan & Syria ● Jordan, Syria & Lebanon travel atlas ● Lebanon ● Middle East on a shoestring ● Turkey ● Turkish phrasebook ● Turkey travel atlas ● Yemen
Travel Literature: The Gates of Damascus ● Kingdom of the Film Stars: Journey into Jordan

NORTH AMERICA Alaska ● Backpacking in Alaska ● Baja California ● California & Nevada ● Canada ● Florida ● Hawaii ● Honolulu ● Los Angeles ● Miami ● New England USA ● New Orleans ● New York City ● New York, New Jersey & Pennsylvania ● Pacific Northwest USA ● Rocky Mountain States ● San Francisco ● Seattle ● Southwest USA ● USA phrasebook ● Washington, DC & the Capital Region
Travel Literature: Drive Thru America

NORTH-EAST ASIA Beijing ● Cantonese phrasebook ● China ● Hong Kong ● Hong Kong, Macau & Guangzhou ● Japan ● Japanese phrasebook ● Japanese audio pack ● Korea ● Korean phrasebook ● Kyoto ● Mandarin phrasebook ● Mongolia ● Mongolian phrasebook ● North-East Asia on a shoestring ● Seoul ● South-West China ● Taiwan ● Tibet ● Tibetan phrasebook ● Tokyo
Travel Literature: Lost Japan

SOUTH AMERICA Argentina, Uruguay & Paraguay ● Bolivia ● Brazil ● Brazilian phrasebook ● Buenos Aires ● Chile & Easter Island ● Chile & Easter Island travel atlas ● Colombia ● Ecuador & the Galapagos Islands ● Latin American Spanish phrasebook ● Peru ● Quechua phrasebook ● Rio de Janeiro ● South America on a shoestring ● Trekking in the Patagonian Andes ● Venezuela
Travel Literature: Full Circle: A South American Journey

SOUTH-EAST ASIA Bali & Lombok ● Bangkok ● Burmese phrasebook ● Cambodia ● Hill Tribes phrasebook ● Ho Chi Minh City ● Indonesia ● Indonesian phrasebook ● Indonesian audio pack ● Jakarta ● Java ● Laos ● Lao phrasebook ● Laos travel atlas ● Malay phrasebook ● Malaysia, Singapore & Brunei ● Myanmar (Burma) ● Philippines ● Pilipino (Tagalog) phrasebook ● Singapore ● South-East Asia on a shoestring ● South-East Asia phrasebook ● Thailand ● Thailand's Islands & Beaches ● Thailand travel atlas ● Thai phrasebook ● Thai audio pack ● Vietnam ● Vietnamese phrasebook ● Vietnam travel atlas

ALSO AVAILABLE: Antarctica ● Brief Encounters: Stories of Love, Sex & Travel ● Chasing Rickshaws ● Not the Only Planet: Travel Stories from Science Fiction ● Travel with Children ● Traveller's Tales

LONELY PLANET

Lonely Planet On-line
www.lonelyplanet.com *or* AOL keyword: lp

Whether you've just begun planning your next trip, or you're chasing down specific info on currency regulations or visa requirements, check out Lonely Planet On-line for up-to-the minute travel information.

As well as mini guides to more than 250 destinations, you'll find maps, photos, travel news, health and visa updates, travel advisories, and discussion of the ecological and political issues you need to be aware of as you travel. You'll also find timely upgrades to popular guidebooks which you can print out and stick in the back of your book.

There's also an on-line travellers' forum where you can share your experience of life on the road, meet travel companions and ask other travellers for their recommendations and advice.

And of course we have a complete and up-to-date list of all Lonely Planet travel products including travel guides, diving and snorkeling guides, phrasebooks, atlases, travel literature and videos, and a simple on-line ordering facility if you can't find the book you want elsewhere.

Lonely Planet Diving & Snorkeling Guides

Known for indispensible guidebooks to destinations all over the world, Lonely Planet's Pisces Books are the most popular series of diving and snorkeling titles available.

There are three series: **Diving & Snorkeling Guides**, **Shipwreck Diving** series and **Dive Into History**. Full colour throughout, the **Diving & Snorkeling Guides** combine quality photographs with detailed descriptions of the best dive sites for each location, giving divers a glimpse of what they can expect both on land and in water. The **Dive Into History** series is perfect for the adventure diver or armchair traveller. The **Shipwreck Diving** series provides all the details for exploring the most interesting wrecks in the Atlantic and Pacific oceans. The list also includes underwater nature and technical guides.

FREE Lonely Planet Newsletters

We love hearing from you and think you'd like to hear from us.

Planet Talk

Our FREE quarterly printed newsletter is full of tips from travellers and anecdotes from Lonely Planet guidebook authors. Every issue is packed with up-to-date travel news and advice, and includes:

- a postcard from Lonely Planet co-founder Tony Wheeler
- a swag of mail from travellers
- a look at life on the road through the eyes of a Lonely Planet author
- topical health advice
- prizes for the best travel yarn
- news about forthcoming Lonely Planet events
- a complete list of Lonely Planet books and other titles

To join our mailing list, residents of the UK, Europe and Africa can email us at go@lonelyplanet.co.uk; residents of North and South America can email us at info@lonelyplanet.com; the rest of the world can email us at talk2us@lonelyplanet.com.au, or contact any Lonely Planet office.

Comet

Our FREE monthly email newsletter brings you all the latest travel news, features, interviews, competitions, destination ideas, travellers' tips & tales, Q&As, raging debates and related links. Find out what's new on the Lonely Planet Web site and which books are about to hit the shelves.

Subscribe from your desktop: www.lonelyplanet.com/comet

Index

Text

A

accommodation 54-7
  camping 55
  hostels 55
  hotels 56-60
  private rooms 55-6
activities 50
  bicycle rental 125, 270
  boat rental 125, 231, 233
diving 223, 227, 231, 233,
    241
  hiking 51, 223, 241
  horse riding 126
  kayaking 51
  rock climbing 53, 185
  scuba diving 51-3, 126,
    256, *52*
  swimming 107, 125, 241
  tennis 233
  water skiing 231
  windsurfing 53, 126, 233
  yachting 50-1
air travel
  departure taxes 64
  to/from Croatia 64-5
  travellers with special needs
    64
  within Croatia 68
arts 30
  architecture 31-4, *150*
  literature 30-1
  music 30
  painting 31-4
  sculpture 31-4

B

Banija-Kordun region 97-9
Barbat 146
Baška 137-9
beaches 35-6
bicycle travel 71
Biševo 228
Blue Grotto 228
boat travel
  coastal ferries 69

  local ferries 70-1
  to Italy & Greece 67
Bol 232-6, **234-5**
books 43-4
  history & politics 44
  travel 43
Boz 190
Brač 228-37, **228-9**
Brela 224-5
Brijuni Islands 157-8
bus travel
  to/from Croatia 65-7
  within Croatia 68
business hours 50

C

car travel
  car rental 71
  road rules 71
  to/from Croatia 67
  within Croatia 70
castles 35
Cavtat 260-1
Charlemagne 15-16
climate 25-30
coastal route 36
courses 53-4
Cres island 122-32, **123**
Cres town 128-30
  getting there & away 130
  information 129
  orientation 129
  places to eat 130
  places to stay 129-30
  things to see 129
Crveni otok 162-3
customs 40

D

Đakovo 109-10
Dalmatia 205-73, **206**, **248-9**
dangers 47
Diocletian's Palace 209-10
disabled travellers 49
drinks 58
Drvenik Mali 221
Drvenik Veli 221
Dubrovnik 246-61, **252-4**
  entertainment 258-9
  getting there & away 259

  information 249-52
  orientation 249
  places to eat 258
  places to stay 256
  things to see 252-6
Dugi Otok 186-90

E

economy 29-30
education 30
Elafiti Islands 260
electricity 44
email 43
embassies & consulates 39-40
  Croatian embassies &
    consulates 39
  embassies & consulates in
    Croatia 40
Emperor Augustus 14-15
Emperor Diocletian 14-15
entertainment 59-60
  cinema 60
  terrace dancing 60
environment 26-30

F

fauna 26-30
fax services 42
Feral Tribune newspaper *45*
festivals 50
flora 26-30
food 57-8, *156*
Franjo Tudjman 28-30

G

galleries 35
gay travellers 49
geography 25-30
government & politics 27-30
Griffon vulture *184*
Grožnjan 169

H

health 46-9
  diarrhoea 48
  heatstroke 47
  insect bites 48
  snake bites 48

Bold indicates maps.
Italics indicates boxed text.

history 13-34
  Austro-Hungaria 19
  Chetniks 20-1
  Croatian Spring 21
  1848 revolution 18-19
  Habsburgs 16-17
  Illyrians 13-14
  independence 22
  Jewish population 20
  Napoleon 18
  Ottoman Empire 16-17
  Krajina 24-30
  Stalin 21
  Tito 20-1
  Ustashe 20
  Yugoslavia 21
hitchhiking 72
Hitler 20
Hrvatsko Zagorje 95-7
Hvar island 237-45
  getting there & away 238,
    238-9
  history 237-8
Hvar town 238-43, **240**
  information 238-40
  orientation 238
  places to eat 242
  places to stay 242
  things to see 240-1

I
Internet resources 43
Istria 147-69, **148**

J
Jelsa 244-5
Jelačic, Ban Josip *81*

K
Katarina island 162-3
Koločep 260
Komiža 227-8
Kopački Rit 110
Kornati Islands 203-4
Korčula 266-71, **264-5**
  information 266-8
  orientation 266
  places to eat 271
  places to stay 270-1
  special events 270
  things to see 268-70

Bold indicates maps.
Italics indicates boxed text.

Korčula Island 264-72, **133**
  getting there & away 265-6
  history 265, *269*
Košljun Island Monastery 139-46
Krajina 195
Krk Island 132-4, **135**
  getting around 134
  getting there & away 134
  history 132-4
Krk town 134-7
Krka National Park 202-3
Kvarner 111-46, **112**

L
landmines 47
laundry 44
legal matters 49
lesbian travellers 49
Lim Fjord 162-3
Lopar 145-6
Lopud 260
Lošinj island 122-32, **123**
Lumbarda 271-2
  getting there & away 272
  information 271
  places to stay & eat 272

M
magazines 44
Makarska 221-4
  getting there & away 224
  information 222-3
  orientation 222
  places to eat 224
  places to stay 223-4
  things to see 223
Mali Lošinj 124-7, **125**
  getting there & away 127
  information 124
  orientation 124
  places to eat 126-7
  places to stay 126-7
  things to see 124-5
maps 37
Meštrović, Ivan *212-13*
Meštrović Gallery (Split) 211
Mljet 261-4, **262-3**
  getting there & away 264
  Malo Jezero 262-3
  orientation 261-2
  places to eat 264
  places to stay 263-4
  things to see & do 262-3
  Veliko Jezero 262-3
money 40
  bargaining 42

changing money 41
  costs 41
  credit cards 41
  currency 40
  exchange rates 41
  tipping 42
motorcycle travel
  within Croatia 70
motorcycle travel
  to/from Croatia 67
Motovun 168-9
Murter 201
museums 35

N
national parks 27-30
  Brijuni Islands 27-30
  Kornati Islands 27-30
  Krka National Park 27-30
  Mljet island 27-30
  Paklenica National Park
    27-30
  Plitvice Lakes National Park
    27-30
  Risnjak National Park 27-30
newspapers 44

O
Opatija 119-22
  getting there & away 122
  information 120-1
  orientation 120
  places to eat 121
  places to stay 121
  things to see 121-2
Orebić 272-3
organised tours 72
Osijek 104-9, **106**
  dangers 106
  getting around 109
  getting there & away 109
  orientation 105
  places to eat 107-9
  places to stay 107
Osor 130-1
  getting there & away 131
  places to stay 131
  special events 131
  things to see 130-1

P
Pag island 190-4
Pag Town 191-4, **192**
  information 192-3
  places to eat 194

places to stay 193-4
things to see 193
Paklenica National Park 181-5, **182**
  park rules *181*
  rock climbing 185
  Velebit Range 185
  walking tours 183-5
  wildlife 182-3
passports 38
Plitvice Lakes National Park 178-81, **179**
  getting there & away 181
  history 179-81
  places to stay & eat 180-1
  wildlife 179-80
Požega 110
politics *see* government & politics
Polo, Marco *269*
population & people 30
Poreč 163-7, **164**
postal services 42
Prevlaka Peninsula 28-30
Primošten 201
Prvić 201
public holidays 50
Pula 151-7, **152**
  information 151-3
  orientation 151
  places to eat 155
  places to stay 154-5
Punat 139

R
Rab Island 139-46, **140**
  getting around 141
  getting there & away 141
Rab town 141-4, **142**
radio 44
religion 34
Rijeka 113-19, **114-15**
  getting there & away 118-19
  information 114-15
  orientation 113-14
  places to eat 117-18
  places to stay 117
  things to see 115-17
Roman Empire 14-15
Rovinj 158-63, *159*
  places to eat 162
  places to stay 161-2
  things to see & do 160-1

S
Sali 187-9, **188**
Samobor 99-100
San Marino *146*

shopping 60
Šibenik 195-201, **198-9**
  information 197
  orientation 197
  places to eat 200
  places to stay 199-200
  things to see 197-9
Šibenik-Knin county 195-204
Šipan 260
Škrip 237
Slavonia 103-10, **104**
Slavonski Brod 110
Sokolovac Hill 110
Solin 14-15, 217-18, **217**
Šolta 216
Southern Dalmatia 246-73
Split 205-7, **208**
  Diocletian's Palace 209-10
  entertainment 215
  getting there & away 215-16
  information 207-9
  orientation 207
  places to eat 214-15
  places to stay 212-14
  things to see 209-11
Stari Grad (Central Dalmatia) 243-4
Stari Grad (Zadar) 186
Stepinac, Cardinal Alojzije *82*
Strossmayer, Bishop Josip *85*
student cards 39
Suha Punta 146
Sumartin 236
Supetar 230-2
  information 230
  orientation 230
  places to eat 232
  places to stay 231-2
  things to see & do 231
Susak island 127

T
taxes 28-30, 42
Telasćica Bay 189-90
telephone services 42
television 44
time 44
Tito *98*
toilets 46
tourist offices 37
train travel
  to/from Croatia 66-7
  within Croatia 68-9
trams
  Osijek 72
  Zagreb 72

travel insurance 39
truffles *168*
Trsat Castle 117
Tribunj 201
Trogir 218-21, **219**
  getting there & away 221
  information 219
  orientation 218
  places to eat 221
  places to stay 220-1
  things to see 219-20

U
Ugljan 178
Ustashe 20

V
Valun 131-2
Varaždin 100-2
Vela Luka 272
  places to stay & eat 272
  Vela Špilje Cave 272
Velebit Range see Paklenica National Park
Veli Lošinj 127-8
  entertainment 128
  information 128
  orientation 128
  places to eat 128
  places to stay 128
  things to see 128
Vis island 225
  getting there & away 225-8
Vis town 226-7
  information 226
  orientation 226
  places to eat 227
  places to stay 227
  things to see & do 226-7
visas 38
Vlachs 196
Vodice 201
Volosko 122
Vrbnik 137
Vukovar *108*

W
War (1991-95) 22-30
water purification 46
weights & measures 44
wildlife *26-7*
women travellers 49
work 54
WWI 20
WWII 21

Y
youth cards 39

Z
Zadar 170-94, **174**
  information 172-3
  orientation 172
  places to eat 177
places to stay 176
Zagreb 73-102, **76-7**
  bookshops 79
  cafés & bars 92-3
  entertainment 93
  getting around 95
  getting there & away 94
  history 74-5
  museums 84-6
orientation 75-8
places to eat 90-3
places to stay 88-90
shopping 94
sport 93
theatre 93
walking tour 80-6
Zlarin 201
Zlatni Rat 232

Boxed Text

Air Travel Glossary 62-3
Ban Josip Jelačić 81
Best Restaurants & Pizzerias on the Coast 214
Bishop Strossmayer 85
Controversial Cardinal Stepinac 82
Delicate & Durable: Pag Lace 191
Did you know ... 33
Dubrovnik: Destruction & Reconstruction 250

An Istrian Feast 156
Ivan Meštrović 212-3
Josip Broz Tito 98
Magic Mushrooms? 168
Marco Polo 269
Morčići 119
Park Rules in Paklenica 181
Responsible Diving 52
Roman Architecture 150
San Marino and San Marino 146
The Siege of Vukovar 108

Street Names 241
Sword Dances 270
The Threatened Griffon Vulture 184
The Trials and Travails of the Feral Tribune 45
Uskoks: The Pirates of Senj 207
Vlachs 196
What's Free 101

MAP LEGEND

BOUNDARIES

▬·▬·▬·▬·· ....International
▬··▬··▬·· ....State
▬ ▬ ▬ ▬ ....Disputed

HYDROGRAPHY

...............Coastline
..............River, Creek
........................Lake
.........Intermittent Lake
.....................Salt Lake
.........................Canal
⊚ ⇥ ....Spring, Rapids
⤙⤙ ⊂▬ ....Waterfalls

ROUTES & TRANSPORT

═══════ ....Freeway
═══════ ....Highway
═══════ ....Major Road
────── ....Minor Road
══════ ....Unsealed Road
═══════ ....City Highway
═══════ ....City Road
▬▬━▬━ ....City Street, Lane

⊐＝＝＝. ....Tunnel
╾┼╾┼╾●┼╾ ....Train Route & Station
╾ ▬ ╾Ⓜ╾ ....Metro & Station
▬▬▬▬▬ ....Tramway
╫╾╫╾╫╾╫╾╫╾ .... Cable Car or Chairlift
─────── .... Walking Track
────────── .... Ferry Route

═══════ ....Pedestrian Mall

AREA FEATURES

▓▓▒▒ ....Building
⚙ ....Park, Gardens
+ + × × ....Cemetery

▓▓▒▒ ....Market
▓▓▒▒ ....Pedestrian Mall
▓▓▓▓ ....Urban Area

MAP SYMBOLS

✈ .... Airport
⌁ ....Ancient or City Wall
∴ ....Archaeological Site
❶ .... Bank
⚲ ....Beach
⚘ .... Border Crossing
⛿ ....Castle or Fort
⌒ ....Cave
▦ 🛈 ....Church
⌒⌒⌒ .... Cliff or Escarpment
◩ ....Dive Site
◎ ....Embassy
✚ ....Hospital
☼ ....Lookout
▲ ....Mountain or Hill

🏛 ....Museum
← ....One Way Street
)(.............................. Pass
★ ....Police Station
✉ .... Post Office
❖ ....Shopping Centre
⛷ ....Ski field
🏛 ....Stately Home
⚑ ....Surf Beach
▭ ....Swimming Pool
✡ ....Synagogue
☎ ....Telephone
❶ ......Tourist Information
◒ .... Transport
🐘 ....Zoo

○ CAPITAL ....National Capital
◉ CAPITAL ....State Capital
● CITY .... City
● Town ....Town
● Village ....Village
○ ....Point of Interest

■ ....Place to Stay
⚑ ....Camping Ground
⌖ ....Caravan Park
⌂ ....Hut or Chalet

▼ ....Place to Eat
🍺 ....Pub or Bar

Note: not all symbols displayed above appear in this book

LONELY PLANET OFFICES

Australia
PO Box 617, Hawthorn, Victoria 3122
☎ (03) 9819 1877 fax (03) 9819 6459
email: talk2us@lonelyplanet.com.au

USA
150 Linden St, Oakland, CA 94607
☎ (510) 893 8555 TOLL FREE: 800 275 8555
fax (510) 893 8572
email: info@lonelyplanet.com

UK
10a Spring Place, London NW5 3BH
☎ (0171) 428 4800 fax (0171) 428 4828
email: go@lonelyplanet.co.uk

France
1 rue du Dahomey, 75011 Paris
☎ 01 55 25 33 00 fax 01 55 25 33 01
email: bip@lonelyplanet.fr
minitel: 3615 lonelyplanet *(1,29 F TTC/min)*

World Wide Web: www.lonelyplanet.com *or* AOL keyword: lp
Lonely Planet Images: lpi@lonelyplanet.com.au